BARRON'S
BUSINESS
TRAVELERS

KOREAN
FOR THE
BUSINESS
TRAVELER

Un-Bok Cheong

Senior Instructor of Korean
Language and Culture
National Foreign Affairs Training Center
U.S. Department of State
Arlington, VA

ACKNOWLEDGMENTS

We would like to thank the following individuals and organizations for their assistance on this project.

Hyun-Sook Cheong, Korean Language Instructor, U.S. government, Hyung-Taek Cheong, and Mia Cheong, Fairfax Station, VA; Dong Kwang Kim, Bilingual Specialist, Fairfax County Public System, Fairfax County, VA; Jae K. Shim, Ph.D., Professor of Accounting, California State University, Long Beach, CA.

Copyright © 1994 by Barron's Educational Series. Prior edition, *Talking Business in Korean,* copyright © 1988 by Barron's Educational Series, Inc.

All rights reserved. No part of this book may be reproduced in any form by photostat, microfilm, xerography, or any other means, or incorporated into any information retrieval system, electronic or mechanical, without the written permission of the copyright owner.

All inquiries should be addressed to:
Barron's Educational Series, Inc.
250 Wireless Boulevard
Hauppauge, NY 11788

International Standard Book No. 0-8120-1772-2

Library of Congress Catalog Card No. 93-34045

Library of Congress Cataloging-in-Publication Data
  Cheong, Un-Bok
  Korean for the business traveler by / Un-Bok Cheong. — 2nd ed.
    p. cm. — (Bilingual business guides)
  ISBN 0-8120-1772-2
  1. Business—Dictionaries. 2. English language—Dictionaries—Korean.
  3. Business—Dictionaries—Korean. 4. Korean language—Dictionaries—English.
  5. Business travel—Korea (South)—Guidebooks. I. Title. II. Series: Barron's bilingual
    business guides.
HF1002.C423 1994   93-34045
650'.03—dc20   CIP

PRINTED IN THE UNITED STATES OF AMERICA

4567   8800   987654321

CONTENTS

Preface v
I. PRONUNCIATION GUIDE 1
II. INTRODUCTION 4
Doing Business in Korean 4
Before you go 7
III. BASIC WORDS AND PHRASES 11
General words and phrases for getting by, including amenities, answers to standard questions, and other essential expressions

IV. BUSINESS DICTIONARY 69
English to Korean 71
Korean to English 162
Key Words for Key Industries 253

V. GENERAL INFORMATION 300
Abbreviations 300
Weights and Measures 307
Temperature and Climate 308
Communication Codes 309
Postal Services 311
Time Zones 311
Major Holidays 312
Currency Information 312
Major Business Periodicals 315
Radio and Television Stations 315
Annual Trade Fairs 316
Travel Times 317
Travel Tips 320
Major Hotels 323
Major Restaurants 328
Major Department Stores 330
Useful Addresses 332
Maps 337

PREFACE

It is the nature of business to seek out new markets for its products, to find more efficient ways to bring its goods to more people. In the global market, this often means traveling to foreign countries where language and customs are different. Even when a business person knows the language of the host country, the specified and often idiosyncratic terminology of the business world can be an obstacle to successful negotiations in a second language. Pocket phrase books barely scratch the surface of these problems, while standard business dictionaries prove too cumbersome.

Now there is a solution-Barron's *Korean for the Business Traveler*. Here is the essential pocket reference for all international business travelers. Whether your business be manufacturing or finance, communications or sales, this three-part guide will put the right words in your mouth and the best expressions in your correspondence.

Barron's *Korean for the Business Traveler* offers you the following features:

- a 6,000-entry list of basic business terms (English-Korean, Korean-English), dealing with accounting, advertising and sales, banking, computers, export/import, finance and investment, labor relations, management, manufacturing, marketing, retail and wholesale, and more.
- a quick guide to basic terms and expressions for getting by when you don't know the language.
- a pronunciation guide for speaking the language.
- a list of common business abbreviations.
- reference words for numbers and amounts, days of the week, months of the year, and seasons.
- conversion tables for metric and customary measurements.
- lists of major holidays, travel times between cities, average temperatures throughout the year.
- addresses and phone numbers of Korean Embassy and consulate, and Korean Trade Association (KOTRA) in the United States.
- lists of major banks, trading companies, department stores, restaurants in Seoul, hotels in major cities and provinces.
- addresses and phone numbers of Tourist Information Center.
- lists of government offices.
- information on international currencies, country and city telephone codes, useful addresses in Korean.

I. PRONUNCIATION GUIDE

This book assumes that you are already somewhat familiar with the basic pronunciation rules of Korean, but for those whose knowledge is a little rusty, here are some tips. Below are tables which give the sounds represented by each Korean letter.

The Hangul alphabet, Korean orthography, is a phonetic writing system that represents the sounds of consonants and vowels. Hangul, a phonetic script, is the official language primarily used in Korea. A limited number of Hanja, Chinese characters, are also used. The Hangul letters consist of 21 vowels and 19 consonants which originally evolved from 24 basic letters (14 consonants and 10 vowels).

The Hangul system, which is scientific, systematic, and practical, is very easy to master within a short period of time.

The following tables show how to pronounce Hangul in romanized letters adapted from those used by the Korean Government and the McCune-Reischauer system.

In 1992, South and North Korea jointly enacted the unified romanized letters that are used in this book excepting a few consonants.

HANGUL	ROMANIZA-TION	ENGLISH SOUND	EXAMPLES
Vowels			
아	*a*	palm	아이 *a-i*
어	*eo*	up	어머니 *eo-meo-ni*
오	*o*	coat	오세요 *o-se-yo*
우	*u*	wood	우리 *u-ri*
으	*eu*	chicken	으뜸 *eu-tteum*
이	*i*	king	이름 *i-reum*
애	*ae*	apple	애국 *ae-guk*
에	*e*	episode	에누리 *e-nu-ri*
외	*oe*	whey	외국 *oe-guk*
위	*wi*	weak	위임장 *wi-im-jjang*
Diphthongs (Combinations of Vowels)			
야	*ya*	yah	야구 *ya-gu*
여	*yeo*	young	여자 *yeo-ja*
요	*yo*	yoga	요구 *yo-gu*
유	*yu*	you	유리 *yu-ri*
얘	*yae*	yam	얘기 *yae-gi*
예	*ye*	yes	예정 *ye-jeong*
의	*eui*	chicken+eat	의견 *eui-gyeon*
와	*wa*	Hawaii	와전 *wa-jeon*
왜	*wae*	wagon	왜요? *wae-yo*
워	*weo*	wonder	워싱턴 *weo-shing-t'eon*
웨	*we*	way	웨이터 *we-i-t'eo*

HANGUL	ROMANIZATION	ENGLISH SOUND	EXAMPLES
		Consonants	
ㄱ	*k, g*	glory	고기 *ko-gi*
ㄴ	*n*	nice	누구 *nu-gu*
ㄷ	*t, d*	donkey	동대문 *tong-dae-mun*
ㄹ	*r, l*	room, tool	일자리 *il-ja-ri*
ㅁ	*m*	mother	모자 *mo-ja*
ㅂ	*p, b*	buy, humble	법인 *peo-bin*
ㅅ	*s, sh*	snack, fish	사람 *sa-ram*
			시험 *shi-heom*
ㅇ	*silent**		아침 *a-ch'im*
ㅇ	*ng*	song	정구 *cheong-gu*
ㅈ	*ch, j*	joke, hinge	지도 *chi-do*
			남자 *nam-ja*
ㅊ	*ch'***	choo-choo	친구 *ch'in-gu*
ㅋ	*k'***	cook	코 *k'o*
ㅌ	*t'***	tank	토요일 *t'o-yo-il*
ㅍ	*p***	people	포도 *p'o-do*
ㅎ	*h*	hope	한국 *hang-guk*
ㄲ	*kk****	garden	꿈 *kkum*
ㄸ	*tt****	dazzle	떡 *tteok*
ㅃ	*pp****	budget	빵 *ppang*
ㅆ	*ss****	scene	쌀 *ssal*
ㅉ	*jj****	jackpot	짠물 *jjan-mul*

*when used as initial sound
**aspirated
***glottal sound

Formation of Syllables

Consonant + Vowel

ㄴ + ㅔ → 네
n + e → ne

ㅇ + ㅏ → 아   ㄴ + ㅣ → 니   ㅇ + ㅗ → 오 = 아니오
silent + *a* → ***a***   *n + i* → ***ni***   silent + *o* → ***o*** = ***an-i-o***

ㅇ + ㅓ → 어   ㄷ + ㅣ → 디 = 어디
silent + *eo* → ***eo***   *d + i* → ***di*** = ***eo-di***

Consonant + Vowel + Consonant

ㅅ + ㅓ + ㄴ → 선   ㅅ + ㅐ + ㅇ → 생   ㄴ + ㅣ + ㅁ = 선생님
s + eo + n → ***seon***   *s + ae + ng* → ***saeng***   *n + i + m* → ***nim*** = ***seonsaengnim***

ㅎ + ㅏ + ㄴ → 한   ㄱ + ㅜ + ㄱ → 국 = 한국
h + a + n → ***han***   *g + u + k* → ***guk*** = ***han-guk*** → ***hang-guk***

Pronunciation Guide

Note: The actual spelling in romanization is *han-guk* but sound ㄴ *n* changes to ㅇ *ng*. There is a phonemic change between syllables when the final sound ㄴ *n* of the syllable is preceded by ㄱ *g* of the next syllable. Beside this, in some other cases, phonemic changes occur between symbols. Therefore, the actual pronunciation differs from the written letter.

In this book the romanization of *hangul* is based on the actual sound.

EXAMPLES:
  관+리 *kwan+ri→**kwalli***
  업+무 *eop+mu→**eommu***
  압+력 *ap+ryeok→**amnyeok***
  식+량 *shik+ryang→**shingnyang***
  앞+날 *ap'+nal→**amnal***

Among consonants, the sounds ㄱ *k, g,* ㄷ *t, d,* ㅂ *p, b* and ㅈ *ch, j* can be either voiced or voiceless depending on its position in the phrase or word. The sounds of these consonants are romanized with two different symbols.

EXAMPLES:
  가격 *ka-gyeok*
  대단히 *tae-dan-hi*
  정거장 *cheong-geo-jang*
  본부 *pon-bu*

Hyphens are sometimes used, when necessary, to distinguish a sound between syllables, to help lengthen sound, and to separate grammatical functions.

EXAMPLES:
  공인 ***kongin**→kong-in*
  상업 ***sangeop**→sang-eop*
  현금 ***hyeongeum**→hyeon-geum*
  종이 ***chongi**→chong-i*
  친구 ***ch'ingu**→ch'in-gu*

II. INTRODUCTION

DOING BUSINESS IN KOREAN

Doing business with another culture and in another language can be a difficult and mystifying experience. Customs and procedures may be quite different from what is perceived as the "normal" way of conducting oneself in a business circumstance.

In this introduction, some of the customs and economic features of Korea are outlined, in order to assist you in effectively conducting business there. Basic knowledge of these factors will help in becoming more accustomed to the business situation of the Korean-speaking world.

Usual Hours of Operation

	Monday-Friday	Saturdays	Sundays & Holidays
Banks	9:30-4:30	9:30-1:30	Closed
Post Offices	9:00-6:00	9:00-1:00	Closed
Department Stores*	10:00-7:30	10:00-7:30	10:00-7:30
Small Shops	10:00-10:00	10:00-10:00	10:00-10:00
Large Companies	8:30-7:00	9:00-1:00	Closed
Government Offices**	9:00-6:00	9:00-1:00	Closed
Foreign Diplomatic Missions	9:00-4:30 or 5:00	Closed	Closed

*closed once a week
**November to February (close at 5:00 PM)

Business Customs

Korea, like any other country, has its unique characteristics and its own culture. Some customs and traditions derived from Confucianism have planted their roots deeply in Korea throughout several thousand years of history. Consequently, manners and life styles are quite different from Western countries. It is very important to understand the culture when doing business or handling other matters with Koreans. Their manner of doing business is not like the business in your country or anywhere else in the world. Therefore, no one expects foreigners to behave exactly like Koreans do. But to do business or to get along well with Koreans, the following cultural notes might give you a hint.

- When you enter someone's home, take off your shoes. This custom should be observed when you enter an *ondol* room, a traditional Korean room that has an under-floor heating system. Koreans prefer to keep their floors

- and carpets free from dirt and other debris that may be stuck on the soles of shoes.
- Try learning how to use chopsticks to eat Korean food. The use of fingers while eating is considered impolite.
- On some occasions, what you say may not be completely comprehended, but a Korean may *pretend* to understand it. If you detect any sign of uneasiness from someone, politely repeat what has just been said; some Koreans would not feel comfortable asking you to repeat it.
- Koreans are fairly culture-generous people. Use any good Western manners when you do not know how to behave or react.
- You should not feel obliged to leave a gratuity at a restaurant because all costs are already included in your bill. If you really want to leave a tip, however, 10% of the bill would be fine.
- A face-to-face meeting is more effective than contact by telephone or a letter when you want to seriously discuss some business.
- It is a good idea to be introduced to government officials or businessmen through your friend or acquaintance. When you are entertained by a person, reciprocate in a similiar way. By doing so you can maintain a positive relationship with him.
- Never write a person's name in red ink. When writing a person's name, Koreans do not use red unless that person is dead. Koreans, however, use red color when they use a *tojang* (*chop* or name seal).
- It is common to exchange business cards. It is advisable to have your card handy when you expect to meet people.
- Koreans write their surname followed by their first name followed by *seonsaengnim* (means "Sir," "Mr.," "teacher"). You may call each individual Mr., or Miss before his or her last name.
- Koreans normally bow when they greet each other. When they bow they also welcome the opportunity to shake hands with others: foreigners, friends or strangers.
- Koreans avoid making direct eye-to-eye contact when in conversation. This is a gesture of politeness and respect. They believe that direct eye contact is impolite and discourteous during conversation.
- When receiving or passing gifts, foods, or goods, Koreans use both hands together as another sign of politeness.
- A suit is more appropriate than casual attire at business meetings and social gatherings.
- Try to avoid jumping right into business matters. Be patient and use a gradual approach. Further, do not expect an immediate "yes" or "no."
- If Korean businessmen take you to a bar or restaurant, consider it part of doing business. In that relaxed and comfortable environment, it is easier to deal with matters related to business. You may reciprocate by taking them out later and discussing other issues with them.
- It is common practice to offer cigarettes to one another.
- *Ki-bun* means feelings, mood, or a state of mind. When someone's *ki-bun* is pleasant, it is easier to deal with him on certain matters.
- *Nunchi* means tact, sense, social sense, or perceptiveness. if one doesn't have *nunchi,* it means that he or she is unresponsive or insensitive.
- *Ch'emyeon* means one's face, prestige, or personal dignity. Koreans treas-

ure this *ch'emyeon*. If *ch'emyeon* is not properly kept, it means that one's reputation has diminished. To keep *ch'emyeon* is to maintain significant interpersonal relationships in society.
- *Put'ak* means making a request, solicitation, or asking a favor. The word *put'ak* is a noun, and is followed by *hamnida* to make a formal polite verb ending, *put'ak-hamnida* means that the speaker is asking his or her counterpart a favor or the speaker wishes that everything goes well with his or her counterpart in the future.

General Government Policy and Economic Situation

Economic Development and Background

Korea, a country that was totally destroyed during the Korean War (1950 to 1953), has achieved remarkable economic success and prosperity from the ruins. Traditionally, as an agricultural country, 60% of the Korean work force was engaged in farming and fishing in 1963, while only 7% of the work force was working in the manufacturing area.

In the early 1960s, the Korean government launched an economic development strategy on export-led industrialization along with the Saema-eul Undong (New Community Movement) that provided the people with vision and hope, and improved rural life with high income and productivity. A vigorous economic development began in the early 1960s, and even though the first few years were slow, Korea's economic growth rate averaged 6.9% by 1971.

Since then, the economic growth has expanded over thirty-four times, and by 1991 the average growth rate was 8.8%. In 1992, the GDP was $294.5 billion, and the GDP per capita was $6,749. Korea now has become the U.S.'s 7th trade partner, and the world's 12th largest exporter and importer.

Current Import and Export Situation

The main exports are electronics and electric products, textiles, steel products, ships, footwear, chemicals, general machinery, motor vehicles, and fishery.

The main imports are general machinery, minerals, fuels, agricultural products, electronic parts, steel products, organic chemicals, industrial electronics, and petroleum products.

In 1992, the total imports and exports were about $81.8 billion and $76.6 billion, respectively. The trade deficit has already reached $5.1 billion contrary to the considerable surpluses during 1986-1989.

For the last three years, the annual increase in exports has averaged 7.1 %, while imports have averaged a 10.2% increase. Korea's import volume has increased in recent years.

Economic Policy

During the 1970s, the Korean government promoted the development of heavy and chemical industries with many tax and financial incentives. This policy, however, failed to achieve its primary objective, which was to promote new export-led industries or to support import-substituting industries. This lesson convinced policy makers to adopt a market-oriented liberalization program in the 1980s. Technological development helped produce quality products. Investment in research and development helped produce quality products. Investment in research and development doubled between 1981 and 1986, from 1-2% of the GDP. This increase was primarily attributable to private-sector investment.

The Korean government's approach to adjustment had three aspects: stabilization, promotion of market efficiency, and balanced growth. Macro-economic tools were used, including a conservative monetary policy and tight fiscal measures to restrain aggregate demand. This resulted in price stability and reduction of the public-sector deficit. The yearly consumer price increase fell dramatically and it has been in the 2-3% range since 1983. The balance of payments also continued to improve, and finally attained a surplus in 1986. The average growth rate was 9.5% between 1981 and 1991.

For the first time in 32 years, a new civilian government, inaugurated on February 25, 1993, has launched a new economic five-year plan (1993-1998). The primary goal is to maintain price stability at 3% within two years, and to change a deficit in the balance of international payments to a favorable one. To resolve current economic problems, the plan will promote economic reform to activate the economy; strengthen global competitiveness; create an open policy for import; stabilize wages, interest rates, and prices; and control speculation in real estate. The overall goal aims to increase GDP per capita growth from $6,749 in 1992 to $15,000 in 1998.

Main imports: agricultural forestry and fishery products, mineral products, chemicals, petroleum products, textiles, articles of iron, steel and metal, machinery and transport equipment, electric and electronics.

Main exports: marine products, chemicals, organic chemicals, articles of plastic, rubber, and leather, non-metalic mineral products, textiles, household goods, footwear, articles of iron, steel and metal, electric and electronics, machinery and transport equipment.

Inflation rate: 6.2%.

Principal trading partners: United States, Japan, China, Hong Kong, Canada, Germany, United Kingdom.

Population: 44 million.

Language: Korean.

Religion: Buddhism, Protestant, Roman Catholic.

GDP: $294.5 billion

Per capita GDP: $6,749.

Unemployment rate: 2.4%.

BEFORE YOU GO

Passports

All permanent U.S. residents must carry a valid passport. Application should be made by mail or in person at least eight (and preferably twelve) weeks in advance to either (1) a U.S. Passport Agency office located in twelve major cities and Washington, D.C., (2) designated U.S. post offices throughout the country, or (3) state and federal courthouses. You may also consult your travel agent or international airline office. All of these offices will let you know what documents you need and the proper procedures to follow. Requirements for citizens and noncitizens differ somewhat. No international travel tickets will be issued by an airline or travel agent to persons without valid passports.

Visas

A visa is required for entry into Korea. But no visas are required for travel to Korea with confirmed outbound tickets for a stay that does not exceed 15 days.

Two types of visas are issued by the Korean embassy or consulate abroad.

- Short-term visa-tourists who want to stay up to 90 days.
- Long-term visa-visitors who want to stay more than 90 days require an entry permit from the Ministry of Justice.

All information concerning applications can be obtained at any Korean consulate or travel agent in the U.S.

Immunizations

There are no immunization requirements (against smallpox or other diseases) for entry into Korea or upon return to the United States. If you plan to include travel outside Korea to any other countries in the southeast, consult your doctor or the nearest U.S. Public Health Service office.

Customs and Currency Regulations

In general, travelers with U.S. passports are allowed to bring in fairly generous amounts of duty-free items for their own personal use. These items include tobacco, alcohol, and perfumes and are typically allowed in the following quantities:

Personal effects: necessary clothing and toilet articles; equipment and tools for direct use in your line of work;
400 cigarettes *or* 50 cigars *or* 200 grams of pipe tobacco and 100 grams of other kinds of tobacco; not to exceed 500 grams.
2 bottles of liquor; not to exceed 1,520cc
2 ounces of perfume
Gifts up to the value of approximately $375.00 (300,000 won)
Articles in excess of these items are subject to customs duty.

When exporting Korean antiques or valuable cultural items, approval is required from the Ministry of Culture. For further information, contact the Art and Antiques Assessment Office (Tel: (02) 662-0106) in Seoul.

Export limits apply to the following ginseng items:
1,200 grams of red ginseng
1,200 grams of white ginseng
900 red ginseng tablets

1,200 grams of sliced ginseng
450 grams of extract ginseng powder
1,200 grams of ginseng powder
1,200 grams of ginseng capsules
2 liters of ginseng drink

For information, Contact the Customs Information Office at Kimp'o International Airport. Tel: (02) 665-3100.

For personal valuables like jewelry or furs and foreign-made items like watches, cameras, typewriters, or tape recorders (acquired before your trip) you should have proof of prior possession or register with U.S. Customs before departure. This will ensure that they are not subject to duty either by the United States upon return or by any country you visit.

Upon return to the United States, each person has a duty-free allowance of $400, including 100 cigars and 1 carton of cigarettes. Each adult may bring in only 1 liter of wine or other liquor duty-free. Gifts worth $50 or less may be sent home subject to certain restrictions. For further up-to-date details, ask your travel agent or airline to provide a copy of U.S. Customs regulation or contact U.S. Customs, P.O. Box 7407, Washington, D.C. 20044 (202) 566-8195.

Travelers can bring foreign currencies equivalent to more than $5,000 into Korea when the amount is declared on arrival on the Foreign Exchange Record. Consult your travel agent about reconversions of unused local currencies.

Traveler's Checks, Credit Cards, Foreign Exchange

All major international traveler's checks and credit cards are accepted by most of the hotels, restaurants, and shops. The most widely recognized and acceptable cards are: American Express, Visa, MasterCard, and Diners Club.

However, be advised that the exchange rate on dollar traveler's checks is almost always disadvantageous. If you want, you can buy foreign currency checks and/or actual currency in the United States before leaving at rates equivalent to or better than the bank rate you will get in Korea.

Currency or checks may be purchased from retail foreign currency dealers. The largest of these, Deak-Perera, will send you information if you contact them at: 29 Broadway, New York, NY 10006 (212) 757-6915.

A warning to credit card users: When charging, make sure that the following information appears on the original and all copies of your bill: the correct date; the official exchange rate for that currency on that date (if possible); and the total amount of the bill. Without this information, you may end up paying at an exchange rate less favorable to you and more favorable to your Korean host, and for a larger bill than you thought!

Drivers' Licenses

A valid American (state) license is usually respected. However, if you have time, and want to rent a car, it is a good idea to get an international drivers' document through the AAA or a local automobile club.

Korean for Business Traveler

Electrical Appliances

Korea's system of electric current and voltage is basically the same as in the United States. But in Korea the voltage current supply is 110 and 220 volts. At hotels both 110 and 220 volts are available. Before using the power, check the current supply.

For further detailed information on foreign electricity, write to: Franzus Company, 352 Park Avenue South, New York, NY 10010 (212) 889-5850.

III. BASIC WORDS AND PHRASES

Greetings

Good morning.	안녕하십니까?
Good afternoon.	*annyeong-hashimnikka?*
Good evening.	안녕하세요?
	annyeong-haseyo?
Good night.	안녕히 주무십시오.
	annyeonghi chumu-shipshiyo.
Pleased to meet you.	만나서 반갑습니다.
	mannaseo ban-gap-seumnida.
How do you do?	처음 뵙겠습니다.
	ch'eoeum boep-kesseumnida.
How do you do? (reply)	네, 처음 뵙겠습니다.
	ne, ch'eoeum boep-kessumnida.
How are you?	안녕하십니까?
	annyeong-hashimnikka?
Fine, thank you.	네, 안녕하십니까?
	ne, annyeong-hasimnikka
Goodbye. (to one who is leaving) (to one who is staying)	안녕히 가십시오.
	annyeonghi ga-shipshiyo.
	안녕히 계십시오.
	annyeonghi gye-shipshiyo.

Common Expressions

Yes.	네.
	ne.
No.	아니오, 아닙니다.
	aniyo, animnida.
Sir.	선생님
	seonsaeng-nim.
Mr.	선생님, 씨, 미스터.
	seonsaeng-nim, ssi, miseut'eo.
Mrs.	씨, 여사, 미세스.
	ssi, yeosa, miseseu.
Miss.	양, 미쓰.
	yang, misseu.
Ms.	여사.
	yeosa.
Thank you.	감사합니다, 고맙습니다.
	kamsa-hamnida, komap-seumnida.
Thank you very much.	대단히 감사합니다.
	taedanhi gamsa-hamnida.
You're welcome.	천만에요, 천만의 말씀입니다.
	ch'eonman-eyo, ch'eonman-eui malsseum-imnida.

I'm sorry.	죄송합니다, 미안합니다.
	choesong-hamnida, mian-hamnida.
Excuse me.	실례합니다.
	shillye-hamnida.
Please.	어서, 좀.
	eoseo, chom.
Hello. (for telephone calls or for getting someone's attention)	여보세요.
	yeobo-seyo.
Of course.	물론입니다, 물론이죠.
	mullon-imnida, mullon-ijyo.
O.K.	좋습니다.
	cho-sseumnida.
Maybe.	아마(그럴거예요).
	ama (geureol-kkeo-yeyo).
Pardon me, but _____.	죄송하지만_____, 미안하지만_____.
	choesong-hajiman_____, mian-hajiman.
It's all right.	좋습니다, 괜찮습니다.
	cho-sseumnida, kwaench'an-seumnida.
It doesn't matter.	상관 없습니다,
	sang-gwan eopsseumnida.
	괜찮습니다.
	kwaench'an-seumnida.
With pleasure.	기꺼이, 즐거이.
	kikkeoi, cheulgeoi.
I don't mind.	저는 상관 없습니다.
	cheo-neun sang-gwan eopsseumnida,
	저는 괜찮습니다.
	cheo-neun gwanench'an-seumnida.
Oh, I see.	아, 알겠습니다.
	a, al-gesseumnida.
Is that so?	그렇습니까? 그래요?
	keureo-sseumnikka? keuraeyo?
Really?	정말입니까? 그래요?
	cheongmal-imnikka? keuraeyo?
Shall we go?	가실까요?
	ka-shilkkayo?
Let's (go/eat/etc.).	(갑/먹읍)시다.
	(kap/meog-eup)shida.
No thank you.	아닙니다, 괜찮습니다.
	ani-mnida, kwaench'an-seumnida.
I don't want it.	그것을 원하지 않습니다.
	keugeoseul weon-haji ansseumnida,
	원치 않습니다.
	weonch'i ansseumnida.
I think so.	(저는)그렇게 생각합니다.
	(cheo-neun)geureok'e saeng-gak-hamnida.

Basic Words and Phrases

I don't think so.	(저는)그렇게 생각하지 않습니다. *(cheo-neun)geureok'e saeng-gak-haji ansseumnida.*
It's interesting/fun.	재미/흥미(가)있습니다. *chaemi/heungmi-(ga) isseumnida.*
It's over/I'm finished.	끝났습니다/저는 끝냈습니다. *kkeun-nasseumnida/cheo-neun kkeun-naesseumnida.*
Yes, it is.	네, 그렇습니다. *ne, geureo-sseumnida.*
No. It isn't.	아니오, 그렇지 않습니다. *aino, geureo-ch'i ansseumnida.*
Just a moment, please.	잠깐만 기다리십시오. *chamkkanman gidarishipshiyo.*
Not yet.	아직 아닙니다. *ajik animnida.*
Soon.	곧. *kot.*
Right away.	즉시, 바로 *cheukshi, paro*
Now.	지금 *chigeum.*
Later.	이따, 후에, 나중에. *itta, hu-e, najung-e.*

Some Questions and Question Words

What's the matter?	왜 그러십니까? *wae geureoshimnikka?*
What's this?	이것이 무엇입니까? *igeoshi mueoshimnikka?*
Where's the _____?	_____이/가 어디에 있습니까? *_____i/ga eodi-e isseumnikka?*
• bathroom	• 화장실 — *hwajangshil*
• dining room	• 식당 — *shikttang*
• entrance	• 입구, 들어가는 곳 — *ipku, deureoga-neun-got*
• exit	• 출구, 나가는 곳 — *ch'ulgu, naga-neun-got*
• telephone	• 전화 — *cheonhwa*
When?	언제? *eonje?*
Where?	어디? *eodi?*
Why?	왜? *wae?*
Who?	누구/누가? *nugu/nuga?*

Korean for Business Traveler 14

Which?	어느?
	eoneu?
What?	무엇, 몇?
	mueot, myeot?
How?	어떻게?
	eotteok'e?
How much?	얼마?
	eolma?
How much (money)?	얼마?
	eolma?

Needs

Could you tell me where the _____ is?	_____이/가 어디에 있는지 말씀해 주십시오.
	_____*i/ga eodi-e inneunji malsseum-hae jushipshiyo.*
Could you give me _____?	_____을/를 좀 주시겠습니까?
	_____*eul/reul jom jushi-gesseumnikka?*
I need _____.	_____이/가 필요합니다.
	_____*i/ga p'iryo-hamnida.*
I want _____.	_____을/를 원합니다.
	_____*eul/reul weon-hamnida.*
I want to go to _____.	_____에 가고 싶습니다.
	_____*e gago/shipseumnida.*
I want to see _____.	_____을/를 보고 싶습니다 (뵙고 싶습니다).
	_____*eul/reul bogo-shipseumnida (boepko-shipseumnida).*
I want to buy _____.	_____을/를 사고 싶습니다.
	_____*eul/reul sago-shipseumnida.*
I want to eat _____.	_____을/를 먹고 싶습니다.
	_____*eul/reul meokko-shipseumnida.*
I want to drink _____.	_____을/를 마시고 싶습니다.
	_____*eul/reul mashigo-shipseumnida.*

Your Personal Condition

I'm thirsty.	(저는)목이 마릅니다.
	(cheo-neun) mogi mareumnida.
I'm hungry.	(저는)배가 고픕니다.
	(cheo-neun) bae-ga gop'eumnida.
I'm full.	(저는)배가 부릅니다.
	(cheo-neun) bae-ga bureumnida.
I'm tired.	(저는)피곤합니다.
	(cheo-neun) p'igon-hamnida.
I'm sleepy.	(저는)졸립니다, 잠이 옵니다.
	(cheo-neun) jollimnida, jam-i omnida.

Basic Words and Phrases

I'm sick.	(저는)아픕니다.
	(cheo-neun) ap'eumnida.
I'm fine.	(저는)좋습니다.
	(cheo-neun) josseumnida.
I'm all right.	(저는)괜찮습니다.
	(cheo-neun) gwaench'anseumnida.

Useful Adjectives and Adverbs

above/below	위에/아래에
	wi-e/arae-e
ahead/behind	먼저/뒤에, 나중에
	meonjeo/twi-e, najung-e
beautiful, pretty/ugly	아름다운, 예쁜/미운
	areumdaun, yeppeun/miun
best/worst	제일 좋은/제일 나쁜
	cheil jo-eun/cheil nappeun
big/small	큰/작은
	k'eun/chageun
dark/light	어두운/밝은
	eodu-un/palgeun
delicious/awful tasting	맛(이) 있는/맛(이) 없는
	mash(i) inneun/mash(i) eomneun
early/late	이른, 일찍/늦은, 늦게
	ireun, iljjik/neujeun, neutkke
easy/difficult	쉬운/어려운
	swi-un/eoryeo-un
expensive/cheap	비싼/싼
	pissan/ssan
few/many	적은/많은
	cheogeun/maneun
first/last	처음/끝(마직막)
	ch'eoeum/kkeut (majimak)
front/back	앞/뒤
	ap/twi
full/empty	가득찬/빈
	kadeukch'an/pin
good/bad	좋은/나쁜
	cho-eun/nappeun
heavy/light	무거운/가벼운
	mugeo-un/kabyeo-un
hot/cold	더운, 뜨거운, 매운/추운, 찬
	teo-un, tteugeo-un, mae-un/ch'u-un, ch'an
high/low	높은/낮은
	nop'eun/najeun
inside/outside	안/밖
	an/pakk
intelligent/stupid	똑똑한/바보같은
	ttottok-han/pabo-gat'eun

Korean for Business Traveler

large/small	큰/작은
	k'eun/chageun
long/short	긴/짧은
	kin/jjalbeun
more/less	더/덜
	teo/teol
near/far	가까운/먼
	kakka-un/meon
old/new	오래된/새
	oraedoen/sae
open/shut	연/닫은
	yeon/tadeun
quiet/noisy	조용한/시끄러운
	choyonghan/shikkeureo-un
right/wrong	맞은/틀린
	majeun/t'eullin
same/differnet	같은/다른
	kat'eun/tareun
slow/fast	느린/빠른
	neurin/ppareun
strong/weak	강한/약한
	kang-han/yak-han
thin/thick	가는/두꺼운
	kaneun/tukkeo-un
warm/cool	따뜻한/시원한, 선선한
	ttateut-han/shiweon-han, seonseon-han
wide/narrow	넓은/좁은
	neolbeun/chobeun
young/old	젊은/늙은
	cheolmeun/neulgeun

Pronouns

I	저, 나
	cheo, na
You	선생님, 당신, 너
	seonsaengnim, tangshin, neo
he/she	그 남자(그분)/그 여자(그분)
	keu-namja (keubun)/keu-yeoja (keubun)
we	우리
	uri
you (plural)	여러분, 당신들
	yeoreobun, tangshin-deul
they	그분들, 그들
	keu-bun-deul, keu-deul
my	제, 내
	che, nae
here/there/over there	여기/거기/저기
	yeogi/keogi/cheogi

Basic Words and Phrases

this/that/that over there (nouns)	이것/그것/저것 *igeot/keugeot/cheogeot*
this/that/that over there (adjectives)	이/그/저 *i/keu/cheo*

Other Useful Words

a, an	하나, 하나의, 어떤 *hana, hana-eui, eotteon*
about	_____에 대해서, _____에 대한, 약, _____에 관해서 _____ *e daehaeseo*, _____ *e daehan, yak,* _____ *e gwanhaeseo*
across	건너서 *keonneoseo*
after	후, _____ㄴ/은 후에 *hu,* _____ *n/eun hu-e*
again	다시, 또 *tashi, tto*
all	모두, 다 *modu, da*
almost	거의 *keo-eui*
also	_____도, 또, 역시 _____ *do, tto, yeokshi*
always	늘, 언제나, 항상 *neul, eonjena, hangsang*
among	중(에), _____가운데 *chung(e),* _____ *ka-unde*
and (between sentences)	_____와/과, _____하고 *wa/kwa,* _____ *hago*
and (with verbs)	_____고 _____ *ko*
and (between sentences)	그리고 *keurigo*
another	다른 *tareun*
around	_____쯤, _____부근, _____주위 _____ *jjeum,* _____ *bugeun,* _____ *chu-wi*
at	_____에, _____에서 _____ *e,* _____ *eseo*
away	멀리 *meolli*
back (of)	뒤 *twi*
because	왜냐하면, _____기 때문에 *waenya-hamyeon,* _____ *ki ttaemun-e*
before	전, _____기전 *cheon,* _____ *ki jeon*

behind	뒤, 뒤에
	twi, twi-e
between	사이, 틈
	sa-i, t'eum
both	둘다, 모두다
	tulda, modu-da
but (with nouns)	____(이)지만
	____*(i)jiman*
but (with verbs)	____지만
	____*chiman*
but (between sentences)	그러나, 그렇지만, 하지만
	keureona, keureoch'iman, hajiman
down	아래
	arae
during	____동안, ____는 동안
	____*tong-an*, ____*neun dong-an*
each	각, ____씩
	kak, ____*ssik*
enough	넉넉하다, 충분하다
	neongneok-hada, ch'ungbun-hada
even	____까지, ____조차
	____*kkaji*, ____*choch'a*
every	매, ____마다
	mae, ____*mada*
except	____외에
	____*oe-e*
for	____을/를 위해서, ____동안
	____*eul/reul wi-haeseo*, ____*tong-an*
from (place)	____에서
	____*eseo*
(time)	____부터
	____*put'eo*
(person)	____에게서, ____한테서
	____*egeseo*, ____*hant'eseo*
however	그러나, 하지만
	keureona, hajiman
if	____(으)면, 만일, 만약
	____*(eu)myeon, manil, manyak*
in	____에, ____안에, ____에서
	____*e*, ____*an-e*, ____*eseo*
instead (of)	____대신에
	taeshin-e
into	____(으)로
	____*(eu)ro*
much	많이
	mani
next (to)	다음(에), 옆(에)
	taeum (e), yeop' (e)

Basic Words and Phrases

of	_____의, _____중에 _____eui, _____chung-e
often	자주 chaju
on	_____에, _____에서, _____위에 _____e, _____eseo, wi-e
only	_____만, 다만 _____man, taman
or	혹은, 또는, _____(이)나 hogeun, ttoneun, _____(i)na
other	다른 tareun
perhaps	아마, 혹시 ama, hokshi
since	_____이래, _____니까 _____irae, _____nikka
some	좀, 조금 chom, chogeum
still (yet)	아직 ajik
to (place)	_____에, _____(으)로 _____e, _____(eu)ro
(time)	_____까지 _____kkaji
(person)	_____에게, _____한테 _____ege, _____hant'e
until	_____까지 _____kkaji
up	위 wi
very	아주, 매우, 대단히, 참, 몹시 aju, mae-u, taedanhi, ch'am, mopshi
with	_____와/과, _____와/과 같이, _____(으)로 _____wa/kwa, _____wa/kwa kach'i, _____(eu)ro

Communicating

Do you understand?	아시겠습니까? *ashi-gesseumnikka?*
Yes, I understand.	네, 알겠습니다. *ne, al-gesseumnida.*
No, I don't understand.	아니오. 모르겠습니다. *aniyo, moreu-gesseumnida.*
Do you understand English?	영어를 아십니까? *yeong-eo-reul ashimnikka?* 영어를 이해하십니까? *yeong-eo-reul ihae-hashimnikka?*

Korean for Business Traveler 20

I speak a little Korean.	한국말을 조금 합니다.
	hang-gung-mal-eul jogeum hamnida.
I know very little Korean.	한국말을 아주 조금 압니다.
	hang-gung-mal-eul aju jogeum amnida.
I don't understand Korean.	한국말을 모릅니다.
	hang-gung-mal-eul moreumnida.
Could you repeat it, please?	다시 말씀해 주시겠습니까?
	tashi malsseum-hae jushigesseumnikka?
Please speak slowly.	좀 천천히 말씀해 주십시오.
	chom ch'eonch'eonhi malsseum-hae jushipshiyo.
Write it down on the paper, please.	종이에 좀 적어 주십시오.
	chong-i-e jom jeogeo jushipshiyo.
Is there anyone who understands English?	영어를 아시는 분 계십니까?
	yeong-eo-reul ashineun bun gyeshimnikka?
Do you speak English?	영어를 아십니까?
	yeong-eo-reul hashimnikka?
What's this called in Korean?	이것을 한국말로 어떻게 말합니까?
	igeoseul hang-gung-mal-lo eotteok'e mal-hamnikka?
What do you call this?	이것을 어떻게 말합니까?
	igeoseul eotteok'e mal-hamnikka?
	이것을 무엇이라고 합니까?
	igeoseul mu-eoshirago hamnikka?
Excuse me, could you help me, please?	실례지만 저를 좀 도와주시겠습니까?
	shillye-jiman jeoreul jom dowa-jushigesseumnikka?
Please point to the phrase in this book.	이 책에서 그 문구를 지적해 주십시오.
	i ch'aegeseo keu munkku-reul jijeok-hae-jushipshiyo.
What did you say?	무엇이라고 말씀하셨습니까?
	mu-eoshirago malsseum-hasyeosseumnikka?

Introductions

Who is that?	저분이 누구십니까?
	cheobun-i nugushimnikka?
Do you know who that is?	저분이 누구인지 아십니까?
	cheobun-i nugu-inji ashimnikka?
I would like to meet him, her (literally, that person)	저분을 만나뵙고 싶습니다.
	cheobun-eul manna-boepko-shipsumnida.
Would you introduce me to him/her (that person)?	저분한테 저를 소개해 주시겠습니까?
	cheobun-hant'e jeo-reul sogae-hae-jushigesseumnikka?
Pardon me, may I introduce myself?	실례지만 저를 소개해도 괜찮습니까?
	shillye-jiman jeo-reul sogae-haedo gwaench'anseumnikka?

Basic Words and Phrases

My name is <u>Bob Smart</u>.	저는 밥 스마트입니다.
	cheo-neun bap seumat'eu-imnida.
How do you do?	처음 뵙겠습니다.
	ch'eo-eum boepkesseumnida.
How do you do (reply)?	네, 처음 뵙겠습니다.
	ne, ch'eo-eum boepkesseumnida.
I'm honored to meet you.	만나뵈서 영광입니다.
	manna-boeseo yeong-gwang-imnida.
I'm glad to meet you.	만나뵈서 반갑습니다.
	manna-boeseo bang-gapseumnida.

Cards

Card.	명함
	myeong-ham.
Here's my card.	제 명함(이) 여기 있습니다.
	che myeong-ham(i) yeogi isseumnida.
Thank you very much.	대단히 감사합니다/고맙습니다.
	taedanhi gamsa-hamnida/komapseumnida
Here's mine.	제것이 여기 있습니다.
	che-geoshi yeogi isseumnida.
May I have your card?	선생님/댁의 명함을 좀 주시겠습니까?
	seonsaengnim/daeg-eui myeong-ham-eul jom jushi-gesseumnikka?

Useful Sentences

Where are you from?	어디서 오셨습니까?
	eodi-seo osyeosseumnikka?
How long will you be staying?	얼마동안 계시겠습니까?
	eolma dong-an gyeshi-gesseumnikka?
Where are you staying?	어디(에) 묵고 계십니까?
	eodi(e) mukko gyeshimnikka?
Where can I reach you?	어디로 선생님께 연락할 수 있습니까?
	eodi-ro seonsaengnim-kke yeollak-halsu isseumnikka?
Here's my address and phone number.	이것이 제 주소와 전화번호입니다.
	igeoshi je juso-wa jeonhwabeonho-imnida.
Could you pick me up at my hotel this evening?	오늘 저녁 호텔에 저를 데리러 오실 수 있습니까?
	oneul jeonyeok hotel-e jeo-reul derireo oshilsu isseumnikka?
See you later.	이따 뵙겠습니다.
	itta boep-kesseumnida.
See you tomorrow.	내일 뵙겠습니다.
	nae-il boep-kesseumnida.

Useful Nouns

address	주소
	chuso
amount	금액, 양(量)
	keumaek, yang
appointment	약속
	yaksok
bargain	바겐
	bagen
bargain sale	바겐 쎄일
	bagen sseil
bill	계산서, 청구서
	kyesanseo, ch'eong-guseo
business	사업, 일
	sa-eop, il
car	자동차, 차
	chadongch'a, ch'a
cashier	회계
	hoegye
check	수표
	sup'yo
city	시
	shi
customs	풍습, 관습
	p'ungseup, kwanseup
date	날, 일
	nal, il
document	서류
	seoryu
elevator	승강기, 엘리베이터
	seung-gang-gi, ellibeit'eo
friend	친구
	ch'in-gu
hanger	옷걸이
	otkeori
key	열쇠
	yeolsoe
list	목록
	mongnok
magazine	잡지
	chapchi
maid	가정부, 파출부
	kajeongbu, p'ach'ulbu
mail	우편물
	up'yeonmul
manager	지배인
	chibae-in

Basic Words and Phrases

map	지도	*chido*
mistake	잘못, 실수, 틀림	*chalmot, shilsu, t'eullim*
money	돈	*ton*
name	이름, 성명, 성함	*ireum, seongmyeong, seongham*
newspaper	신문	*shinmun*
office	사무실	*samushil*
package	소포, 짐	*sop'o, chim*
paper	종이	*chong-i*
passport	여권	*yeokkweon*
pen	펜	*p'en*
pencil	연필	*yeonp'il*
porter	짐꾼, 포터	*chimkkun, p'ot'eo*
postage	우편 요금	*up'yeon yogeum*
post office	우체국	*uch'eguk*
price	값	*kap*
raincoat	비옷, 우비	*pi-ot, ubi*
reservation	예약	*yeyak*
restaurant	식당, 음식점	*shiktang, eumshikcheom*
restroom	화장실	*hwajangshil*
road	길, 도로	*kil, toro*
room	방	*pang*
shirt	셔쓰	*syeosseu*
shoes	구두, 신	*kudu, shin*
shower	샤워	*syaweo*

store	상점 *sangjeom*
street	거리, 길 *keori, kil*
suit	양복 *yangbok*
suitcase	가방 *kabang*
taxi	택시 *t'aekshi*
telegram	전보 *cheonbo*
telephone	전화 *cheonhwa*
ticket	표 *p'yo*
time	시간 *shigan*
tip	팁 *t'ip*
train	기차 *kich'a*
train station	역, 정거장 *yeok, cheong-geojang*
trip	여행 *yeohaeng*
umbrella	우산 *usan*
waiter	웨이터, 종업원 *weit'eo, chong-eob-weon*
watch	시계 *shigye*
water	물 *mul*

Useful Verbs

accept	받다, 수락하다 *patta, surak-hada*
answer	대답하다 *taedap-hada*
arrive	도착하다 *toch'ak-hada*
ask	묻다, 물어보다 *mutta, mureor-boda*
assist	도와주다 *towajuda*
bargain	흥정하다 *heungjeong-hada*

Basic Words and Phrases

be	이다, 있다 *ida, issta*
begin (vt)	시작하다 *shijak-hada*
(vi)	시작되다 *shijak-doeda*
bring	가지고 오다, 가져오다 *kajigo-oda, kajyeo-oda*
buy	사다 *sada*
call	전화걸다/전화하다, 부르다 *cheonhwa keolda/cheonhwa hada, pureuda*
carry	나르다, 운반하다 *nareuda, unban-hada*
change	바꾸다 *pakkuda*
close (vt)	닫다 *tatta*
(vi)	가깝다 *kakkapta*
come	오다 *oda*
confirm	확인하다 *hwagin-hada*
continue	계속하다 *kyesok-hada*
cost	돈이 들다 *ton-i deulda*
cut down (price)	(값을)깎다 *(kapseul)kkakkta*
deliver	전달하다 *cheondal-hada*
direct	지시하다, 가리키다 *chishi-hada, karik'ida*
do	하다 *hada*
eat	먹다, 들다 *meokta, teulda*
end	끝나다 *kkeunnada*
enter	들어가다 *teureo-gada*
examine	검사하다, 시험치다/보다 *keomsa-hada, shiheom ch'ida/boda*
exchange	바꾸다, 교환하다 *pakkuda, kyohwan-hada*
feel	느끼다 *neukkida*

finish	끝내다 *kkeunaeda*
fix	고치다, 수리하다 *koch'ida, suri-hada*
follow	따르다 *ttareuda*
forget	잊어버리다 *ijeobeorida*
forward	전하다 *cheon-hada*
get	얻다 *eotta*
give	주다 *chuda*
go	가다 *kada*
hear	듣다 *teutta*
help	돕다, 도와주다 *topta, towajuda*
keep	간직하다, 지키다 *kanjik-hada, chik'ida*
know	알다 *alda*
learn	배우다 *pae-uda*
leave	떠나다 *tteonada*
like	좋아하다 *cho-a-hada*
listen	듣다 *teutta*
look	보다 *poda*
lose	잃다 *ilt'a*
make	만들다 *mandeulda*
mean	뜻하다, 의미하다 *tteut'ada, euimi-hada*
meet	만나다 *mannada*
miss (transportation)	놓치다 *noch'ida*
need	필요하다 *p'iryo-hada*
open (vt)	열다 *yeolda*

Basic Words and Phrases

open (vi)	열리다 *yeollida*
order	주문하다, 시키다 *chumun-hada, shik'ida*
pay	내다, 지불하다 *naeda, chibul-hada*
prefer	____을/를 좋아하다, ____을/를 택하다 *____eul/reul jo-a-hada, ____eul/reul t'aek-hada*
prepare	준비하다 *chunbi-hada*
present	제출하다, 내놓다 *chech'ul-hada, naenot'a*
prove	증명하다 *cheungmyeong-hada*
put	놓다, 두다 *not'a, tuda*
read	읽다 *ikta*
receive	받다 *patta*
recommend	추천하다 *ch'uch'eon-hada*
register	등록하다 *teungnok-hada*
repair	고치다, 수리하다 *koch'ida, suri-hada*
repeat	반복하다, 되풀이하다, 따라하다, 다시하다 *panbok-hada, toep'uri-hada, ttara-hada, tashi-hada*
rest	쉬다 *swida*
return	돌아가다 *tora-gada*
run	뛰다 *ttwida*
say	말하다 *mal-hada*
see	보다 *poda*
send	보내다 *ponaeda*
show	보이다 *poida*
sit	앉다 *antta*
speak	말하다 *mal-hada*

Korean for Business Traveler 28

stand	서다 *seoda*
start	시작하다 *shijak-hada*
stay	머물다, 있다, 체류하다 *meomulda, issta, ch'eryu-hada*
stop (vt)	세우다 *se-uda*
(vi)	서다 *seoda*
take	가져가다 *kajyeo-gada*
talk	이야기하다 *iyagi-hada*
tell	말하다/이야기하다 *mal-hada/iyagi-hada*
think	생각하다 *saeng-gak-hada*
try	해보다, 노력하다 *hae-boda, noryeok-hada*
turn	돌리다, 틀다, 돌다 *tollida, t'eulda, tolda*
use	쓰다, 사용하다 *sseuda, sayong-hada*
visit	방문하다 *pangmun-hada*
wait	기다리다 *kidarida*
walk	걷다 *keotta*
want	원하다 *weon-hada*
wear	입다 *ipta*
work	일하다 *il-hada*
write	쓰다 *sseuda*

Directions

north	북 *puk*
south	남 *nam*
east	동 *tong*
west	서 *seo*

at the corner	모퉁이에서, 구석에서
	mot'ung-i-eseo, kuseog-eseo
on the corner	모퉁이에, 구석에
	mot'ung-i-e, kuseog-e
straight ahead	똑바로
	ttokparo
left	좌측, 왼쪽
	chwach'euk, oenjjok
right	우측, 오른쪽/바른쪽
	uch'euk, oreunjjok/pareunjjok
middle	중간, 가운데
	chung-gan, kaunde

Days of the Week

Sunday	일요일
	iryoil
Monday	월요일
	weoryoil
Tuesday	화요일
	hwayoil
Wednesday	수요일
	suyoil
Thursday	목요일
	mogyoil
Friday	금요일
	keumyoil
Saturday	토요일
	t'oyoil
day	일, 날
	il, nal
today	오늘
	oneul
yesterday	어제
	eoje
the day before yesterday	그저께
	keujeokke
tomorrow	내일
	naeil
the day after tomorrow	모레
	more
week	주
	chu
this week	이(번)주, 금주
	i(beon)-ju, keum-ju
last week	지난 주, 전주
	chinan-ju, cheon-ju
next week	다음 주, 내주
	ta-eum-ju, nae-ju

for one week	일주일(동안)
	il-jjuil (dong-an)
for two weeks	이주일(동안)
	i-juil (dong-an)
in one week	일주일 후에
	il-jjuil hu-e
in two weeks	이주일 후에
	i-juil hu-e
for two days	이틀, 이일(동안)
	it'eul, i-il (dong-an)
in one day	하루 (일일) 후에
	haru,(iril) hu-e
in two days	이틀후에
	it'eul-hu-e
three days ago	사흘전, 삼일전
	saheul-jeon, sam-il-jeon
this morning	오늘 아침
	oneul ach'im
this afternoon	오늘 오후
	oneul ohu
tonight	오늘 밤
	oneul-pam
tomorrow night	내일 밤
	naeil-pam
in the morning	아침에
	ach'im-e
in the afternoon	오후에
	ohu-e
in the early evening	초저녁에
	ch'o-jeonyeog-e
in the evening	저녁에
	cheonyeog-e
by morning	아침까지
	ach'im kkaji
by Tuesday	**화요일까지**
	hwayoil kkaji
What day is today?	오늘이 며칠입니까?
	oneuri myeoch'irimnikka?
It's ____.	____일입니다.
	____*irimnida.*
weekday	주일, 주중
	chuil, chujung
weekend	주말
	chumal
every day	매일, 날마다
	maeil, nal-mada
a week from today	일주일후
	il-jjuil-hu

Basic Words and Phrases

from today on	오늘부터
	oneul but'eo
day off	휴일, 비번일, 휴무
	hyuil, pibeon-il, hyumu
holiday	공휴일
	konghyu-il
work day	근무일
	keunmu-il
per day	하루에
	haru-e
during the day	낮에
	naje
during the week	주중에
	chujung-e

The Four Seasons

spring	봄
	pom
summer	여름
	yeoreum
autumn	가을
	ka-eul
winter	겨울
	kyeo-ul

Counting Days

one day	하루, 일일
	haru, iril
two days	이틀, 이일
	it'eul, i-il
three days	사흘, 삼일
	saheul, sam-il
four days	나흘, 사일
	naheul, sa-il
five days	닷새, 오일
	tassae, o-il
six days	엿새, 육일
	yeossae, yug-il
seven days	이레, 칠일
	ire, ch'iril
eight days	여드레, 팔일
	yeodeure, p'aril
nine days	아흐레, 구일
	aheure, ku-il
ten days	열흘, 십일
	yeoreul, shibil

eleven days   열 하루, 십일일
yeol-haru, shibiril
twelve days   열이틀, 십이일
yeol-it'eul, shibi-il

Months of the Year

January	일월 *irweol*
February	이월 *i-weol*
March	삼월 *sam-weol*
April	사월 *sa-weol*
May	오월 *o-weol*
June	유월 *yu-weol*
July	칠월 *ch'irweol*
August	팔월 *p'arweol*
September	구월 *ku-weol*
October	시월 *shi-weol*
November	십일월 *shibirweol*
December	십이월 *shibi-weol*

Days of the Month

1st	일일 *iril*
2nd	이일 *i-il*
3rd	삼일 *sam-il*
4th	사일 *sa-il*
5th	오일 *o-il*
6th	육일 *yug-il*
7th	칠일 *ch'iril*

8th	팔일	*p'aril*
9th	구일	*ku-il*
10th	십일	*shib-il*
11th	십일일	*shibiril*
12th	십이일	*shibi-il*
13th	십삼일	*shipsam-il*
14th	십사일	*shipsa-il*
15th	십오일, 보름	*shibo-il, poreum*
16th	십육일	*shimnyug-il*
17th	십칠일	*shipch'iril*
18th	십팔일	*ship'aril*
19th	십구일	*shipku-il*
20th	이십일	*ishib-il*
21st	이십일일	*ishibiril*
22nd	이십이일	*ishibi-il*
23rd	이십삼일	*ishipsam-il*
24th	이십사일	*ishipsa-il*
25th	이십오일	*ishibo-il*
26th	이십육일	*ishimnyug-il*
27th	이십칠일	*ishipch'iril*
28th	이십팔일	*iship'aril*
29th	이십구일	*ishipku-il*
30th	삼십일	*samshib-il*
31st	삼십일일	*samshibiril*

month	월, 달
	weol, tal
two months ago	두달 전
	tu-dal jeon
last month	지난 달
	chinan-dal
this month	이달
	i-dal
next month	다음 달, 내 달
	ta-teum-ttal, nae-tal
during the month of ____	____(달)에
	____*(tal)e*
since the month of ____	____(달)부터, ____(달)이래
	____*(tal)but'eo,* ____*(tal)irae*
for the month of ____	____(달)에, ____(달)동안
	____*(tal)e,* ____*(tal) dong-an*
every month	매월, 달마다
	mae-weol, tal-mada
per month	한달에
	han-dare
one month	한달
	han-dal
a few months	몇달
	myeot-tal

Telling Time

A.M.	오전, 상오
	ojeon, sang-o
P.M.	오후, 하오
	ohu, ha-o
noon	정오, 열두시
	cheong-o, yeoldu-shi
midnight	자정, 밤중
	chajeong, pamjjung
o'clock	시
	shi

First a list of hours, then a list of minutes, then we'll put them together.

1 o'clock	한시
	han-shi
2 o'clock	두시
	tu-shi
3 o'clock	세시
	se-shi
4 o'clock	네시
	ne-shi

Basic Words and Phrases

5 o'clock	다섯시	*taseot-shi*
6 o'clock	여섯시	*yeoseot-shi*
7 o'clock	일곱시	*ilgop-shi*
8 o'clock	여덟시	*yeodeol-shi*
9 o'clock	아홉시	*ahop-shi*
10 o'clock	열시	*yeol-shi*
11 o'clock	열한시	*yeolhan-shi*
12 o'clock	열두시	*yeoldu-shi*
1 minute	일 분	*il-bun*
2 minutes	이 분	*i-bun*
3 minutes	삼 분	*sam-bun*
4 minutes	사 분	*sa-sbun*
5 minutes	오 분	*o-bun*
6 minutes	육 분	*yuk-bun*
7 minutes	칠 분	*ch'il-bun*
8 minutes	팔 분	*p'al-bun*
9 minutes	구 분	*ku-bun*
10 minutes	십 분	*ship-bun*
11 minutes	십일 분	*shibil-bun*
12 minutes	십이 분	*shibi-bun*
13 minutes	십삼 분	*shipsam-bun*
14 minutes	십사 분	*shipsa-bun*
15 minutes	십오 분	*shipo-bun*
16 minutes	십육 분	*shipyuk-bun*

17 minutes	십칠 분	*shipch'il-bun*
18 minutes	십팔 분	*ship'albun*
19 minutes	십구 분	*shipku-bun*
20 minutes	이십 분	*iship-bun*
21 minutes	이십일 분	*ishibil-bun*
22 minutes	이십이 분	*ishibi-bun*
23 minutes	이십삼 분	*ishipsam-bun*
24 minutes	이십사 분	*ishipsa-bun*
25 minutes	이십오 분	*ishibo-bun*
26 minutes	이십육 분	*ishimnyuk-bun*
27 minutes	이십칠 분	*ishipch'll-bun*
28 minutes	이십팔 분	*iship'al-bun*
29 minutes	이십구 분	*ishipku-bun*
30 minutes	삼십분, 반	*samship-bun, pan*
31 minutes	삼십일 분	*samshibil-bun*
32 minutes	삼십이 분	*samshibi-bun*
33 minutes	삼십삼 분	*samshipsam-bun*
34 minutes	삼십사 분	*samshipsa-bun*
35 minutes	삼십오 분	*samshibo-bun*
36 minutes	삼십육 분	*samshimnyuk-bun*
37 minutes	삼십칠 분	*samshipch'il-bun*
38 minutes	삼십팔 분	*samship'al-bun*
39 minutes	삼십구 분	*samshipku-bun*
40 minutes	사십 분	*saship-bun*

Basic Words and Phrases

41 minutes	사십일 분 *sashibil-bun*
42 minutes	사십이 분 *sashibi-bun*
43 minutes	사십삼 분 *sashipsam-bun*
44 minutes	사십사 분 *sashipsa-bun*
45 minutes	사십오 분 *sashibo-bun*
46 minutes	사십육 분 *sashimnyuk-bun*
47 minutes	사십칠 분 *sashipch'il-bun*
48 minutes	사십팔 분 *sashhip'al-bun*
49 minutes	사십구 분 *sashipku-bun*
50 minutes	오십 분 *oship-bun*
51 minutes	오십일 분 *oshibil-bun*
52 minutes	오십이 분 *oshibi-bun*
53 minutes	오십삼 분 *oshipsam-bun*
54 minutes	오십사 분 *oshipsa-bun*
55 minutes	오십오 분 *oshibo-bun*
56 minutes	오십육 분 *oshimnyuk-bun*
57 minutes	오십칠 분 *oshipch'il-bun*
58 minutes	오십팔 분 *oship'al-bun*
59 minutes	오십구 분 *oshipku-bun*
a quarter after ten	열시 십오분 *yeol-shi shibo-bun*
a quarter to ten	열시 십분전 *yeol-shi ship-pun-jeon*

Note: Start using *jeon* which means "to" or "before" at 15 minutes before the hour.

half past ten	열시반 *yeol-shi-bun*

Note: *ban* means "half."

Korean for Business Traveler 38

What time is it?	지금 몇 시입니까?
	chigeum myeot-shi-imnikka?
It's 5:00 o'clock.	다섯시입니다.
	taseot-shi-imnida.

- 1:05 · 한시 오분   *han-shi o-bun*
- 2:10 · 두시 십분   *tu-shi ship-pun*
- 3:15 · 세시 십오분   *se-shi shibo-bun*
- 4:20 · 네시 이십분   *ne-shi iship-bun*
- 5:25 · 다섯시 이십오분   *taseot-shi ishibo-bun*
- 6:30 · 여섯시 삼십분/ 여섯시 반   *yeoseot-shi samship-pun/ yeoseot-shi-bun*
- 7:35 · 일곱시 삼십오분   *ilgop-shi samshibo-bun*
- 8:40 · 여덟시 사십분   *yeodeol-shi saship-pun*
- 9:45 · 아홉시 사십오분/ 열시 십오분전   *ahop-shi sashibo-bun/ yeol-shi shibo-bun-jeon*
- 10:50 · 열시 오십분/ 열한시 십분전   *yeol-shi oship-pun/ yeolhan-shi ship-pun-jeon*
- 11:55 · 열한시 오십오분/ 열두시 오분전   *yeolhan-shi oshibo-bun/ yeoldu-shi o-bun-jeon*
- 8:00 · 여덟시   *yeodeol-shi*

Note: For time schedules (as in railway and airline time-tables) numbers 1-59 are used for minutes, not "a quarter to," or "ten to" the hour. Hours are based on the 24-hour clock.

My train leaves at 1:48 P.M.	기차가 오후 한시 사십팔분에 떠납니다.
	kich'a-ga ohu han-shi saship'al-bun-e tteonamnida.
My plane arrives at 10:53 A.M.	비행기가 오전 열시 오십 삼분에 도착합니다.
	pihaeng-gi-ga ojeon yeol-shi oshipsam-bun-e doch'ak-hamnida.
per hour	시간마다/매시, 매시간
	shigan-mada/mae-shi, mae-shigan
three hours ago	세 시간 전
	se-shigan-jeon
early (adj)	이른/빠른
	ireun, ppareun
(adv)	일찍
	iljjik

late (adj)	늦은
	neujeun
late (adv)	늦게
	neutke
on time	제시간, 정시
	che-shigan, cheong-shi
in the morning	오전에
	ojeon-e
in the afternoon	오후에
	ohu-e
in the evening	저녁에
	cheonyeog-e
at night	밤에
	pam-e
second	초
	ch'o
minute	분
	pun
hour	시간
	shigan

Arrival/Hotel

My name is _____. 제 이름은 _____입니다.
che ireum-eun _____ imnida.

I'm American. 저는 미국사람입니다.
cheo-neun miguksaram-imnida.

I'm staying at_____. 저는 _____에 머물고 있습니다/
_____에 있습니다.
*cheo-neun _____e meomulgo isseumnida/
_____e isseumnida.*

Here's my passport. 여기 제 여권이 있습니다.
yeogi je yeokkweoni isseumnida.

• business card • 명함 *myeongham*

I'm on a business trip. 저는 출장 중입니다.
cheo-neun ch'uljjang-jung-imnida

I'm just passing through. 저는 그저 지나가는 길입니다.
cheo-neun geujeo jinaganeun-girimnida.

I'll be staying here a few days. 저는 여기 며칠 머물겠습니다/
있겠습니다, 묵겠습니다.
*cheo-neun yeogi myeoch'il
meomul-gesseumnida/
it-kesseumnida, muk-kesseumnida.*

• a week • 일주일 *il jjuil*
• a few weeks • 몇주일 *myeot-chuil*
• a month • 한달 *han-dal*

I have nothing to declare. 저는 신고할 것이 없습니다.
*cheo-neun shin-go-hal-geoshi
eop-seumnida.*

Korean for Business Traveler

I'd like to go to the _____ hotel.	저는 _____ 호텔에 가고 싶습니다. *cheo-neun _____ hot'ere gago-shipseumnida.*
Where can I get a taxi?	어대서 택시를 탑니까? *eodiseo t'aekshi-reul t'amnikka?*
I have a reservation.	저는 예약을 했습니다. *cheo-neun yeyak-eul haesseumnida.*
I need a room for one night.	저는 하루밤 머물겠습니다. *cheo-neun haru-ppam meomul-gesseumnida.*
I want a double room with a bath.	저는 목욕탕이 있는 이인용 방을 원합니다. *cheo-neun mogyokt'ang-i inneun i-inyong-bang-eul weon-hamnida.*
What is the rate for the room?	그 방값은 얼마입니까? *keu bangkkapseun eolma-imnikka?*
Where is the elevator?	엘리베이터가 어디에 있습니까? *ellibeit'eo-ga eodi-e isseumnikka?*
Please wake me tomorrow at_____.	내일 _____시에 좀 깨워주십시오. *naeil _____shi-e jom kkaeweo-jushipshiyo.*
Did anyone call for me?	저한테 전화온 것 있습니까? *cheo-hant'e jeonhwa ongeot isseumnikka?*
I'd like to put this in the hotel safe.	이것을 호텔 보관함에 두고 싶습니다. *igeoseul hot'el bogwanham-e dugo-shipseumnida.*
Can you please make this call for me?	이 전화 좀 걸어주시겠습니까? *i jeonhwa jom georeo-jushi-gesseumnikka?*
Please send someone up for the bags.	짐꾼 좀 올려 보내주십시오. *chimkkun jom ollyeo bonae-jushipshiyo.*
Please send up some mineral water.	생수 좀 올려 보내주십시오. *saengsu jom ollyeo bone-jushipshiyo.*
I'd like the bill, please.	계산서 좀 주십시오. *kyesanseo jom jushipshiyo.*

Transportation: General Expressions

taxi	택시 *t'aekshi*
car with driver	운전기사 딸린 차 *unjeongisa ttallin ch'a*
bus	버스 *peoseu*
subway	지하철, 전철 *chihach'eol, cheonch'eol*
train	기차 *kich'a*
plane	비행기 *pihaeng-gi*

Basic Words and Phrases

English	Korean	Romanization
Where is the taxistand?	택시 타는 곳이 어디에 있습니까?	t'aekshi t'aneun-goshi eodi-e isseumnikka?
• bus stop	• 버스 정류장	peoseu jeong-nyu-jang
• subway station	• 지하철 역, 전철역	chichach'eol-yeok, cheonch'eol-yeok
• train station	• 기차역, 역	kich'a-yeok, yeok
• airport	• 공항	konghang
Where can I get a car with driver?	운전기사 딸린 차를 어디서 빌릴 수 있습니까?	unjeongisa ttallinch'a-reul eodiseo billilsu-isseumnikka?
Is the rate by the hour?	요금은 시간당 얼마입니까?	yogeum-eun shigan-dang eolma-imnikka?
• the half-day	• 반나절(에)	bannajeol(e)
• the day	• 하루(에)	haru(e)
I'd like to get one.	하나 빌렸으면 좋겠습니다.	hana billyeosseumyeon jok'esseumnida.
How much is a ticket to ____?	____까지 표가 얼마입니까?	____kkaji p'yo-ga eolma-imnikka?
Is this seat taken?	이 자리 누가 있습니까?	i jari nuga isseumnikka?
How long does it take?	얼마(나) 걸립니까?	eolma(na) geollimnikka?
Do I have to change ____?	____을/를 갈아 타야 합니까?	____eul/reul gara t'a-ya-hamnikka?
	____을/를 바꿔 타야 합니까?	____eul/reul bakkweo t'a-ya-hamnikka?

Note: If you travel by bus or taxi, it's a good idea to have someone write down your destination so you can show it to the driver, who may not understand English.

Taxi

English	Korean	Romanization
Please call a taxi.	택시 좀 불러 주십시오.	t'aekshi jom bulleo-jushipshiyo.
Please take me to this address.	이 주소로 좀 데려다 주십시오.	i juso-ro jom deryeoda-jushipshiyo.
I want to go to ____.	____에 가고 싶습니다.	____e gago-shipseumnida.
Stop here, at the corner, please.	여기서/모퉁이에서 세워주십시오.	yeogiseo/mot'ung-i-eseo seweo-jushipshiyo.
Please wait for me. I'll be right back.	좀 기다려주십시오. 곧 돌아오겠습니다.	chom gidaryeo-jushipshiyo. kot tora-o-gesseumnida.
I have some baggage.	제가 짐이 있습니다.	che-ga jim-i isseumnida.

Korean for Business Traveler 42

Urban

Where is the nearest bus stop/subway station?	가까운 버스정류장/지하철역이 어디 있습니까? *kakkaun peoseu jeong-nyu-jang/jihach'eol-yeok-i eodi isseumnikka?*
Is there a subway in this city?	이 도시에 지하철이 있습니까? *I doshi-e jihach'eori isseumnikka?*
Is there a subway map in English?	영어로 된 지하철 지도가 있습니까? *yeong-eo-ro doen jihach'eol jido-ga isseumnikka?*
Which line goes to_____?	어느 노선이 _____에 갑니까? *eoneu noseon-i _____e gamnikka?*
Does this bus go to_____?	이 버스가 _____에 갑니까? *i beoseu-ga_____e gamnikka?*
Where do I get off for_____?	_____에 가려면 어디서 내립니까? *_____e ga-ryeomyeon eodiseo naerimnikka?*
How many stops to_____?	_____은/는 몇번째 정거장입니까? *_____eun/neun myeot-peonjjae jeong-geo-jang-imnikka?*
I want to get off here.	여기서 내리고 싶습니다. *yeogiseo naerigo-shipseumnida.*
Please tell me when we get to_____.	_____에서 저한테 말씀해 주십시오. *_____eseo jeo-hant'e malsseum-hae-jushipshiyo.*
How often do the buses run?	버스는 얼마나 자주 다닙니까? *peoseu-neun eolmana jaju danimnikka?*

Train

Is there a timetable in English?	영어로 된 열차 시간표가 있습니까? *yeong-eo-ro doen yeolch'a shiganp'yo-ga isseumnikka?*
I'd like a <u>one-way ticket</u> to_____.	_____로 가는 편도표를 원합니다. *_____ro ga-neun p'yondop'yo-reul weon-hamnida.*

- round-trip ticket
- ticket with reserved seat
- first-class ticket
- economy-class ticket

- 왕복표   *wangbok-p'yo*
- 지정 좌석표   *chijeong jwaseok-p'yo*
- 일등표   *iltteung-p'yo*
- 일반석표   *ilbanseok-p'yo*

Where is the dining car?	식당 칸은 어디입니까? *shiktang-k'an-eun eodi-imnikka?*

Plane

When is there a flight to_____?	_____행 비행기는 언제 있습니까? *_____haeng bihaeng-gi-neun eonje isseumnikka?*

Basic Words and Phrases

Where do I pick up my luggage?	제 짐을 어디서 찾습니까? *che jim-eul eodiseo ch'at-seumnikka?*
That flight has been <u>delayed</u>.	그 비행기가 연착됐습니다. *keu bihaeng-gi-ga yeonch'ak-twaesseumnida.*
• cancelled	• 취소 *ch'wiso*
May I carry this bag in the plane?	이 가방을 비행기에 가지고 타도 괜찮습니까? *i gabang-eul bihaeng-gi-e gajigo t'a-do gwaench'an-seumnikka?*
Your bags are overweight.	선생님의 가방 무게가 초과되었습니다. *seonsaengnim-eui gabang muge-ga ch'ogwa-doe-eosseumnida.*
I'd like a seat in the <u>nonsmoking section</u>.	금연석을/를 원합니다. *keumyeon-seog-eul/reul weon-hamnida.*
• smoking area	• 흡연석 *heubyeon-seog*
• near the window	• 창 가까운 자리 *ch'ang gakkaun jari*
• on the aisle	• 통로 자리 *t'ongno jari*
What time does the plane leave?	비행기가 몇시에 떠납니까? *pihaeng-gi-ga myeot-shi-e tteonamnikka?*
What's my flight number?	제 비행기(번호)는 몇번입니까? *che bihaeng-gi(beonho)-neun myeot-peon-imnikka?*
What's the gate number?	탑승구(번호)는 몇번입니까? *t'apseung-gu(beonho)-neun myeot-peon-imnikka?*
I'd like to confirm my flight reservation.	제 비행기 예약을 확인하고 싶습니다. *che bihaeng-gi yeyak-eul hwagin-hago-shipseumnida.*

Renting a Car

I would like to rent a small car.	작은 차를 빌리고 싶습니다. *chageun ch'a-reul billigo-shipseumnida.*
• with automatic transmission.	• 자동기아가 있는 *chadong-gia-ga inneun*
How much does it cost <u>per day</u>?	하루에 얼마입니까? *haru-e eolma-imnika?*
• per week	• 일주일에 *il-jjuire*
• per kilometer	• 킬로당 *k'illo-dang*
How much is the insurance?	보험료는 얼마입니까? *poheomnyo-neun eolma-imnikka?*
Do you accept credit cards?	신용카드를 받습니까? *shinyong-k'adeu-reul bat-seumnikka?*
Do I have to leave a deposit?	보증금을 내야 합니까? *pojeung-geum-eul nae-ya-hamnikka?*

Korean for Business Traveler 44

I want to rent the car here and leave it someplace else.

여기서 차를 빌리고 다른 곳에다 두고 싶습니다.
yeogiseo ch'a-reul billigo dareun-goseda dugo-shipseumnida.

Where is the gas station?

주유소가 어디에 있습니까?
chuyuso-ga eodi-e isseumnikk?

Fill'er up with premium.

고급으로 넣어주십시오.
kogeub-euro neoeo-jushipshiyo.

Please check the <u>battery</u>.

밧테리를/을 좀 봐 주십시오.
pat'eri-reul/eul jom bwa-jushipshiyo.

• brakes	• 브레이크	*peureik'eu*
• carburetor	• 캬브레터	*k'yabeuret'eo*
• hood	• 보네트	*ponet'eu*
• oil	• 오일	*oil*
• spark plugs	• 스파크 플러그	*seup'ak'eu p'eulleogeu*
• tires	• 타이아	*t'aia*
• water	• 물	*mul*

Some Korean Road Signs

 Road Closed

 No Bicycles

 No Entry

 No Automobiles

Basic Words and Phrases

 No Right Turn

 No U Turn

 No Passing

 No Vehicles Carrying Inflammables

 Minimum Speed

 Maximum Speed

 No Stopping

 No Parking

Korean for Business Traveler 46

 Stop

 Slow Down

 Use of Horn Prohibited

 Crossing by Pedestrians Prohibited

 School Crossing

 Straight and Right Turn

 Left Turn

 Traffic Circle

Basic Words and Phrases

 Automobiles Only

 Sound Horn

 Go Straight

 Pedestrian Crossing

  One Way

 Road Divides

 Bicycle Only

 Pedestrian Path

Korean for Business Traveler 48

 Snow Tires or Chains

 Keep Right

 Parking

 Safety Zone

Leisure Time

Where can I buy an English-language newspaper?	영자신문을 어디서 살 수 있습니까? *yeongjja shimmun-eul eodiseo sal-su-isseumnikka?*
I'd like to see a <u>baseball game</u>.	야구시합을 보고 싶습니다. *yagu-shihab-eul bo-go-shipseumnida.*

- folk village ・ 민속촌 *minsokch'on*
- Panmunjeom ・ 판문점 *p'anmunjeom*
- Lotte World ・ 롯데 월드 *rotte weoldeu*
- Secret Garden ・ 비원 *piweon*

Where can I buy the tickets?	표를 어디서 살 수 있습니까? *p'yo-reul eodiseo sal-su-isseumnikka?*
Is there a pool near the hotel?	호텔 근처에 수영장이 있습니까? *hot'el geunch'eo-e suyeong-jang-i isseumnikka?*
Is it far?	멉니까? *meomnikka?*
Is there a discotheque here?	여기 디스코 클럽이 있습니까? *yeogi diseuk'o k'eulleob-i isseumnikka?*
Is there one at the hotel?	이 호텔에 있습니까? *i hot'ere isseumnikka?*
I would like to reserve a table.	자리(테이블)를(을) 예약하고 싶습니다. *chari(t'eibul)-reul(eul) yeyak-ha-go-shipseumnida.*

Restaurants

Breakfast	아침 *ach'im*
Lunch	점심 *cheomshim*
Dinner	저녁 *cheonyeok*
Korean food	한식 *hanshik*
Chinese food	중국음식 *chung-guk eumshik*
Japanese food	화식, 일본음식 *hwashik, ilbon eumshik*
Western food	양식 *yangshik*
Korean restaurant	한식집 *hanshik-chip*
Chinese restaurant	중국집 *chung-guk-chip*
Japanese restaurant	일식집, 화식집 *ilshik-chip, hwashik-chip*

Western restaurant	양식집 *yangshik-chip*
Do you know a good restaurant?	좋은 음식점을 아십니까? *cho-eun eumshikcheom-eul a-shimnikka?*
Is it very expensive?	아주 비쌉니까? *aju pissamnikka?*
Waiter!/Waitress!	웨이터/웨이트레스, 아가씨, 여보세요. *weit'eo/weit'eureseu, agassi, yeoboseyo.*
We'd like to have lunch.	점심을 들고 싶습니다. *cheomshim-eul deul-go-shipseumnida.*
I'd like to try Korean food.	한식을 먹어보고 싶습니다. *hanshig-eul meogeo-bo-go-shipseumnida.*
The menu, please.	메뉴 좀 주십시오. *menyu jom jushipshiyo.*
What's today's special?	오늘 특별한 음식은 무엇입니까? *oneul t'eukpyeol-han eumshig-eun mu-eoshimnikka?*
What do you recommend?	무슨 음식을 권하시겠습니까? *museun eumshig-eul gweon-ha-shi-gesseumnikka?*
To begin, please bring us a cocktail.	먼저 칵테일 좀 갖다 주십시오. *meonjeo k'akt'eil jom gatta jushipshiyo.*
• a bottle of mineral water	• 생수/약수 한병 *saengsu/yaksuhan-byeong*
• a beer	• 맥주 한병 *maekchu han-byeong*
Do you have a house wine?	포도주 있습니까? *p'odoju isseumnikka?*
I'd like to order now.	지금 주문하겠습니다. *chigum jumun-ha-gesseumnida.*
Show me the menu again, please.	메뉴 좀 다시 보여 주십시오. *menyu jom dashi boyeo-jushipshiyo.*
I'd like some coffee, please.	커피 좀 주십시오. *k'eop'i jom jushipshiyo.*
Do you have American cigarettes?	양담배/미국담배 있습니까? *yangdambae/miguk tambae isseumnikka?*
Please give me a pack of matches also.	성냥도 좀 주십시오. *seongnyang-do jom jushipshiyo.*
Do you mind if I smoke?	담배 피워도 괜찮습니까? *tambae p'iweodo kwaench'an-seumnikka?*
Check, please.	계산서 좀 주십시오. *kyesanseo jom jushipshiyo.*
Do you take <u>credit cards</u>?	신용카드를 받습니까? *shinyong-k'adeu-reul bat-seumnikka?*
• traveler's checks	• 여행자수표 *yeohaengja sup'yo*
Which credit cards do you take?	어느 신용카드를 받습니까? *eoneu shinyong-k'adeu-reul bat-seumnikka?*
Are the tax and service charge included?	세금과 서비스요금이 포함됐습니까? *segeum-gwa seobiseu-yogeum-i p'oham-dwaesseumnikka?*

Basic Words and Phrases

Is this correct?	이것이 맞습니까?
	igeoshi mat-seumnikka?
May I have a receipt, please?	영수증 좀 주시겠어요?
	yeongsujeung jom jushi-gesseoyo?
We don't have much time.	우리는 시간이 없습니다.
	uri-neun shigan-i ep-seumnida.
Where are the restrooms?	화장실이 어디있습니까?
	hwajangshiri eodi isseumnikka?
Could you bring me a knife please?	칼 좀 갖다 주시겠습니까?
	k'al jom gatta-jushi-gesseumnikka?
• a fork	• 포크　　　　　　*p'ok'eu*
• a spoon	• 숟가락　　　　　*sutkkarak*
• a teaspoon	• 작은술/차 숟가락　*chageunsul/ch'a sutkkarak*
• a tablespoon	• 큰 술/큰 숟가락　*k'eunsul/k'eun sutkkarak*
• a glass	• 잔　　　　　　　*chan*
• a cup	• 잔, 컵　　　　　*chan, k'eop*
• a saucer	• 잔대, 잔받침　　 *chanttae, chanbatch'im*
• a plate	• 접시　　　　　　*cheopshi*
• a bowl	• 그릇, 사발　　　*keureut, sabal*
• a napkin	• 냅킨　　　　　　*nap'euk'in*
• some toothpicks	• 이쑤시개　　　　*i-ssushigae*
• an ashtray	• 재떨이　　　　　*chaetteori*

Shopping

How much is it?	그것은 얼마입니까?
	keugeoseun eolma-imnikka?
Where can I find _____?	_____을/를 어디서 찾을 수 있습니까?
	_____*eul/reul eodiseo ch'ajeul-su isseumnikka?*
Can you help me?	좀 도와 주실 수 있습니까?
	chom dowa-jushil-su isseumnikka?
I need _____.	_____이/가 필요합니다.
	_____*i/ga p'iryo-hamnida.*
Do you have any others?	다른 것이 있습니까?
	tareun-geoshi isseumnikka?
Do you have anything smaller?	작은 것이 있습니까?
	chag-eun-geoshi isseumnikka?
• larger	• 큰 것　　　　　*k'eun-geosh*
Can I pay with a traveler's check?	여행자 수표를 드려도 됩니까?
	yeohaengja sup'yo-reul deuryeo-do doemnikka?

Names of Shops and Stores

store	상점, 가게
	sangjeom, kage
market	시장
	shijang
department store	백화점
	paekhwajeom
bakery	제과점
	chegwajeom
shoe store	양화점
	yanghwajeom
tailor shop	양복점
	yangbokcheom
dressmaking store	양장점
	yangjangjeom
barber shop	이발소
	ibalso
beauty parlor	미장원
	mijang-weon
stationery	문방구
	munbang-gu
souvenir store	기념품 가게/상점
	kinyeomp'um gage/sangjeom
book store	서점, 책방
	seojeom, ch'aekpang
drug store	약국, 약방
	yakkuk, yakpang
gas station	주유소
	chuyuso
florist	화원, 꽃가게, 꽃집
	hwaweon, kkotkage, kkotchip
antique store	골동품점
	kolttongp'umjeom
laundry	세탁소
	set'akso
tobacco store	담배가게
	tambae gage
street stall	노점
	nojeom
general store, miscellaneous store	잡화점
	chaphwajeom

Medical Care

Where is the nearest pharmacy? 가까운 약국이 어디 있습니까?
kakkaun yakkug-i eodi isseumnikka?

Basic Words and Phrases

Is there a pharmacy that carries American/European products?	미제/유럽제 약을 파는 약국이 있습니까? *mije/yureopche yag-eul p'aneun yakkug-i isseumnikka?*
I need something for a <u>cold</u>.	감기약이 필요합니다. *kamgi-yag-i p'iryo-hamnida.*
• constipation	• 변비　　　*pyeonbi*
• a cough	• 기침　　　*kich'im*
• diarrhea	• 설사　　　*seolsa*
• a headache	• 두통　　　*tut'ong*
• indigestion	• 소화불량　*sohwa-bullyang*
• insomnia	• 불면증　　*pulmyeonjjeung*
• a toothache	• 치통　　　*ch'it'ong*
• an upset stomach	• 위통　　　*wit'ong*
I don't feel well. I need a doctor who speaks English.	몸이 좀 불편합니다. *mom-i jom bulp'yeon-hamnida.* 영어를 할 수 있는 의사가 필요합니다. *yeong-eo-reul hal-su-inneun euisa-ga p'iryo-hamnida.*
I'm dizzy.	(제가) 어지럽습니다. *(che-ga)eojireop-seumnida.*
I feel weak.	기운이 없습니다. *kiun-i eop-seumnida.*
I have a pain in my chest around my heart.	심장 부근 가슴이 아픕니다. *shimjang-bugeun gaseum-i ap'eumnida.*
I had a heart attack some years ago.	몇년 전 심장마비에 걸렸었습니다. *myeonnyeon-jeon shimjang-mabi-e geollyeosseosseumnida.*
I'm taking this medicine.	이 약을 쓰고 있습니다. *i yag-eul sseu-go-isseumnida.*
Do I have to go to the hospital?	병원에 가야 합니까? *pyeong-weon-e gaya-hamnikka?*
I have a toothache.	치통이 있습니다. *ch'it'ong-i isseumnida.*
Could you recommend a dentist?	치과의사를 소개해 주시겠습니까? *ch'ikkwa-euisa-reul sogae-hae-jushi-gesseumnikka?*
I just broke my glasses.	제 안경이 방금 깨졌습니다. *che an-gyeong-i bang-geum kkaejyeosseumnida.*
Can you repair them while I wait?	기다리는 동안 고쳐주실 수 있습니까? *kidarineun-dong-an goch'yeo-jushil-su-isseumnikka?*

Telephones

Where is a public telephone?	공중전화가 어디에 있습니까? *kongjung-jeonhwa-ga eodi-e isseumnikka?*

Is there an English telephone directory?	영어로 된 전화번호부가 있습니까? *yeong-eo-ro doen jeonhwa-beonhobu-ga isseumnikka?*
I'd like to make a phone call. Could you give me some change?	전화를 걸려고 합니다. 잔돈(동전)좀 주시겠습니까? *cheonhwa-reul geollyeo-go-hamnida. chan-don(tongjeon) jom jushi-gesseumnikka?*
May I use your phone?	댁의 전화 좀 써도 괜찮습니까? *taeg-eui jeonhwa jom sseo-do gwaench'an-seumnikka?*
How do you call the United States?	미국에 어떻게 전화합니까? *migug-e eotteok'e jeonhwa-hamnikka?*
I'd like to talk to the operator.	교환수와 이야기하고 싶습니다. *kyohwansu-wa iyagi-hago-shipseumnida.*
May I speak to _____?	_____좀 바꿔 주시겠습니까? *_____jom bakkweo-jushi-gesseumnikka?*
Who's calling?	누구십니까? *mugu-shimnikka?*
Speak slowly, please.	천천히 말씀해 주십시오. *ch'eonch'eonhi malsseum-hae-jushipshiyo.*
Speak louder, please.	크게 말씀해 주십시오. *k'euge malsseum-hae-jushipshiyo.*
Don't hang up.	끊지 마십시오. *kkeunch'i-masipshiyo.*
I got a wrong number.	잘못 걸었습니다. *chalmot keoreosseumnida.*
I was disconnected.	끊어졌습니다. 연결이 안됐습니다. *kkeuneojyeosseumnida. yeon-gyeori an-dwaesseumnida.*
I'd like to leave a message.	말씀 좀 전해 주시겠습니까? *malsseum jom jeon-hae-jushi-gesseumnikka?*
He/she isn't here.	(그분이)여기 안계십니다. *(keu-bun-i)yeogi an-gyeshimnida.*
He/she'll be back at _____.	(그분이)_____에 돌아오십니다. *(keu-bun-i) _____e dora-oshimnida.*
He's <u>in a meeting</u>.	(그분이) 회의중입니다. *(keu-bun-i) hoe-eui-jung-imnida.*
• on vacation	• 휴가　　　hyuga
• out to lunch	• 점심식사　jeomshim-shiksa
The line is busy.	통화중입니다. *t'onghwa-jung-imnida.*

Postal Services

post office	우체국 *uch'eguk*

Basic Words and Phrases

post card	엽서	
	yeopseo	
letter	편지	
	p'yeonji	
telegram	전보	
	cheonbo	
air mail letter	항공 편지	
	hang-gong-p'yeonji	
registered letter	등기 편지	
	teung-gi-p'yeonji	
special delivery letter	속달 편지	
	soktal-p'yeonji	
package	소포, 짐	
	sop'o, chim	
Where is a mailbox?	우체통이 어디에 있습니까?	
	uch'et'ong-i eodi-e isseumnikka?	
Where is a post office?	우체국이 어디에 있습니까?	
	uch'egug-i eodi-e isseumnikka?	
I'd like to buy some stamps.	우표를 사려고 합니다.	
	up'yo-reul sa-ryeogo-hamnida.	
Which window is it?	어느 창구입니까?	
	eoneu ch'ang-gu-imnikka?	
What's the postage to the United States?	미국까지 우편요금은 얼마입니까?	
	miguk-kkaji up'yeon-yogeum-eun eolma-imnikka?	
I'd like to send a telex.	텔렉스를 치려고 합니다.	
	t'elekseu-reul ch'i-ryeogo-hamnida.	
How late are you open?	몇시까지 엽니까?	
	myeot-shi-kkaji yeomnikka?	
How much is it <u>per minute</u>?	<u>일분에</u> 얼마입니까?	
	<u>*il-bun-e eolma-imnikka?*</u>	
• per word	• 한자에	*han-ja-e*

Signs

Entrance	입구, 들어가는 곳
	ipku, deureo-ganeun-got
Exit	출구, 나가는 곳
	ch'ulgu, naganeun-got
East exit	동쪽 출구
	tong-jjok ch'ulgu
West exit	서쪽 출구
	seo-jjok ch'ulgu
South exit	남쪽 출구
	nam-jjok ch'ulgu
North exit	북쪽 출구
	puk'jjok ch'ulgu
Lavatory	공중 변소
	kongjung-byeonso

Elevator	엘리베이터, 승강기	
	ellibeit'eo, seung-gang-gi	
Men	신사, 남자	
	shinsa, namja	
Women	숙녀, 여자	
	sungnyeo, yeoja	
Adult	어른, 성인	
	eoreun, seong-in	
Child	어린이	
	eorini	
Danger	위험	
	wiheom	
Keep out	출입 금지	
	ch'urip geumji	
Under construction	공사중	
	kongsa-jung	
Fire extinguisher	소화기	
	sohwagi	
Fee required	유료	
	yuryo	
Free admission	무료 입장	
	muryo ipchang	
Business hours	영업 시간	
	yeong-eop-shigan	
Closed today	금일 휴업, 오늘 쉽니다.	
	keumil-hyu-eop, oneul swimnida.	
Temporarily closed	임시 휴업	
	imshi-hyu-eop	
Staying open	야간 영업	
	yagan-yeong-eop	
No smoking	금연	
	keumyeon	
Full	만원	
	manweon	
Parking place	주차장	
	chuch'ajang	
No parking	주차 금지, 주차 엄금	
	chuch'a-geumji, chuch'a-eomgeum	
Waiting room	대기실	
	taegi-shil	
Hospital	병원	
	pyeong-weon	
Please ring	벨을 누르시오	
	pereul nuru-shiyo.	
Pull	당기시오	
	tang-gi-shiyo	
Push	미시오	
	mi-shiyo	

Basic Words and Phrases

Caution	주의
	chu-eui
Emergency exit	비상구
	pisang-gu
Don't touch	손대지 마시오
	son dae-ji-mashiyo
Information	안내소
	annaeso
Beware of dog	개주의, 맹견주의, 개조심
	kae ju-eui, maeng-gyeon ju-cui, kaejoshim
Beware of fire	불조심
	pul-joshim
Cashier	계산대
	kyesandae
For rent	세 놓음
	se no-eum
No entry	입장 금지
	ipchang-geumji
No admittance	입장 금지
	ipchang-geumji
Private	개인용
	kaein-yong
Private property	사유지
	sayuji
Ticket booth	매표소, 표 파는곳
	maep'yoso, p'yo p'aneun-got
Open	열음, 열었음
	yeoreum, yeoreosseum
Closed	닫음, 닫았음
	tadeum, tadasseum
For sale	매품
	maep'um
Warning	경고
	kyeong-go
Stop	멈춤, 중지
	meomch'um, chungji
Sold out	매진
	maejin
Out of order	고장
	kojang
Not in use	사용 불가, 사용 금지
	sayongbulga, sayong-geumji
Fit for drinking	음료수
	eumnyosu
Don't drink the water	마시지 못함
	mashi-ji-mot'am
Shoes off	신을 벗으시오
	shin-eul beoseushiyo

Now in session	회의중, 강의중	
	hoe-eui-jung, kang-eui-jung	
Keep off the grass	잔디에 들어가지 마시오	
	chandi-e deureo-ga-ji-mashiyo	

Numbers

Note: There are two kinds of numerals, of Korean origin and Chinese origin. Korean numerals are generally used in counting hours, times, ages, months and with specific classifiers; Chinese numerals are usually used in dealing with money matters, the metric system, and counting floors of buildings, minutes, days, and years. Refer to counters using Korean and Chinese numerals. Up to 99 both numerals are used; for 100 and up, Chinese numerals are used.

	Korean Origin	**Chinese Origin**
0	영	
	yeong	
1	하나	일
	hana	*il*
2	둘	이
	tul	*i*
3	셋	삼
	set	*sam*
4	넷	사
	net	*sa*
5	다섯	오
	taseot	*o*
6	여섯	육
	yeoseot	*yuk*
7	일곱	칠
	ilgop	*ch'il*
8	여덟	팔
	yeodeol	*p'al*
9	아홉	구
	ahop	*ku*
10	열	십
	yeol	*ship*
11	열 하나	십 일
	yeol-hana	*shib-il*
12	열 둘	십 이
	yeol-ttul	*shib-i*
13	열 셋	십 삼
	yeol-set	*ship-sam*
14	열 넷	십 사
	yeol-net	*ship-sa*
15	열 다섯	십 오
	yeol-ttasseot	*ship-o*

16	열 여섯	십육	
	yeol-yeoseot	*shim-nyuk*	
17	열 일곱	십칠	
	yeol-ilgop	*ship-ch'il*	
18	열 여덟	십팔	
	yeol-yeodeol	*ship-p'al*	
19	열 아홉	십구	
	yeol-ahop	*ship-ku*	
20	스물	이십	
	seumul	*i-ship*	
30	서른	삼십	
	seoreun	*sam-ship*	
40	마흔	사십	
	maheun	*sa-ship*	
50	쉰	오십	
	swin	*o-ship*	
60	예순	육십	
	yesun	*yuk-ship*	
70	일흔	칠십	
	ireun	*ch'il-ship*	
80	여든	팔십	
	yeodeun	*p'al-ship*	
90	아흔	구십	
	aheun	*ku-ship*	
100		백, 일백	
		paek, il-baek	
200		이백	
		i-baek	
300		삼백	
		sam-baek	
400		사백	
		sa-baek	
500		오백	
		o-baek	
600		육백	
		yuk-baek	
700		칠백	
		ch'il-baek	
800		팔백	
		p'al-baek	
900		구백	
		ku-baek	
1,000		천, 일천	
		ch'eon, il-ch'eon	
2,000		이천	
		i-ch'eon	
3,000		삼천	
		sam-ch'eon	

4,000	사천	*sa-ch'eon*
5,000	오천	*o-ch'eon*
6,000	육천	*yuk-ch'eon*
7,000	칠천	*ch'il-ch'eon*
8,000	팔천	*p'al-ch'eon*
9,000	구천	*ku-ch'eon*
10,000	만, 일만	*man, il-man*
20,000	이만	*i-man*
30,000	삼만	*sam-man*
40,000	사만	*sa-man*
50,000	오만	*o-man*
60,000	육만	*yuk-man*
70,000	칠만	*ch'il-man*
80,000	팔만	*p'al-man*
90,000	구만	*ku-man*
100,000	십만, 일십만	*shim-man, il-shim-man*
200,000	이십만	*i-shim-man*
300,000	삼십만	*sam-shim-man*
400,000	사십만	*sa-shim-man*
500,000	오십만	*o-shim-man*
600,000	육십만	*yuk-shim-man*
700,000	칠십만	*ch'il-shim-man*
800,000	팔십만	*p'al-shim-man*
900,000	구십만	*ku-shim-man*

Basic Words and Phrases

1,000,000	백만, 일백만	paeng-man, il-baeng-man
2,000,000	이백만	i-baeng-man
3,000,000	삼백만	sam-baeng-man
4,000,000	사백만	sa-baeng-man
5,000,000	오백만	o-baeng-man
6,000,000	육백만	yuk-baeng-man
7,000,000	칠백만	ch'il-baeng-man
8,000,000	팔백만	p'al-baeng-man
9,000,000	구백만	ku-baeng-man
10,000,000	천만, 일천만	ch'eon-man, il-ch'eon-man
20,000,000	이천만	i-ch'eon-man
100,000,000	억, 일억	eok, ireok
1,000,000,000	십억	shib-eok
10,000,000,000	백억	paeg-eok
100,000,000,000	천억	ch'eon-eok
1,000,000,000,000	조	cho

Examples

540	**오백 사십**	o-baek-sa-ship
1,540	천 오백 사십	ch'eon-o-baek-sa-ship
11,540	만 천 오백 사십	man-ch'eon-o-baek-sa-ship
1,611,540	백 육십 일만 일천 오백 사십	paeng-yuk-shib-il-man-il-ch'eon-o-baek-sa-ship

Ordinal Numbers

Note: There are two sets of ordinal numbers, Korean and Chinese.

Korean ordinal numbers

first	첫째
	ch'eot-jjae

second	둘째
	tul-jjae
third	셋째
	set-jjae
fourth	넷째
	net-jjae
fifth	다섯째
	taseot-jjae
sixth	여섯째
	yeoseot-jjae
seventh	일곱째
	ilgop-jjae
eighth	여덟째
	yeodeol-jjae
ninth	아홉째
	ahop-jjae
tenth	열째
	yeol-jjae

Chinese ordinal numbers

first	제일
	che-il
second	제이
	che-i
third	제삼
	che-sam
fourth	제사
	che-sa
fifth	제오
	che-o
sixth	제육
	che-yuk
seventh	제칠
	che-ch'il
eighth	제팔
	che-p'al
ninth	제구
	che-gu
tenth	제십
	che-ship

Quantities

a half	반, 이분의 일
	pan, i-bun-eui il
a quarter	사분의 일
	sa-bun-eui il
three quarters	사분의 삼
	sa-bun-eui sam
a third	삼분의 일
	sam-bun-eui il

Basic Words and Phrases

two thirds	삼분의 이
	sam-bun-eui i
a cup	잔, 컵
	chan, k'eop
a dozen	다스, 타
	taseu, t'a
a kilo	킬로
	k'illo
a liter	리터
	rit'eo
a little	조금
	chogeum
a lot	많이
	mani
a pair	쌍, 벌
	ssang, peol
enough	넉넉히
	neongneokhi

Counting Different Kinds Of Things

Counters Using Korean Numerals

one	*two*	*three*	*four*	*five*
o-clock — 시 — shi				
한시	두시	세시	네시	다섯시
han-shi	*tu-shi*	*se-shi*	*ne-shi*	*taseot-shi*
hours — 시간 — shigan				
한시간	두시간	세시간	네시간	다섯시간
han-shigan	*tu-shigan*	*se-shigan*	*ne-shigan*	*taseot-shigan*
times — 번 — beon				
한번	두번	세번	네번	다섯번
han-beon	*tu-beon*	*se-beon*	*ne-beon*	*taseot-peon*
ages — 살 — sal				
한살	두살	세살	네살	다섯살
han-sal	*tu-sal*	*se-sal*	*ne-sal*	*taseot-sal*
packs (of cigarettes, etc.) — 갑 — gap				
한갑	두갑	세갑	네갑	다섯갑
han-gap	*tu-gap*	*se-gap*	*ne-gap*	*taseot-kap*
people — 사람 — saram — 명 — myeong				
한사람	두사람	세사람	네사람	다섯사람
han-saram	*tu-saram*	*se-saram*	*ne-saram*	*taseot-saram*
한명	두명	세명	네명	다섯명
han-myeong	*tu-myeong*	*se-myeong*	*ne-myeong*	*taseot-myeong*
people (honorific) — 분 — bun				
한분	두분	세분	네분	다섯분
han-bun	*tu-bun*	*se-bun*	*ne-bun*	*taseot-pun*

Korean for Business Traveler

one	two	three	four	five

animals, fish — 마리 ___ mari

한마리	두마리	세마리	네마리	다섯마리
han-mari	tu-mari	se-mari	ne-mari	taseot-mari

bound objects (books, notebooks, etc.) — 권 ___ gweon

한권	두권	세권	네권	다섯권
han-gweon	tu-gweon	se-gweon	ne-gweon	taseot-kweon

houses, buildings — 채 ___ ch'ae

한채	두채	세채	네채	다섯채
han-ch'ae	tu-ch'ae	se-ch'ae	ne-ch'ae	taseot-ch'ae

vehicles, machines — 대 ___ dae

한대	두대	세대	네대	다섯대
han-dae	tu-dae	se-dae	ne-dae	taseot-tae

bottles — 병 ___ byeong

한병	두병	세병	네병	다섯병
han-byeong	tu-byeong	se-byeong	ne-byeong	taseot-byeong

items, units, objects — 개 ___ gae

한개	두개	세개	네개	다섯개
han-gae	tu-gae	se-gae	ne-gae	taseot-kae

small sticks (pencil, brush, etc.) — 자루 ___ jaru

한자루	두자루	세자루	네자루	다섯자루
han-jaru	tu-jaru	se-jaru	ne-jaru	taseot-jaru

months — 달 ___ dal

한달	두달	석/세달	넉/네달	다섯달
han-dal	tu-dal	seok/se-dal	neok/ne-dal	taseot-tal

sheets, tickets — 장 ___ jang

한장	두장	석/세장	넉/네장	다섯장
han-jang	tu-jang	seok/se-jang	neok/ne-jang	taseot-chang

liquid (glasses or cups of.) — 잔 ___ jan

한잔	두잔	석/세잔	넉/네잔	다섯잔
han-jan	tu-jan	seok/se-jan	neok/ne-jan	taseot-chan

pairs of things to wear on feet or legs — 켤레 ___ k'yeolle

한켤레	두켤레	세켤레	네켤레	다섯켤레
han-k'yeolle	tu-k'yeolle	se-k'yeolle	ne-k'yeolle	taseot-k'yeolle

suits (of clothes) — 벌 ___ beol

한벌	두벌	세벌	네벌	다섯벌
han-beol	tu-beol	se-beol	ne-beol	taseot-peol

a pair, a couple — 쌍 ___ ssang

한쌍	두쌍	세쌍	네쌍	다섯쌍
han-ssang	tu-ssang	se-ssang	ne-ssang	taseot-ssang

bowls — 그릇 ___ geureut

한그릇	두그릇	세그릇	네그릇	다섯그릇
han-geureut	tu-geureut	se-geureut	ne-geureut	taseot-keureut

dishes — 접시 ___ jeopshi

한접시	두접시	세접시	네접시	다섯접시
han-jeopshi	tu-jeopshi	se-jeopshi	ne-jeopshi	taseot-cheopshi

Basic Words and Phrases

one	two	three	four	five
minutes — 분__bun				
일분	이분	삼분	사분	오분
il-bun	*i-bun*	*sam-bun*	*sa-bun*	*o-bun*
years — 년__nyeon				
일년	이년	삼년	사년	오년
il-nyeon	*i-nyeon*	*sam-nyeon*	*sa-nyeon*	*o-nyeon*
won(Korean monetary unit) — 원__won				
일원	이원	삼원	사원	오원
irwon	*i-won*	*sam-won*	*sa-won*	*o-won*
ages — 세__se				
일세	이세	삼세	사세	오세
il-se	*i-se*	*sam-se*	*sa-se*	*o-se*
floors of building — 층__ch'eung				
일층	이층	삼층	사층	오층
il-ch'eung	*i-ch'eung*	*sam-ch'eung*	*sa-ch'eung*	*o-ch'eung*
months (January, February, etc.) — 월__weol				
일월	이월	삼월	사월	오월
irweol	*i-weol*	*sam-weol*	*sa-weol*	*o-weol*
portions, servings — 인분__inbun				
일인분	이인분	삼인분	사인분	오인분
irinbun	*i-inbun*	*sam-inbun*	*sa-inbun*	*o-inbun*

Years

1900	천구백년
	ch'eon-gubaeng-nyeon
1987	천구백팔십칠년
	ch'eon-gubaek-p'alship-ch'il-nyeon
1988	천구백팔십팔년
	ch'eon-gubaek-p'alship-p'al-nyeon
1989	천구백팔십구년
	ch'eon-gubaek-p'alship-ku-nyeon
1990	천구백구십년
	ch'eon-gubaek-kushim-nyeon

The Hangul Alphabet

Vowels / Consonants	ㅏ a	ㅑ ya	ㅓ eo	ㅕ yeo	ㅗ o	ㅛ yo	ㅜ u	ㅠ yu	ㅡ eu	ㅣ i
ㄱ k, g	가 ka	갸 kya	거 keo	겨 kyeo	고 ko	교 kyo	구 ku	규 kyu	그 keu	기 ki
ㄴ n	나 na	냐 nya	너 neo	녀 nyeo	노 no	뇨 nyo	누 nu	뉴 nyu	느 neu	니 ni
ㄷ t, d	다 ta	댜 tya	더 teo	뎌 tyeo	도 to	됴 tyo	두 tu	듀 tyu	드 teu	디 ti
ㄹ r, l	라 ra	랴 rya	러 reo	려 ryeo	로 ro	료 ryo	루 ru	류 ryu	르 reu	리 ri
ㅁ m	마 ma	먀 mya	머 meo	며 myeo	모 mo	묘 myo	무 mu	뮤 myu	므 meu	미 mi
ㅂ p, b	바 pa	뱌 pya	버 peo	벼 pyeo	보 po	뵤 pyo	부 pu	뷰 pyu	브 peu	비 pi
ㅅ s, sh	사 sa	샤 sya	서 seo	셔 syeo	소 so	쇼 syo	수 su	슈 syu	스 seu	시 si
ㅇ silent	아 a	야 ya	어 eo	여 yeo	오 o	요 yo	우 u	유 yu	으 eu	이 i
ㅈ ch, j	자 cha	쟈 chya	저 cheo	져 chyeo	조 cho	죠 chyo	주 chu	쥬 chu	즈 cheu	지 chi
ㅊ ch'	차 ch'a	챠 ch'ya	처 ch'eo	쳐 ch'yeo	초 ch'o	쵸 ch'yo	추 ch'u	츄 ch'yu	츠 ch'eu	치 ch'i
ㅋ k'	카 k'a	캬 k'ya	커 k'eo	켜 k'yeo	코 k'o	쿄 k'yo	쿠 k'u	큐 k'yu	크 k'eu	키 k'i
ㅌ t'	타 t'a	탸 t'ya	터 t'eo	텨 t'yeo	토 t'o	툐 t'yo	투 t'u	튜 t'yu	트 t'eu	티 t'i
ㅍ p'	파 p'a	퍄 p'ya	퍼 p'eo	펴 p'yeo	포 p'o	표 p'yo	푸 p'u	퓨 p'yu	프 p'eu	피 p'i
ㅎ h	하 ha	햐 hya	허 heo	혀 hyeo	호 ho	효 hyo	후 hu	휴 hyu	흐 heu	히 hi

Basic Words and Phrases

Koreans are deservedly proud of their phonetic writing system called *han-gul*. Developed by King Sejong of the Yi Dynasty in 1443, it was designed to make Korean easy to read. Until *han-gul* was invented, Koreans relied on adaptations of Chinese characters with *han-gul,* primarily in newspapers and magazines.

With the advent of *han-gul,* the literacy rate in Korea improved dramatically to what is now one of the highest in the world. One of the most remarkable aspects of the system is the way in which the shape of the consonants resembles the shape of the mouth and tongue as they form the corresponding sounds. Koreans continue to celebrate the development of this original invention, *Han-gul* Day, on October 9.

BUSINESS DICTIONARY

ENGLISH TO KOREAN

KOREAN TO ENGLISH

BUSINESS DICTIONARY

The 3,000-entry list of basic business terms (English-Korean) presents the entry in English in the left column. The center column provides the Hangul symbols. In the right column, the romanized letters enacted jointly by South and North Korea appear. The romanization, which uses hyphens to separate syllables of words, provides a guide to the pronunciation of the Hangul. The letter *v* in parentheses is used to indicate that the word which it follows is defined as a verb.

In the 3,000-entry Korean to English list, the words are alphabetized using the romanized form. Thus, you will find the romanization in the left column, the English in the center, and the Hangul on the right.

IV. BUSINESS DICTIONARY

ENGLISH TO KOREAN

A

abandon (v)	포기하다, 위부(委付)하다, 인도(引渡)하다	p'ogi-hada, wibu-hada, indo-hada
abandonment	소유권 포기, 위부(委付)	so-yu-kkweon p'ogi, wibu
abatement	인하(引下), 감소(減少)	inha, kamso
ability-to-pay concept	지불 유자격 개념	jibul yujakyeok kae-nyeom
above-mentioned	상술한, 상기의	sangsul-han, sang-gi-eui
above par	액면 가격 이상	aengmyeon ga-gyeok
above-the-line	표준 이상의	p'yojun i-sang-eui
absentee ownership	부재자 소유권	pujaeja soyukkweon
absenteeism	부재 지주 제도, 상습적 결근	pujae jiju jedo, sangseu-pcheok kyeol-geun
absolute temperature	절대 온도	cheolttae ondo
absorb (v)/absorb the loss	부담시키다, 손해를 부담하다	pudam si-k'ida, sonhae-reul pudam-hada
absorption costing	전부원가계산(全部原價計算)	cheonbu weonkka gyesan
abstract of title	권리 증서 요약서	kweolli jeungseo yo-yakseo
accelerated amortization	가속 분할 상환	kasok pun-hwal sang-hwan
accelerated depreciation	가속 감가 상각	kasok kamkka sang-gak
acceleration clause	상환 가속 조항, 촉진 조항	sanghwan kasok chohang, ch'okchin johang
acceleration premium	가속 할증금, (증권의) 액면 초과액	kasok haljeung-geum, (cheungkkweon-eui) aengmyeon ch'ogwa-aek
accelerator	가속 장치, 액셀	kasok changch'i, aeksel
accept (v)	(어음을)인수하다	(eo-eum-eul) insu-hada
acceptable quality level	합격 품질 수준	hapkyeok p'umjil su-jun
acceptance	수락, 어음의 인수	surak, eo-eum-eui insu
acceptance agreement	인수 승낙	insu seung-nak
acceptance bill	인수 어음	insu eo-eum
acceptance credit	인수 신용	insu sinyong
acceptance house	어음 인수 업자, 인수자	eo-eum insu eopcha, insuja
acceptance sampling	인수 견본 추출(抽出)	insu gyeonbon ch'u-ch'ul
acceptance test	합격 판정 시험	hapkyeok p'anjeong si-heom
acceptor	인수인(引受人)	insu-in
accession rate	증가율	cheung-ga-yul
accessory	액세서리, 부속품	aekseseori, pusokp'um
accidental damage	우발적 손해	ubaljeok sonhae
accommodation bill	융통 수표(融通手票)	yungt'ong su-p'yo
accommodation credit	융통 신용	yungt'ong sin-yong
accommodation endorsement	융통 보증, 융통 배서	yungt'ong bo-jeung, yungt'ong bae-seo
accommodation paper	융통 어음	yungt'ong eo-eum

accommodation parity

accommodation parity	조절 등가, 형평 가격	chojeol deungkka, hyeongp'yeong gagyeok
accommodation platform	조절 강령	chojeol gangnyeong
accompanied goods	부수 상품, 휴대품	pusu sangp'um, hyudaep'um
accord and satisfaction	협정과(빚의) 변제, 의무의 이행	hyeopcheong-gwa (pij-eui) byeonje, euimu-eui i-haeng
account	구좌, 계정(計定)	kujwa, kyejeong
account balance	계정 잔고	kyejeong jan-go
account current	경상 계정(經常計定)	kyeongsang gyejeong
account day	결산일(決算日)	kyeolsanil
account executive	구좌 담당	kujwa damdang
account for (v)	계정하다	kyejeong-hada
account number	구좌 번호	kujwa beonho
account period	거래 기간	keorae gigan
account, secured	담보 계정	tamppo gyejeong
accountability	책무, 책임	ch'aengmu, ch'aegim
accountant	계리사, 회계사	kyerisa, hoegyesa
accountant, chief	회계 주임	hoegye ju-im
accounting cost	원가 회계(原價會計)	weonkka hoegye
accounting department	회계과, 경리과	hoegyekkwa, kyeongnikkwa
accounting, management	관리 회계	gwalli hoegye
accounting method	회계 방법	hoegye bangbeop
accounting period	계정 기간, 회계 기간	kyejeong gigan, hoegye gigan
accounting ratio	회계 비율	hoegye bi-yul
accounts, group	집단 회계	chiptan hoegye
accounts payable	지불 계정(줄돈)	chilbul gyejeong(chultton)
accounts receivable	수취 계정(받을돈)	such'wi gyejeong(padeultton)
accretion	자연 증가	cha-yeon jeung-ga
accrual	발생, 경과(經過)	balsaeng, kyeong-gwa
accrual method	발생주의 원칙	palsaeng-ju-eui weonch'ik
accrue (v)	(이자가)붙다, 발생하다	(ija-ga)butta, palsaeng-hada
accrued assets	선급 자산(先給資產)	seon-geup chasan
accrued depreciation	축적 감가 상각	ch'ukcheok gamkka sang-gak
accrued expenses	미지급 비용(未支給費用)	mi-jigeup piyong
accrued interest	미지급 이자(未支給利子), 미수 이자(未收利子)	mi-jigeup ija, misu ija
accrued revenue	미수 수입(未收收入)	misu su-ip
accrued taxes	미지급세(未支給稅)	mi-jigeupse
accumulated depreciation	감가 상각 충당금, 누적 감가 상각	kamkka sang-gak ch'ungdang-geum, nujeok kamkka sanggak
acetaldehyde	흡반(吸盤)	heuppan
acetate	아세트 산염	aset'eu sanyeom
acetic acid	아세트 산(酸)	aset'eu san
acetone	아세톤	aset'on
acid (adj)	산(酸)의	san-eui
acid-test ratio	당좌 비율, 정밀 검사 비율, 산성 검사 비율 (酸性檢査比率)	tangjwa biyul, cheongmil geomsa biyul, sanseong geomsa biyul

acknowledge (v)/acknowledge receipt of (v)	승인하다/(수령을)통지하다	seung-in-hada, (su-ryeong-eul) t'ongji-hada
acoustic coupler	음향 연결기	eumhyang yeon-gyeolgi
acquire (v)	취득하다	ch'wideuk-hada
acquired rights	기득권	kideukkweon
acquisition	취득, 습득	ch'wideuk, seupteuk
acquisition, data	정보 획득, 정보 수집	cheongbo hoekteuk, cheongbo sujip
acquisition profile	취득 윤곽, 취득 측면	ch'wideuk yun-gwak, ch'wideuk ch'eungmyeon
acreage allotment	(경작)면적 할당	(kyeongjak) myeonjeok halttang
across-the-board settlement	전면적인 결산, 지불 양도	cheonmyeonjeog-in gyeolsan, chibul yangdo
across-the-board tariff negotiations	전면 관세 협상	cheonmyeon gwanse hyeopsang
act of God	불가항력	pulga-hangnyeok
action plan	활동 계획	hwalttong gyehoek
action research	활동 연구	hwalttong yeon-gu
active account	유효 계정	yuhyo gyejeong
active assets	유효 자산	yuhyo jasan
active debt	유효 채무	yuhyo ch'aemu
active trust	유효 외상(판매)	yuhyo oesang (p'anmae)
activity chart	활동 도표	hwalttong do-p'yo
activity on arrow	화살표의 활동	hwasalp'yo-eui hwalttong
actual cash value	실제 현금 가치	shilje hyeon-geum gach'i
actual cost	실제 비용	shilje biyong
actual income	실제 소득, 실수입	shilje sodeuk, shilsuip
actual liability	실제 부채	shilje buch'ae
actual market volume	실제 시장 거래량	shilje shijang georae-ryang
actual total loss	추정 전손(推定全損)	ch'ujeong jeonson
actuals	실제, 실질, 실정	shilje, shiljil, shiljeong
actuary	보험 회계사	poheom hoegyesa
add-on sales	가산 판매	kasan p'anmae
addendum	추가(사항)	ch'uga(sahang)
address commission	주선료	chuseollyo
adjudge (v)	선정하다, 판정하다	seonjeong-hada, p'anjeong-hada
adjudication	(파산 등의)선고	(p'asan-deung-eui) seon-go
adjust (v)	(계산따위를) 청산하다, 조정하다	(kyesan ttawi-reul) ch'eongsan-hada, chojeong-hada
adjustable peg	조절 억제책	chojeol eokchech'aek
adjusted CIF price	운임 보험료 포함 조정 가격	unim boheomnyo p'oham jojeong gagyeok
adjusted earned income	조정 수입	chojeong su-ip
adjusted rate	조정 비율	chojeong biyul
adjusting entry	조정 기입 사항	chojeong gi-ip sahang
adjustment process	조정 과정	chojeong gwajeong
adjustment trigger	조절 제동기	chojeol jedong-gi

administration

administration	유산 관리, 행정 기관	yusan-gwalli, haengjeong-gigwan
administrative	관리(경영)의	kwalli (kyeong-yeong)-eui
administrative expense	관리 비용	kwalli biyong
administrator	관재인(管財人), 관리자	kwanjae-in, kwanllija
administratrix	여성 관리(관재)인	yeoseong gwalli (kwanjae)-in
advance (v)	선불하다, 선대하다	seonbul-hada, seondae-hada
advance freight	선불 운임	seonbul unim
advance notice	사전 통고	sajeon t'ong-go
advance payments	선불	seonbul
advance refunding	선도 상환	seondo sanghwan
advanced technology	첨단기술	ch'eomdan gisul
advantage, competitive	경쟁상의 이점	kyeongjaengsang-eui it-jeom
adverse balance	역수지(逆收支)	yeoksuji
advertising	광고	kwang-go
advertising agency	광고 대행업(자)	kwang-go daehaeng eop (cha)
advertising budget	광고 예산	kwang-go yesan
advertising campaign	광고 선전	kwang-go seonjeon
advertising drive	대대적인 판매, 대선전	taedaejeog-in p'anmae, taeseonjeon
advertising expenses	광고비	kwang-go
advertising manager	광고 부장	kwang-go bujang
advertising media	광고 매체	kwang-go maech'e
advertising research	광고 연구	kwang-go yeon-gu
advice note	안내 통지	an-nae t'ongji
advise (v)	조언하다, 충고하다, 자문하다	cho-eon-hada, ch'ung-go-hada, chamun-hada
advisory council	자문 위원회, 자문 회의	chamun wiweonhoe, chamun hoeeui
advisory funds	자문 기금	chamun gigeum
advisory service	자문 사무(봉사)	chamun samu(bongsa)
aerial photographic camera	항공 사진 카메라	hang-gong sajin k'amera
affidavit	선서서(宣誓書), 재정 보증서	seonseo-seo, chaejeong bojeungseo
affiliate (v)	제휴하다	chehyu-hada
affiliates	계열(系列)회사	kyeyeol hoesa
affiliation	제휴	chehyu
affirmative action	고용 차별 수정 조치	koyong ch'abyeol sujeong joch'i
affreightnment	용선(傭船)	yongseon
afloat	(어음따위가) 유통하여	(eoeum ttawi-ga) yut'ong-hayeo
after-hours-trading	영업 시간 외의 무역	yeong-eop shigan-oe-eui muyeok
after-sales-service	아프터 써비스	ap'eut'eo sseobiseu
after-sight	열람후	yeollamhu
after-tax real rate of return	납세후 실제 배당율	napsehu shilje baedang-yul
afterdate (v)	후불하다	hubul-hada

alternator

against all risks (adv)	각종 위험에 반해서	kakchong wiheom-e banhaeseo
agency	대리점	daerijeom
agency bank	대리 은행	daeri eunhaeng
agency fee	대리점 수수료	daerijeom susu-ryo
agenda	안컨, 의사 일정	ankkeon, euisa iljjeong
agent	대리인(점)	daeri-in(jeom)
agent bank	업무 대행 은행	eommu daehaeng euehaeng
aggregate demand	총 수요	ch'ong suyo
aggregate risk	총 위험	ch'ong wiheom
aggregate supply	총 공급	ch'ong-gong-geup
agreement	합의, 협정, 무역 거래 조건 협정서, 합의서	habeui, hyeop cheong, muyeok keorae jokkeon hyeopcheongseo, habeuiseo
agricultural paper	농업 어음	nong-eop eoeum
agricultural products	농산물	nongsanmul
agriculture	농업	nong-eop
air bag	에어백	e-eobaek
air conditioner	에어콘	e-eo-k'on
air express	항공 속달, 지급	hang-gong soktal, chigeup
air freight	항공 화물	hang-gong hwamul
air shipments	항공 적하	hang-gong jeokha
algorithm	연산(演算) 방식	yeonsan bangshik
algorithmic language	연산 언어	yeonsan eoneo
alien corporation	외국 회사	oeguk hoesa
alkaline (adj)	알카리성(염기성)	alk'alliseong (yeomgiseong)
all in cost	전 비용을 들여	cheon biyong-eul deuryeo
all or none	전부 인수 혹은 부분 인수	cheonbu insu hogeun bubun insu
allocation of costs	비용 할당	piyong halttang
allocation of responsibilities	책임 분담, 책임 할당	ch'aegim bundam, ch'aegim halttang
allocation, resource	자원 배분	chaweon baebun
allonge	부전지(附箋紙)	pujeonji
allot (v)	할당하다	halttang-hada
allotment	할당, 배당	halttang, baedang
allotment letter	주식 배당 통지서	chushik baedang t'ongjiseo
allow (v)	주다, 공급하다, 허용하다	chuda, kong-geup-hada, heoyong-hada
allowance	충당금, 용돈	ch'ungdnag-geum, yongtton
allowance, depreciation	감가 상각 충당금	kamkka sang-gak ch'ungdang-geum
alloy	합금(合金)	hapkeum
alloy steel	합금강(合金鋼)	hapkeumgang
all-weather camera	전천후 카메라	cheonch'eonhu k'amera
alongside	선측(船側)에	seonch'eug-e
alteration	변경, 개조	pyeon-gyeong, kaejo
alternating current	교류	kyoryu
alternative order	양자 택일의 주문서, 환어음	yangja t'aegil-eui jumunseo, hwaneoeum
alternator	교류기	kyoryugi

English	Korean	Romanization
alumina	알루미나(산화알미늄)	allumina(sanhwa alminyum)
aluminum	알루미늄	alluminyum
amalgamation	합동, 합병	hap-tong, hap-pyeong
amend (v)	개정하다, 수정하다	kaejeong-hada, sujeong-hada
amendment	개정, 수정	kaejeong, sujeong
amine	아민	amin
ammonia	암모니아	ammonia
amorphous semiconductor	비정질(非定質) 반도체	pijeongjil bandoch'e
amorphous silicon	비결정 규소	pi-gyeoljjeong gyuso
amortization	분할 상환	punhal sanghwan
amount	총계, 원리 합계, 총액, 금액	ch'ong-gye, weolli hapkye, ch'ong-aek, keumaek
amount due	지불 예정 총액, 지불액	chibul yejeong ch'ong-aek, chilbul-aek
amplifier	증폭기	cheungp'okki
amplitude modulation	진폭 변조	chinp'ok pyeonjo
anaesthetic	마취의	mach'wi-eui
analgesic	무통성의	mut'ongseong-eui
analogue computer	유사형 전자 계산기	yusahyeong jeonja gyesan-gi
analysis	분석, 해석	punseok, haeseok
analysis, breakeven	손익 분기 분석, 채산 분석	sonik pun-gi bunseok, ch'aesan bunseok
analysis, competitor	경합자 분석	kyeonghapcha bunseok
analysis, cost	원가 분석	weonkka bunseok
analysis, cost-benefit	비용 효과 분석	piyong hyokkwa bunseok
analysis, critical path	주요 경로 분석 (主要經路分析)	chuyo gyeongno bunseok
analysis, depth	심층 분석	shimch'eung bunseok
analysis, financial	재정 분석, 재무 분석	chaejeong bunseok, chaemu bunseok
analysis, functional	기능 분석	kineung bunseok
analysis, input-output	투입 산출 분석	t'u-ip sanch'ul bunseok
analysis, investment	투자 분석	t'uja bunseok
analysis, job	작업 분석	chageop bunseok
analysis, needs	필요도 분석	p'iryodo bunseok
analysis, product	생산품 분석	saengsanp'um bunseok
analysis, profitability	수익성 분석	suikseong bunseok
analysis, risk	위험도 분석	wiheomdo bunseok
analysis, sales	판매 분석	p'anmae bunseok
analysis, systems	체계 분석, 조직 분석	ch'egye bunseok, chojik punseok
analyst	분석자(가), 통계 전문가	punseokcha(ka), t'ong-gye jeonmun-ga
anchorage (dues)	정박(세)	cheongbak(se)
ancillary operations	부수 운용, 보조 효과	pusu unyong, pojo hyokkwa
angle of incidence	입사각(入射角)	ipsagak
annealing	소둔(燒鈍)	sodun
annual	1년마다의, 연례의	ilnyeonmada-eui, yeollye-eui
annual accounts	연례 계정	yeollye gyejeong

annual audit	연례 회계 감사	yeollye hoegye gamsa
annual report	연례 보고서	yeollye bogoseo
annuitant	연금 수령인	yeon-geum suryeong-in
annuity	연금(수령권)	yeon-geum (suryeongkkwon)
antacid	제산성의	chesanseong-eui
anti-dumping duty	반 덤핑 관세	pan deomp'ing gwanse
anti-inflammatory (adj)	항 염증의	hang yeomjjeung-eui
antibiotic	항생의	hangsaeng-eui
anticholinergic	항 혈압 강하제	hang hyeorap kanghaje
antique authenticity certificate	골동품 감정 증명서	kolttongp'um gamjeong jeungmyeongseo
antiseptic	방부(防腐)의	pangbu-eui
antitrust laws	독점 금지법	tokcheom geumjibeop
aperture	구경	kugyeong
apparel	의류, 기성복	euiryu, kiseongbok
application form	신청 용지, 신청서	shinch'eong yongji, shinch'eongseo
applied proceeds swap	적용된 수익 교환	cheogyong doen su-ik kyohwan
appointment	임명, (재산의)지정	immyeong, (chaesan-eui) jijeong
appraisal	감정, 평가	kamjeong, p'yeongkka
appraisal, capital expenditure	자본금 지출 평가(감정)	chabon-geum jich'ul p'yeongkka (gamjeong)
appraisal, financial	재정 평가	chaejeong p'yeongkka
appraisal, investment	투자 감정	t'uja gamjeong
appraisal, market	시장 감정	shijang gamjeong
appraisal, self-	자체 감정	chach'e gamjeong
appreciation	가치 증가, 평가, 판단	kach'i jeung-ga, p'yeong kka, p'andan
apprentice	도제, 초심자	toje, ch'oshimja
appropriation	예산 금액	yesan geumaek
approval	결재, 인가, 승인	kyeoljae, in-ga, seung-in
approve (v)	결재하다, 인가하다	kyeoljae-hada, in-ga-hada
approved delivery facility	인가된 양도 시설	in-ga-doen yangdo shiseol
approved securities	공인 유가 증권	kong-in yukka jeungkkwon
arbitrage	중개 거래	chung-gae georae
arbitration	중재(仲裁)	chungjae
arbitration agreement	중재 협정	chungjae hyeopcheong
arbitrator	중재인	chungjae-in
area manager	지역 관리인	chiyeok kwalli-in
arithmetic mean	산술 평균	sansul p'yeong-gyun
armaments	군비, 장비	kunbi, changbi
arms length	이익 거래	i-ik keorae
around (exchange term)	약, 근처의	yak, keunch'eo-eui
arrears	체불(滯拂), 체화(滯貨)	ch'ebul, ch'ehwa
artificial intelligence	인공 두뇌	in-gong dunoe
ASA speed	미국 규격 협회 속도	miguk kyugyeok hyeophoe sokto

as if and when	처럼, 조건 및 시기대로	ch'eoreom, chogeon mit shigi-daero
as is goods	현상태 물품	hyeonsangt'ae mulp'um
as per advice	통지대로, 통지에 의하여	t'ongjidaero, t'ongji-e euihayeo
as soon as possible (shipment)	가능한 한, 조속한 시일내에	kaneunghanhan, chosokhan shi-ilnae-e
asking price	요구가격	yogu gagyeok
aspirin	아스피린	aseup'irin
assay	분석, 평가	punseok, p'yeongkka
assemble (v)	조립하다	chorip-hada
assembly	조립, 조립품	chorip, chorip-p'um
assembly factory	조립 공장	chorip kongjang
assembly line	(조립 공장의) 일관작업선(一貫作業線)	(chorip kongjang-eui) ilgwanjageopseon
assess (v)	견적하다, 과세하다	kyeonjeok-hada, kwase-hada
assessed valuation	사정(査定)가격, 감정가격	sajeong gagyeok, kamjeong gagyeok
assessment	사정액, 불입금지정	sajeong-aek, puripkeum jijeong
asset	자산, 유산	chasan, yusan
asset turnover	자산 회전율	chasan hoejeonnyul
asset value	자산 가치	chasan gach'i
assets accrued	증식 자산	cheungshik chasan
assets, current	유동 자산	yudong jasan
assets, deferred	거치 자산	keoch'i jasan
assets, fixed	고정 자산	kojeong jasan
assets, intangible	무형 자산	muhyeong jasan
assets, liquid	유동 자산	yudong jasan
assets, net	순수 자산	sunsu jasan
assets, tangible	유형 자산	yuhyeong jasan
assign (v)	배당하다, 할당하다	paedang-hada, halttang-hada
assignee	양수인, 수탁자, 관재인(管財人)	yangsu-in, sut'akcha, kwanjae-in
assignor	양도인(讓渡人)	yangdo-in
assistant	조수, 보좌역	chosu, pojwa-yeok
assistant general manager	총지배인 보좌역	ch'ong-jibae-in bojwa-yeok
assistant manager	차장, 부지배인, 부관리인	ch'ajang, pujibae-in, pu-gwalli-in
associate company	동업사, 관련회사	tong-eopsa, kwallyeon hoesa
assumed liability	인수 책임액	insu ch'aegimaek
at and from	입하 및 선적지	ipha mit seonjeokchi
at best	최고 조건으로	ch'oego jokkeon-euro
at call	청구하는 대로	ch'eong-gu-haneundaero
at or better	현수준 혹은 그 이상	hyeonsujun hogeun geu-isang
at par	액면 가격으로	aengmyeon gagyeog-euro
at sight	일람불(一覽拂)	illambul
at the close	체결시, 종장(終場)에	ch'egyeolshi, chongjang-e

English	Korean	Romanization
at the market	싯가로, 시장가격으로	shitkka-ro, shijang gagyeog-euro
at the opening	개장시(開場時)	kaejangshi
attach (v)	부착하다, 압류하다	puch'ak-hada, amnyu-hada
attache case	서류 가방	seoryu gabang
attended time	참석 시간	ch'amseok shigan
attestation	증명서	cheungmyeongseo
attorney	변호사, 대리인	pyeonhosa, taeri-in
attorney, power of	위임권, 위임장, 대리인	wi-imkkweon, wi-imjjang, daeri-in
attrition	마손, 소모	mason, somo
audio component system	오디오 전축 시스템	odio jeonch'uk siseut'em
audio response equipment	청력 반응 장치	ch'eongnyeok baneung jangch'i
audit (v)	(회계를)감사하다	(hoegye-reul) gamsa-hada
audit, internal	내부 감사	naebu gamsa
audit trail	감사 추적	kamsa ch'ujeok
auditing balance sheet	감사 대차 대조표	kamsa daech'a daejop'yo
auditor	회계 감사관	hoegye gamsagwan
autarky	자급 자족	chageup chajok
authenticity (gold)	정금(正金)	cheong-geum
authority (to have)	수권서(授權書)	sukkweonseo
authorize (v)	위임하다, 허가하다	wi-im-hada, heoga-hada
authorized dealer	공인(인가)증권업자, 공인업자	kong-in(in-ga) jeungkkweon eopcha, kong-in eopcha
authorized shares	수권 주식(증권)	sukkweon jushik (jeungkkweon)
authorized signature	수권 서명, 공인(인가)된 서명	sukkweon seomyeong, kong-in(in-ga)doen seomyeong
auto parts	자동차 부품	chadongch'a bup'um
auto-loading	자동 장치, 자동 장전	chadong jangch'i, chadong jangjeon
automatic	자동, 자동 기계	chadong, chadong gigye
automatic aperture control device	자동 구경 조절 장치	chadong gugyeong jojeol jangch'i
automatic developing machine	자동 현상기	chadong hyeonsang-gi
automatic exposure	자동 노출	chadong noch'ul
automatic focusing	자동 촛점	chadong ch'otcheom
automatic gearshift	자동 변속 기어	chadong byeonsok kieo
automatic printing machine	자동 인화기	chadong inhwagi
automatic rewinding	자동 되감기	chadong doegamkki
automatic teller machine (ATM)	현금 자동 출납기	hyeon-geum jadong ch'ulnapki
automation	오토메이션, 자동(自動)	ot'omeisyeon, chadong
automobile	자동차	chadongch'a
autonomous	자율의, 자발적인	chayureui, chabaljeogin
autoreverse	자동 역회전	chadong yeok-hoejeon
auxiliary lens	보조 렌즈	pojo renjeu

A

availability, subject to	이용 가능 조건하에	*iyong ganeung jokkeonha-e*
average	평균, 해손(海損)	*p'yeong-gyun, haeson*
average cost	평균 원가	*p'yeong-gyun weonkka*
average life	평균 수명	*p'yeong-gyun sumyeong*
average price	평균 가격	*p'yeong-gyun gagyeok*
average unit cost	평균 단위 비용	*p'yeong-gyun danwi biyong*
averaging	평균하다, 균분하다	*p'yeong-gyun-hada, kyunbun-hada*
avoidable costs	회피 가능 비용	*hoep'i ganeung biyong*
axle	차축	*ch'ach'uk*

B

back date	연체일(延滯日)	*yeonch'e-il*
back haul	체화(滯貨), 연체(延滯)화물	*ch'ehwa, yeonch'e hwamul*
back order	연체 주문	*yeonch'e jumun*
back selling	연체 판매	*yeonch'e p'anmae*
back taxes	연체 세금	*yeonch'e segeum*
back-to-back credit	동시 발행 신용장	*tongshi balhaeng shinyongjjang*
back-to-back loan	동시 발행 대부	*tongshi balhaeng daebu*
back-up-bonds	보조 공채 증서	*pojo gongch'ae jeungseo*
backed note	배서 어음, 증권	*paeseo eoeum, cheungkkweon*
backing and filling	배서 및 보충	*paeseo mit poch'ung*
backing support	보증 서류	*pojeung seoryu*
backlog	주문 잔고	*chumun jan-go*
backwardation	수도유예(受渡猶豫)	*sudo yuye*
backwash effect	반향 효과	*panhyang hyokkwa*
bad debt	불량 부채	*pullyang buch'ae*
balance, bank	은행 잔고	*eunhaeng jan-go*
balance, credit	대변 잔액	*taebyeon janaek*
balance of payments	국제 수지(國際收支)	*kukche suji*
balance of trade	무역 수지(貿易收支)	*muyeok suji*
balance ratios	차감 비율(差減比率)	*ch'agam biyul*
balance sheet	대차 대조표	*taech'adaejop'yo*
bale capacity	화물 수용량	*hwamul suyongnyang*
bale cargo	화물 적하(貨物積荷)	*hwamul jeokha*
ballast bonus	밸러스트 보너스	*paelleoseut'eu boneoseu*
balloon (payment)	풍선 지불금	*p'ungseon jibulgeum*
balloon note	풍선 증권, 어음	*p'ungseon jeungkkweon, eo-eum*
bank	은행	*eunhaeng*
bank acceptance	은행 보증 어음	*eunhaeng bojeung eo-eum*
bank account	당좌 예금	*tangjwa yegeum*
bank balance	은행 잔고	*eunhaeng jan-go*
bank carnet	은행 허가증	*eunhaeng heogajjeung*
bank charges	은행 부과금	*eunhaeng bugwageum*
bank check	은행 수표	*eunhaeng sup'yo*
bank deposit	은행 예금	*eunhaeng yegeum*

bank draft	은행 환어음, 지불 명령서	eunhaeng hwaneo-eum, chibul myeongnyeongseo
bank examiner	은행 감독관	eunhaeng gamdokkwan
bank exchange	은행환(시세), 은행환전	eunhaenghwan(shise), eunhaeng hwanjeon
bank holiday	은행 휴무	eunhaeng hyumu
bank letter of credit	은행 신용장	eunhaeng shinyongjjang
bank loan	은행 대부	eunhaeng daebu
bank money order	은행환	eunhaenghwan
bank note	은행권	eunhaengkkweon
bank rate	은행 할인율	eunhaeng harinyul
bank release	은행 양도증서	eunhaeng yangdo jeungseo
bank statement	은행 명세서(보고서)	eunhaeng myeongseseo (bogoseo)
bankruptcy	파산	p'asan
bar chart	막대형 도표	makttaehyeong dop'yo
barbiturate	진정, 수면제	chinjeong, sumyeonje
bareboat charter	용선(傭船) 계약,(매매) 계약, 거래 조건, 바겐	yongseon gyeyak (maemae) gyeyak, keorae jokkeon, pagen
bargaining, collective	(노사의)단체 교섭	(nosa-eui)danch'e kyoseop
bargaining power	교섭권, 계약권	kyoseopkweon, kyeyak-kweon
barratry	선원의 비행(非行)	seonweon-eui bihaeng
bars	봉강(棒鋼)	pong-gang
barter (v)	물물교환하다	mulmul kyohwan-hada
base	염기(鹽基)	yeomgi
base currency	기준화폐(통화)	kijun hwap'ye(t'ong-hwa)
base price	기준 단가, 기준가	kijun dankka, kijunkka
base rate	기본 요금	kibon yogeum
base year	기준 년도	kijun nyeondo
basic point (1/100%)	기준치	kijunch'i
basket	바구니, 소쿠리	paguni, sok'uri
batch processing	일괄 처리	ilgwal ch'eo-ri
batch production, batten fitted	일괄 생산	ilgwal saengsan
battery	밧데리	patteri
baud	보(1 bit)	bo
bear (v), bear (securities)	(비용을)부담하다, 파는 쪽	(piyong-eul)budam-hada, p'aneunjjok
bear market	하락세, 약세	harakse, yakse
bearer	지참인, 소지인(所持人)	chich'amin, soji-in
bearer bond	무기명 채권	mugimyeong ch'aekkweon
bearer security	무기명 증권	mugimyeong jeungkkweon
bell-shaped curve	종모양의 곡선	chong moyang-eui gokseon
below par	액면 이하로	aengmyeon iha-ro
below the line	표준 이하의 항목	ph'yojun iha-eui hangmok
bends	곡손(曲損)	kokson
benzene	벤젠	penjen
bequest	유증(遺贈), 유산(遺産), 유물(遺物)	yujeung, yusan, yumul

berth terms

berth terms	버스 텀즈 조건	*peoseu t'eomjeu jokkeon*
bid (takeover)	입찰, 경매 가격 신고	*ipch'al, kyeongmae gagyeok sin-go*
bid and asked	입찰 및 청구	*ipch'al mit ch'eong-gu*
bill	청구서, 증서, 증권	*ch'eong-guseo, cheungseo, cheungkkweon*
bill broker	어음(증권) 중개인	*eoeum(cheungkkweon) chung-gae-in*
bill of exchange	환어음	*hwan-eoeum*
bill of lading	선하(船荷) 증권	*seonha jeungkkweon*
bill of sale	매도증	*maedojjeung*
bill of sight	임시 양륙 신고서	*imshi yangnyuk shin-goseo*
billboard	게시판, 광고판	*keship'an, kwang-gop'an*
billets	철봉	*ch'eolbong*
binary notation	2진법	*ijinppeop*
binder	가계약, 구두 약속	*kagyeyak, kudu yaksok*
bio-ceramics	생(生)요업(窯業)	*saeng yo-eop*
biochemistry	생화학	*saeng-hwahak*
bio-computer	생 컴퓨터	*saeng-k'eomp'yut'eo*
bit	비트	*pit'eu*
black and white film	흑백 필름	*heukpaek p'illeum*
black and white TV	흑백 테레비	*heukpaek t'erebi*
black market	암시장	*amshijang*
blanket bond	포괄적 보증금	*p'ogwaljjeok pojeung-geum*
blanket order	포괄적 주문서, 포괄적 환어음	*p'ogwaljjeok chumunseo, p'ogwaljjeok hwan-eoeum*
blast funace	용광로	*yong-gwangno*
bleed (v)	출혈하다	*ch'ulhyeol-hada*
blockage of funds	재원(財源)의 봉쇄, 자금 봉쇄	*chaeweon-eui bongswae, chakeum bongswae*
blocked currency	봉쇄 통화	*pongswae t'onghwa*
blood	혈액, 피	*hyeoraek, p'i*
blue chip stock	우량 주식(증권)	*uryang jushik(jeungkkweon)*
blue collar worker	육체 노동자	*yukch'e nodongja*
blueprint	청사진, 설계도	*ch'eongsajin, seolgyedo*
board, executive	중역 간부 임원	*chung-yeok kanbu imweon*
board meeting	이사 회의	*isa hoe-eui*
board of directors	이사회	*isahoe*
board room	이사 회의실, (증권거래소의) 입회장	*isa hoe-euishil, (cheungkkweon georaeso-eui) iphoejang*
body	차체	*ch'ach'e*
boiler plate	보일러 강(鋼)판	*poilleo gangp'an*
bond	채권, 보증계약	*ch'aekkweon, pojeung gyeyak*
bond areas	보세구역(保稅區域)	*pose guyeok*
bond issue	채권 발행	*ch'aekkweon balhaeng*
bond power	채권 효력	*ch'aekkweon hyoryeok*
bond rating	채권 등급	*ch'aekkweon deung-geup*
bonded carrier	보세 화물 운송인	*pose hwamul unsong-in*
bonded goods	보세 화물, 보세품	*pose hwamul, posep'um*
bonded warehouse	보세 창고	*pose ch'angkko*

bone china	골제(骨製) 그릇	*koljje geureut*
bonus (premium)	액면 초과액, 이익 배당	*aengmyeon ch'ogwa-aek, i-ik paedang*
book inventory	장부 목록	*changbu mongnok*
book value	장부 가격	*changbu gagyeok*
book value per share	증권의 장부 가격	*cheungkkweon-eui jangbu gagyeok*
bookkeeping	부기, 경리	*pugi, kyeongni*
boom	폭등, 호황	*p'oktteung, hohwang*
border	국경	*kukkyeong*
border tax adjustment	국경 세금 조정	*kukkyeong segeum jojeong*
borrow (v)	차용(借用)하다, 빌리다	*ch'ayong-hada, pillida*
borrowing name system	차명제(借名制)	*ch'amyeongje*
botanic	식물(학)의	*shingmul(hag)-eui*
bowl	그릇, 사발	*keureut, sabal*
boycott	보이콧, 불매 운동	*poik'ot, pulmae undong*
brainstorming	최선책 결정	*ch'oeseonch'aek kyeoljjeong*
branch office	지점, 분점	*chijeom, punjeom*
brand	상표, 유명 상품	*sangp'yo, yumyeong sangp'um*
brand acceptance	품질 인수, 상표 인정	*p'umjil insu, sangp'yo injeong*
brand image	상표 모양	*sangp'yo moyang*
brand loyalty	상표 선호(商標選好)	*sangp'yo seonho*
brand manager	품질 책임자, 상표 담당인	*p'umjil ch'aegimja, sangp'yo damdang-in*
brand recognition	상표 인식	*sangp'yo inshik*
brake	제동기, 브레이크	*chedong-gi, peureik'eu*
Braun tube	브라운관	*peuraun gwan*
breadbasket	빵 바구니	*ppang baguni*
breakeven (v)	본전이다, 손익(損益)이 없다	*ponjeon-ida, sonig-i eopta*
breakeven analysis	손익 분기점 분석	*sonik pun-gijjeom bunseok*
breakeven point	손익 분기점, 채산점(採算點)	*sonik pun-gijjeom, ch'aesanjeom*
briefcase	서류 가방	*seoryu gabang*
broken lot	단주(端株)	*tanju*
broken stowage	(약속이 파기된)적하료	*(yakso-gi p'agidoen) jeokharyo*
broker	중개인	*chung-gae-in*
broker, software	소프트 웨어 부로커	*sop'eut'eu we-eo burok'eo*
budget	예산	*yesan*
budget, advertising	광고(선전)예산	*kwang-go (seonjeon) yesan*
budget appropriation	예산 지출금	*yesan jich'ulgeum*
budget, capital	자본 지출 예산	*chabon jich'ul yesan*
budget, cash	현금(현찰)예산	*hyeon-geum (hyeonch'al) yesan*
budget forecast	예산 예측	*yesan yech'euk*
budget, investment	투자 예산	*t'uja yesan*
budget, marketing	시장 조사 예산, 시장 개척비	*shijang josa yesan, shijang gaech'eokpi*
budget, sales	판매 예산	*p'anmae yesan*
buffer memory	완충 기억 장치	*wanch'ung gieok changch'i*

bug (defect in computer program)	(예기치 않은 잘못) 버그	(yegich'i-aneun jalmot) peo-geu
bull (securities)	(시세 상승을 예상) 사는 쪽	(shise sangseung-eul yesang) saneun-jjok
bull market	강세 시장	kangse shijang
bumper	완충기, 범퍼	wanch'ung-gi, peomp'eo
burden rate	적재율	cheokchae-yul
bureaucrat	관료, 관료주의자	kwallyo, kwallyo ju-euija
business activity	경기(景氣), 사업활동	kyeong-gi, sa-eop hwalttong
business card	명함	myeongham
business cycle	경기 순환	kyeong-gi sunhwan
business management	사업 경영	sa-eop kyeong-yeong
business plan	사업 계획, 경영 계획	sa-eop kyehoek, kyeong-yeong gyehoek
business policy	사업 방침	sa-eop pangch'im
business strategy	사업(경영)전략	sa-eop (kyeong-yeong) jeollyak
butanol	부타놀	put'anol
butter dish	버터 접시	peot'eo jeopshi
butter knife	버터 나이프	peot'eo naip'eu
buy at best (v)	최고 유리한 가격에 사다	ch'oego yurihan gagyeok-e sada
buy back (v)	되사다	toe-sada
buy on close (v)	종가(終價)에 사다	chongkka-e sada
buy on opening (v)	초장(初場)에 사다	ch'ojang-e sada
buyer	구매자, 바이어	kumaeja, ba-i-eo
buyer, chief	구매 책임자	kumae ch'aegimja
buyer, credit	크레딧 바이어(신용 구매자)	k'euraedit pa-i-eo (shinyong gumaeja)
buyer, potential	예상 구매자, 살사람	yesang gumaeja, salsaram
buyer's market	매주(買主) 시장, 구매자 시장	maeju shijang, kumaeja shijang
buyer's option	매주(買主) 선택	maeju seont'aek
buyer's premium	매주의 할증금	maeju-eui haljeung-geum
buyer's responsibility	매주 책임	maeju ch'aegim
buyout	매점(買占)	maejeom
by-laws	규칙, 세칙, 정관(定款)	kyuch'ik, sech'ik, cheong-gwan
by-product	부산물(副產物)	pusanmul
byte	바이트(8비트)	pa-i-t'eu (p'al bi-t'eu)

C

cable	외국 전보, 외신	oeguk cheonbo, oeshin
cable transfer	전신환	cheonshinhwan
calcium	칼슘	k'alsyum
calculator	**계산기**	kyesan-gi
call back	회수(回收)	hoesu
call feature	요구불 성격을 지닌, 요구불성(要求佛性)	yogubul seongkkyeog-eul jinin, yogubul seong
call loan	요구불 단기 대부금	yogubul dan-gi daebugeum

call money	요구불 단기 차입금	yogubul dan-gi ch'aipkeum
call option	주식 매수 선택권	chushik maesu seont'aekkweon
call price	요구불 가격	yogubul gagyeok
call protection	요구불 보호	yogubul boho
call rate	요구불 비율	yogubul biyul
call rule	요구불 규정	yogubul kyujeong
camera body	사진기 몸체	sajinkki momch'e
campaign, advertising	광고 선전, 광고전	kwang-go seonjeon, kwang-gojeon
campaign, productivity	생산품 판매 촉진 운동	saengsanp'um p'anmae ch'okchin undong
camshaft	캠축	k'aemch'uk
cancel (v)	삭제하다, 취소하다	sakje-hada, ch'wiso-hada
cancelled check	입금 수표	ipkeum sup'yo
candlestick	촛대	ch'ottae
capacity	능력, 법정 자격	neungnyeok, peopcheong jagyeok
capacity, manufacturing	생산(제조) 능력	saengsan(chejo) neungnyeok
capacity, plant	공장 생산 능력	kongjang saengsan neungnyeok
capacity, utilization	이용 능력	iyong neungnyeok
capital	자본	chabon
capital account	자본 계정	chabon gyejeong
capital allowance	자본 수당	chabon sudang
capital asset	고정 자산(固定資產)	kojeong jasan
capital budget	자본 지출 예산	chabon jich'ul yesan
capital expenditure	자본 지출	chabon jich'ul
capital expenditure appraisal	자본 경비 감정(사정)	chabon gyeongbi gamjeong (sajeong)
capital exports	자본 수출	chabon such'ul
capital gain/loss	자산 매각 소득/손실	chasan maegak sodeuk/sonshil
capital goods	자본재	chabonjae
capital increase	자본 증가	chabon jeung-ga
capital market	자본 시장	chabon shijang
capital, raising	자본 조달	chabon jodal
capital, return on	수익 자본	suik chabon
capital, risk	모험 자본	moheom jabon
capital spending	자본 지출	chabon jich'ul
capital stock	주식 자본	chushik chabon
capital structure	자본 구조	chabon gujo
capital surplus	자본 잉여금	chabon ing-yeogeum
capital, working	운영 자본	unyeong jabon
capital-intensive (adj)	자본 집약적(集約的)	chabon jibyakjjeok
capital-output ratio	자본 산출율(算出率)	chabon sanch'ullyul
capitalism	자본 주의	chabon ju-eui
capitalization	자본화, 주식자본	chabonhwa, chushik chabon
capsule	캡슐	k'aepsyul
car	자동차	chadongch'a

car telephone	자동차용 전화, 카폰	chadongch'a-yong jeonhwa, ko-p'on
carbon steel	탄소강	t'ansogang
carburetor	기화기, 캬뷰레터	kihwagi, k'yaburet'eo
cargo	적하(積荷), 뱃짐	cheokha, paetjim
carload	차량 한대분 화물	ch'aryang handaebun hwamul
carnet	무관세 특별 허가증	mugwanse t'eukpyeol heogajjeung
carrier	운송 업자	unsong eopja
carrier's rish	운송 업자 위험	unsong eopja wiheom
carry forward (v)	차기로 이월하다	ch'agi-ro i-weol-hada
carryback	대월분(貸越分)	taeweolbun
carrying charge	유지비(維持費), 월부 판매 할증금	yujibi, weolbu p'anmae haljjeung-geum
carrying value	유지치(維持値)	yujich'i
carryover	이월(移越), 이월금	iweol, iweolgeum
cartel	기업 연합	ki-eop yeonhap
cartridge	필름통	p'illeumt'ong
carving knife	고기써는 칼	kogi sseoneun k'al
cash	현찰, 현금	hyeonch'al, hyeon-geum
cash-and-carry	현금 판매, 현금 자국선 수송 주의	hyeon-geum p'anmae, heyon-geum jagukseon susongju-eui
cash balance	현금 잔고	hyeon-geum jan-go
cash basis	현금 기준, 현금 주의 원칙	hyeon-geum gijun, hyeon-geum ju-eui weonch'ik
cash before delivery	인도전 현찰 지불	indojeon hyeonch'al jibul
cash book	현금 출납부	hyeon-geum ch'ulnappu
cash budget	현금 예산	hyeon-geum yesan
cash delivery	현금 인도, 당일결제	hyeon-geum indo, tang-il gyeoljje
cash discount	현금 할인	hyeon-geum harin
cash dividend	현금 이익 배당	hyeon-geum i-ik paedang
cash entry	현금 기장(記帳)	hyeon-geum gijang
cash flow	현금 유출입(유통)(流出入)	hyeong-geum yuch'urip(yut'ong)
cash flow statement	현금 유출입 명세서	hyeon-geum yuch'urip myeongseseo
cash in advance	선불(先拂)	seonbul
cash management	현찰 관리	hyeonch'al kwalli
cash on delivery	대금 상환 인도	taegeum sanghwan indo
cash register	금전등록기	keumjeon deungnok-ki
cash surrender value	현금 중도 해약 환급금(還給金)	hyeon-geum jungdo haeyak hwan-geupkeum
cashier's check	자기앞 수표, 보증 수표	chagi-ap sup'yo, pojeung sup'yo
cassette	카세트(테이프)	k'aset'eu (t'e-i-p'eu)
cast iron	주철, 무쇠	chuch'eol, musoe
cast steel	주강(鑄鋼)	chugang

casualty insurance	재해 보험	chaehae boheom
catalog	카다로그, 색인 목록	k'adarogeu, saegin mongnok
catalyst	촉매(觸媒)	ch'ongmae
CB	자동차용 무선 통신기	chadongch'a-yong museon t'ongshin-gi
ceiling	최고 한도, 상한선	ch'oego hando, sanghanseon
cement	도성(陶性)합금	toseong hapkeum
central bank	중앙 은행	chung-ang eunhaeng
central processing unit (computers)	중앙 연산 처리 장치	chung-ang yeonsan ch'eori jangch'i
central rate	공정 금리	kongjeong geumni
centralization	중앙화, 집중화	chung-anghwa, chipchunghwa
ceramic condenser	자기 축전기	chagi ch'ukcheon-gi
certificate	증명서 증권, 주식	cheungmyeongseo
certificate (securities)		cheungkkweon, chushik
certificate of deposit	정기 예금 증서	cheong-gi yegeum jeungseo
certificate of incorporation	법인 설립 인가증	peobin seollip in-gajjeung
certificate of origin	원산지 증명서	weonsanji jeungmyeong seo
certified check	보증 수표	pojeung sup'yo
certified public accountant	공인 회계사	kong-in hoegeysa
chain of command	지휘(명령) 계통	chihwi (myeongnyeong) gyet'ong
chain store	연쇄점	yeonswaejeom
chain store group	연쇄망, 연쇄점군(群)	yeonswaemang, yeonswaejeom-gun
chairman of the board	이사회 회장, 이사장	i-sahoe hoejang, isajang
chamber of commerce	상공 회의소	sang-gong hoe-euiso
champagne glass	샴페인 잔	syamp'ein jan
channel of distribution	유통 경로, 분배 경로	yut'ong gyeongno, punbae gyeongno
charge account	외상 거래 계정	oesang georae gyejeong
charge-off	손실 공제	sonshil gongje
charges	차변 기입(借邊記入), 요금	ch'abyeon gi-ip, yogeum
chart, activity	활동 도표	hwalttong dop'yo
chart, bar	막대 도표	makttae dop'yo
chart, flow	작업 공정도, 순서도	chageop kongjeongdo, sunseodo
chart, management	운영 도표	unyeong dop'yo
charter	면허장, 특허장	myeonheojjang, t'eukheojjang
charter (shipping)	용선(傭船)	yongseon
charter party agency	용선 계약 대행자(점)	yongseon gyeyak taehaengja (jeom)
chartered accountant	공인 회계사	kong-in hoegyesa
chassis	차대	ch'adae
chattel	동산(動産), 가재(家財)	tongsan, kajae
chattel mortgage	동산 양도 저당	tongsan yangdo jeodang

cheap (adj)

cheap (adj)	싼, (구매력이 저하한)	ssan, (kumaeryeong-i) jeohahan
check	수표, 회계 전표	sup'yo, hoegye jeonp'yo
checking account	당좌 예금 구좌	tanjwa yegeum guiwa
checklist	대조표, 점검표	taejop'yo, cheomgeomp'yo
cheese tray	치즈 쟁반	ch'ijeu jaengban
chemical	화학 제품	hwahak chep'um
chemical fertilizer	화학 비료	hwahak piryo
chief accountant	회계 주임	hoegye juim
chief buyer	구매관, 구매 주임	kumaegwan, kumae juim
chief executive	최고 경영인, 최고 경영 책임자	ch'oego gyeongyeong-in, ch'oego gyeong-yeong ch'aegimja
china	도자기, 자기	tojagi, chagi
chip	칩, 직접 회로	ch'ip, chikcheop hoero
chip condenser	반도체 축전기	pandoch'e ch'ukcheon-gi
chloride	염화물	yeomhwamul
chloroform	클로로 포름	k'eulloro p'oreum
chromium	크롬	k'eurom
circuit breaker	회로 차단기	hoero ch'adan-gi
civil action	민사소송	minsa sosong
civil engineering	토목 공학	t'omok konghak
claim	청구, 손해 배상 청구서, 지불 청구권	ch'eong-gu, sonhae baesang ch'eong-guseo, chibul ch'eong-gukkweon
classified ad	구인, 구직 광고	kuin, kujik kwang-go
clearing house	어음 교환소	eoeum gyohwanso
closed account (accounting)	차액이 없는 대차 계정	ch'a-aeg-i eomneun daech'a gyejeong
closely held corporation	비공개 회사	pi-gong-gae hoesa
close-up lens	근접 거리 렌즈	keunjeop keori renjeu
closing entry (accounting)	결산 기재(決算記載)	kyeolssan gijae
closing price	파장 시세(罷場時勢), 폐장(廢場) 시세	p'ajang shise, p'yejang shise
clutch	전동 장치, 클러치	cheondong jangch'i, k'euleoch'i
co-ownership	공유권, 공동 소유권	kong-yukkweon, kongdong soyukkweon
coal	석탄	seokt'an
coaster	바퀴달린 쟁반	pak'wi-dallin jaengban
codicil	유언 보족서(補足書), 일반 추가 조항, 부록	yu-eon bojokseo, ilban ch'uga johang, purok
coffee break	휴게 시간, 휴식 시간	hyuge shigan, hyushik shigan
coffeepot	커피 주전자	k'eop'i jujeonja
coil	코일(螺管 : 나관)	k'oil (nagwan)
coinsurance	공동 보험	kongdong boheom
cold rolling	냉간압연(冷間壓延)	naeng-gan-abyeon
collar	깃	kit
collateral	부가 저당(附加抵當)	puga jeodang
colleague	동료, 동업자	tongnyo, tong-eopja

competitive strategy

collect on delivery	대금 교환 인도(引渡)	tae-geum gyohwan indo
collection period	징수 기간, 수금 기간	chingsu gigan, sugeum gigan
collections	수집품, 소장품	sujipp'um, sojangp'um
collective agreement	단체 협약	tanch'e hyeobyak
collective bargaining	단체 교섭	tanch'e gyoseop
collector of customs	관세 징수원	kwanse jingsu-weon
color	물감, 색	mulkkam, saek
color film	천연색(컬러) 필름	ch'eonyeonsaek (k'eolleo) p'illeum
color liquid crystal	색무늬 수정	saengmuni sujeong
color print	천연색(컬러) 인화(印畵)	ch'eonyeonsaek (k'eolleo) inhwa
color slide	천연색 슬라이드	ch'eonyeonsaek seullaideu
color TV	컬러 테레비	k'eolleo t'erebi
combination	기업 결합, 단체 행동, 연합	ki-eop kyeolhap, tanch'e haengdong, yeonhap
combination duty	공동 직책	kongdong jikch'aek
commerce	통상, 무역, 교섭	t'ongsang, muyeok, kyoseop
commercial bank	상업 은행	sang-eop eunhaeng
commercial grade	상업(무역)상 등급	sang-eop (muyeok) sang deung-geup
commercial invoice	상업(무역) 송장(送狀)	sang-eop (muyeok) songjjang
commission (agency)	중개점, 중개(대리)권	chung-gaejeom, chung-gae (taeri) kkweon
commission (fee)	수수료, 중개료	susuryo, chung-gaeryo
commitment	(거래소의)매매 계약, 약정	(keoraeso-eui) maemae gyeyak, yakcheong
commodity	상품, 일용품	sangp'um, iryongp'um
commodity exchange	상품 거래소	sangp'um georaeso
common carrier	일반 운송업자(회사)	ilban unsong eopja (hoesa)
common market	공동 시장	kongdong shijang
common stock	보통 주식	pot'ong jushik
compact disc (CD)	콤팩 디스크	k'omp'aek diseuk'eu
compact disc player	휴대용 디스크 연주 장치	hyudae-yong diseuk'eu yeonju jangch'i
company	회사, 상사	hoesa, sangsa
company goal	회사 목표	hoesa mokp'yo
company, holding	지주(持株) 회사	chiju hoesa
company, parent	모회사(母會社)	mohoesa
company policy	회사 정책	hoesa jeongch'aek
compensating balance	보상 예금	posang yegeum
compensation	보상, 배상, 보수	posang, paesang, posu
compensation trade	구상(求償) 무역	kusang muyeok
competition	경쟁	kyeongjaeng
competitive advantage	경쟁상의 유리(이점)	kyeongjaengsang-eui yuri(ijjeom)
competitive edge	경쟁적 우세, 강점	kyeongjaengjeok u-se, kangjjeom
competitive price	경쟁 가격	kyeongjaeng gagyeok
competitive strategy	경쟁 전략	kyeongjaeng jeollyak
competitiveness	경쟁력	kyeongjaengnyeok

competitor

competitor	경쟁자, 경쟁 상대	kyeongjaengja, kyeongjaeng sangdae
competitor analysis	경쟁 상대 분석, 경합자 분석	kyeongjaeng sangdae bunseok, kyeonghapcha bunseok
component	구성 요소, 성분(成分)	kuseong yoso, seongbun
composite index	종합 지수(指數)	chonghap chisu
compound	배합 원료	paehap weollyo
compound interest	복리(複利)	pongni
compounds	합성물	hapseongmul
comptroller	경리 부장, 회계 감사관	kyeongni bujang, hoegye gamsagwan
computer	컴퓨터, 전자 계산기	k'eomp'yut'eo, cheonja gyesan-gi
computer, analog	상사형(아날로그) 전자 계산기	sangsahyeong (analogeu) jeonja gyesan-gi
computer bank	컴퓨터 은행	k'eomp'yut'eo eunhaeng
computer center	컴퓨터 센터	k'eomp'yut'eo sent'eo
computer, digital	계수형(디지탈) 전자 계산기	kyesuhyeong (dijit'al) jeonja gyesan-gi
computer input	컴퓨터 입력(入力)	k'eomp'yut'eo imnyeok
computer language	컴퓨터 언어	k'eomp'yut'eo eoneo
computer memory	컴퓨터 기억장치(용량)	k'eomp'yut'eo gi-eok changch'i (yongnyang)
computer output	컴퓨터 출력(出力)	k'eomp'yut'eo ch'ullyeok
computer program	컴퓨터 프로그램	k'eomp'yut'eo p'eurogeuraem
computer storage	컴퓨터 저장 장치	k'eomp'yut'eo jeojang jangch'i
computer terminal	컴퓨터 터미날	k'eomp'yut'eo t'eominal
computerized numerical control	전산 수치 조종	cheonsan such'i jojong
condenser	축전기	ch'ukcheon-gi
condenser lens	집광 렌즈	chipkwang renjeu
conditional acceptance	조건부 어음 인수	chokkeonbu eoeum insu
conditional sales contract	조건부 매매 계약	chokkeonbu maemae gyeyak
conductivity	도전율	tojeonnyul
conference room	회의실	hoe-euishil
confidential (adj)	기밀의	kimireui
confirmation of order	수주(受注) 확인, 환어음의 확인	suju hwagin, hwan-eoeum-eui hwagin
conflict of interest	이해 상반(충돌)	ihae sangban(ch'ungdol)
conglomerate	복합 기업	pokhap ki-eop
connecting rod	연접봉	yeonjeop-pong
connnector	접속기	cheopsokki
consideration (bus. law)	대가(對價)	taekka
consignee	하수인(荷受人), 수탁 판매자	hasuin, sut'ak p'anmaeja
consignment	위탁 판매, 탁송	wit'ak p'anmae, t'aksong
consignment note	위탁 화물 송장(送狀)	wit'ak hwamul songjjang
consolidated financial statement	연결 재정 결산서	yeon-gyeol jaejeong gyeolsanseo

consolidation	합병(合倂), 정리 통합	happyeong, cheongni t'onghap
consortium	협회, 조합	hyeophoe, chohap
consular invoice	영사 증명 송장	yeongsa jeungmyeong songjjang
consultant	고문, 상담역	komun, sangdamnyeok
consultant, management	경영 고문	kyeong-yeong gomun
consumer	소비자, 수요자	sobija, suyoja
consumer acceptance	소비자 승인	sobija seung-in
consumer credit	소비자 신용	sobija shinyong
consumer goods	소비재(消費財)	sobijae
consumer price index	소비자 물가 지수	sobija mulkka jisu
consumer research	소비자 조사	sobija josa
consumer satisfaction	소비자 만족	sobija manjok
contact	접촉	cheopch'ok
container	컨테이너	k'eont'eineo
content	함유량	hamnyu-ryang
contingencies	우발 사고(偶發事故)	ubal sago
contingent fund	우발 대비 자금	ubal daebi jageum
contingent liability	우발 채무	ubal ch'aemu
continuous caster	부단한 주조자	pudan-han jujoja
contract	계약, 계약서	kyeyak, kyeyakseo
contract carrier	계약(전속) 수송업자, 청부 수송업자	kyeyak (cheonsok) susong-eopcha, ch'eongbu susong-eopcha
contract month	계약월	kyeyagweol
control, cost	원가 관리, 원가 통제	weonkka gwalli, weonkka t'ongje
control, financial	재정 통제, 재정 관리	chaejeong t'ongje, chaejeong gwalli
control, inventory	재고품 관리, 상품 목록 관리	chaegop'um gwalli, sangp'um mongnok kwalli
control, manufacturing	제조 관리	chejo gwalli
control, production	생산 관리	saengsan gwalli
control, quality	품질 관리	p'umjil gwalli
control, stock	주식 관리	chushik kwalli
controllable costs	관리(조종) 가능 비용	kwalli (chojong) ganeung biyong
controller	경리 부장	kyeongni bujang
controlling interest	지배 주주(支配株主)	chibae juju
converter	전로(轉爐), 컨버터	cheollo, k'eonbeot'eo
convertible debentures	전환 사채(轉換社債)	cheonhwan sach'ae
convertible preferred stock	전환 우선주(株)	cheonhwan useonju
cooperation agreement	협업 협정(協業協定)	hyeobeop hyeopcheong
cooperative	협동 조합	hyeoptong johap
cooperative advertising	협동 광고	hyeoptong gwang-go
copper	구리, 동(銅)	kuri, tong
copy (text)	광고 문안(文案)	kwang-go munan
copy testing	광고 효과 조사	kwang-go hyokkwa josa

copyright	판권, 저작권	p'ankkweon, cheojakkweon
cordless phone	무선 전화기	museon jeonhwagi
corporate growth	법인(기업) 성장	peobin (ki-eop) seongjang
corporate image	법인(기업) 이미지	peobin (ki-eop) imiji
corporate planning	기업 기획(企業企劃)	ki-eop kihoek
corporate structure	법인 구조(형태)	peobin gujo (hyeongt'ae)
corporation	법인, 사단 법인	peobin, sadan beobin
corporation tax	법인세	peobinse
corpus	원금(元金), 자본금	weon-geum, chabon-geum
correspondence	서신 왕래, 통신	seoshin wangnae, t'ongshin
correspondent bank	거래 은행	keorae eunhaeng
cortisone	코티손	k'ot'ison
cost	원가	weonkka
cost (v)	원가를 계산하다	weonkka-reul gyesan-hada
cost accounting	원가 회계	weonkka hoegye
cost analysis	원가 분석	weonkka bunseok
cost and freight	비용 및 화물 수송	piyong mit hwamul susong
cost, average	평균 원가(비용)	p'yeong-gyun weonkka(biyong)
cost control	비용 관리	piyong gwalli
cost, direct	직접비	chikcheop-pi
cost effective (adj)	비용 효과적인	piyong hyokkwajeogin
cost factor	비용 요소	piyong yoso
cost, indirect	간접비	kanjeop-pi
cost of capital	자본 비용	chabon biyong
cost of goods sold	판매 상품 비용	p'anmae sangp'um biyong
cost of living	생계비, 생활비	saeng-gyebi, saenghwalbi
cost reduction	비용 절감	piyong jeolgam
cost, replacement	대체(對替)비용	taech'e biyong
cost-benefit analysis	비용-효과분석	piyong-hyokkwa bunseok
cost-plus contract	원가-가산 계약	weonkka-gasan gyeyak
cost-price squeeze	원가-가격 이문	weonkka-gagyeok imun
costs, allocation of	원가 배당, 경비 할당	weonkka baedang, kyeongbi halttang
costs, fixed	고정비	kojeongbi
costs, managed	관리비	kwallibi
costs, production	생산비	saengsanbi
costs, set-up	설치비, 설립비	seolch'ibi, seollippi
costs, standard	표준 원가	p'yojun weonkka
costs, variable	변동비(變動費)	pyeondongbi
cotton	면직물, 면	myeonjingmul, myeon
cough drop	기침약(드롭), 진해정(鎭咳錠)	kich'imnyak (deurop), chinhaejeong
cough syrup	기침약(시럽), 진해시럽	kich'imnyak (shireop), chinhae shireop
counterfeit	모조품, 위조품	mojop'um, wijop'um
countervailing duty	상쇄 관세(相殺關稅)	sangswae gwanse
country of origin	원산지, 원산국	weonsanji, weonsan-guk
country of risk	위험국, 국별 위험도	wiheomguk, kukpyeol wiheomdo
coupon (bond interest)	이권부(利權付) 채권	ikkweonbu ch'aekkweon

courier service	배달 봉사(편의)	paedal bongsa(p'yeon-eui)
covenant (promises)	계약, 서약	kyeyak, seoyak
cover	책 표지	ch'aek p'yoji
cover charge	서비스료	seobiseu-ryo
cover letter	표지 서한	p'yoji seohan
cover ratio	보증금 비율, 고정비 부담 비율	pojeung-geum biyul, kojeongbi budam biyul
coverage (insurance)	보험 계약 범위, 보험 범위, 제한 금액	poheom gyeyak peomwi, poheom beomwi jehan geumaek
crankshaft	크랭크축	k'euraengk'eu ch'uk
crawling peg	평가(平價)의 소폭 조정	p'yeongkka-eui sop'ok chojeong
credit	신용, 대변 기입(貸邊記入)	shinyong, taebyeon gi-ip
credit (v)	외상 판매하다, 외상 거래하다	oesang p'anmae-hada, oesang georae-hada
credit balance	신용 대부 잔고 (信用貸付殘高)	shinyong daebu jan-go
credit bank	신용 대부 은행	shinyong daebu eunhaeng
credit bureau	(상업) 흥신소, 신용 조사소	(sang-eop) heungshinso, shinyong josaso
credit card	신용 카드, 크레딧 카드	shinyong k'a-deu, k'euredit k'a-deu
credit control	신용 대부 통제	shinyong daebu t'ongje
credit insurance	신용 보험	shinyong boheom
credit line	대출 한도액	taech'ul hando-aek
credit management	신용 관리	shinyong gwalli
credit note	대변 전표	taebyeon jeonp'yo
credit rating	신용도, 신용 평가	shinyongdo, shinyongp'yeongkka
credit reference	신용 조회(처)	shinyong johoe (ch-eo)
credit terms	신용 조건, 약정	shinyong jokkeon, yakcheong
credit union	신용 조합	shinyong johap
creditor	채권자	ch'aekkweonja
critical path analysis	주요 경로 분석(主要經路分析)	chu-yo gyeongno bunseok
crop (v)	잘라내다	challa-naeda
crosslicensing	상호 특허 사용허가, 특허 사용 교환	sangho t'eukheo sayong heoga, t'eukheo sayong gyohwan
crucible	도가니	togani
crystal glass	수정 그래스	sujeong geuraeseu
cufflink	소맷부리 단추	somaetpuri danch'u
cultural export permit	문화재 수출 허가서	munhwajae such'ul heogaseo
cultural property	문화재	munhwajae
cum dividend	배당부(配當附)	paedangbu
cumulative	누가적(累加的)인, 누적(累積)하는	nugajeongin, nujeokhaneun
cumulative preferred stock	누적 우선주	nujeok useonju
cup	컵	k'eop
cupola	용선로(溶銑爐)	yongseollo

currency	통화, 화폐, 통화 유통액	t'onghwa, hwap'ye, t'onghwa yut'ong-aek
currency bond	화폐(통화) 밴드	hwap'ye (t'onghwa) baendeu
currency clause	화폐 조항, 약정	hwap'ye johang, yakcheong
currency conversion	화폐 차환(借換)	hwap'ye ch'ahwan
currency exchange	화폐 교환	hwap'ye gyohwan
current assets	유동 자산(流動資産)	yudong jasan
current liabilities	유동 부채	yudong buch'ae
current ratio	현행 비율	hyeonhaeng biyul
current yield	현행 산출고, 유동 비율	hyeonhaeng sanch'ulgo, yudong biyul
curriculum vitae	이력(서) 고객, 교섭 상대	iryeok (seo)
customer	고객, 교섭 상대	kogaek, kyoseop sangdae
customer service	고객 봉사	kogaek pongsa
customs	세관	segwan
customs broker	세관 화물 취급인, 통관사	segwan hwamul ch'wigeub-in, t'ong-gwansa
customs duty	관세 제도	kwanse jedo
customs entry	통관 신고	t'ong-gwan shin-go
customs union	관세 동맹	kwanse dongmaeng
cut (v)	자르다	chareuda
cutback	삭감, 축소	sakkam, ch'ukso
cutlery	식탁용 절제품(칼, 포크 등)	shikt'ang-yong ch'eolje-p'um (k'al, p'ok'eu deung)
cutting tool	깎는 연장	kkangneun yeon-jang
cycle billing	주기 선하 증서 작성	chugi seonha jeungseo jakseong
cycle, business	경기 순환	kyeong-gi sunhwan
cycle, life (of a product)	제품 수명 주기	chep'um su-myeong jugi
cycle, work	작업 주기	chakeop chugi
cylinder boring machine	실린더 천공기	shillindeo ch'eon-gong-gi
cylindrical coordinates robot	원통형 조정 로보트	weont'ong-hyeong jojeong robot'eu
cylindrical grinder	원통형 분쇄기	weont'onghyeong bunswaegi

D

daily (adj), (adv)	매일의, 매일	maeil-eui, maeil
dairy products	낙농 제품(酪農製品)	nangnong jep'um
damage	손해, 손상(損傷)	sonhae, sonsang
data	데이터, 자료(資料)	deit'eo, charyo
data acquisition	자료 취득, 자료 습득	charyo ch'wideuk, charyo seupdeuk
data bank	데이터 뱅크, 경영 정보 은행	deit'eo baengk'eu, kyeong-yeong jeongbo eunhaeng
data base	정보(자료) 기저(基底)	cheongbo (charyo) gijeo
data processing	정보 유효화 과정	cheongbo yuhyohwa gwajeong
data of delivery	(매매 화물의) 수도일자(受渡日字)	(maemae hwamul-eui) sudo iljja

delay (n)

day loan	일일 대부(貸付), 일일 대출(貸出)	iril daebu, iril daech'ul
day order (stock market)	일일 수주(受注)	iril suju
DC machine	직류계	chingnyugye
dead freight	부적 운임(不積運賃), 위약 배상금	pujeok unim, wiyak paesang-geum
dead rent	확정 채굴료(確定採掘料)	hwakcheong ch'aegullyo
deadline	(은행의) 준비금 한계선, 마감	(eunhaeng-eui) junbigeum han-gyeseon, magam
deadlock	교착 상태, 정돈(停頓) 상태	kyoch'ak sangt'ae, cheongdon sangt'ae
deal	거래, 밀약(密約)	keorae, milyak
deal, package	일괄 취급, 일괄 거래	ilgwal ch'wigeup (georae)
dealer	상인, 증권 업자	sang-in, cheungkkwon eopcha
dealership	판매권	p'anmaekkwon
debentures	사채(社債), 환세 증명서(還稅證明書)	sach'ae, hwanse jeungmyeongseo
debit	차변(借邊), 부채(負債)	ch'abyeon, puch'ae
debit entry	차변 기입(借邊記入)	ch'abyeon gi-ip
debit note	차변표, 매매 환표	ch'abyeonp'yo, maemae hwanp'yo
debt	부채, 채무, 빛	puch'ae, ch'aemu, pit
debug (v)	디버그하다, 오류를 수정하다	dibeogeu-hada, oryureul sujeong-hada
deductible (adj)	공제 대상(控除對象)의	kongje daesang-eui
decanter	식탁용 마개있는 유리병	shikt'ang-yong magae-inneun yuribyeong
deduction	공제(액)	kongje(aek)
deed	행위, 증서(證書)	haengwi, cheungseo
deed of sale	매약 증서(賣約證書)	maeyak cheungseo
deed of transfer	주식 매매 증서	chushik maemae jeungseo
deed of trust	신탁 증서	shint'ak cheungseo
default (v)	지불을 소홀히 하다, 위탁금을 소비하다	chibureul sohori-hada, wit'akkeum-eul sobi-hada
defective (adj)	결함있는	kyeolham inneun
deferred annuities	거치(据置) 연금	keoch'i yeon-geum
deferred assets	(대차대조표 중의) 거치 자산(据置資産)	(taech'a daejop'yo jung-eui) geoch'i jasan
deferred charges	거치 비용(据置費用)	keoch'i biyong
deferred deliveries	거치 인수, 거치 교부	keoch'i insu, keoch'i gyobu
deferred income	거치 수익	keoch'i su-ik
deferred liabilities	거치 부채, 채무	keoch'i buch'ae, ch'aemu
deferred tax	거치 세금	keoch'i segeum
deficit	결손(缺損), 적자(赤字)	kyeolson, cheokja
deficit financing	적자 재정(赤字財政)	cheokja jaejeong
deficit spending	적자 재정 소비	cheokja jaejeong sobi
deflation	통화 수축, 디프레, 물가 하락	t'onghwa such'uk, tip'eure, mulkka harak
defroster	서리 제거 장치	seori jegeo jangch'i
delay (n)	지연, 연기	chiyeon, yeon-gi

delinquent account	체납 계정	ch'enap kyejeong
delivered price	인수(引受) 가격	insu gagyeok
delivery	배달, 송달, 인도(引渡)	paedal, songdal, indo
delivery date	배달 일자	paedal iljja
delivery notice	화물 인도 통지서	hwamul indo t'ongjiseo
delivery points	배달 지점	paedal jijeom
delivery price	인도가격	indo gagyeok
demand	요구, 청구	yogu, ch'eong-gu
demand (v)	요구(청구)하다	yogu (ch'eong-gu)-hada
demand deposit	요구불 예금	yogubul yegeum
demand line of credit	신용 요구 한도	shinyong yogu hando
demographic (adj)	인구 통계학상의	in-gu t'onggyehaksang-eui
demotion	강등, 격하	kangdeung, kyeokha
demurrage	초과 정박, 체선료(滯船料)	ch'ogwa jeongbak, ch'eseonryo
density	밀집 상태	miljjip sangt'ae
department	(company)부(部), (U.S. government)성(省)	pu, seong
department store	백화점	paekhwajeom
depletion accounting	소모(감소) 계정	somo (kamso) gyejeong
depletion control	소모(감소) 통제	somo (kamso) t'ongje
deposit	예금, 공탁금(供託金)	yegeum, kongt'akkeum
deposit account	예금 계정	yegeum gyejeong
deposit, bank	은행 예금	eunhaeng yegeum
depository	공금 수탁소, 금고	kong-geum sut'akso, keumgo
depreciation	감가 상각(減價償却), 가치 저감(價値低減)	kamkka sang-gak, kach'i jeogam
depreciation, accelerated	가속 감각 상각	kasok kamkka sang-gak
depreciation, accrued	축적 감가 상각	ch'ukcheok kamkka sang-gak
depreciation allowance	감가 상각 충당	kamkka sang-gak ch'ungdang
depreciation of currency	통화 가치 하락	t'onghwa gach'i harak
depression	불경기, 불황(不況)	pulgyeong-gi, pulhwang
depth analysis	심도 분석(深度分析)	shimdo bunseok
deputy chairman	부회장	puhoejang
deputy manager	부지배인	pujibae-in
design (v)	도안하다	toan-hada
design engineering	설계 공학	seolgye gonghak
designer	디자이너	tijaineo
desk-top calculator	탁상용 계산기	t'aksang-yong gyesan-gi
dessert plate	후식용(後食用) 그릇	hushing-yong geureut
devaluation	평가 절하	p'yeongkka jeolha
develop	현상하다	hyeonsang-hada
diabetes	당뇨병	tangnyoppyeong
die	다이	ta-i
die casting	주조	chujo
diesel	디젤 기관	dijel gigwan
differential, price	가격 차별(격차)	kagyeok ch'abyeol (keokch'a)
differential, tariff	차별 관세, 차별 세율	ch'abyeol gwanse, ch'abyeol seyul
differential, wage	차별 임금	ch'abyeol imgeum

English	Korean	Romanization
digital (adj)	계수형의 디지탈의	kyesu-hyeong-eui, dijit'areui
digital	디지탈, 계수형(計數形)	dijit'al, kyesuhyeong
digital audio disc	계수형 가청 디스크	kyesu-hyeong gach'eong diseuk'eu
digital audio tape recorder	계수형 청취 테이프 녹음기	kyesu-hyeong ch'eongch'wi t'eip'eu nogeumgi
digital computer	디지탈(계수형) 계산기	dijit'al (gyesu-hyeong) gyesan-gi
dilution of equity	지주 비율 저하 (持株比率低下)	chiju biyul jeoha
dilution of labor	노농 희석(稀釋)	nodong heuiseok
diode	이극 진공관	igeuk chin-gonggwan
direct access storage	직접 접촉 기억 장치	chikcheop cheopch'ok ki-eok changch'i
direct cost	직접 비용	chikcheop piyong
direct expenses	직접 경비(지출)	chikcheop kyeongbi (chich'ul)
direct investment	직접 투자	chikcheop t'uja
direct labor (accounting)	직접 노동	chikcheop nodong
direct mail	직접 가정 배달 광고	chikcheop kajeong baedal gwang-go
direct paper	직접 환어음	chikcheop hwan-eo-eum
direct quotation	직접 시세표	chikcheop shisep'yo
direct reduction process	직접 환원 과정	chikcheop hwanweon gwajeong
direct selling	직접 판매	chikcheop p'anmae
director	이사(理事)	isa
disbursement	지출, 지불(금)	chich'ul, chibul(geum)
disc brake	원판 제동 장치	weonp'an jedong jangch'i
discharge (v)	하물(荷物)을 양륙(揚陸)하다	hamu-reul yangnyuk-hada
discount	할인, 할인액	harin, harinaek
discount rate	할인율	harinyul
discount securities	**할인 유가 증권**	harin yukka jeungkkweon
discounted cash flow	현금 수지(收支) 할인	hyeon-geum suji harin
discounting	할인, 감가	harin, kamkka
discretionary account	(주식의)임의 주문(任意注文)	(chushig-eui) imeui chumun
discretionary order	임의 주문	imeui chumun
dish	접시	cheopshi
dishonor (as a check)	부도, 인수 거절	pudo, insu geojeol
disincentive	행동(활동) 억제(抑制)	haengdong (hwalttong) eokche
disk	디스크, 평원반(平圓盤)	diseuk'eu, p'yeongweonban
disk drive	디스크 드라이브	diseuk'eu deuraibeu
dispatch	발송, 특파	palsong, t'eukp'a
display unit	표시 단위	p'yoshi danwi
disposable income	가처분 소득(可處分所得)	kach'eobun sodeuk
dispute	쟁의(爭議), 논쟁(論爭)	chaeng-eui, nonjaeng
dispute (v)	논쟁하다, 논박하다	nonjaeng-hada, nonbak-hada
dispute, labor	노동 쟁의(勞動爭議)	nodong jaeng-eui
distillation	증류(蒸溜)	cheungnyu
distribution, channel of	판매 경로(통로), 유통 경로	p'anmae gyeongno(t'ongno), yut'ong gyeongno

distribution costs	판매비, 유통비	p'anmaebi, yut'ongbi
distribution network	판매망, 유통망	p'anmaemang, yut'ongmang
distribution policy	판매 정책, 유통 정책	p'anmae jeongch'aek, yut'ong jeongch'aek
distributor	판매인, 배급업자	p'anmae-in, paegeup eopcha
diuretic	이뇨제	inyoje
diversification	경영 다양화(多樣化) (다각화-多角化)	kyeong-yeong dayanghwa(dagakhwa)
divestment	환투자(還投資)	hwan-t'uja
dividend	배당금, 배당율	paedang-geum, paedangyul
dividend yield	배당금 수익	paedang-geum su-ik
division of labor	분업(分業)	puneop
dock (ship's receipt)	선거 하수증(船渠荷受證)	seon-geo hasujjeung
dock handling charge	선거 사용료(船渠使用料)	seon-geo sayongnyo
document	서류, 선적 서류	seoryu, seonjeok seoryu
dollar cost averaging	달러 비용 평균화	dalleo biyong p'yeong-gyunhwa
domestic bill	국내 어음	kungnae eoeum
domestic corporation	국내 법인, 주식회사	kungnae beobin, chushik hoesa
domestic product	국산품, 국내생산품	kuksan-p'um, kungnae saengsan-p'um
door-to-door (sales)	호별 방문 판매	hobyeol bangmun p'anmae
dose	1회분	ilhoebun
double dealing	이중 거래	ijung georae
double-entry bookkeeping	복식 기장법 부기 (複式記帳法簿記)	pokshik kijangbeop pugi
double pricing	이중 가격	ijung gagyeok
double taxation	이중 과세(課稅)	ijung gwase
double time	이중 시간	ijung shigan
down payment	기본금, 맞돈	kibon-geum, mat-ton
down period	공장 폐쇄 기간	kongjang p'yeswae gigan
down swing	하강(下降)	hagang
down the line (adj), (adv)	전면적인, 대폭적인, 전면적으로, 대폭적으로	cheonmyeonjeog-in, taep'okcheog-in, cheonmyeon-jeog-euro, taep'okcheog-euro
down time	가동 중지 시간	kadong jungji shigan
down turn	침체	ch'imch'e
draft	환어음, 지불 명령서	hwaneoeum, chibul myeong nyeongseo
drawback	환불세(還拂稅)	hwanbulse
drawdown	삭감(削減)	sakkam
drawee	어음 지정인, 지불인	eoeum jijeong-in, chiburin
drawer	어음 발행인	eoeum balhaeng-in
drayage	운반비, 운임(運賃)	unbanbi, unim
dress	의복, 드레스	euibok, teureseu
drilling machine	천공기	ch'eon-gong-gi
drop	소량	soryang
drop shipment	생산자 직송(直送)	saengsanja jiksong
drug	약제	yakche

dry cargo	건화(乾貨)	keonhwa
dry goods	곡류, 직물류	kongnyu, chingmullyu
dummy	견본	kyeonbon
dumping (goods in foreign market)	덤핑, 투매(投賣)	teomp'ing, t'umae
dun (v)	지불을 심히 독촉하다	chibul-eul shimhi dokch'ok-hada
dunnage	짐깔개	chimkkalgae
duopoly	복점(複占), 이인점(二人占)	pokcheom, i-injeom
durable goods	내구재(耐久財)	naegujae
duress	협박, 감금	hyeoppak, kamgeum
duty	세, 관세	se, kwanse
duty ad valorem	종가세(從價稅)	chong-gase
duty, anti-dumping	부당 염매 대항세 (不當廉賣對抗稅)	pudang yeommae daehangse
duty, combination	종합 관세	chonghap kwanse
duty, countervailing	상쇄 관세, 균형세	sangswae gwanse, kyunhyeongse
duty, export	수출 관세, 수출세	such'ul gwanse, such'ulse
duty, remission	경감 관세(輕減關稅)	kyeong-gam gwanse
duty, specific	종량세(從量稅)	chongnyangse
duty-free	면세(免稅), 무세(無稅)	myeonse, muse
dynamic memory	역학 기억 장치	yeokhak kieok changch'i
dynamics, group	집단 역학	chiptan yeokhak
dynamics, market	시장 활기(活氣)	shijang hwalgi
dynamics, product	생산 활기(活氣)	saengsan hwalgi
dynamo	발전기, 전선(電線)	paljeon-gi, cheonseon

E

earmark (v)	(금을 중앙은행의 보유금에서)빼내다	(keum-eul jung-ang eunhaeng-eui boyugeum-eseo) ppaenaeda
earnings	소득(所得), 수익고(收益高)	sodeuk, su-ikko
earnings on assets	수익 자산(收益資產)	su-ik chasan
earnings per share	주당(株當) 소득	chudang sodeuk
earnings performance	수익 이행, 수익 작업	su-ik ihaeng, su-ik chageop
earnings report	수익 보고	su-ik pogo
earnings, retained	유보 수익(留保收益)	yubo su-ik
earnings yield	수익 이율(利率)	su-ik iyul
earnings/price ratio	수익 주가 비율 (收益株價比率)	su-ik chukka biyul
earthenware	토기, 질그릇	t'ogi, chil-geureut
econometrics	계량 경제학	kyeryang gyeongjehak
economic (adj)	경제(상)의, 경제학의, 경제적	kyeongje(sang)-eui, kyeongjehak-eui, kyeongjejeok
economic indicators	경제 지표	kyeongje jip'yo
economic life	경제 생활	kyeongje saenghwal

English	Korean	Romanization
economic order quantity (EOQ)	경제 발주량(發注量)	(EOQ) kyeongje baljuryang
economics	경제학	kyeongjehak
economy of scale	규모 경제	kyumo gyeongje
edit (v)	편집하다	p'yeonjip-hada
edition	판, 간행	p'an, kanhaeng
editor	편집자	p'yeonjipcha
EE camera	광전관 사진기	kwangjeon-gwan sajinkki
effective yield	실질 이윤(實質利潤)	shiljjil iyun
efficiency	능률, 효율	neungnyul, hyoyul
egg cup	계란용 컵	kyeran-yong doen
elasticity (of supply of demand)	(수요나 공급의)탄력성	(suyo-na gong-geup-eui) t'allyeokseong
electric cable	전선(電線)	cheonseon
electric circuit	전기 회로	cheon-gi hoero
electric furnace	전기로(電氣爐)	cheon-gi-ro
electric heater	전기 난방기	cheon-gi nanbang-gi
electric interlocking maching	전기 연결 기계	cheon-gi yeon-gyeol gigye
electric line telephone	유선 전화기	yuseon jeonhwagi
electric resistance	전기 저항	cheon-gi jeohang
electric shaver	전기 면도기	cheon-gi myeondo-gi
electric tools	전기 공구	cheon-gi gong-gu
electrical engineering	전기 공학	cheon-gi gonghak
electro-conductive glass	전기 전도 유리	cheon-gi jeondo yuri
electro-conductive polymer	전기 전도 중합체	cheon-gi jeondo junghapch'e
electro-magnetic shielding	전자기 보호물	cheonjagi bohomul
electrode	전극	cheon-geuk
electrolysis	전기 분해	cheon-gi bunhae
electrolytic process	전기 분해 과정	cheon-gi bunhae gwajeong
electromagnet	전자석	cheonjaseok
electron beam	전자선	cheonjaseon
electron gun	전자총	cheonjach'ong
electron microscope	전자 현미경	cheonja hyeonmigyeong
electronic cash register	전자 금전 등록기	cheonja geumjeon deungnok-ki
electronic desk calculator	전자 탁상용 계산기	cheonja t'aksang-yong gyesan-gi
electronic home appliance	가정용 전자	kajeong-yong jeonja
electronic musical instruments	전자 악기(樂器)	cheonja akki
electronic organ	전자 오르간	cheonja oreugan
electronic sewing machine	전자 재봉틀	cheonja jaebongt'eul
electronic typewriter	전자 타자기	cheonja t'ajagi
electronics	전자 공학	cheonja gonghak
embargo	수출 금지, 금수(禁輸)	such'ul geumji, keumsu
embezzlement	착복, 횡령	ch'akpok, hoengnyeong

employee	고용인, 사용인, 종업원	*koyong-in, sayong-in, chong-eopweon*
employee counseling	고용인 상담	*koyong-in sangdam*
employee relations	고용인 관계	*koyong-in gwan-gye*
employment agency	직업 소개소	*chikeop sogaeso*
encumbrance (liens, liabilities, commitments)	부담(負擔), 채무(債務)	*pudam, ch'aemu*
end of period	기말(期末), 결말(結末)	*kimal, kyeolmal*
end mill	말단부 제작 기계	*malttanbu jejak kigye*
end product	최종 생산품	*ch'oejong saengsanp'um*
end-use certificate	최종 용도 증명서	*ch'oejong yongdo jeungmyeongseo*
endorsement	배서(背書)	*paeseo*
endowment	기부(寄附)	*kibu*
enforce (v)	집행하다	*chiphaeng-hada*
engine	엔진	*enjin*
engineering	공학(工學)	*konghak*
engineering and design department	공학 설계과	*konghak seolgyekkwa*
engineering, design	설계 공학	*seolgye gonghak*
engineering, industrial	생산 관리	*saengsan gwalli*
engineering, plastic	공학 합성 수지	*konghak hapseong suji*
engineering, systems	조직 공학	*chojik konghak*
engineering, value	평가 공학	*p'yeongkka gonghak*
engrave (v)	파다, 새기다	*p'ada, saegida*
enlarge (v)	확대하다	*hwaktae-hada*
enlargement	확대	*hwakttae*
enlarger	확대기	*hwakttaegi*
enterprise	기업, 사업	*ki-eop, sa-eop*
entrepreneur	기업가, 사업가	*ki-eopkka, sa-eopkka*
entry, cash	보통 수입 신고	*pot'ong su-ip sin-go*
entry, debit	차변 기입(借邊記入)	*ch'abyeon gi-ip*
entry permit	통관 면허	*t'ong-gwan myeonheo*
enzyme	효소(酵素)	*hyoso*
EP · ROM	도넛형 판독 전용 기억 장치	*doneot-hyeong p'andok cheonyong gieok changch'i*
equal pay for equal work	균등 작업, 균등 임금	*kyundeung jageop, kyundeung imgeum*
equalizer	균압선, 균형 장치	*kyunapseon, kyunhyeong jangch'i*
equipment	장치(裝置), 장비(裝備)	*changch'i, changbi*
equipment leasing	장비 임대(裝備賃貸)	*changbi imdae*
equity	순가(純價), 공평(公平), 지주(支柱)	*sunkka, kongp'yeong, chiju*
equity, dilution of	지주비율 저하(持株比率低下)	*chiju biyul jeoha*
equity investments	지주 투자(持株投資)	*chiju t'uja*
equity, return on	지주 투자 수익율 (持株投資收益率)	*chiju t'uja suingnyul*
equity share	몫, 순가 할당(純價割當)	*mok, sunkka halttang*
ergonomics	인체 공학(人體工學)	*inch'e gonghak*

error

error	오산(誤算), 오류(誤謬)	osan, oryu
escalator clause	신축 조항(伸縮條項)	shinch'uk chohang
escape clause	면책 약관, 예외 규정	myeonch'aek yakkwan, ye-oe gyujeong
escheat	귀속(歸屬), 몰수(沒收)	kwisok, molsu
escrow	에스크로, 조건부 날인 증서(條件附捺印證書)	eseuk'euro, chokkeonbu narin jeungseo
escrow account	기탁 계정(寄託計定)	kit'ak kyejeong
espresso cup	에스프레스 컵	eseup'eureseu k'eop
estate	소유지, 자산	soyuji, chasan
estate agent	토지 관리인	t'oji gwalli-in
estate tax	유산세(遺產稅)	yusanse
estimate	견적, 평가	kyeonjeok, pyeongkka
estimate (v)	평가하다	p'yeongkka-hada
estimate, sales	매매 평가	maemae p'yeongkka
estimated, price	견적 가격	kyeonjeok kagyeok
estimated time of arrival	도착 예정 시간	toch'ak yejeong shigan
estimated time of departure	출발 예정 시간	ch'ulbal yejeong shigan
ethane	에탄	et'an
ether	에테르	e'tereu
ethylene	에틸렌	et'illen
ethylene dichloride	에틸렌 이염화물	et'illen iyeomhwamul
ethylene glycol	에틸렌 그리콜	et'illen geurik'ol
ethylene oxide	에틸렌 옥시드	et'illen okshideu
Eurobond	구주 증권	kuju jeungkkwon
Eurocurrency	유로 통화	yuro t'onghwa
Eurodollar	유로 달러	yuro dalleo
evaluation	평가	p'yeongkka
evaluation, job	업무(직무)평가	eommu (chingmu) p'yeongkka
ex dividend	배당락(配當落)	paedangnak
ex dock	수입항 부두도(輸入港埠頭渡)	su-iphang bududo
ex factory	공장 인도	kongjang indo
ex mill	제작소 인도, 제분소 인도	chejakso indo, chebunso indo
ex mine	광업소 인도	kwang-eopso indo
ex rights	(신주 할당-新株割當-의) 권리락(權利落)	(shinju halttang-eui) gweollirak
ex ship	수입항 본선 인도 (輸入港本船引渡)	su-iphang bonseon indo
ex warehouse	창고 인도	ch'angkko indo
ex works	현장 인도	hyeonjang indo
exchange (n) (stock, commodity)	거래소	keoraeso
exchange (v)	교환하다	kyohwan-hada
exchange control	외국환 관리	oegukhwan gwalli
exchange discount	환할인(換割引)	hwan-harin
exchange loss	환손실(換損失)	hwan-sonsil
exchange rate	환시세(換時勢)	hwan-shise
exchange risk	환위험(換危險)	hwan-wiheom
exchange value	교환 가치	kyohwan gach'i

excise duty	물품세	*mulp'umse*
excise license	소비세 면허	*sobise myeonheo*
excise tax	국내 소비세	*kungnae sobise*
executive	경영 간부, 중역(重役)	*kyeong-yeong ganbu, chung-yeok*
executive board	상임 이사회	*sang-im isahoe*
executive, chief	최고 경영 책임자	*ch'oego gyeong-yeong ch'aekimja*
executive committee	실행(집행)위원회	*shilhaeng (chiphaeng) wiweonhoe*
executive compensation	간부 역원 보수	*kanbu yeokweon bosu*
executive director	전무(專務)	*cheonmu*
executive, line	직계 간부 역원	*chikkye ganbu yeogweon*
executive search	행정 조사	*haengjeong josa*
executor	지정 유언 집행자	*chijeong yu-eon jiphaengja*
exemption	면제, 해제	*myeonje, haeje*
expectations, up to our	우리의 기대에 부응하는	*uri-eui gidae-e bu-eung-haneun*
expected results	예상 결과, 예상 이익	*yesang gyeolgwa, yesang i-ik*
expenditure	지출, 경비	*chich'ul, kyeongbi*
expense account	교제비(交際費), 소요 경비(所要經費)	*kyojebi, soyo gyeongbi*
expenses	경비(經費), 비용	*kyeongbi, piyong*
expenses, direct	직접 비용	*chikcheop piyong*
expenses, indirect	간접 비용	*kanjeop piyong*
expenses, running	조업비(操業費)	*cho-eop-pi*
expenses, shipping	적송비(積送費)	*cheoksongbi*
expiry date	종료일, 만기일	*chongnyo-il, man-gi-il*
export (v)	수출하다	*such'ul-hada*
export agent	수출 대리점	*such'ul daerijeom*
export credit	수출 신용장	*such'ul sinyongjjang*
export duty	수출세	*such'ulse*
export entry	수출 통관 수속	*such'ul t'ong-gwan susok*
export, for	수출용	*such'ulyong*
export house	수출 상사	*such'ul sangsa*
export manager	수출 부장	*such'ul bujang*
export middleman	수출 중간상, 중개인	*such'ul jung-gansang, chung-gae-in*
export permit	수출 허가(서)	*such'ul heoga (seo)*
export quota	수출 할당(쿼터)	*such'ul halttang (k'weot'eo)*
export regulation	수출 규정, 수출 규칙	*such'ul gyujeong, such'ul gyuch'ik*
export sales contract	수출 매매 계약	*such'ul maemae gyeyak*
export taxes	수출품세	*such'lp'umse*
export-import bank	수출입 은행	*such'urip eunhaeng*
exposure	노출	*noch'ul*
exposure meter	노출계	*noch'ulgye*
expropriation	수용(收用), 징수(徵收)	*suyong, chingsu*
extra dividend	특별 배당금	*t'eukpyeol baedang-geum*

F

fabric	직물	chingmul
face value	액면가(額面價)	aengmyeonkka
facilities	시설, 설비	shiseol, seolbi
facsimile	팩시밀리, 팩스	p'aekshimilli, p'aekseu
factor	대리점, 도매상	taerijeom, tomaesang
factor analysis	인자(因子)/요인(要因) 분석(分析)	inja/yoin bunseok
factor rating	요소(인자, 등급)결정	yoso (inja, teung-geup) gyeoljjeong
factor, cost	원가 요소(原價要素)	weonkka yoso
factor, load	부하율(負荷率)	puhayul
factor, profit	이윤 요소(利潤要素)	iyun yoso
factoring	환불 이자 계산	hwanbul ija gyesan
factory	공장, 제조장	kongjang, chejojang
factory overhead	공장 총경비(工場總經費)	kongjang ch'ong-gyeongbi
fail (v)	실패하다, 파산하다	shilp'ae-hada, p'asan-hada
failure	실패, 파산, 불이행	shilp'ae, p'asan, pulihaeng
fair market value	공정 시장가(公正市場價)	kongjeong sijangkka
fair return	공정 수익(公正收益), 반환(返還)	kongjeong su-ik, panhwan
fair trade	공정 거래(公正去來)	kongjeong-georae
false name system	가명제(假名制)	kamyeongje
family-run business	가족 경영 사업	kajok kyeong-yeong sa-eop
farm out (v)	대여(貸與)하다, (작업을) 외부에 맡기다	taeyeo-hada, (chakeop-eul) oebu-e matkkida
fashion	유행	yuhaeng
favorable balance	흑자	heukcha
feed ratio	공급율	kong-geumnyul
feedback	환부(還附), 귀환(歸還), 피이드백	hwanbu, kwihwan, p'i-ideubaek
fender	바퀴 덮개	pak'wi deopkkae
ferrite	아철 산염	ach'eol sanyeom
ferroalloys	합금질	hapkeumch'eol
ferrochromium	철과 크롬의 합금	ch'eol-gwa k'eurom-eui hapkeum
ferromanganese	망간철	mang-gan-ch'eol
ferronickel	니켈철	nik'elch'eol
ferrosilicon	규소철	kyusoch'eol
fiber-optic communication	광학 섬유 통신	kwanghak seomyu t'ongshin
fiber-reinforced plastics	섬유 보강 합성 수지	seomyu bogang hapseong suji
fidelity bond	성실 계약, 성실 증권	seongshil gyeyak, seongshil jeungkkweon
fiduciary (adj)	신용상의, 신탁의	shinyongsang-eui, shint'ak-eui
fiduciary issue	신용 발행, 무준비 발행	shinyong balhaeng, mujunbi balhaeng
fiduciary loan	신용 대부(信用貸付)	shinyong daebu

fixed costs

English	Korean	Romanization
field warehousing	산지 입고(產地入庫)	sanji ipko
fifth-generation computer	5세대 컴퓨터	o-sedae k'eomp'yut'eo
file	서류철	seoryuch'eol
film	필름	p'illeum
filter	필터	p'ilt'eo
finalize (v)	결말을 짓다	kyeolmal-eul jitta
finance (v)	융자하다	yungja-hada
finance company	융자(금융) 회사	yungja (keumyung) hoesa
financial analysis	재무 분석, 금융 분석	chaemu bunseok, keumnyung bunseok
financial appraisal	재정 감정(鑑定)	chaejeong gamjeong
financial clique	재벌(財閥)	chaebeol
financial control	금융(재정) 통제	keumyung (chaejeong) t'ongje
financial director	재무 이사, 재정 부장	chaemu isa, chaejeong bujang
financial highlights	재정적 중요점	chaejeongjeok chung-yojjeom
financial incentive	재정 장려, 재정 동기	chaejeong jangnyeo, chaejeong dong-gi
financial management	재무 관리(財務管理)	chaemu gwalli
financial period	회계 기간	hoegye gigan
financial planning	재정 계획	chaejeong gyehoek
financial services	재정 사무, 재무 관계 서비스	chaejeong samu, chaemu gwan-gye seobiseu
financial statement	재무 제표(財務諸表)	chaemu jep'yo
financial year	회계 년도(會計年度)	hoegye nyeondo
fine ceramics	정교 섬세한 도자기류	cheong-gyo seomsehan dojagiryu
fine (penalty)	벌금, 과료(科料, 過料)	peolgeum, kwaryo
fine polymer	정교 섬세한 중합체	cheong-gyo seomsehan junghapch'e
finished goods inventory	제품 재고 목록	chep'um chaego mongnok
fire (v)	해고(解雇)하다, 파면(罷免)하다	haego-hada, p'amyeon-hada
firm	회사, 상점	hoesa, sangjeom
first in-first out	선입 선출법(先入先出法)	seonip seonch'ulppeop
first preferred stock	제일 우선주(第一優先株)	cheil useonju
fiscal agent	재무 대리인	chaemu daeri-in
fiscal drag	재정 지연(遲延)	chaejeong jiyeon
fiscal year	회계 년도	hoegye nyeondo
fish-eye lens	어안 렌즈	eo-an renjeu
fishy-back service (container)	컨테이너 선박 수송 서비스	k'eont'eineo seonbak susong seobiseu
fixed assets	고정 자산(固定資產)	kojeong jasan
fixed capital	고정 자본(固定資本)	kojeong jabon
fixed charges	확정 부채(確定負債), 고정비(固定費)	hwakcheong buch'ae, kojeongbi
fixed costs	고정 비용	kojeong biyong

English	Korean	Romanization
fixed expenses	고정 지출	kojeong jich'ul
fixed focus camera	고정 촛점 카메라	kojeong ch'otcheom k'amera
fixed income security	고정 수입 보장	kojeong su-ip pojang
fixed investment	고정 투자	kojeong t'uja
fixed price	정가(定價), 정찰 가격(正札價格)	cheongkka, cheongch'al gagyeok
fixed rate of exchange	고정 환율(固定換率)	kojeong hwannyul
fixed resistor	고정 정보 기억 사용 장치	kojeong jeongbo gi-eok sayong jangch'i
fixed sequence robot	고정 반복 진행 로보트	kojeong banbok chinhaeng robot'eu
fixed term	정기(定期), 확정 조건(確定條件)	cheong-gi, hwakcheong jokkeon
fixture (on balance sheet)	정기 대부금(定期貸付金)	cheong-gi daebugeum
flannel	면 플란넬	myeon p'eullannel
flash bulb	섬광 전구	seomgwang jeon-gu
flash cube	섬광 전구 발광 장치	seomgwang jeon-gu balgwang jangch'i
flat bond	무이식 공채(無利息公債)	mu-ishik kongch'ae
flat car	대차(臺車), 화물차(貨物車)	taech'a, hwamulch'a
flat rate	균일 요금(均一僚金)	kyunil yogeum
flat yield	균일 이윤(利潤)	kyunil iyun
fleet policy	회사 차량 보험 가입 증서	hoesa ch'aryang boheom ga-ip jeungseo
flexible tariff	신축성 관세율(伸縮性關稅率)	shinch'ukseong gwanseyul
float (outstanding checks, stock)	부동 증권(浮動證券)	pudong jeungkkweon
float (v) (issue stock)	공채(公債)를 발행하다	kongch'ae-reul balhaeng-hada
floating asset	유동 자산(流動資產)	yudong jasan
floating charge	유동 담보(流動擔保)	yudong dambo
floating debt	유동 부채, 일시 차입금	yudong buch'ae, ilshi ch'a-ipkeum
floating exchange rate	변동 환율	pyeondong hwannyul
floating rate	변동 시세	pyeondong shise
floating rates	적하세(積荷稅)	cheokhase
floor (of exchange)	입회장(立會場)	iphoejang
floppy disk	플로피 디스크, 얇은 디스크	p'eullop'i diseuk'eu, yalbeun diseuk'eu
flow chart	플로우 차아트, 유도(流圖)	p'eullou ch'aat'eu, yudo
flute	긴 술잔	kin suljjan
focus	촛점	ch'otcheom
follow-up (v)	사후(事後) 검토(檢討)하다	sahu geomt'o-hada
follow-up order	추구 주문(追求注文)	ch'ugu jumun
font	활자	hwaljja
food processor	식품 가공기	shikp'um gagong-gi
foodstuffs	식량, 식료품	shingnyang, shingnyop'um
footing (accounting)	합계, 총계	hapkye, ch'ong-gye
for export	수출용	such'ulyong
force majeure	불가항력(不可抗力)	pulgahangnyeok

free of particular average

forecast	예측, 예보	yech'euk, yebo
forecast (v)	예측하다, 예보하다	yech'euk-hada, yebo-hada
forecast, budget	예산 예측	yesan yech'euk
forecast, market	시장 예측	sijang yech'euk
forecast, sales	판매 예측	p'anmae yech'euk
foreign bill of exchange	외국환 어음	oegukhwan eoeum
foreign corporation	외국 회사(법인)	oeguk hoesa (peobin)
foreign currency	외국 화폐, 외화	oeguk hwap'ye, oehwa
foreign debt	외채(外債)	oech'ae
foreign exchange	외국환	oegukhwan
foreign product	외제(外製), 외제품, 외국산품	oeje, oejep'um, oeguksanp'um
foreign securities	외국 유가 증권	oeguk yukka jeungkkeon
foreign tax credit	외국세 감면(外國稅減免)	oegukse gammyeon
foreign trade	외국(해외) 무역	oeguk (hae-oe) muyeok
foreman	직장(職長), 조장(組長)	chikchang, chojang
forgery	위조(僞造), 변조(變造)	wijo, pyeonjo
fork	포크	p'ok'eu
form	조판	chop'an
form letter	포옴레터, 기정(既定) (기성-既成) 편지	p'o-om ret'eo, kijeong (kiseong) p'yeonji
formaline	포르말린	p'oreumallin
format	체재, 형(型)	ch'ejae, hyeong
forward contract	선물 계약(先物契約), 예약(豫約)	seonmul gyeyak, yeyak
forward cover	선물 지불(先物支拂)	seonmul jibul
forward margin	선물(先物) 마진, 선물 수익(先物收益)	seonmul majin, seonmul su-ik
forward market	선물 시장(先物市場)	seonmul shijang
forward purchase	선물 구입(先物購入)	seonmul gu-ip
forward shipment	선적송(先積送), 미리 싣기	seonjeoksong, miri shitki
forwarding agent	운송 대리점(업자)	unsog daerijeom (eopcha)
foul bill of lading	고장부 선하 증권 (故障附船荷證券)	kojangbu seonha jeungkkweon
foundry	주조공장	chujo gongjang
four colors	4색	sa-saek
four-wheel drive	4륜 구동 전동 장치	saryun gudong jeondong jangch'i
franchise	독점 판매권, 총판권(總販權)	dokcheom p'anmaekkweon, ch'ongp'ankkweon
fraud	사기(詐欺)	sagi
free alongside ship	선측도(船側渡)	seonch'eukto
free and clear (adj)	부채없는, 저당이 들어 있지 않은	puch'ae eomneun, cheodang-e deureo itchi-aneun
free enterprise	자유 기업(自由企業)	chayu gi-eop
free list (commodities without duty)	무세품표(無稅品表)	musep'ump'yo
free market	자유 시장(自由市場)	chayu shijang
free market industry	자유 시장 기업	chayu shijang gi-eop
free of particular average	단독 해손 부담보 (単獨海損不擔保)	tandok haeson buldambo

English	Korean	Romanization
free on board	본선도(本船渡)	ponseondo
free on rail	화차도(貨車渡)	hwach'ado
free port	자유항(自由港)	chayuhang
free time	자유 시간	chayu shigan
free trade zone	자유 무역 지역	chayu muyeok chiyeok
freeboard	건현(乾舷)	keonhyeon
freelance	자유 계약의, 자유업의	chayu gyeyak-eui, chayu-eop-eui
freight	화물 운송, 화물	hwamul unsong, hwamul
freight all kinds	다종의 화물	tajong-eui hwamul
freight allowed	허가된 화물	heogadoen hwamul
freight collect	운임 도착 지불	unim doch'ak chibul
freight forwarder	운송 업자	unsong eopcha
freight included	화물(운임) 포함	hwamul (unim) p'oham
freight prepaid	운임 선불	unim seonbul
french cuff	샤쓰 꺾어 접는 커프스	syasseu kkeokkeo jeomneun k'eop'euseu
frequency curve	반도 곡선	pindo gokseon
frequency modulation	주파수 변조	chup'asu byeonjo
friction press	마찰 압착기	mach'al apch'akki
fringe benefits	부가급(附加給)	pugageup
fringe market	이차(二次) 시장, 부가 시장	ich'a shijang, puga shijang
front-end fee	선불 비용	seonbul biyong
front-end financing	선불 재정	seonbul jaejeong
front-end loading	우선 선적	useon seonjeok
front-wheel drive	전륜 구동 전동 장치	cheollyun gudong jeondong jangch'i
frozen assets	동결 자산	tong-gyeol jasan
fuel consumption	연료 소비	yeollyo sobi
fuel injection system	연료 분사 체계	yeollyo bunsa
full settlement	완전 결산, 청산	wanjeon gyeolsan, ch'eongsan
functional analysis	기능 분석	kineung bunseok
fund	자금, 기금	chageum, kigeum
fund, contingent	임시 기금	imshi gigeum
fund, sinking	감채(減債) 기금	kamch'ae gigeum
fund, trust	공탁금(供託金)	kongt'akkeum
funded debt	공채빚	kongch'aebit
funds, public	공금(公金), 공공 기금	kong-geum, kong-gong gigeum
funds, working	운영 자금	unyeong jageum
fungible goods	대체 가능 식품	taech'e ganeung sangp'um
furnace	용광로	yong-gwangno
futures	선물(先物), 선물 계약	seonmul, seonmul gyeyak
futures option	선물(先物) 선택	seonmul seont'aek

G

English	Korean	Romanization
galley proof	교정쇄(校正刷)	kyojeongswae
garnishment	채권 압류 통고, 출정 명령	ch'aekkwon amnyu t'ong-go, ch'uljjeong myeongnyeong

English	Korean	Romanization
gas laser	개스 레이저	gaeseu reijeo
gas pedal	휘발류 공급 발판, 패달	hwiballyu gong-geup palp'an, p'aedal
gasoline	휘발류, 가솔린	hwiballyu, kasollin
gasoline tank	휘발류 통, 가솔린 탱크	hwiballyu t'ong, kasollin t'aengk'eu
GATT (General Agreement on Tariffs and Trade)	일반 무역 관세 협정	ilban muyeok kwanse hyeopcheong
gear cutting machine	톱니 바퀴 깎는 기계	t'omni bak'wi kkangneun gigye
gearing	전동 장치(傳動裝置)	cheondong jangch'i
gearless	무전동 장치의	mujeondong jangch'i-eui
gearshift	기어, 변속지레	kieo, pyeonsok chire
general acceptance	보통 인수	pot'ong insu
general average loss	공동 해손 분실	kongdong haeson bunshil
general manager	총 지배인	ch'ong jibae-in
general meeting	(주주)총회	(chuju)ch'onghoe
general partnership	합명 회사	hammyeong hoesa
general strike	총 파업	ch'ong p'a-eop
generator	발전기	paljjeon-gi
gentlemen's agreement	신사 협정	shinsa hyeopcheong
gilt (British govt. security)	금박(金嚙), 금분(金粉)	keumbak, kuembun
glass	유리잔	yuri-jan
glass fiber	유리 섬유	yuri seomyu
glass laser	유리 레이저	yuri reijeo
glass-reinforced cement	유리 보강 시멘트	yuri bogang siment'eu
glassy semiconductor	유리질 반도체	yurijil bandoch'e
global competitiveness	국제 경쟁력	kukche gyeongjaengnyeok
glossy (adj)	광택있는	kwang'aeginneun
glut	공급 과다(과잉)	kong-geup kwada (kwa-ing)
go around	우회하다, 회피하다	uhoe-hada, hoep'i-hada
go public (v)	주식을 공개하다	chushik-eul gong-gae-hada
godown	창고, 광	ch'ang-go, kwang
gogo fund	(주식의) 단기 투자 자금	(chushik-eui) dan-gi t'uja jageum
going concern value	계속 영업 가치	kyesok yeong-eop kach'i
going rate (or price)	현행 요율	hyeonhaeng yoyul
gold clause	금약관(金約款)	keumyakkwan
gold price	금가(金價)	keumkka
gold reserves	정화 준비	cheonghwa junbi
goldplated (adj)	금 도금된	keum dogeum-doen
good delivery (securities)	적법 수도(適法受渡)	cheokpeop sudo
good will	영업권	yeong-eopkkweon
goods	상품, 재화(財貨)	sangp'um, chaehwa
goods, capital	자본재	chabonjae
goods, consumer	소비재	sobijae
goods, durable	내구재(耐久財)	naegujae
goods, industrial	산업품	saneop-p'um

government	정부	*cheongbu*
government agency	정부 기관	*cheongbu gigwan*
government bank	정부 은행	*cheongbu eunhaeng*
government bonds	국채(國債)	*kukch'ae*
grace period	유예 기간(猶豫期間)	*yuye gigan*
grade, commercial	상업의 등급	*sang-eop-eui deung-geup*
graft	수회(收賄), 독직(瀆職)	*suhoe, tokchik*
grain	곡물	*kongmul*
graph	도표, 도식	*dop'yo, doshik*
gratuity	보수, 상금	*posu, sang-geum*
gravy boat	고기 국물 그릇	*kogi gungmul geureut*
gray market	준 암거래 시장	*chun amgeorae shijang*
grid	격자(格子)	*kyeokcha*
grievance procedure	불평 처리 절차	*pulp'yeong ch'eori jeolch'a*
grinder	분쇄기	*punswaegi*
gross domestic product	국내 총생산	*kungnae ch'ong saengsan*
gross income	총 소득	*ch'ong sodeuk*
gross investment	총 투자	*ch'ong t'uja*
gross loss	총 손실	*ch'ong sonshil*
gross margin	총 판매 수익	*ch'ong p'anmae su-ik*
gross national product	국민 총생산	*kungmin ch'ongsaengsan*
gross price	총 가격	*ch'ong gagyeok*
gross profit	총 이익	*ch'ong i-ik*
gross sales	총 매상고	*ch'ong maesang-go*
gross spread	총 값차이	*ch'ong gapch'a-i*
gross weight	총 중량	*ch'ong jungnyang*
gross yield	총 수익	*ch'ong su-ik*
ground (adj)	가루로 만든	*karu-ro mandeun*
group accounts	집단 계정	*chiptan gyejeong*
group dynamics	집단 역학	*chiptan yeokhak*
group insurance	단체 보험	*tanch'e boheom*
group, product	생산 집단(단체)	*saengsan jiptan (tanch'e)*
group, training	훈련 집단(단체)	*hullyeon jiptan (tanch'e)*
growth	성장	*seongjang*
growth, corporate	회사 성장	*hoesa seongjang*
growth index	성장 지수(指數)	*seongjang jisu*
growth industry	성장 산업	*seongjang saneop*
growth potential	성장 잠재력	*seongjang jamjaeryeok*
growth rate	성장율	*seongjangyul*
growth stock	성장 주식	*seongjang jushik*
guarantee	보증, 인수, 담보	*pojeung, insu, tambo*
guaranty bond	보증서	*pojeungseo*
guaranty company	보증 회사	*pojeung hoesa*
guesstimate	추정량(推定量)	*ch'ujeongnyang*
guidelines	유도 지표, 지침(指針)	*yudo jip'yo, jich'im*

H

half-life (bonds)	반감(半減)(증권)	*pan-gam (cheungkkweon)*
handbag	핸드백	*haendeubaek*

hydrochloric acid

English	Korean	Romanization
handblown glass	손으로 부풀려 만든 유리 제품	son-euro bup'ullyeo mandeun yuri jep'um
handicap	불리, 장애	pulli, chang-ae
hand-knit (adj)	손으로 짠, 뜨게질 한	son-euro jjan, tteugejil-han
handmade (adj)	수세공(手細工)의	susegong-eui
handpainted (adj)	손으로 칠한	son-euro ch'ilhan
hand-sewn (adj)	손으로 꿰맨	son-euro kkwemaen
hand-woven (adj)	손으로 뜬	son-euro tteun
harbor dues	항세(港稅)	hangse
hard copy	지면 복사	chimyeon boksa
hard currency	경화(硬貨), 교환 가능 통화	kyeonghwa, kyohwan ganeung t'onghwa
hard sell	적극 판매	cheokkeuk p'anmae
hardcover	양장본	yangjangbon
hardware	철물, 기계	ch'eolmul, kigye
head office	본점(本店), 본사(本社)	ponjeom, ponsa
headhunter	인재 선발 담당자	injae seonbal damdangja
headline	표제	p'yoje
headload	머리에 얹는 짐, 머리짐	meori-e eonneun jim, meorijim
headquarters	본사	ponsa
heat-resistant ceramics	내열(耐熱) 도자기류	naeyeol dojagiryu
heavy industry	중공업	chung-gong-eop
heavy lift charges	특별 중량 화물 양육료	t'eukpyeol jungnyang hwamul yang-yungnyo
hedge (v)	양다리 걸치다	yangdari geolch'ida
hem	감침질	kamch'imjil
hexachlorophene	6가 엽록소	yukka yeomnokso
hidden assets	은익 자산(隱匿資産)	eunik chasan
highest bidder	최고 입찰자	ch'oego ipch'aljja
hoard (v)	저장하다	cheojang-hada
holder (negotiable instruments	주주, 주인	chuju, chu-in
holder in due course	유상 소유인(有償所有人)	yusang soyu-in
holding company	모회사(母會社)	mohoesa
holding period	보유 기간	poyu gigan
holographic memory	레이저 사진술 기억장치	reijeo sajinsul gi-eok changch'i
home market	국내 시장	kungnae shijang
hormone	호르몬	horeumon
horsepower	마력	maryeok
hot money	국제간 단기 자금	kukchegan dan-gi jageum
hot rolling	열회전	yeol hoejeon
hot strip coil	내열(耐熱) 코일	naeyeol k'oil
hourly earnings	시간당 수입	shigandang su-ip
housing authority	주택 담당 부서	chut'aek tamdang buseo
human resources	인력 자원	illyeok chaweon
hybrid computer	하이브리드 전자 계산기	haibeurideu jeonja gyesan-gi
hybrid materials	혼성 물질	honseong muljjil
hydrocarbon	탄화수소	t'anhwa suso
hydrochloric acid	염산	yeomsan

hydrolysis

hydrolysis	가수분해	*kasu bunhae*
hypothecation	담보 계약	*tambo gyeyak*

I

ice bucket	얼음통	*eoreum-t'ong*
idle capacity	유휴 능력	*yuhyu neungnyeok*
ignition	점화	*cheomhwa*
illegal (adj)	위법의, 불법의	*wibeop-eui, pulbeop-eui*
illegal shipments	불법 선적	*pulbeop seonjeok*
illustration	삽화, 도해	*saphwa, tohae*
imitation	모방, 모조	*mobang, mojo*
impact on (v)	영향(충격)을 주다	*yeonghyang (ch'unggyeok) -eul juda*
impact, profit	이윤 효과	*iyun hyokkwa*
impending changes	절박한 변화	*cheolbakhan byeonhwa*
implication	내포, 함축	*naep'o, hamch'uk*
implied agreement	묵계(默契), 묵시적 동의	*mukkye, mukshijeok tong-eui*
import	수입	*suip*
import (v)	수입하다	*suip-hada*
import declaration	수입 신고	*suip shin-go*
import deposits	수입 예치	*suip yech'i*
import duty	수입 관세	*suip kwanse*
import entry	수입 수속	*suip susok*
import license	수입 승인증	*suip seung-injjeung*
import of record	음반 수입자	*eumban suipcha*
import quota	수입 할당	*suip halttang*
import regulations	수입 규정	*suip kyujeong*
import tariff	수입 세율	*suip seyul*
impound	예치 자금, 몰수(沒收)	*yech'i jageum, molsu*
improve upon (v)	개선하다	*kaeseon-hada*
improvements	개선, 호전	*kaeseon, hojeon*
impulse buying	충동 구매	*ch'ungdong gumae*
imputed (adj)	귀속된	*kwisok-toen*
in transit	운송중	*unsongjung*
in-the-red	적자의	*cheokcha-eui*
inadequate (adj)	불충분한	*pulch'ungbunhan*
incentive	유인(誘因), 동기	*yuin, tong-gi*
inchoate interest	미종결 이자	*mijong-gyeol ija*
incidental expenses	임시비	*imshibi*
income	소득, 수입	*sodeuk, suip*
income account	수입 계정(收入計定)	*suip kyejeong*
income bonds	수익(收益) 채권	*suik ch'aekkweon*
income bracket	소득 계층	*sodeuk keych'eung*
income, gross	총 소득	*ch'ong sodeuk*
income, net	순 소득	*sunsodeuk*
income statement	소득 계산서	*sodeuk kyesanseo*
income tax	소득세	*sodeukse*
income yield	소득 수익	*sodeuk suik*

English	Korean	Romanization
incorporate (v)	유한 책임 회사로 등록하다	yuhan ch'aegim hoesa-ro deungnok-hada
increase	증액	cheung-aek
increase (v)	증대(증가)하다	cheungdae (cheung-ga)-hada
increased costs	증가 비용	cheung-ga biyong
incremental cash flow	증분된 현금 유출	cheungbun-doen hyeon-geum yuch'ul
incremental cost	증가 비용	cheung-ga biyong
indebtedness	부채액	puch'ae-aek
indemnity	면책(免責), 보상, 보험	myeonch'aek, posang, poheom
indenture	채권 증서	ch'aekkweon cheungseo
independent suspension	독립 차대 버팀 장치	tongnip ch'adae beot'im jangch'i
index (indicator)	지수(指數)	chisu
index (v)	색인을 달다	saegin-eul dalda
index, growth	성장 지수	seongjang jisu
index option	주가 지수(株價指數)옵션	chukka jisu opsyeon
indexing	지수화	chisuhwa
indirect claim	간접 청구	kanjeop ch'eong-gu
indirect cost	간접 비용	kanjeop piyong
indirect expenses	간접비	kanjeop-pi
indirect labor	간접 노동	kanjeop nodong
indirect tax	간접세	kanjeopse
induction furnace	유도 전기로	yudo jeon-giro
industrial accident	노무 재해	nomu jaehae
industrial arbitration	산업 중재	saneop chungjae
industrial engineering	산업 공학	saneop konghak
industrial goods	산업 상품	saneop sangp'um
industrial insurance	공업 종업원 보험	kong-eop chong-eobweon boheom
industrial planning	산업 계획	saneop kyehoek
industrial relations	노사 관계	nosa gwangye
industral union	산업별 노동 조합	saneoppyeol nodong johap
industry	산업, 생산업	saneop, saengsaneop
industry-wide (adj)	산업 전체의	saneop cheonch'e-eui
inefficient (adj)	비능률적(非能率的)	pineungnyulcheok
inelastic demand or supply	비탄력성 수요 공급	pit'allyeokseong suyo gong-geup
infant industry	신흥 산업(新興產業)	shinheung saneop
inflation	통화 팽창, 인프레, 물가 상승	t'onghwa p'aengch'ang, inp'eure, mulkka sangseung
inflationary (adj)	통화 팽창의, 인프레성	t'onghwa p'aengch'ang-eui, inp'eureseong
infrared filmg	적외선 필름	cheog-oeseon p'illeum
infrastructure	하부 조직, 사회 간접 자본	habu jojik, sahoe ganjeop chabon
ingot	금은괴	keum-eun-goe
inheritance tax	상속세	sangsokse
injection	주입	chuip
injection molding machine	분사틀 기계	punsa-t'eul gigye

I

injection pump	분사 펌프	punsa p'eomp'eu
injunction	명령, 강제 명령	myeongnyeong, kangje myeongnyeong
ink	잉크	ingk'eu
inland bill of lading	국내 운송 적하 증권	kungnae unsong jeokha jeungkkweon
innovation	혁신	hyeokshin
input	입력, 투입	imnyeok, t'uip
input-output analysis	투입 산출 분석	t'uip sanch'ul bunseok
insert	삽입물	sabimmul
insert machine	삽입기	sabipki
insolvent (adj)	지불 불능의	chibul bulneung-eui
inspection	검사(檢査), 감사(監査)	keomsa, kamsa
inspector	검사관, 검열관	keomsagwan, keomyeolgwan
instability	불안정	puranjeong
installment credit	분할 신용대(分割信用貸)	punhal shinyongdae
installment plan	분할 계획	punhal gyehoek
institutional advertising	기업 광고	kieop kwang-go
institutional investor	기관 투자가(機關投資家)	kigwan t'ujaga
instruct (v)	지명하다, 지시하다	chimyeong-hada, chishi-hada
instrument	기계, 기구	kigye, kigu
instrumental capital	증권상의 자본, 제조 자본	cheungkkweonsang-eui jabon, chejo jabon
insulin	인슐린	insyullin
insurance	보험(保險)	poheom
insurance broker	보험 중개인	poheom jung-gaein
insurance company	보험 회사	poheom hoesa
insurance fund	보험 자금	poheom jageum
insurance policy	보험 증권	poheom jeungkkweon
insurance premium	보험료	poheomnyo
insurance underwriter	보험 인수 업자	poheom insu eopcha
intangible assets	무형 자산	muhyeongjasan
integrated management system	통합 운영 체계	t'onghap unyeong ch'egye
intellectual property right	지적(知的) 소유권	chijeok soyukkweon
intelligent robot	지능 로보트	chi-neung robot'eu
interact (v)	상호 작용하다	sangho jagyong-hada
interbank	은행간의	eunhaeng-gan-eui
interchangeable lens	교환 가능 렌즈	kyohwan ganeung renjeu
interest	이자, 이권, 권익	ija, ikkweon, kweonik
interest arbitrage	이자 재정(利子裁定)	ija jaejeong
interest, compound	복리(複利)	pongni
interest expenses	이자 비용	ija biyong
interest income	이자 소득	ija sodeuk
interst parity	이자 평형(평가)	ija p'yeonghyeong (p'yeongkka)
interest period	이자 기간	ija gigan
interest rate	금리, 이율	keumni, iyul
interface	공유 영역	kong-yu yeong-yeok

invoice, commercial

English	Korean	Romanization
interim	잠시(暫時)	chamshi
interim budget	임시 예산	imshi yesan
interim statement	임시 계산서	imshi gyesanseo
interlocking directorate	겸임 중역회	kyeomim jungyeokhoe
intermediary	중개 조정자	chung-gae jojeongja
intermediary goods	매개 상품(媒介商品)	maegae sangp'um
internal	내부의, 국내의	naebu-eui, kungnae-eui
internal audit	내부 감사(監査)	naebu gamsa
internal funding	내부 자금 조달	naebu jageum jodal
internal grinder	내부 분쇄기	naebu bunswaegi
internal rate of return	내부 수익율	naebu suingnyul
internal revenue tax	내국세	naegukse
international conference	국제 회의	kukche hoe-eui
International Date Line	국제 날짜 변경선	kukche naljja byeon-gyeongseon
interstate commerce	주간 무역(州間貿易)	chugan muyeok
intervene	개입(介入)하다	kaeip-hada
interview	회견, 회담	hoegyeon, hoedam
intestate	무유언 사망자(無遺言死亡者)	muyueon samangja
intrinsic value	실재 가치, 고유 가치	shiljjae gach'i, koyu gach'i
introduction	서언, 서문	seo-eon, seomun
invalidate (v)	무효로 하다	muhyo-ro-hada
inventory	재고품 목록	chaegop'um mongnok
inventory control	재고품 관리	chaegop'um kwalli
inventory, perpetual	영속적 재고 관리	yeongsokcheok chaego gwalli
inventory, physical	실지 재고	shiljji jaego
inventory turnover	재고품 회전율	chaegop'um hoejeonnyui
inverted market	역(逆)시장	yeokshijang
invest (v)	투자하다	t'uja-hada
invested capital	투자 자본	t'uja jabon
investment	투자, 투자금	t'uja, t'ujageum
investment adviser	투자 고문	t'uja gomun
investment analysis	투자 분석	t'uja bunseok
investment appraisal	투자 평가 감정	t'uja p'yeongkka gamjeong
investment bank	투자 은행	t'uja eunhaeng
investment budget	투자 예산	t'uja yesan
investment company	신탁 회사	shint'ak hoesa
investment credit	투자 신용	t'uja shinyong
investment criteria	투자 기준	t'uja gijun
investment grade	투자 등급	t'uja deung-geup
investment letter	투자 서류, 인가장	t'uja seoryu, in-gajjang
investment policy	투자 정책	t'uja jeongch'aek
investment program	투자 계획	t'uja gyehoek
investment, return on	투자 이윤	t'uja iyun
investment strategy	투자 전략	t'uja jeollyak
investment trust	투자 신탁	t'uja shint'ak
investor relations	투자자 이해(利害)	t'ujaja ihae
invisibles	무역외 수지(貿易外收支)	muyeogoe suji
invitation to bid	입찰(入札) 권유(초대)	ipch'al gweonyu (ch'odae)
invoice	송장(送狀), 매입서(買入書)	songjjang, maeipseo
invoice, commercial	상업 송장	sang-eop songjjang

invoice, consular	영사 송장	*yeongsa songjjang*
invoice cost	송장 비용	*songjjang biyong*
invoice, pro forma	매입 견적 송장	*maeip kyeonjeok songjjang*
iodine	옥소(沃素)	*okso*
iron	철제	*ch'eolche*
iron ore	철광석	*ch'eolgwangseok*
issue (stock)	발행	*palhaeng*
issue (v)	발행하다	*palhaeng-hada*
issue price	매출 가격	*maech'ul gagyeok*
issued shares	발행 주식	*palhaeng jushik*
italic	이탤릭체	*it'aerik-ch'e*
item	조항, 품목	*chohang, p'ummok*
itemize	항목별로 기장(記帳)하다	*hangmokpyeol-lo gijang-hada*
itemized account	명세 정산서(明細精算書)	*myeongse jeongsanseo*

J

jacket	(가제본의)표지	*(ka-jebon-eui)p'yoji*
Jason clause	제이슨 조항(條項)	*cheiseun johang*
jawbone	신용	*shinyong*
jet condenser	분출 축전기	*punch'ul ch'ukcheon-gi*
jet lag	시차로 인한 피로	*shich'a-ro inhan p'iro*
jewel	보석, 장신구	*poseok, changshin-gu*
jig	선광기(選鑛機)	*seon-gwang-gi*
jig (production)	선광기(選鑛機)	*seon-gwang-gi*
job	직무, 역할	*chingmu, yeokhal*
job analysis	직무 분석	*chingmu bunseok*
job description	직종, 직무 분석 기록	*chikchong, chingmu bunseok kirok*
job evaluation	직무 평가	*chingmu p'yeongkka*
job hopper	상습 전직자(常習轉職者)	*sangseup cheonjikcha*
job lot	무더기로 파는 염가품(廉價品)	*mudeogi-ro p'aneun yeomkkap'um*
job performance	직무 수행 성적	*chingmu suhaeng seongjeok*
job security	직업 안정 보장	*chigeop anjeong bojang*
job shop	직업 찾기	*chigeop ch'atkki*
jobber	장내 중개인, 도매상	*changnae jung-gaein, tomaesang*
jobber's turn	장내 중개인이 수취하는 차익금(差益金)	*changnae jung-gaein-i such' wi-haneun ch'aikkeum*
joint account	공동 구좌	*kongdong gujwa*
joint cost	공동 비용	*kongdong biyong*
joint estate	공동 자산, 공동 소유지	*kongdong jasan, kongdong soyuji*
joint liability	공동 의무, 공동 책임	*kongdong euimu, kongdong ch'aegim*
joint owner	공동 소유	*kongdong soyu*
joint stock company	주식 공사(株式公社)	*chushik kongsa*

joint venture	합작회사, 공동 사업체	*hapchak hoesa, kongdnog sa-eopch'e*
Josephson device	죠셉슨 장치	*chyosepseun jangch'i*
journal	장부(帳簿)	*changbu*
journeyman	직공(職工)	*chikkong*
joystick	조종간(操縱桿)	*chojong-gan*
junior partner	일반 사원, 후순위 동업자	*ilban saweon, husunwi dong-eopcha*
junior security	후순위 유가 증권	*husunwi yukka jeungkkweon*
jurisdiction	관할권(管轄權)	*kwanhalkkweon*
justify (v)	(-의 행을) 가지런히 하다	*(-eui haeng-eul) gajireonhi-hada*

K

key exports	주요 수출품	*chuyo such'ulp'um*
key man insurance	사업가 보험	*sa-eopka boheom*
keyboard	건반, 키보드	*keonban, k'ibodeu*
Keynesian economics	케인즈 경제학	*k'einjeu gyeongjehak*
keypunch	키펀치	*k'ip'eonch'i*
kickback	상납(上納), 반환	*sangnap, panhwan*
kiting (banking)	융통 어음 발행	*yungt'ong eo-eum balhaeng*
knife	칼	*k'al*
knot (nautical)	노트, 해리(海里)	*not'eu, haeri*
know-how	노-하우, 요령, 비법(秘法)	*no-hau, yoryeong, pibeop*
knurling tool	마디 공구	*madi gong-gu*

L

labor	노동, 작업	*nodong, chageop*
labor code	노동 법전, 규칙	*nodong beopcheon, kyuch'ik*
labor dispute	노동 쟁의	*nodong jaeng-eui*
labor force	노동력	*nodongnyeok*
labor law	노동법	*nodongpeop*
labor leader	노동 지도자	*nodong jidoja*
labor market	노동 시장	*nodong shijang*
labor relations	노사 관계	*nosa gwan-gye*
labor turnover	노동 이동	*nodong idong*
labor union	노동 조합	*nodong johap*
labor-intensive (adj)	노동 집약형의	*nodong jibyakhyeong-eui*
labor-saving (adj)	노동 절약의	*nodong jeoryak-eui*
laborer	노동자, 인부(人夫)	*nodongja, inbu*
lace	가장자리 장식	*kajangjari jangshik*
ladle	국자	*kukcha*
lagging indicator	지연(遲延) 표시기	*chiyeon p'yoshigi*
laissez-faire	자유 방임 주의, 무간섭 주의	*chayu bang-im jueui, muganseop-chueui*
land	토지	*t'oji*
land grant	무상 토지 불하	*musang t'oji bulha*

land reform

land reform	토지 개혁	t'oji gaehyeok
land tax	지세(地稅)	chise
landed cost	양륙비(揚陸費) 포함 원가	yangnyukpi p'oham weonkka
landing certificate	양륙(揚陸) 증명서	yangnyuk cheungmyeongseo
landing charges	화물 양륙비(揚陸費)	hwamul yangnyukpi
landing costs	양륙비(揚陸費)	yangnyukpi
landowner	지주(地主)	chiju
lapping machine	접는 기계	cheomneun gigye
large-scale (adj)	대규모의	taegyumo-eui
large-scale integrated circuit	대형 집적 회로	taehyeong chipcheok hoero
laser	레이저	reijeo
laser beam printer	레이저 광 인쇄기	reijeo-gwang inswaegi
laser fusion	레이저 핵융합	reijeo haeng-yunghap
laser processing	레이저 처리	reijeo ch'eori
lash (v)	낭비하다	nangbi-hada
last in-first out	후입 선출법(後入先出法)	hu-ip seonch'ulbeop
lathe	선반(旋盤)	seonban
law	법률, 법규	peomnyul, peopkyu
law of diminishing returns	수익 점감 법칙	su-ik cheomgam beopch'ik
lawsuit	소송, 고소	sosong, koso
lawyer	변호사, 법률가	pyeonhosa, peomnyulga
lay time	정박 시간	cheongbak shigan
lay up	휴항(休航)	hyuhang
lay-off	일시 해고, 강제 휴업, 해고 휴직 기간	ilshihaego, kangje hyu-eop, haego hyujik kigan
laydays	정박 기간(碇泊期間)	cheongbak kigan
layout	배치, 계획	baech'i, kyehoek
lead time	조달 기간	chodal gigan
leader	지도자, 인기있는 주식	chidoja, inkki-inneun jushik
leading indicator	선행 지표(先行指標)	seonhaeng jip'yo
leads and lags	수지의 시간적 차질, 진도와 지연	suji-eui shiganjeok ch'ajil, chindo-wa jiyeon
leakage	누손(漏損)	nuson
learning curve	학습 곡선, 경험 곡선	hakseup kokseon, kyeongheom gokseon
lease	임대차 계약(賃貸借契約)	imdaech'a gyeyak
lease (v)	임대(賃貸)하다	imdae-hada
leased department	임대한 부문	imdaehan bumun
leave of absence	휴가	hyuga
ledger	원부(原簿), 대장	weonbu, taejang
ledger account	원장 계정(元帳計定)	weonjang gyejeong
ledger entry	원장 기입	weonjang gi-ip
legacy	유증(遺贈)	yujeung
legal capital	법률상의 자본금	peomnyulsang-eui jabon-geum
legal entity	법률상의 실체물	peomnyulsang-eui shilch'emul
legal holiday	법정 휴일	peopcheong hyuil

English	Korean	Romanization
legal list (fiduciary investments)	신용상의 투자	shinyongsang-eui t'uja
legal monopoly	법정 독점	peopcheong dokcheom
legal tender	법정 통화	peopcheong t'onghwa
lending margin	대출 최저 수익금	taech'ul ch'oejeo suikkeum
length	길이, 장단	kiri, changdan
lens	렌즈	renjeu
less-than-carload	소량 취급 화물	soryang ch'wigeup hwamul
less-than-truckload	한 트럭 미만 적재 화물	han t'eureok miman jeokchae hwamul
lessee	임차인(賃借人)	imch'ain
lessor	임대인(賃貸人)	imdaein
letter	서한, 증서	seohan, cheungseo
letter of credit	신용장	shinyongjjang
letter of guaranty	외화 조건 보증서	oehwa jokkeon bojeungseo
letter of indemnity	무고장 선하 증권 (無故障船荷證券)	mugojang seonha jeungkkweon
letter of introduction	소개장(紹介狀)	sogaejjang
letterpress	인쇄 자구, 활판 인쇄기	inswae jagu, hwalp'an inswaegi
level out (v)	평평히 하다	p'yeongp'yeonghi-hada
leverage	부채 사용	puch'ae sayong
leveraged lease	안전한 임대	anjeonhan imdae
levy taxes (v)	세금을 과하다	segeum-eul gwa-hada
liability	의무, 책임	euimu, ch'aegim
liability, actual	실질 채무(實質債務)	shiljjil ch'aemu
liability, assumed	인수 채무(引受債務)	insu ch'aemu
liability, contingent	임시 부채(臨時負債)	imshi buch'ae
liability, current	당좌 부채(當座負債)	tangjwa buch'ae
liability, fixed	고정 부채(固定負債)	kojeong buch'ae
liability insurance	책임 보험	ch'aegim boheom
liability, secured	담보(擔保)채무	tambo ch'aemu
liability, unsecured	무담보 채무	mudambo ch'aemu
liable for tax	세금 지불 의무	segeum jibul euimu
liable to (adj)	의무가 있는	euimu-ga inneun
liaison	연락, 접촉	yeollak, cheopch'ok
libel	문서 명예 훼손 (文書名譽毁損), 모욕(侮辱)	munseo myeong-ye hweson, moyok
license	면허, 인가서	myeonheo, in-gaseo
license fees	특허권 사용료	t'eukheokkweon sayongnyo
licensed warehouse	사설 보세 창고	saseol bose ch'angkko
lien	선취 특권(先取特權), 유치권	seonch'wi t'eukkweon, yuch'ikkweon
life cycle (of a product)	(제품) 수명(壽命)	(chep'um) sumyeong
life insurance policy	생명 보험 보증권	saengmyeong boheom bojeungkkweon
life member	종신 회원	chongshin hoeweon
life of a patent	전매 특허권 유효 기간	cheonmae t'eukheokkweon yuhyo gigan
lighterage	부선운반(船運搬)	puseon unban

English	Korean	Romanization
light emitting diode	방사 이극 진공관	pangsa igeuk chin-gong-gwan
limit order (stock market)	제한 주문	chehan jumun
limited liability	유한 책임	yuhan ch'aegim
limited partnership	합자 회사(合資會社)	hapcha hoesa
line	행	haeng
line, assembly	일관 작업	ilgwan jageop
line drawing	선화	seonhwa
line executive	업종 경영 간부	eopchong gyeong-yeong ganbu
line management	노선(업종)경영	noseon (eopchong) gyeong-yeong
line of business	영업 품목, 사업 노선	yeong-eop p'ummok, sa-eop noseon
line printer	행(行) 인쇄기	haeng inswaegi
line, product	제품(생산) 종목	chep'um (saeng-san) jongmok
linear	선상(線上)의, 직선(直線)의	seonsang-eui, chikseon-eui
linear estimation	선형식 견적	seonhyeongshik kyeonjeok
linear programming	선형 계획법(線形計劃法)	seonhyeong gyehoek-peop
linear terms	선형형(線形型)	seonhyeong-hyeong
linen	린네르, 아마포	rinnereu, amap'o
linen (adj)	린네르제(製)의	rinnereuje-eui
lining	안감	ankkam
liquid assets	유동 자산	yudong jasan
liquid crystal	액정(液晶)	aekcheong
liquid helium	액체 헬륨	aekch'e hellyum
liquidation	변제, 청산	pyeonje, ch'eongsan
liquidation value	변제 가치	pyeonje gach'i
liquidity	유동성	yudongseong
liquidity preference (economics)	유동성 선호(選好)	yudongseong seonho
liquidity ratio	유동 비율	yudong biyul
list price	표시 가격	p'yoshi gagyeok
listed securities	상장주(上場株)	sangjangju
listing	목록 기입(目錄記入)	mongnok ki-ip
litigation	소송, 기소	sosong, kiso
living trust	생존 신탁(生存信託)	saengjon shint'ak
load (sales charge)	부가료(附加料)	pugaryo
load factor	부하율(負荷率)	puhayul
load, work	일량, 업무량	illyang, eommuryang
loan	대부(貸付), 차관	taebu, ch'agwan
loan stock	대여 주식	taeyeo jushik
lobbying	로비 활동, 원외 운동	robi hwalttong, weonoe undong
local customs	지방 세관	chibang segwan
local taxes	지방세	chibangse
lock in (rate of interest) (v)	이자율을 고정하다	ijayul-eul gojeong-hada
lock out	공장 폐쇄	kongjang p'yeswae
logistics	비품, 병참품	pip'um, pyeongch'amp'um

logo	약호, 어표	yakho, eop'yo
long hedge	장기 양다리 걸치기	chang-gi yangdari geolch'igi
long interest	강세측, 시황(市況)	kangsech'euk, shihwang
long ton	영톤(英톤)	yeongt'on
long sleeves	긴 소매	kin somae
long-focus lens	장거리 촛점 렌즈	chang-geori ch'otcheom renjeu
long-range planning	장기 계획	chang-gi gyeheok
long-term capital account	장기 자본 계정	chang-gi jabon gyejeong
long-term debt	장기 부채	chang-gi buch'ae
loss	손(損), 손실, 분실	son, sonshil, punshil
loss, gross	총 손실	ch'ong sonshil
loss leader	유객(유인용) 상품(誘客商品)	yugaek (yuinyong) sangp'um
loss, net	순 손실	sun sonshil
loss-loss ratio	손실 비율	sonshil piyul
lot	대지, 획지(劃地), 택지	taeji, hoekchi, t'aekchi
lower case	소문자	somunjja
low-income	저소득	cheosodeuk
low-interest loans	저리 대부(低利貸付)	cheori daebu
low-yield bonds	저리 증권(低利證券)	cheori jeungkkweon
lump sum	총계 금액, 일시불	ch'ong-gye geumaek, ilshibul
luxury goods	사치품(奢侈品)	sach'ip'um
luxury tax	사치 품목세	sach'i p'ummokse

M

machine tools	기계 공구	kigye gong-gu
machinery	기계류	kigyeryu
machining center	기계 공작소(工作所)	kigye gongjakso
macro lens	매크로 렌즈	maek'euro renjeu
macroeconomics	거시 경제학(巨視經濟學)	keoshi gyeongjehak
made in U.S.A.	미제(美製), 미국산(美國産)	mije, miguksan
magnetic bubble memory	자기(磁器) 기포 기억 장치	chagi gip'o gieok changch'i
magnetic disc unit	자기 디스크 장치	chagi diseuk'eu jangch'i
magnetic fluid	자기 유동체	chagi yudongch'e
magnetic memory	자기(磁氣) 기억 장치	chagi gieok changch'i
magnetic tape	자기(磁氣) 테이프	chagi t'eip'eu
magnetic tape unit	자기 테이프 장치	chagi t'eip'eu jangch'i
mail order	우편 주문, 통신 판매	up'yeon jumun, t'ongshin p'anmae
mailing list	우편 발송 대장	up'yeon balsong daejang
mainframe computer	메인 프레임 컴퓨터	mein p'eureim k'eomp'yut'eo
maintenance	유지(維持), 관리	yuji, kwalli
maintenance contract	유지 관리 계약	yuji gwalli gyeyak
maintenance margin	증권 구입 유지 부채율	cheung-kkweon gu-ip yuji buch'ae-yul
maize	옥수수	oksusu

major statistics	주요 지표(主要指標)	chuyo jip'yo
majority interest	다수 이익	tasu i-ik
make available (v)	입수 가능하다	ipsu kaneung-hada
make-or-buy decision	생산 구입 결정	saengsan guip kyeolcheong
make-ready	준비	chunbi
maker (of a check, draft, etc.)	약속 어음 발행인	yaksok eoeum balhaeng-in
makeshift	미봉책, 임시 변통 수단	mibongch'aek, imshibyeont'ong sudan
man (gal) Friday	충복(忠僕), 심복	ch'ungbok, shimbok
man hours	인시(人時), 노동 시간	inshi, nodong shigan
manage (v)	관리하다, 경영하다	kwalli-hada, kyeong-yeong-hada
managed costs	관리 비용	kwalli biyong
managed economy	통제 경제	t'ongje gyeongje
managed float	관리 부동 증권 (管理浮動證券)	kwalli budong jeungkkweon
management	관리, 경영	kwalli, kyeong-yeong
management accounting	관리 회계	kwalli hoegye
management, business	경영 관리	kyeong-yeong kwalli
management by objectives	목표에 의한 관리	mokp'yo-e euihan kwalli
management chart	관리 도표	kwalli dop'yo
management consultant	경영 자문, 고문	kyeong-yeong jamun, komun
management, credit	신용 관리	shinyong kwalli
management fee	관리비	kwallibi
management, financial	재정 관리	chaejeong kwalli
management group	관리단	kwallidan
management, line	품목 관리	p'ummok kwalli
management, market	판매 시장 관리	p'anmae shijang kwalli
management, middle	중간 경영 관리	chung-gan gyeong-yeong kwalli
management, office	사무 관리	samu kwalli
management, personnel	인사 관리	insa kwalli
management, product	제품 관리	chep'um kwalli
management, sales	판매 관리	p'anmae kwalli
management, systems	조직 관리	chojik kwalli
management team	운영진	unyeongjin
management, top	최고 경영진	ch'oego gyeong-yeongjin
manager	관리인, 경영인, 지배인	kwalli-in, kyeong-yeong-in, chibae-in
mandate	위임(委任)	wi-im
mandatory redemption	강제 상환	kangje sanghwan
manganese ore	망간 광석	mang-gan gwangseok
manganese steel	망간강	mang-gan-gang
manifest	적하 목록, 송장(送狀)	cheokha mongnok, songjjang
manipulator	위험 물질 취급 장치	wiheom muljjil ch'wigeup changch'i
manmade fibers	인조 섬유	injo seomyu
manpower	인력, 노동력	illyeok, nodongnyeok

market value

English	Korean	Romanization
manual workers	육체 노동자	yukch'e nodongja
manufacturer	제조 업자(업체)	chejo eopcha, chejo-eopch'e
manufacturer's agent	제조 업자 대리점	chejo eopcha daerijeom
manufacturer's representative	제조 업체 대리	chejo eopch'e dae-ri
manufacturing capacity	제조(생산) 능력	chejo (saengsan) neungnyeok
manufacturing control	제조 통제	chejo t'ongje
margin call	(주식의)추력 증거금 (追力證據金)	(chushik-eui) ch'uryeok cheung-geogeum
margin, gross	총 이익	ch'ong i-ik
margin, net	순 이익	sun i-ik
margin of safety	안전 여유(安全餘裕)	anjeon yeoyu
margin, profit	마진, 이윤폭, 이윤	marjin, iyun-p'ok, iyun
margin rate	마진율	majin-yul
margin requirements	보증금 수요	pojeung-geum suyo
marginal account	최저회계, 한계계정	ch'oejeo hoegye, han-gye gyejeong
marginal cost	한계(限界) 비용	han-gye biyong
marginal pricing	한계 가격	han-gye gagyeok
marginal productivity	한계 생산력	han-gye saengsannyeok
marginal revenue	한계 수입(收入)	han-gye suip
marine cargo insurance	해상 화물 보험	haesang hawmul boheom
marine underwriter	해상 보험 업자	haesang boheom eopcha
maritime contract	해운 계약	haeun gyeyak
markdown	가격 인하	kagyeok inha
market	시장, 판매 시장	shijang, p'anmae shijang
market (v)	판매하다	p'anmae-hada
market access	시장 접근	shijang jeopkeun
market appraisal	판매 시장 평가	p'anmae shijang p'yeongkka
market, buyer's	구매자(매주-買主) 시장	kumaeja (maeju) shijang
market concentration	시장 집중	shijang jipchung
market dynamics	시장 활기(活氣)	shijang hwalgi
market forces	시장력(市場力)	shijangnyeok
market forecast	시장 예측	shijang yech'euk
market, fringe	외변(外邊)(부가-附加) 시장	oebyeong (puga) shijang
market index	시장 지표(지수)	shijang jip'yo(jisu)
market management	판매 시장 관리	p'anmae shijang kwalli
market penetration	판매 시장 침투	p'anmae shijang ch'imt'u
market plan	판매 계획	p'anmae gyehoek
market position	시장 위치, 시장 상황	shijang wich'i, shijang sanghwang
market potential	잠재 시장	chamjae shijang
market price	시가(市價), 시세(時勢)	shikka, shise
market rating	시장율	shijang-yul
market report	시황 보고	shihwang bogo
market research	판로(시장) 조사	p'allo (shijang) jo-sa
market saturation	시장 포화 상태	shijang p'ohwa sangt'ae
market share	시장 분배	shijang bunbae
market survey	시장 조사	shijang josa
market trends	시가(市價)의 추세(趨勢)	shikka-eui ch'use
market value	시장 가격, 시가(市價)	shijang gagyeok, shikka

market-maker (securities)	시장 어음 발행인, 주도주(主導株)	shijang eo-eum balhaeng-in, chudoju
marketable securities	환가 가능 증권 (換價可能證券)	hwankka ganeung jeungkkwon
marketing	마켓팅	mak'et'ing
marketing budget	마케팅 예산	mak'et'ing yesan
marketing concept	판매 개념	p'anmae gaenyeom
marketplace	시장(市場)	shijang
markup	가격 인상	kagyeok insang
mass communications	매스콤, 언론	maeseuk'om, eollon
mass marketing	대량 마켓팅	taeryang mak'et'ing
mass media	매스 미디어, 대중 매체(大衆媒體)	maeseu midieo, taejung maech'e
mass production	대량 생산	taeryang saengsan
matched samples	대응 견본	tae-eung gyeonbon
material handling robot	재료 취급 로보트	chaeryo ch'wigeup robot'eu
materials	재료, 자료	chaeryo, charyo
maternity leave	출산 휴가	ch'ulsan hyuga
mathematical model	수학적 모형(模型)	suhakcheok mohyeong
matrix	자모, 모형	chamo, mohyeong
matrix management	매트릭스 관리	maet'eurikseu gwalli
matt	매트	maet'eu
maturity	만기(滿期)	man-gi
maturity date	만기일	man-gi-il
maximize (v)	극대화하다, 최대한 활용하다	keuktaehwa-hada, ch'oe-daehan hwallyong-hada
mean (average)	평균치, 비례 중항	p'yeong-gyunch'i, pirye junghang
measure (v)	측정하다	ch'eukcheong-hada
mechanical	기계적인	kigyejeogin
mechanical engineering	기계 공학	kigye gonghak
mechanical press	기계 압착기	kigye apch'akki
mechanics' lien	기계공 유치권 (機械工留置權)	kigyegong yuch'ikkweon
median	중위수(中位數)	chungwisu
mediation	조정(調整), 중개(仲介)	chojeong, chung-gae
medication	약물치료	yangmul ch'iryo
medicine	약	yak
medium of exchange	교환 수단(중개물)	kyohwan sudan (chung-gaemul)
medium term	중기(中期)	chung-gi
meet the price (v)	가격이 맞다	kagyeogi matta
meeting	회의	hoe-eui
meeting, board	이사회	isahoe
member firm	회원사(會員社)	hoeweonsa
member of firm	회사원, 사원	hoesaweon, saweon
memorandum	회람(回覽), 메모	hoeram, memo
mercantile	상인, 무역 업자, 상업	sang-in, muyeogeopcha, sang-eop
mercantile agency	상업 흥신소	sang-eop heungshinso
mercantile law	상법	sangppeop

merchandise	상품	sangp'um
merchandising	상품화 정책(계획)	sangp'umhwa jeongch'aek (kyehoek)
merchant	상인	sang-in
merchant bank	상업 은행	sang-eop eunhaeng
merchant guild	상인 조합	sang-in johap
merger	합병(合倂)	happyeong
metal alloys for hydrogen storage	수소 저장을 위한 금속 합금	suso jeojang-eul wi-han geumsok hapkeum
metal hydride	금속 수소 화물	keumsok suso hwamul
metal processing machine	금속 공작 기계	keumsok kongjak kıgye
metallic fiber	금속질 섬유	keumsokchil seomyu
metals	금속(金屬)	keumsok
methane	메탄	met'an
methanol	메탄올	met'anol
method	방법, 절차	pangbeop, cheolch'a
metrification	미터화	mit'eohwa
micro camera	현미경 사진용 카메라	hyeonmigyeong sajinyong k'amera
micro cassette recorder	마이크로 카세트 녹음기	maik'euro k'aset'eu nogeumgi
micro computer	소형 컴퓨터	sohyeong k'eomp'yut'eo
micro processor	소형 중앙 처리 장치	sohyeong jung-ang ch'eori jangch'i
microchip	전자 기능 회로	cheonja gineung hoero
microfiche	소형 필름 카드	sohyeong p'ileum k'adeu
microfilm	축소 복사용(縮小複寫用) 필름, 마이크로 필름	ch'ukso boksayong p'illeum, maik'euro p'illeum
microwave	마이크로 웨이브	maik'euro-weibeu
microwave oven	전자 오븐, 전자 렌지	cheonja obeun, cheonja renji
middle management	중간 경영 관리	chung-gan gyeong-yeong gwalli
middleman	중개인, 중간상	chung-gaein, chung-gansang
mileage	마일수	mail-su
milling	제분(製粉), 축융(縮絨)	chebun, ch'ugyung
milling machine	금속 절삭기	keumsok cheolsak-ki
mini component system	소형 구조 시스템	sohyeong gujo siseut'em
mini computer	소형 컴퓨터	sohyeong k'eomp'yut'eo
minimum reserves	최소 예비금	ch'oeso yebigeum
minimum wage	최저 임금	ch'oejeo imgeum
minority interest	소수 주주 소유분 (小數株主所有分)	sosu juju soyubun
mint	조폐국, 부원(富源)	chop'yeguk, puweon
miscalculation	오산(誤算)	osan
miscellaneous (adj)	기타의, 잡동사니의	kit'a-eui, chapttongsani-eui
misleading	오도(誤導)	odo
misunderstandg	오해(誤解)	ohae
mixed cost	혼합 비용	honhap piyong
mixed sampling	혼합된 견본 적출	honhaptoen gyeonbon jeokch'ul

mobility of labor	노동 가동성(유동성)	nodong gadongseong (yudongseong)
mock-up	실물 크기 모형	shilmul k'eugi mohyeong
mode	방법, 방식	pangbeop, pangshik
model	모형, 모델	mohyeong, model
modern	현대	hyeondae
modular production	변조기 생산	pyeonjogi saengsan
moire	물결 무늬 옷감의 일종	mulkkyeol muni otkkam-eui iljjong
molding machine	주조기	chujo-gi
mom and pop store	구멍가게	kumeong gage
monetary base	통화 기준	t'onghwa gijun
monetary credits	화폐 신용	hwap'ye shinyong
monetary policy	금융 정책	keumnyung jeongch'aek
money	금융, 금전	keumnyung, keumjeon
money broker	화폐 중개인	hwap'ye jung-gae-in
maney manager	현금 관리자	hyeon-geum gwallija
money market	금융 시장	keumnyung shijang
money order	우편환(郵便換)	up'yeonhwan
money shop	화폐상, 금융 회사	hwap'yesang, keumnyung hoesa
money supply	통화 공급량	t'onghwa gong-geupnyang
monitor	감시 장치, 컴퓨터 스크린	kamshi jangch'i, k'eomp'yut'eo seuk'eurin
monopoly	전매(專賣), 공급 독점	cheonmae, kong-geup tokcheom
monopsony	수요 독점(需要獨占)	suyo dokcheom
Monte Carlo technique	몬테 칼로법	mont' ek'allobeop
moonlighting	부업(副業)	pu-eop
morale	사기(士氣)	sagi
moratorium	지불 정지, 활동 중지	chibul jeongji, hwalttong jungji
morphine	모르핀	moreup'in
mortgage	주택 융자	chut'aek yungja
mortgage bank	주택 융자 은행	chut'aek yungja eunhaeng
mortgage bond	담보부 채권(擔保附債券)	tambobu ch'aekkweon
mortgage certificate	담보 증서	tambo jeungseo
mortgage debenture	담보 사채권(社債權)	tambo sach'aekkweon
most-favored nation	조건부 최혜국	chokkeonbu ch'oehyeguk
motion	운동, 명령 신청	undong, myeongnyeong shinch'eong
motivation study	동기 조사	tong-gi josa
motor drive	모터 드라이브	mot'eo deuraibeu
movement of goods	상품 동향(動向)	sangp'um donghyang
moving average	이동 평균법	idong p'yeong-gyunppeop
moving expenses	이사비, 이전비	isabi, ijeonbi
moving parity	이동 등가(移動等價)	idong deungkka
mug	원통형 찻잔	weont'onghyeong ch'atchan
multicurrency	복수 통화(複數通貨)	poksu t'onghwa
multicut lathe	복수 절단 선반	poksu jeolttan seonban
multilateral agreement	다변 협정	tabyeon hyeopcheong

negotiable securities

multilateral trade	다변 무역	tabyeon muyeok
multinational corporation	다국적 회사	tagukcheok hoesa
multiple exchange rate	복식 환율	pokshik hwannyul
multiple taxation	복식 과세(複式課稅)	pokshik kwase
multiples	배수(倍數), 배량(倍量)	paesu, paeryang
multiplier	승수(乘數)	seungsu
multiprogramming	다중 프로그래밍	tajung p'eurogeuraeming
multispindle drilling machine	복수 방추 천공기	poksu bangch'u ch'ong-gong-gi
municipal bond	시채권(市債券)	shich'aekkweon
muslin	옥양목	ogyangmok
mutual fund	투자 신탁	t'uja shint'ak
mutual savings bank	상호 저축 은행	sangho jeoch'uk eunhaeng
mutually exclusive classes	상호 배제 조항	sangho baeje johang

N

named inland point in country of importation	수입국내 지정 지점	suipkungnae jijeong jijeom
named point of destination	지정 도착 지점 (指定到着地點)	chijeong doch'ak chijeom
named point of exportation	지정 수출 지점	chijeong such'ul jijeom
named point of origin	지정 원산(原産) 지점	chijeong weonsan jijeom
named port of importation	지정 수입항	chijeong suiphang
named port of shipment	지정 선적항	chijeong seonjeokhang
naphtha	나프타	nap'eut'a
napkin	나프킨	nap'euk'in
narcotic	마취성의	mach'wiseong-eui
national bank	국립 은행	kungnip eunhaeng
national debt	국가 채무(債務)	kukka ch'aemu
nationalism	민족 주의, 국가 주의	minjokchueui, kukkajueui
nationalization	국유화, 국영화	kugyuhwa, kugyeonghwa
native produce	현지 농산물	hyeonji nongsanmul
natural resources	천연 자원	ch'eonyeon jaweon
near money	근사 통화(近似通貨)	keunsa t'onghwa
needs analysis	필수품 분석	p'ilsup'um bunseok
negative	원판	weonp'an
negative cash flow	적자 현금 유출 (赤字現金流出)	cheokcha hyeon-geum yuch'ul
negative pledge	부정적 언질(否定的言質)	pujeongjeok eonjil
negligent (adj)	태만(怠慢)한	t'aemanhan
negotiable	양도할 수 있는, 유통되는, 협상 가능한	yangdohal su inneun, yut'ongdoeneun, hyeopsang ganeung-han
negotiable securities	유통 유가 증권	yut'ong yukka jeungkkweon

negotiate (v)	교섭하다, 협상하다, 유통시키다	kyoseop-hada, hyeopsang-hada, yut'ongshik'ida
negotiated sale	상담(商談)된 판매	sangdamdoen p'anmae
negotiation	교섭, 협상, 유통	kyoseop, hyeopsang, yut'ong
net (adj)	순익의, 순(純)	sunig-eui, sun
net asset value	순 자산가(純資產家)	sun jasankka
net asset worth	순 자산 가치	sun jasan gach'i
net assets	순 자산	sun jasan
net borrowed reserves	순차용(借用)준비금	sun ch'ayong junbigeum
net cash flow	순 현금 유출(유통)	sun hyeon-geum yuch'ull (yut'ong)
net change	순 변화	sun byeonhwa
net equity assets	순 형평 자산(純衡平資產)	sun hyeongp'yeong jasan
net income	순 소득	sun sodeuk
net investment	순 투자	sun t'uja
net loss	순손(純損)	sun son
net margin	순 이익	sun i-ik
net position (of a trader)	(무역업자의) 정위치 (正位置)	(muyeogeopcha-eui) jeongwich'i
net present value	순수 현재 가치 (현가-現價)	sunsu hyeonjae gach'i (hyeonkka)
net profit	순 이익	sun i-ik
net sales	순 매상고	sun maesang-go
net working capital	순 운전 자본, 순 영업 자본	sun unjeon jabon, sun yeong-eop chabon
net worth	순 자산(純資產)	sun-jasan
network (to)	연쇄점, 연락망	yeonswaejeom, yeollangmang
neutral (adj)	중성(中性)의	chungseong-eui
new ceramics	새 제도술(製陶術)	sae jedosul
new issue	신규 발행	shin-gyu balhaeng
new materials	새 재료(材料)	sae jaeryo
new money	새 화폐	sae hwap'ye
new product development	신제품 개발	shinjep'um gaebal
newsprint	신문 용지	shinmun yongji
nickel-cadmiun battery	니켈 카드늄 전지	nik'el k'adeunyum jeonji
nitrate	질산염	chilsanyeom
nitric acid	질산	chilsan
nitrite	아질산염	a-jilsanyeom
night depository	야간 보관소(입금)	yagan bogwanso (ipkeum)
no load fund	무하중(無荷重) 투자 신탁 기금	muhajung t'uja shint'ak kigeum
no par value	액면 미상(額面未詳)	aengmyeon misang
no problem	문제 없는, 별 문제 없는	munje eomneun, pyeol munje eomneun
nominal price	명목상 가격	myeongmoksang gagyeok
nominal yield	명목상 수익	myeongmoksang suik
noncumulative preferred stock	불축적 배당(주)	pulch'ukcheok paedang (ju)
noncurrent assets	비유동 자산	pi yudong jasan

nondurable goods	비 내구재(非耐久財)	pi naegujae
nonfeasance	의무 불이행, 태만	euimu bulihaeng, t'aeman
nonmember	비 회원	pi hoeweon
nonprofit	비 영리	pi yeongni
nonresident	비 거주자	pi geojuja
nonvoting stock	무의결권 주식	mueuigyeolkweon jushik
norm	기준, 규범	kijun, kyubeom
not otherwise indexed by name	이름 순으로 나열되지 않은	ireumsun-euro nayeoldoeji aneun
notary	공증인(公證人)	kongjeung-in
note, credit	대변표(貸邊表)	taebyeonp'yo
note, debit	차변표(借邊表)	ch'abyeonp'yo
note, promissory	약속 어음	yaksok eoeum
note receivable	수취 약속 어음	such'wi yaksok eoeum
notebook computer	노트 북 컴퓨터	not'eubuk k'eomp'yut'eo
novation	경개(更改)	kyeong-gae
null and void	무효	muhyo
nullify (v)	무효로 하다, 취소하다	muhyoro-hada, ch'wiso-hada
numerical control	수치 제어(數値制御)	such'i je-eo
numerical control machine	수치 제어기	such'i je-eogi
numerical control robot	수치 제어 로보트	such'i je-eo robot'eu
nylon	나일론	naillon

O

objective lens	대물 렌즈	taemul renjeu
obligation	의무, 채무	euimu, ch'aemu
obsolescence	폐기, 퇴화	p'yegi, t'oehwa
occupation	직업, 점유권	chigeop, cheomyukkweon
occupational hazard	직업상의 위험	chigeopsang-eui wiheom
odd lot	단주(端株)	tanju
odd lot broker	단주 중개인	tanju jung-gae-in
odometer	주행 거리계	chuhaeng geori-gye
off board (stock market)	장외	chang-oe
off line	직결되지 않은	chikkyeoldoeji aneun
off-the-books (adj)	장부에 남기지 않은	changbu-e namgiji aneun
offer (v)	제의하다, 신청하다	che-eui-hada, shinch'eong-hada
offer for sale	판매 제의 가격	p'anmae je-eui gagyeok
offered price	신청 가격	shinch'eong gagyeok
offered rate	신청율	shinch'eong-yul
office	사무실	samushil
office, branch	지점, 분점, 분실	chijeom, punjeom, punshil
office, head	본사, 본점	ponsa, ponjeom
office management	사무 관리	samu gwalli
offset printing	오프셋 인쇄	op'euset inswae

offshore company	연안 회사, 해외 회사	yeonan hoesa, hae-oe hoesa
ohm	오옴, 전기 저항 단위	o-om, cheongi jeohang danwi
oil pump	기름 펌프	kireum p'eomp'eu
ointment	연고, 고약	yeon-go, koyak
oligopoly	소수 독점, 과점(寡占)	sosu dokcheom, kwajeom
oligopsony	소수 구매 독점	sosu gumae dokcheom
omit (v)	생략하다	saengnyak-hada
on account (adv)	외상으로, 계약금으로서, 증거금으로서	oesang-euro, kyeyakkeum-euroseo, cheung-geo-geum-euroseo
on consignment (adv)	위탁 판매(계약)(으)로	wit'ak p'anmae (kyeyak)-(eu) ro
on cost (adv)	간접비로	kanjeoppi-ro
on demand (adv)	청구(請求)에 따라	ch'eong-gu-e ttara
on line	온라인	onrain
on-the-job training	직장 훈련, 현장 연수	chikchang hullyeon, hyeonjang yeonsu
open account	청산 계정, 당좌 계정	ch'eongsan gyejeong, tangjwa gyejeong
open cover	포괄적 예정 보험	p'ogwaljeok yejeong boheom
open door policy	문호 개방 정책	munho gaebang jeongch'aek
open market	일반 시장, 공개 시장	ilban shijang, kong-gae shijang
open market operations (money policy)	공개 시장 조작	kong-gae shijang jojak
open order	재량 주문	chaeryang jumun
open shop	개방적 공장	kaebangjeok kongjang
opening balance	이월 잔고(移越殘高)	iweol jan-go
opening price	초장 가격(初場價格)	ch'ojang gagyeok
operating budget	영업 예산	yeong-eop yesan
operating expenses	영업비	yeong-eoppi
operating income	영업 소득	yeong-eop sodeuk
operating profit	영업 이윤	yeong-eop iyun
operating statement	영업 손익 계산서	yeong-eop sonik kyesanseo
operations audit	영업 감사(監査)	yeong-eop kamsa
operations headquarters	경영 본부	kyeong-yeong bonbu
operations management	업무 관리	eommu gwalli
operator	증권업자, 투기 중매인	cheungkkwon eopcha, t'ugi jungmaein
opium	아편	ap'yeon
opportunity costs	기회 비용	kihoe biyong
optical cable	광(光) 케이블	kwang k'eibeul
optical character reader	광학 문자 판독기	kwanghak munjja p'andokki
optical computer	광 컴퓨터	kwang k'eomp'yut'eo
optical disc	광 디스크	kwang diseuk'eu
optical fiber	광 섬유	kwang seomyu
optical integrated circuit	광 직접 회로	kwangjikcheop hoero

optical magnetic memory	광 자기 기억 장치	kwang jagi gieok changch'i
optical mark reader	광학 기호 판독기	kwanghak kiho p'andokki
optical transmission	광 전송장치(光電送裝置)	kwang jeonsong jangch'i
option	선택권	seont'aekkweon
option, stock	주(株) 선택권	chu-seont'aekkweon
optional	임의의, 수의의	imeui-eui, su-eui-eui
optional equipment	선택 장치	seont'aek changch'i
opto-electronics	광학 전자학	kwanghak cheonjahak
opto-electronics industry	광학 전자 산업	kwanghak cheonja saneop
order	주문(注文)	chumun
order (v)	주문하다	chumun-hada
order form	주문 양식(注文樣式)	chumun yangshik
order number	주문 번호	chumun beonho
order of the day	일정(日程)	iljjeong
order, to place on	주문하다, 발주(發注)하다	chumun-hada, palju-hada
ordinary capital	경상 자본(經常資本)	kyeongsang jabon
organic chemicals	유기(有機)화학품	yugi hwahakp'um
organization	조직(組織), 기관(機關), 기구(機構)	chojik, kigwan, kigu
original cost	취득 원가(取得原價)	ch'wideuk weonkka
original entry	초기입(初記入)	ch'o-gi-ip
original maturity	최초 만기(滿期)	ch'oech'o man-gi
other assets (and liability)	기타 자산(및 부채)	kit'a jasan (mit puch'ae)
outbid (v)	경매(競賣)에 이기다, 고가(高價)를 매기다	kyeongmae-e igida, kokka-reul maegida
out-of-pocket expense	초과 경비(經費)	ch'ogwa gyeongbi
outlay	비용, 경비, 지출	piyong, kyeongbi, chich'ul
outlet	판로(販路)	p'allo
outlook	전망, 형세	cheonmang, hyeongse
output	산출고, 산출량	sanch'ulgo, sanch'ullyang
outsized articles	특대형 상품	t'euktaehyeong sangp'um
outstanding contract	미해결 계약	mihaegyeol gyeyak
outstanding debt	차월(借越)금	ch'aweolgeum
outstanding stock	미결제 재고품, 채권 발행고	migyeolje jaegop'um, ch'aekkweon balhaeng-go
outturn	생산고, 산출액	saengsan-go, sanch'uraek
overage	매과고(買過高), 견적 이상 생산액	maegwago, kyeonjeok isang saengsanaek
overbought	과매입(過買入)	kwamaeip
overcapitalized	자본 과잉	chabon gwa-ing
overcharge	과잉 청구	kwa-ing ch'eong-gu
overdraft	당좌 대월, 초과 발행	tangjwa daeweol, ch'ogwa balhaeng
overdue (adj)	기한 경과의, 지체의	kihan gyeong-gwa-eui, chich'e-eui
overhang	과잉	kwa-ing
overhead	간접 경비, 오버 헤드	kanjeop gyeongbi, obeohedeu

overlap	중복, 겹침	chungbok, kyeopch'im
overnight (adj)	일박(一泊)의	ilbag-eui
overpaid (adj)	과불(過拂)의	kwabul-eui
overseas private investment corporation	해외 민간 투자 공사	hae-oe min-gan t'uja gongsa
oversold	초과 판매	ch'ogwa p'anmae
overstock	재하 과잉(在荷過剩), 초과 재고(在庫)	chaeha gwa-ing, ch'ogwa jaego
oversubscribed (adj)	응모(신입), 초과의	eungmo (shinip), ch'ogwa-eui
oversupply	공급 과잉	kong-geup kwa-ing
over-the-counter quotation	장외 거래 시세	chang-oe georae shise
overtime	초과 근무, 시간외 근무	ch'ogwa geunmu, shiganoe geunmu
overvalued (adj)	과대 평가된	kwadae p'yeongkkadoen
owner	소유자, 하주(荷主)	soyuja, haju
owner's equity	선주의 순가(純價)	seonju-eui sunkka
ownership	소유권	soyukkweon
ownership, absentee	부재 지주	pujae jiju
oxidation	산화	sanhwa

P

p/e ratio	주가 수익 비율 (株價收益比率)	chukka su-ik piyul
package deal	포장 거래, 일괄 (一括) 거래	p'ojang georae, ilgwal georae
packaging	내장(內裝) 무역 상품, 포장(包裝)	naejang muyeok sangp'um, p'ojang
packing case	포장 상자	p'ojang sangja
packing list	포장 명세서	p'ojang myeongseseo
page	페이지	p'eiji
page makeup	페이지 조판	p'eiji jop'an
pagination	페이지 매김	p'eiji maegim
paid holiday	유급 휴가	yugeup hyuga
paid in full	완불(完拂)	wanbul
paid up capital	불입필(拂入畢) 자본금	pulip-p'il jabon-geum
paid up shares	불입필주(拂入畢株)	pulip-p'ilju
paid-in surplus	불입 잉여금	pulip ing-yeogeum
paint	칠	ch'il
pallet	제륜기, 하대	cheryun-gi, hadae
palletized freight	제륜기 수송(輸送)	cheryun-gi susong
pamphlet	팜플렛, 작은 책자	p'amp'eullet, chageun ch'aekcha
paper	지폐, 어음류	chip'ye, eo-eumnyu
paper profit	장부상 이익	changbusang i-ik
paper tape	종이 테이프	chong-i t'eipeu
paperback	반양장본	pan-yangjangbon

English	Korean	Romanization
par	동가(同價), 액면 가격	tongkka, aengmyeon gagyeok
par, above (adv)	액면 이상으로	aengmyeon isang-euro
par, below (adv)	액면 이하로	aengmyeon iha-ro
par value	환평가	hwan-p'yeongkka
parcel post	소포 우편	sop'o up'yeon
parent company	모회사(母會社)	mo-hoesa
parity	평형 가격(平衡價格), 동가(同價)	p'yeonghyeong gagyeok, tongkka
parity income ratio	평형 소득율	p'yeonghyeong sodeungnyul
parity price	패리티 가격	p'aerit'i gagyeok
part cargo	부분 하물(部分荷物)(뱃짐)	pubun hamul (paetchim)
partial payment	어음 내입금(內入金), 분할 불입금	eo-eum naeipkeum, punhal buripkeum
participating preferred stock	참가 우선주(參加優先株)	ch'amga useonju
participation fee	참가비	ch'amgabi
participation loan	참가 대부(參加貸付)	ch'amga daebu
particular average loss	단독 해손(單獨海損)	tandok haeson
partner	동업자, (출자)조합원	tong-eocha, (ch'ulja) johabweon
partnership	동업, 조합	tong-eop, chohap
parts	부품	pup'um
passbook	예금 통장, 외상 장부	yegeum t'ongjang, oesang jangbu
passed dividend	보류, 배당	poryu, paedang
past due	지불 기한 경과	chibul gihan gyeong-gwa
pastry server	과자 쟁반	kwaja jaengban
patent	특허권, 전매 특허품	t'eukheokkweon, cheonmae t'eukheop'um
patent application	특허 출원	t'eukheo ch'urweon
patent law	특허법	t'eukheobeop
patent pending	특허 출원중	t'eukheo ch'urweonjung
patent royalty	특허권 사용료	t'eukheokkweon sayongnyo
patented process	특허권이 있는 생산 과정	t'eukheokkweon-i inneun saengsan gwajeong
pattern	견본, 모형	kyeonbon, mohyeong
pattern recognition	패턴 인식	p'aeteon inshik
pay (v)	지불하다	chibul-hada
pay as you go	현금불 주의	hyeon-geumbul jueui
pay off	급료 지불, 이익 분배	keumnyo jibul, i-ik punbae
pay up (v)	청산해 버리다, 전액 납입하다	ch'eongsan hae-beorida, cheonaek nabip-hada
payable on demand	청구불, 요구불	ch'eong-gubul, yogubul
payable to bearer	지참인불(持參人拂)	chich'amin-bul
payable to order	지시인불(指示人拂)	chishi-in-bul
payback period	갚는 기간, 회수(回收) 기간	kamneun gigan, hoesu gigan
payee	수취인(受取人)	such'wi-in
payer	지불인, 매도인(賣渡人)	chiburin, maedoin

payload

payload	유료 하중(荷重), 임금 부담	yuryo hajung, imgeum budam
paymaster	회계 주임, 지불계	hoegye juim, chibulgye
payment	지불, 납부	chibul, nappu
payment in full	전액 지불	cheonaek chibul
payment in kind	현금불	hyeon-geumbul
payment refused	지불 거절	chibul geojeol
payout period	지불(지출) 기간	chibul (chich'ul) gigan
payroll	급료 지불부	keumnyo jibulbu
payroll tax	급료 지불세	keumnyo jubulse
peak load	최대량 부하(負荷)	ch'oedaeryang buha
pegged price	고정 가격(固定價格)	kojeong gagyeok
pegging	고정 하기, 억제 하기	kojeonghagi, eokchehagi
pellet	작은 알약	chageun allyak
penalty clause	위약 조항(違約條項)	wiyak chohang
penalty-fraud action	사기 행위 벌금 조치	sagi haeng-wi beolgeum joch'i
penicillin	페니실린	p'enishillin
penny stock	1페니 주식	ilp'eni jushik
pension fund	연금(年金), 은급(銀給), 기금(基金)	yeon-geum, eun-geup, kigeum
pepper mill	후추 제분기	huch'u jebun-gi
pepper shaker	후춧가루통	huch'ut karu-t'ong
per capita	일인당	irindang
per diem	일당(日當)	ilttang
per share	일주당(一株當)	iljudang
percentage earnings	비율 수익고, 소득	piyul su-ikko, sodeuk
percentage of profit	이윤 비율	iyun biyul
perfect crystal device technology	완전 광석 검파 장치 기술	wanjeon gwangseok keomp'a jangch'i gisul
performance bond	계약 보증	kyeyak pojeung
periodic inventory	주기적 재고품 목록	chugijeok chaegop'um mongnok
peripheral equipment	주변 장치	chubyeon jangch'i
peripherals	부수 장치(附隨裝置)	pusu jangch'i
perks	팁, 이익, 수당	t'ip, i-ik, sudang
permit	허가, 인가	heoga, in-ga
perpetual inventory	영속적 재고 관리	yeongsokcheok chaego gwalli
personal cassette player	개인용 카세트 전축	kaein-yong k'aset'eu jeonch'uk
personal computer	개인용 컴퓨터, 퍼스컴	kaein-yong k'eomp'yut'eo, p'eoseuk'eom
personal deduction	개인 공제(控除)	kaein gongje
personal exemption	기초 공제	kich'o gongje
personal income tax	개인 소득세	kaein sodeukse
personal liability	개인 의무	kaein euimu
personal property	동산(動産), 개인 재산	tongsan, kae-in jaesan
personal stereo radio	개인용 입체 음향 라디오	kaein-yong ipch'e eumhyang radio
personal TV	개인용 테레비	kaein-yong t'erebi
personality test	성격 검사	seongkkyeok keomsa

personnel administration	인사 행정	insa haengjeong
personnel department	인사과	insakkwa
personnel management	인사 관리	insa gwalli
petrochemical	석유 화학	seogyu hwahak
petrochemicals	석유 화학 제품	seogyu hwahak chep'um
petrodollars	석유 달러	seogyu dalleo
petroleum	석유	seogyu
pharmaceutical	석유 화학 제품	chojehag-eui
pharmacist	약제사	yakchesa
phase in (v)	취하다, 단계직으로 투입하다	ch'wi-hada, tan-gyejeog-euro t'u-ip-hada
phase out (v)	단계적으로 제거(除去)하다	tan-gyejeog-euro jegeo-hada
phenol	석탄산	seokt'ansan
phone-answering machine	자동 응답 전화기	chadong eungdap cheonhwagi
photoconductive materials	사진 전도 물질	sajin jeondo muljjil
photoconductivity	사진 전도력	sajin jeondoryeok
photoelectro-magnetic effect	사진 전자기 효과	sajin jeonjagi hwyokkwa
physical inventory	실지 물량 재고 조사법	shiljji mullyang jaego josappeop
physician	의사	euisa
phytosanitary regulations	식물 위생 규칙	shingmul wisaeng gyuch'ik
pick up and delivery	입수 후 배달	ipsuhu baedal
picket line	파업 시위(罷業示威), 파업	p'a-eop shiwi, p'a-eop
pie chart	파이형 도표	p'a-i-hyeong dop'yo
piecework	삯일, 청부일	sangnil, ch'eongbu-il
pig iron	선철	seonch'eol
piggyback service	등으로 나르는 일, 등짐 서비스	teung-euro nareuneun il, teungjjim seobiseu
pigment	그림 물감	keurim mulkkam
pilferage	좀도둑, 장물(臟物)	chomdoduk, changmul
pill	알약	allyak
pilotage	수로 안내(水路案內), 조종술	suro annae, chojongsul
pinion	작은 톱니바퀴	chageun t'omni bak'wi
pipage	수송관, 소송료	susong-gwan, susongnyo
piston	피스톤	p'iseut'on
pitcher	물주전자	mul-jujeonja
place an order (v)	주문하다, 발주(發注)하다	chumun-hada, paljju-hada
place of business	영업 장소, 상업지	yeong-eop changso, sang-eopchi
place mat	(접시) 장식용 받침	(cheopshi) jangshing-yong bach'im
place setting	식기 한벌	shikki hanbeol
placement (personnel)	채용, 고용	ch'aeyong, koyong
plan	계획, 설계	kyehoek, seolgye
plan, action	사업 계획	sa-eop kyehoek
plan, market	시장 계획	shijang gyehoek

English	Korean	Romanization
planetary gear train	차동 기어 장치	ch'adong gieo jangch'i
planned obsolescence	계획적 폐기 (노후화-老朽化)	kyehoekcheok p'yegi (nohuhwa)
plant capacity	공장 생산 능력	kongjang saengsan neungnyeok
plant location	공장 위치	kongjang wich'i
plant manager	공장 관리자, 공장장	kongjang gwallija, kongjangjang
plasma cutting machine	플라즈마 절단기	p'eullajeuma jeolttan-gi
plasma etching	플라즈마 부식동판술	p'eullajeuma bushik tongp'ansul
plate	접시, 식기류	cheopshi, shikkiryu
platter	큰 접시	k'eun jeopshi
playback robot	녹음 장치 로보트	nogeum jangch'i robot'eu
pleat	주름	chureum
pledge	저당, 담보물	cheodang, tamppomul
plenary meeting	본회의(本會議), 총회(總會)	ponhoe-eui, ch'onghoe
plow back (earnings) (v)	재투자하다	chae-t'uja-hada
plus accrued interest	여분의 경과 이자	yeobun-eui gyeong-gwa ija
plutes	재벌(財閥)	chaebeol
pocket-sized TV	포켓용 소형 테레비	p'ok'ennong sohyeong t'erebi
point	포인트	p'oint'eu
point (percentage) (mortgage term)	부동산 융자 수수료	pudongsan yungja susuryo
point, breakeven	채산점, 손익 분기점	ch'aesanjjeom, sonik pun-gijjeom
point of order	의사 진행에 관한 건	euisa jinhaeng-e gwanhankkeon
point of sale	판매 시점(販賣時點)	p'anmae shijjeom
polar coordinates robot	극좌표 로보트	keukchwap'yo robot'eu
policy	방침, 보험 증권	pangch'im, poheom jeungkkweon
policyholder	보험 계약자, 증권 용지	poheom gyeyakjja, cheungkkweon yongji
poly-crystal silicon	다결정 규소	ta-gyeoljjeong gyuso
polyester	폴리에스테르 섬유	p'ollieseutereu seomyu
polymer	중합체	chunghapch'e
polystyrene	폴리스틸렌	polliseut'illen
polyurethane	폴리우레탄	p'olliuret'an
pool (of funds)	공동 출자	kongdong ch'uljja
pool (v)	공동 출자하다	kongdong ch'uljja-hada
pooling of interests	공동 출자식 합병법 (共同出資式合倂法)	kongdong ch'uljashik happyeongbeop
poplin	포프린	p'op'eurin
portable TV	휴대용 테레비	hyudae-yong t'erebi
portfolio	유가 증권 명세서	yukka jeungkkweon myeongseseo
portfolio management	유가 증권 관리	yukka jeungkkweon gwalli
portfolio, stock	주식 명세서	chushik myeongseseo
portfolio theory	자산 선택론	chasan seont'aengnon
position limit	거래 한계	keorae han-gye

English	Korean	Romanization
positive	양화	yanghwa
positive cash flow	흑자 현금 유출, 현금 유입(現金流入)	heukcha hyeon-geum yuch'ul, hyeon-geum yuip
post (bookkeeping) (v)	원장(元帳)으로 옮겨쓰다	weonjang-euro omgyeo sseuda
postdated (adj)	사후 일부(事後日附)	sahu ilbu
postpone (v)	연기하다	yeon-gi-hada
potential buyer	구입 예정자	ku-ip yejeongja
potential sales	판매 가능성	p'anmae ganeungseong
pottery	도기	togi
powder metallurgy	분말 야금	punmal yageum
power of attorney	위임장(委任狀)	wi-imjjang
power steering	동력 조타 장치	tongnyeok chot'a jangch'i
practical	실제적인, 실용적인	shiljjejeogin, shiryongjeong-in
precision machinery	정밀 기계류	cheongmil gigyeryu
pre-emptive right	선매권(先買權)	seonmaekkweon
prefabrication	조립식 가옥 부품 제조	choripshik kaok pup'um jejo
preface	서문, 서언	seomun, seo-eon
preferential debts	우선 채무(優先債務)	useon ch'aemu
preferred stock	우선주(優先株)	useonju
preferred tariff	우선 세율, 우선 관세	useon seyul, useon gwanse
preliminary prospectus	예비 사업 계획 요강	yebi sa-eop kyehoek yogang
premises	경내(境內), 가옥 및 대지, 구내(構內)	kyeongnae, kaok mit taeji, kunae
premium, acceleration	가속 보험료	kasok poheomnyo
premium, insurance	보험료	poheomnyo
premium offer	수수료 제의 신청	susuryo je-eui shinch'eong
premium payment	보험료 불입	poheomnyo burip
premium pricing	보험료 평가	poheomnyo p'yeongkka
prepaid credit card	선불 카드	seonbul k'adeu
prepaid expenses (balance sheet)	선불 비용(先拂費用)	seonbul biyong
prepay (v)	선불하다	seonbul-hada
prescription	처방	ch'eobang
president	사장, 총재, 회장	sajang, ch'ongjae, hoejang
preventive maintenance	예방 유지비	yebang yujibi
price	가격, 대금	kagyeok, taegeum
price (v)	값을 매기다(정하다)	kapseul maegida (jeong-hada)
price cutting	할인, 에누리	harin, enuri
price differential	가격차(격차)	kagyeok ch'a (kyeokch'a)
price elasticity	가격 탄력성	kagyeok t'allyeokseong
price fixing	정가 매기기, 가격 조작	cheongkka maegigi, kagyeok chojak
price index	물가 지수	mulkka jisu
price limit	지정가(指定價)	chijeongkka
price list	가격표	kagyeokp'yo
price, competitive	경쟁 가격	kyeongjaeng kagyeok
price, market	시장 가격	shijang kagyeok
price range	가격 범위	kagyeok peomwi

English	Korean	Romanization
price stability	물가 안정	mulkka anjeong
price support	가격 유지	kagyeok yuji
price tick	가격 점검	kagyeok cheomgeom
price war	가격 전쟁, 물가 경쟁	kagyeok cheonjaeng, mulkka gyeongjaeng
price-earnings ratio	주가 수익률	chukka su-ingnyul
primary market	주요 시장	chuyo shijang
primary reserves	제1차 적립금, 준비금	che ilch'a jeongnipkeum, chunbigeum
prime costs	구입 원가	ku-ip weonkka
prime rate	기준 이자율	kijun ijayul
prime time	주요 시간, 최고조 시간	chuyo shigan, ch'oegojo shigan
principal	원금(元金), 원금 계정	weon-geum, weon-geum gyejeong
print	날염하다, 프린트하다	nalyeom-hada, p'eurint'eu-hada
printed matter	인쇄물	inswaemul
printing	인화	inhwa
printing shop	인쇄소	inswaeso
printout	출력 정보 지시 테이프, 인쇄	ch'ullyeok cheongbo jishi t'eip'eu, inswae
priority	우선권, 선취권	useonkkweon, seonch'wi kkweon
private fleet	개인 선단(船團), 선대(船隊)	kaein seondan, seondae
private label (or brand)	개인 상표	kaein sangp'yo
private placement (finance)	사적 배치, 개인 배치	sajjeok paech'i, kaein baech'i
pro-forma invoice	견적 송장	kyeonjeok songjjang
pro-forma statement	견적 명세서	kyeonjeok myeongseseo
probate	유언 검증(遺言檢證)	yu-eon geomjeung
problem	문제, 의문	munje, euimun
problem, analysis	문제 분석	munje bunseok
problem, no	문제 없음	munje eopseum
problem solving	문제 해결	munje haegyeol
proceeds	매상고, 수익(收益)	maesang-go, su-ik
process (v)	가공 처리(加工處理)하다	kagong ch'eori-hada
process, production	생산 과정	saengsan gwajeong
processing error	가공 오류(加工誤謬)	kagong oryu
procurement	조달(調達)	chodal
product	제품(製品), 생산품	chep'um, saengsanp'um
product analysis	제품 분석	chep'um bunseok
product design	제품 설계	chep'um seolgye
product development	제품 개발	chep'um gaebal
product dynamics	제품 활력	chep'um hwallyeok
product group	제품 계열	chep'um gyeyeol
product life	제품 수명	chep'um sumyeong
product line	제품 종목	chep'um jongmok
product management	제품 관리	chep'um gwalli
product profitability	제품의 수익성	chep'um-eui su-ikseong
production	생산	saengsan

protest (banking, law)

production control	공정 관리(工程管理), 생산 관리	kongjeong gwalli, saengsan gwalli
production costs	생산비	saengsanbi
production line	생산선, 일관작업(一貫作業)	saengsanseon, ilgwan jageop
production process	생산 과정	saengsan gwajeong
production schedule	생산 예정표	saengsan yejeongp'yo
productivity	생산성	saengsanseong
productivity	생산력 추진 운동	saengsannyeok ch'ujin undong
profession	직업, 전문직	chigeop, cheonmunjik
profiler	측면도, 프로파일러	ch'eungmyeondo, p'europ'ailleo
profit	이윤, 이익금	iyun, i-ikkeum
profit factor	이윤 요소	iyun yoso
profit, gross	총 이익	ch'ong-i-ik
profit impact	이윤 효과	iyun hyokkwa
profit margin	이윤 마진, 이윤폭	iyun majin, iyunp'ok
profit, net	순 이익	sun-i-ik
profit projection	이윤 예측(豫測)	iyun yech'euk
profit sharing	이익 분배(分配)	i-ik punbae
profit-and-loss account	손익 계정	sonik kyejeong
profit-and-loss statement	손익 계산서	sonik kyesanseo
profit-taking	이익 취득	i-ik ch-wideuk
profitability	수익성	suikseong
profitabilty analysis	수익성 분석	suikseong bunseok
program	프로그램, 계획	peurogeuraem, kyehoek
program (v)	계획을 세우다	kyehoeg-eul se-uda
prohibited goods	(수입) 금지품	(suip) keumjip'um
project	계획, 기획, 사업	kyehoek, kihoek, sa-eop
project (v)	기획하다	kihoek-hada
project planning	프로젝트 기획	p'eurojekt'eu gihoek
projector	영사기	yeongsagi
promissory note	약속 어음	yaksok eo-eum
promotion	승진, 증진, 촉진	seungjin, jeungjin, ch'okchin
promotion, sales	판매 증진 (촉진)	p'anmae jeungjin (ch'okchin)
prompt (n)	직시 적재(直時積載)	chikshi jeokchae
prompt (adj)	신속(迅速)한	shinsokhan
proof of loss	손해 증명	sonhae jeungmyeong
proofreading	교정	kyojeong
property	재산, 소유물	chaesan, soyumul
proprietary	소유의, 독점의	soyu-eui, tokcheom-eui
proprietor	소유자, 경영자	soyuja, kyeong-yeongja
propylene	프로필렌	p'europ'illen
prosecute (v)	제소하다, 기소하다	cheso-hada, kiso-hada
prospectus	설립 취지서, 계획서	seollip ch'wijiseo, kyehoekseo
protectionism	보호 무역 주의	poho muyeokchu-eui
protest (banking, law) (v)	이의(異議)를 제기(提起)하다	ieui-reul jegi-hada

proxy	대리(권), 위임장	taeri (kweon), wi-imjjang
proxy statement	위임장, 대리인 명세서	wi-imjjang, taeri-in myengseseo
prudent man rule	신중한 투자 규칙	shinjunghan t'uja gyuch'ik
public auction	공매(公賣), 경매(競賣)	kongmae, kyeongmae
public company	주식 공개 회사, 주식 공모 회사	chushik kong-gae hoesa, chushik kongmo hoesa
public domain	공유지, 권리 소멸 상태	kong-yuji, kweolli somyeol sangt'ae
public funds	국채, 공채, 공금	kukch'ae, kongch'ae, kong-geum
public offering	공모(公募)	kongmo
public opinion poll	여론 조사	yeoron josa
public property	공유 재산	kong-yu jaesan
public relations	섭외, 홍보	seoboe, hongbo
public sale	공매, 경매	kongmae, kyeongmae
public sector	공공 부문	kong-gong bumun
public utility	공익 사업	kong-ik sa-eop
public works	공공 토목 사업	kong-gong t'omok sa-eop
publicity	선전(宣傳), 광고(廣告), 주지(周知)	seonjeon, kwang-go, chuji
publisher	발행인, 출판인	palhaeng-in, ch'ulp'an-in
pulse	파동, 진동(振動)	p'adong, chindong
pump priming	경제 부흥 촉진	kyeongje buheung ch'okchin
punch card	펀치 카드	p'eonch'i k'adeu
punch press	구멍 뚫는 기구	kumeong ttulneun gigu
purchase (v)	구입하다	kuip-hada
purchase money mortgage	매입 대금 저당	mae-ip taegeum jeodang
purchase order	매입(구매) 주문	mae-ip (kumae) jumun
purchase price	구매 가격	kumae gagyeok
purchasing agent	구매원, 구매 대리점	kumae-weon, kumae daerijeom
purchasing manager	구매 관리자	kumae gwallija
purchasing power	구매력	kumaeryeok
pure risk	위험 부담	wiheom budam
purgative	하제(下劑)	haje
put and call	특권부 매매	t'eukkweonbu maemae
put in a bid (v)	입찰에 붙이다	ipch'al-e buch'ida
put into	(배가) 입항하다	(pae-ga) iphang-hada
put option	해소 특권(解消特權)	haeso t'eukkweon
pyramid selling	피라밋식 판매	p'iramit-shik p'anmae
pyramiding	이익 편승 거래	i-ik p'yeonseung georae

Q

qualifications	자격	chagyeok
qualified acceptance endorsement	조건부 인수 배서(背書)	chokkeonbu insu baeseo
quality control	품질 관리	p'umjil gwalli

English	Korean	Romanization
quality goods	우량품(優良品)	uryangp'um
quality management	품질 경영	p'umjil gyeong-yeong
quantity	양, 분량, 수량	yang, pullyang, suryang
quantity discount	수량 할인	suryang harin
quasi-public company	준(準) 공모 회사(公募會社)	chun-gongmo hoesa
quench (v)	쇠 담금질하다	soe damgeumjil-hada
quick assets	급속 환가 자산	keupsok hwankka jasan
quit claim deed	권리 포기 증서	kweolli p'ogi jeungseo
quorum	정족수	cheongjoksu
quota	몫, 할당액	mok, halttang-aek
quota, export	수출 할당	such'ul halttang
quota, sales	판매 할당	p'anmae halttang
quota system	할당제	halttangje
quotation	시세, 시세표	shise, shisep'yo

R

English	Korean	Romanization
rack jobber	장내 중개인	changnae jung-gaein
radar	레이다, 전파 탐지기	reida, cheonp'a t'amjigi
radial drilling machine	방사상 천공기	pangsasang ch'eon-gong-gi
radial tire	레이디얼 타이어	reidieol t'aieo
radiator	방열기, 라지에타	pang-yeolgi, rajiet'a
radio	라디오	radio
radio cassette player	라디오 카세트 전축	radio k'aset'eu jeonch'uk
rail shipment	철도 적송(積送)	ch'eoltto jeoksong
rain check	인환권(引換卷)	inhwankkweon
raincoat	비옷	pi'ot
raising capital	자본 조달	chabon jodal
rally	회복(回復), 반등(反騰), 대회(大會)	hoebok, pandeung, taehoe
RAM	등속 호출 기억 장치, 램	teungsok hoch'ul gieok changch'i, raem
random access memory	등속 호출 기억 장치	teungsok hoch'ul gieok changch'i
random sample	무작위 추출	mujagwi ch'uch'ul
rangefinder	거리계	keorigye
rate	비율, 운임, 요금	piyul, unim, yogeum
rate, base	기준율	kijun-nyul
rate of growth	성장율	seongjang-nyul
rate of increase	증가율	cheung-gayul
rate of interest	이자율	ijayul
rate of return	수익율, 이윤율	suing-nyul, iyun-nyul
rating, credit	신용 등급	shinyong deung-geup
rating, market	시장 등급	shijang deung-geup
ratio	비, 비율	pi, piyul
rationing	배급(配給)	paegeup
raw materials	원료, 원자재(原資材)	weollyo, weonjajae
rayon	인조견사	injo gyeonsa
re-export	재수출, 역수출	chaesuch'ul, yeoksuch'ul
ready cash	현금 즉시불	hyeon-geum jeukshibul

English	Korean	Romanization
ready-to-wear	기성복	kiseongbok
real assets	실질 자산	shiljjil jasan
real estate	부동산	pudongsan
real income	실질 소득	shiljjil sodeuk
real investment	실제 투자	shiljje t'uja
real name financial system	금융실명제(金融實名制)	keumnyung shilmyeongje
real price	실제 가격	shiljje gagyeok
real time	즉석 응답 방식	cheukseok eungdap pangshik
real wages	실질 임금	shiljjil imgeum
ream	연(連: 종이 500매)	yeon(chong-i obaengmae)
reamer	확공기(擴孔機)	hwakkong-gi
rear axle	뒤 차축	twi ch'ach'uk
reasonable care	상당(相當)한 주의(注意)	sangdanghan ju-eui
rebate	환불	hwanbul
recapitalization	자본 재구성(資本在構成)	chabon jaeguseong
receipt	영수증, 수령(受領)	yeongsujeung, suryeong
recession	경기 후퇴	kyeong-gi hut'oe
rechargeable (adj)	재충전 가능한	chae-ch'ungjeon ganeung-han
reciprocal training	호혜 연수(互惠研修)	hohye yeonsu
record date	기록일, 등록일	kirogil, teungnogil
record player	전축	cheonch'uk
recourse	의뢰(依賴), 상환 청구	euiroe, sanghwan ch'eong-gu
recovery (acct. receivable)	회수(回收), 회복(回復)	hoesu, hoebok
recovery of expenses	비용 만회	piyong manhoe
rectifier	정류기	cheongnyugi
red tape	관청식 번잡한 수속	kwanch'eongshik beonjaphan susok
redeemable bond	수시 상환 공채	sushi sanghwan gongch'ae
redemption allowance	상환 급여	sanghwan geubyeo
redemption fund	상환 적립금	sanghwan jeongnipkeum
redemption premium	상환 수수료, 상환 할증금	sanghwan susuryo, sanghwan haljeung-geum
rediscount rate	재할인율	chaeharinyul
reduction	환원법	hwanweonppeop
reference, credit	신용 조회처	shinyong johoech'eo
reference number	조회 번호, 참조 번호	chohoe beonho, ch'amjo beonho
refinancing	재융자(再融資)	chaeyungja
reflation	통화 재팽창	t'onghwa jaep'aengch'ang
reflex camera	반사 증폭 장치 카메라	pansa jeungp'ok jangch'i k'amera
reform	개혁(改革)	kaehyeok
refractories	내화 벽돌	naehwa byeoktol
refrigerator	냉장고	naengjang-go
refund	상환금, 반환물	sanghwan-geum, panhwanmul
refuse acceptance (v)	인수를 거절하다	insu-reul geojeol-hada
refuse payment (v)	지불을 거절하다	chibul-eul geojeol-hada

resident buyer

English	Korean	Romanization
regard (with regard to)	-에 관해 중시하다	-e gwanhae jungshi-hada
register	인쇄 지면의 안팎의 일치	inswae jimyeon-eui anp'akk-eui ilch'i
registered check	기명 수표(記名手票)	kimyeong sup'yo
registered mail	등기 우편	teung-gi up'yeon
registered representative	등록된 대리인	teungnoktoen daeri-in
registered security	기명 증권(記名證券)	kimyeong jeungkkweon
registered trademark	등록 상표	teungnok sangp'yo
regression analysis	회귀 분석(回歸分析)	hoegwi bunseok
regressive tax	누감세(累減稅)	nugamse
regular warehouse	정규 창고	cheong-gyu ch'ang-kko
regulation	규칙, 규제, 조정(調整)	kyuch'ik, kyuje, chojeong
reimburse	지불하다, 변상하다	chibul-hada, pyeonsang-hada
reinsures	재보험 가입자	chae-boheom gaipcha
reliable source	정통한 소식통	cheongt'onghan soshikt'ong
remedies	치료	ch'iryo
remedy (law)	변상, 구제	pyeonsang, kuje
remission duty	면제세	myeonjese
remission of a tax	세금 면제	segeum myeonje
remote control	원격 조정 장치, 리모콘	weonkkyeok chojong jangch'i, remok'on
remuneration	보수, 보상, 급료	posu, posang, keumnyo
renegotiate (v)	재교섭하다	chae-gyoseop-hada
renew (v)	갱신하다, 연장하다	kaengshin-hada, yeonjang-hada
rent	임대, 사용료	imdae, sayongnyo
reorder (v)	추가 주문하다	ch'uga jumun-hada
reorganization	재편성, 개조(改組)	chae-p'yeonseong, kaejo
repay (v)	갚다	kapta
repeat order	재주문하다	chae-jumun-hada
repeatable robot	반복 로보트	panbok robot'eu
replacement cost	신품 교체비	shinp'um gyoch'ebi
replacement parts	교체 부품	kyoch'e bup'um
reply (v)	회답하다, 답변하다	hoedap-hada, tappyeon-hada
reply, in...to	-에 답하여	-e dap-ha-yeo
report	보고, 보도	pogo, podo
repossession	되찾음, 회복	toech'ajeum, hoebok
representative	대표, 대리(代理)	taep'yo, taeri
reproduction costs	재생산 비용	chae-saengsan biyong
request for bid	입찰 신청	ipch'al shinch'eong
requirements	필수, 소요 요건, 필요 물건	p'ilsu, soyo yokkeon, p'iryo mulgeon
resale	재판매	chae-p'anmae
research	조사, 연구	chosa, yeon-gu
research and development	연구 개발	yeon-gu gaebal
reserve	준비금, 적립금	chunbigeum, cheongnipkeum
resident buyer	주재 구매원	chujae gumaeweon

resolution (legal document)	결의, 해결	kyeoreui, haegyeol
resource allocation	자원 배분(資源配分)	chaweon baebun
restrictions on export	수출 제한	such'ul jehan
restrictive labor practices	제한적 노동 관습(慣習)	chehanjeok nodong gwanseup
restructure	재구성	chae-guseong
resume	이력서	iryeokseo
retail	소매(小賣)	somae
retail bank	소매 은행	semae eunhaeng
retail merchandise	소매 상품	somae sangp'um
retail outlet	소매점, 소매 판로(販路)	somaejeom, somae p'allo
retail price	소매 물가	somae mulkka
retail sales tax	소매 판매세	somae p'anmaese
retail trade	소매업	somae-eop
retained earnings	유보 소득(留保所得)	yubo sodeuk
retained profits	유보 이익(留保利益)	yubo i-ik
retirement	은퇴, 퇴직	eunt'oe, t'oejik
retroactive (adj)	소급하는	sogeuphaneun
return on assets managed	관리 자산 수익(收益)	kwalli jasan su-ik
return on capital	자본 수익	chabon su-ik
return on equity	순가 수익(純價收益)	sunkka su-ik
return on investment	투자 수익	t'uja su-ik
return on sales	판매 수익	p'anmae su-ik
return, rate of	수익율	su-ingnyul
revaluation	평가 절상(評價切上)	p'yeongkka jeolsang
revenue	세입(歲入), 수입(收入)	se-ip, su-ip
revenue bond	수입 담보(收入擔保) 채권(債權)	suip tambo ch'aekkweon
reverse stock split	역주식 분할(逆株式分割)	yeok-chushik punhal
revocable trust	취소 가능 신탁	ch'wiso ganeung shint'ak
revolving credit	순환 신용(循環信用)	sunhwan shinyong
revolving fund	순환 기금, 회전 기금	sunhwan gigeum, hoejeon gigeum
revolving letter of credit	순환 신용장	sunhwan shinyongjjang
rider (contracts)	추가 조항, 첨부 서류	ch'uga johang, ch'eombu seoryu
right of recourse	상환 청구권	sanghwan ch'eonggukkweon
right of way	통행권	t'onghaengkkweon
risk	위험, 모험	wiheom, moheom
risk analysis	위험도 분석	wiheomdo bunseok
risk assessment	위험 평가(사정-査定)	wiheom p'yeongkka (sajeong)
risk capital	위험 자본	wiheom jabon
rod	측량간	ch'eungnyang-gan
roll turning lathe	회전 세공 선반	hoejeon segong seonban
rollback	물가 인하 정책	mulkka inha jeongch'aek
rolling mill	압연기	abyeon-gi
rolling stock	차량(車輛)	ch'aryang

rollover	반환(返還)	panhwan
ROM	판독 전용 기억 장치, 롬	p'andok cheonyong gieok changch'i, rom
rough draft	초고(草稿), 초안(草案)	ch'ogo, ch'o-an
rough estimate	개략 견적서(概略見積書)	kaeryak kyeonjeokseo
round lot	모개 흥정	mogae heungjeong
routine	일상 사무(日常事務)	ilsang samu
royalty (payment)	특허권 사용료	t'eukheokkwon sayongnyo
rubber	고무	komu
running expenses	경상비(經常費)	kyeongsangbi
rush order	급주문(急注文)	keup-chumun

S

saccharin	사카린	sak'arin
safe deposit box	귀중품 보관함	kwijungp'um bogwanham
safeguard	보호, 안전 장치	poho, anjeon jangch'i
salad bowl	샐러드용 접시	saelleodeu-yong jeopshi
salad plate	샐러드 접시	saelleodeu jeopshi
salary	봉급(俸給)	pong-geup
sales	매상고, 판매액	maesang-go, p'anmae-aek
sales analysis	판매 분석	p'anmae bunseok
sales budget	판매 예산	p'anmae yesan
sales estimate	판매 예상고(豫想高)	p'anmae yesang-go
sales force	판매원(販賣員)	p'anmaeweon
sales forecast	판매 예측	p'anmae yech'euk
sales management	판매 관리	p'anmae gwalli
sales promotion	판매 촉진	p'anmae ch'okchin
sales quota	판매 할당액	p'anmae halttang-aek
sales tax	물품 판매세	mulp'um p'anmaese
sales territory	판매 영역(領域)	p'anmae yeong-yeok
sales volume	판매량	p'anmaeryang
salt	염(鹽), 소금	yeom, sogeum
salt shaker	소금 가루통	sogeum garu-t'ong
salts	약용염	yagyong-yeom
salvage (v)	회수(回收)하다, 구출(救出)하다	hoesu-hada, kuch'ul-hada
salvage charges	해난 구조비(海難救助費), 회수 비용(回收費用)	haenan gujobi, hoesu biyong
salvage value	해난 구조품 가격, 회수 가치(回收價值)	haenan gujop'um gagyeok, hoesu gach'i
salve	연고	yeon-go
sample (v)	견본을 만들다	kyeonbon-eul mandeulda
sample line	견본 종목	kyeonbon jongmok
sample size	견본 크기	kyeonbon k'eugi
saponification	비누화	pinuhwa
saucer	받침 접시	pach'im jeopshi
save of the future	장래 구제(將來救濟)	changnae guje
savings	저금, 저축, 예금	cheogeum, cheoch'uk, yegeum

savings account

savings account	저축 계정, 저축(예금) 구좌	cheoch'uk kyejeong, cheoch'uk (yegeum) kujwa
savings bank	저축 은행(貯蓄銀行)	cheoch'uk eunhaeng
savings bond	저축 공채(公債)	cheoch'uk kongch'ae
scalper	암매자(暗賣者)	am-maeja
scanner	정밀 조사자	cheongmil josaja
scarf	목도리, 스카프	moktori, seuk'ap'eu
schedule	예정(豫定), 일람표	yejeong, illamp'yo
scrap	쇠 부스러기	soe buseureogi
screen	그물 판유리	keumul p'an-yuri
screw cutting lathe	나사 절단 선반	nasa jeolttan seonban
script	원본, 정본(正本)	weonbon, cheongbon
sealed bid	봉함 입찰(封緘入札)	pongham ipch'al
seasonal (adj)	계절적인, 주기적인	kyejeoljeogin, chugijeogin
seat	좌석	chwaseok
seatbelt	좌석벨트	chwaseok pelt'eu
second mortgage	제이차 저당(抵當)	che-i-ch'a jeodang
second position	두번째 위치	tu-beon-jjae wich'i
secondary market (securities)	유통 시장(流通市場)	yut'ong shijang
secondary offering (securities)	재매출(再賣出)	chae-maech'ul
secret fund	비자금(秘資金)	pijageum
secretary	비서, 서기관	piseo, seogigwan
secured accounts	담보부 계정(擔保附計定)	tamppobu-gyejeong
securities	유가 증권	yukka jeungkkweon
security	보증, 담보	pojeung, tamppo
sedative	진정제	chinjeongje
self-appraisal	자체 평가 조사	chach'e p'yeongkka josa
self-employed	자가 취업자, 자영인(自營人)	chaga ch'wieopcha, chayeong-in
self-service	셀프 서비스	selp'eu seobiseu
self-timer	자동 개폐기	chadong gaep'yegi
sell (to) (v)	팔다, 판매하다	p'alda, p'anmae-hada
sell and leaseback	매도(賣渡) 및 임대(賃貸)	maedo mit imdae
sell direct	직매하다	chingmae-hada
sell, hard	적극적 판매	cheokkeukcheok p'anmae
sell, soft	소극적 판매	sogeukcheok p'anmae
semiconductor laser	반도체 레이저	pandoch'e reijeo
semi-variable costs	준변동 비용(準變動費用)	chun-byeondong biyong
senior issue	상위 주식(上位株式)	sang-wi jushik
seniority	선임권(先任權), 서열(序列)	seonimgweon, seoyeol
sensitometer	감광 도계	kamgwang dogye
separation	이직(離職), 부부 별거(夫婦別居)	ijik, pubu byeolgeo
sequence robot	연속 진행 로보트	yeonsok chinhaeng robot'eu
sequential control	순차 조절	sunch'a jojeol
serial bonds	연속 사채(連續社債)	yeonsok sach'ae
serial storage	직렬 기억 장치 (直列記憶裝置)	chingnyeol gi-eok changch'i
serum	혈청	hyeolch'eong

English	Korean	Romanization
service (v)	봉사하다(奉仕), 점검하다	pongsa-hada, cheomgeom-hada
service, advisory	자문 봉사(諮問奉仕)	chamun bongsa
service contract	봉사 계약, 정기 점검 계약	pongsa gyeyak, cheong-gi jeomgeom gyeyak
service, customer	고객 봉사	kogaek pongsa
serving spoon	음식 숟가락	eumshik sutkkarak
set	한 벌	han beol
set-up costs	조립 비용, 설비 비용	chorip piyong, seolbi biyong
settlement	청산, 결산	ch'eongsan, kyeolsan
settlement, full	총(완전) 결산	ch'ong (wanjeon) gyeolsan
severance pay	해직 수당, 퇴직금	haejik sudang, t'oejikkeum
sew	바느질하다, 봉재하다	paneujil-hada, pongjae-hada
sewing machine	재봉틀	chaebongt'eul
sewn (adj)	철한, 맨	ch'eol-han, maen
shaft lather	샤프트 선반공	syap'eut'eu seonban-gong
shape-memory alloy	형(型) 기억 합금	hyeong gieok hapkeum
shaping machine	형삭반(形削盤)	hyeongsakpan
shareholder	주주(株主)	chuju
shareholders' equity	주주의 순가(純價)	chuju-eui sunkka
shareholder's meeting	주주 회의	chuju hoe-eui
shares	주식(株式)	chushik
shearing machine	전단기(剪斷機)	cheondan-gi
sheet	장	chang
sheet bar	박판 봉강(棒鋼)	pakp'an bong-gang
sheet pile	박판 더미	pakp'an deomi
shift (labor)	교대 시간(交代時間)	kyodae shigan
shipment	선적, 적송(積送)	seonjeok, cheoksong
shipper	하주(荷主)	haju
shipping agent	선적 대행 업자	seonjeok taehaeng eopjja
shipping charges	선적비	seonjeokpi
shipping expenses	선적 비용	seonjeok piyong
shipping instructions	선적 지시서	seonjeok chishiseo
shirt	셔쓰	syeosseu
shock absorber	완충 장치	wanch'ung jangch'i
shoe	구두	kudu
short delivery	인도품 부족(引渡品不足)	indop'um bujok
short position	공매 상태(公賣狀態)	kongmae sangt'ae
short sale	단기 예측 매각, 공매(公賣)	tan-gi yech'euk maegak, kongmae
short shipment	잔적품(殘積品)	chanjeokp'um
short sleeves	짧은 소매	jjalbeun somae
short supply	공급 부족(供給不足)	kong-geup pujok
shortage	부족, 부족액	pujok, pujogaek
short-term capital account	단기 자본 계정	tan-gi jabon gyejeong
short-term debt	단기 부채(負債)	tan-gi buch'ae
short-term financing	단기 융자	tan-gi yungja
shoulder pad	어깨심	eokkae shim
shrink-wrapped	수축 포장(收縮包裝)	such'uk p'ojang
shutter	셔터	syeot'eo

shutter speed	셔터 속도	syeot'eo sokto
sick leave	질병 휴가, 병가(病暇)	chilbyeong hyuga, pyeong-ga
sight draft	일람불(一覽拂) 어음	illambul eo-eum
signature	서명(署名), 조인(調印)	seomyeong, choin
silent partner	익명 사원(匿名社員)	ingmyeong saweon
silk	비단	pidan
silverplate (adj)	은 그릇의	eun geureuseui
silverware	식탁용 은제품	shikt'ang-yong eun-jep'eum
simulate (v)	모의 실험(模擬實驗)하다	mo-eui shilheom-hada
sinking fund	감채 기금(減債基金)	kamch'ae gigeum
sinus	공동(空洞)	kongdong
size	크기	k'eugi
skilled labor	숙련 노동	sungnyeon nodong
skirt	스커트, 치마	seuk'eot'eu, chi'ma
sky lens	스카이 렌즈	seuk'ai renjeu
slacks	바지	paji
sleeping pill	수면제	sumyeonje
slide	슬라이드	seullaideu
slide projector	슬라이드 영사기	seullaideu yeongsagi
sliding parity	변동 등가(變動等價)	pyeondong deungkka
sliding scale	순응율(順應率), 신축법(伸縮法)	suneung-nyul, shinch'ukpeop
slotting machine	자동 판매기	chadong p'anmaegi
slump	경기 침체(景氣沈滯), 폭락(暴落)	kyeong-gi ch'imch'e, p'ongnak
small business	소기업(小企業)	sogieop
soft cover	종이 표지	chong-i p'yoji
soft currency	연화(軟貨)	yeonhwa
soft focus lens	연 촛점 렌즈	yeon ch'otcheom renjeu
soft goods	직물류	chingmullyu
soft loan	연화 차관	yeonhwa ch'agwan
soft sell	은근한 상술(商術)	eun-geunhan sangsul
software	소프트 웨어	sop'eut'eu we-eo
software broker	소프트 웨어 중개인(仲介人)(브로커)	sop'eut'eu we-eo jung-gae-in (beurok'eo)
sole agent	총 대리점	ch'ong-daerijeom
sole proprietorship	개인 점주(個人店主), 개인 업주	kae-in jeomju, kae-in eopchu
sole rights	독점권	tokcheomkkweon
solid-state laser	고체 레이저	koch'e reijeo
solubility	용해도	yonghaedo
solute	용질	yongjil
solution	용액	yong-aek
solvency	지불 능력	chibul neungnyeok
solvent	용매	yongmae
soup dish	수프 접시	sup'eu jeopshi
soup spoon	수프용 숟가락	sup'euyong sutkkarak
spark plug	스파크 플러그, 발화 장치 마개	seup'ak'eu p'eulleogeu, palhwa jangch'i magae
speaker	확성기, 스피커	hwakseong-gi, seup'ik'eo

starch

specialist (stock exchange)	전문가	cheonmun-ga
specialty goods	특제품, 전문품	t'eukchep'um, cheonmunp'um
specific duty	종량세(從量稅)	chongnyangse
speculator	투기꾼, 투기자	t'ugikkun, t'ugija
speed up (v)	속도를 내다, 가속(加速)하다	sokto-reul naeda, kasok-hada
speedometer	속도계	soktogye
spin off (v)	분리 신설(分離新設)하다	pulli shinseol-hada
spine	(책의) 등	(ch'aeg-eul) deung
spiral tube	나선형 강철관	naseon-hyeong gangch'eol-gwan
spline milling machine	키홈 절삭 기계	k'ihom jeolsak kigye
split, stock	주식 분할	chushik punhal
spoilage	손상품(損傷品)	sonsangp'um
sponge	스폰지	seup'onji
sponsor (of fund, partnership)	보증인, 후원자	pojeung-in, huweonja
spoon	숟가락	sutkkarak
sportswear	운동복	undong-bok
spot delivery	현장 인도	hyeonjang indo
spot market	현물 시장	hyeonmul shijang
spread	주가폭(株價幅), 가격 차이, 차액	chukkap'ok, kagyeok ch'ai, ch'a-aek
spreadsheet	부기 계산표, 정산표(精算表)	pugi gyesanp'yo, cheongsanp'yo
staff	직원, 참모	chigweon, ch'ammo
staff and line	참조 직계식(參謀直系式)	ch'ammo jikkyeshik
staff assistant	보좌 참모	pojwa ch'ammo
staff organization	참조 조직, 참모진	ch'ammo jojik, ch'ammojin
stagflation	스태그 플레이션	seut'aegeup'euleisyeon
stainless steel	스텐레스	seut'entreseu
stale check	지연 수표(遲延手票)	chiyeon sup'yo
stand-alone text processor	독립형 원문 프로세서	tongniphyeong weonmun p'euroseseo
stand-alone workstation	독립형 작업장	tongniphyeong jageopchang
standard costs	표준 비용	p'yojun biyong
standard deviation	표준 편차(標準偏差)	p'yojun p'yeoncha
standard equipment	표준 장치	p'yojun jangch'i
standard lens	표준 렌즈	p'yojun renjeu
standard of living	생활 수준	saenghwal sujun
standard practice	표준 관례(標準慣例)	p'yojun gwallye
standard time	표준시, 표준 노무 시간	p'yojunshi, p'yojun nomu shigan
standardization	표준화	p'yojunhwa
standing charges	고정 경비	kojeong gyeongbi
standing costs	고정 비용	kojeong biyong
standing order	계속 판매 주문	kyesok p'anmae jumun
starch	전분	cheonbun

start-up cost	조업 개시 비용 (操業開始費用)	cho-eop kaeshi biyong
statement	성명서, 계산서	seongmyeongseo, kyesanseo
statement, financial	재무 제표(財務諸表)	chaemu jep'yo
statement of account	계산서	kyesanseo
statement, pro forma	견적 계산서	kyeonjeok kyesanseo
statement, profit and loss	손익 계산서	sonik kyesanseo
statistics	통계	t'ong-gye
statute	법령	peomnyeong
statute of limitations	출소 기한법	ch'ulso gihanppeop
steel foil	강철박편	kangch'eol bakp'yeon
steel mill	제강소	chegangso
steeling wheel	타륜 핸들	t'aryun haendeul
stereo TV	스테레오(입체음향) 테레비	seut'ereo (ipch'e eumhyang) t'erebi
stereophonic (adj)	입체 음향 장치의	ipch'e eumhyang jangch'i-eui
stimulant	흥분제	heungbunje
stock	증권, 주식	cheungkkweon, chushik
stock certificate	주권(株券)	chukkweon
stock control	주식 통제	chushik t'ongje
stock exchange	증권 거래, 주식 거래	cheungkkweon georae, chushik keorae
stock index	주식 지표	chushik chip'yo
stock market	증권 시장, 주식 시장	cheungkkweon shijang, chushik shijang
stock option	주식 매입, 매매 선택권(옵션)	chushik mae-ip maemae seont'aekkweon (opsyeon)
stock power	주권 양도 위임장	chukkweon yangdo wi-imjjang
stock profit	주식 이윤(株式利潤)	chushik iyun
stock puchase	주식 구입(購入)	chushik kuip
stock split	주식 분할(分割)	chushik punhal
stock takeover	주식 인계 인수	chushik in-gye insu
stock turnover	증권 회전율(回轉率)	cheungkkweon hoejeonnyul
stock-in-trade	재고(在庫) 영업 용품	chaego yeong-eop yongp'um
stockbroker	주식 중개인 (仲介人)(브로커)	chushik chung-gae-in (beurok'eo)
stockholder	주주(株主)	chuju
stockholders' equity	주주의 순가(純價)	chuju-eui sunkka
stoneware	석기(石器), 돌그릇	seokki, tol geureut
stop-loss order	손실 방지 주문	sonshil bangji jumun
storage	저장, 창고	cheojang, ch'angkko
store (v)	저장하다, 보관하다	cheojang-hada, pogwan-hada
stowage	적하(積荷), 짐싣기	cheokha, chimsitki
stowage charges	적하 비용(積荷費用)	cheokha biyong
straddle	양립(兩立)	yangnip
strapping	끈, 가죽끈	kkeun, kajuk-kkeun
strategic articles	전략품(戰略品)	cheollyakp'um
streamline (v)	능률적으로 하다, 합리화하다	neungnyuljeog-euro hada, hamnihwa-hada

switching charges

English	Korean	Romanization
stress management	스트레스 관리	seut'eureseu gwalli
strike (v)	동맹 파업하다	tongmaeng p'a-eop-hada
strike, wildcat	무모(無謀)한 파업	mumohan p'a-eop
strikebreaker	파업 파기(罷業破棄)	p'a-eop p'agi
strobe	섬광 전구	seomgwang jeon-gu
stuffing	채워 넣는 물건, 박제(剝製)	ch'aeweo neonneun mulgeon, pakche
style	유행(형)	yuhaeng (hyeong)
subcontract	하청 계약(下請契約)	hach'eong gyeyak
subcontractor	하청인, 하청 업자	hach'eong-in, hach'eong-eopcha
sublet	전대(轉貸)	cheondae
subscription price	예약 가격	yeyak kagyeok
subsidiary	자회사(子會社)	chahoesa
subsidy	보조금, 장려금	pojogeum, changnyeogeum
substandard	규격(표준)이하	kyugyeok (p'yojun) iha
suede	수에드	suedeu
sugar bowl	설탕 그릇	seolt'ang geureut
suit	양복	yangbok
sulfate	황산염	hwangsanyeom
sulfuric acid	황산	hwangsan
sulphamide	설파제	seolp'aje
sum-of-the years digits	급수 체감법(級數遞減法)	keupsu ch'egambeop
super alloys	초 합금(超合金)	ch'o hapkeum
super lattice	초 격자	ch'o gyeokcha
superconduction ceramics	초 전도 제도술	ch'o jeondoch'e jedosul
superconductive coil	초 전도 코일	ch'o jeondo k'oil
superconductive materials	초 전도 물질	ch'o jeondo muljjil
superconductive phenomena	초 전도 현상	ch'o jeondo hyeonsang
superconductor	초 전도체	ch'o jeondoch'e
supersede (v)	지위를 박탈(剝奪)하다	chiwi-reul bakt'al-hada
supervisor	관리자, 감독자	kwallija, kamdokcha
supplier	공급자	kong-geupcha
supply and demand	수요 공급	suyo gong-geup
support activities	지원 활동(支援活動)	chiweon hwalttong
surcharge	초과 청구, 추가 요금	ch'ogwa ch'eong-gu, ch'uga yogeum
surety company	보증 회사	pojeung hoesa
surface grinder	표면 분쇄기	p'yomyeon bunswaegi
surplus capital	잉여 자본(剩餘資本)	ing-yeo jabon
surplus goods	잉여 상품, 잉여품	ing-yeo sangp'um, ing-yeop'um
surtax	부가세(附加稅)	pugase
suspend payment (v)	지불 중지하다	chibul jungji-hada
suspension	차대 버팀 장치	ch'adae beot'im jangch'i
sweater	스웨터	seuwet'eo
switch	스위치	seuwich'i
switching charges	전철 수송료(轉轍輸送料)	cheonch'eol susongnyo

English	Korean	Romanization
syndicate	기업가 합동, 신디케이트	kieopkka haptong, shindik'eit'eu
synthesis	접골	cheopkol
synthetic (adj)	합성의, 인조의	hapseong-eui, injo-eui
synthetic suede	합성 수에드	hapseong suedeu
syringe	관장기	kwanjang-gi
systems analysis	시스템 분석, 조직 분석	siseut'em bunseok, chojik bunseok
systems design	시스템 디자인(설계)	shiseut'em dijain (seolgye)
systems engineering	시스템(조직) 공학	siseut'em (chojik) konghak
systems management	시스템(조직) 관리	siseut'em (chojik) kwalli

T

English	Korean	Romanization
table of contents	목차, 차례	mokch'a, ch'arye
tablecloth	식탁보	shikt'akpo
tablet	정제	cheongje
tachometer	회전 속도	hoejeon sokto
taffeta	호박단(琥珀緞)	hobaktan
tailor	재단사	chaedansa
take down	분해 장치(分解裝置)	punhae jangch'i
take off (v)	값을 깍다	kaps-eul kkakta
take out	꺼내다	kkeonaeda
take-home pay	실급료(實給料)	shilgeumnyo
takeover	이어 받다, 인수(引受)하다	ieo batta, insu-hada
takeover bid	회사 인수 신청	hoesa insu shinch'eong
tangible assets	유체 자산(有體資産), 유형 자산(有形資産)	yuch'e jasan, yuhyeong jasan
tanker	유조선(油槽船), 탱커	yujoseon, t'aengk'eo
tape recorder	녹음기	nogeumgi
target price	목표 가격	mokp'yo gagyeok
tariff	세율, 관세	seyul, kwanse
tariff barriers	관세 장벽	kwanse jangbyeok
tariff charge	관세 비용	kwanse biyong
tariff classification	관세 등급 분류	kwanse deun-geup pullyu
tariff commodity	관세 상품(용품)	kwanse sangp'um (yongp'um)
tariff differential	관세율 격차(格差)	kwanseyul gyeokch'a
tariff war	관세 전쟁(분쟁)	kwanse jeonjaeng (bunjaeng)
task force	대책 본부, 특별 전문 위원회	taech'aek ponbu, t'eukpyeol jeonmun wiweonhoe
tax	세, 조세(租稅)	se, chose
tax allowance	세금 공제(控除)	segeum gongje
tax base	과세 기준	kwase gijun
tax burden	세금(조세) 부담	segeum (chose) budam
tax collector	수세리(收稅利)	suseri
tax deduction	세금 공제(액)	segeum gongje (aek)
tax evasion	탈세(脫稅)	t'alse
tax, excise	국내 소비세, 물품세	kungnae sobise, mulp'umse
tax, export	수출세	such'ulse

English	Korean	Romanization
tax haven	세금 탈피처	segeum t'alp'ich'eo
tax, import	수입세	suipse
tax, sales	판매세, 매상세	p'anmaese, maesangse
tax shelter	감세 수단(減稅手段)	kamse sudan
tax-free income	면세 소득	myeonse sodeuk
taxation	과세, 세수(稅收)	kwase, sesu
team management	팀 관리, 작업조 관리	t'im gwalli, jageopcho gwalli
telecommunications	전기 통신	cheon-gi t'ongshin
telemarketing	텔레 마케팅	t'elle mak'et'ing
telephoto lens	망원 렌즈	mang-weon renjeu
teleprocessing	전신 회선, 텔레 프로세싱	cheonshin hoeseon, t'ellep'eurosesng
television	테레비	t'erebi
telex	텔렉스, 전송식 통신문	t'elekseu, cheonsongshik t'ongshinmun
tender	입찰, 제출	ipch'al, chech'ul
tender, legal	법화(法貨)	peophwa
tender offer	주식 공개 매입 제의	chushik kong-gae maeip che-eui
term bond	정기 채권	cheong-gi ch'aekkweon
term insurance	정기 보험	cheong-gi boheom
term loan	기한부 융자	kihanbu yungja
terminal	터미널, 단말 장치	t'enmineol, tanmal jangch'i
terminate (v)	종결(終結)시키다	chong-gyeolshik'ida
terms of sale	판매 조건	p'anmae jokkeon
terms of trade	교역 조건	kyoyeok chokkeon
territorial waters	영해	yeonghae
territory	영토	yeongt'o
textile	직물, 섬유	chingmul, seomyu
thermostat	온도 조절 장치	ondo jojeol jangch'i
thin market	약세 시황(弱勢市況)	yakse shihwang
third-party exporter	제3 수출자	chesam such'ulja
third window	제3 창구	chesam ch'ang-gu
35mm camera	35밀리 사진기(카메라)	samshibo milli sajinkki (k'amera)
through bill of lading	통용 선하 증권	t'ongyong seonha jeungkkweon
throughput	정보 처리, 드르풋트	cheongbo ch'eori, deureup'ut'eu
tick, price	증권 시세 표시	cheungkkweon shise p'yoshi
ticker tape	주식 상장 표시 테이프	chushik sangjang p'yoshi t'eip'eu
tie	넥타이, 타이	nekt'ai, t'ai
tied aid	조건부 원조	chokkeonbu weonjo
tied loan	구속 대부(拘束貸付)	kusok taebu
tight market	긴축 시장	kinch'uk shijang
time and motion	작업(作業)시간 및 동작(動作)	chageop shigan mit tongjak
time bill (of exchange)	기한부 환어음	kihanbu hwan-eo-eum
time deposit	정기 예금	cheong-gi yegeum
time, down	중지 시간, 다운 타임	chungji shigan, daun t'aim

time, lead	소요 시간, 리드 타임	soyo shigan, rideu t'aim
time order	시한 주문(時限注文)	shihan jumun
time sharing	시분할 제도(時分割制度)	shi bunhal jedo
time zone	시간대(時間帶)	shigandae
timetable	시간표	shiganp'yo
tip (inside information)	내부 정보(內部情報)	naebu jeongbo
tire	바퀴, 타이어	pak'wi, t'aieo
titanium	티타늄	t'it'anyum
titanium metal	티타늄 금속	t'it'anyum geumsok
title	제목, 칭호, 소유권	chemok, ch'ingho, soyukkweon
title insurance	소유권 보험	soyukkweon boheom
toluene	톨루엔	t'olluen
tombstone	묘석(墓石), 묘비(墓碑)	myoseok, myobi
tonnage	적량, 용적 톤수	cheongnyang, yongjeok t'onsu
tool	공구(工具)	kong-gu
tools	공구, 기구	kong-gu, kigu
top management	최고 경영층(진)	ch'oego gyeong-yeongch'eung (jin)
top price	최고 가격	ch'oego kagyeok
top quality	최고 품질	ch'oego p'umjil
topping up	마무리, 완성	mamuri, wanseong
torque	비트는 힘	pit'euneun him
tort	불법 행위	pulbeop haeng-wi
toxicology	독물학	tongmulhak
toxin	독소	tokso
trade	무역, 통상, 교역, 거래	muyeok, t'ongsang, kyoyeok, keorae
trade (v)	매매하다, 교환하다	maemae-hada, kyohwan-hada
trade acceptance	무역 인수 어음	muyeok insu eo-eum
trade agreement	통상(무역) 협정	t'ongsang (muyeok) hyeopcheong
trade association	무역 협회, 동업 조합	muyeok hyeophoe, ton-eop chohap
trade barrier	무역 장벽(障壁)	muyeok changbyeok
trade commission	무역(통상) 위원회	muyeok (t'ongsang) wiweonhoe
trade credit	무역 신용장	muyeok shinyongjjang
trade date	무역 일자	muyeok iljja
trade discount	동업자 할인	tong-eopcha harin
trade, fair	공정 거래, 대등 무역	kongjeong georae, taedeung muyeok
trade house	상사(商社)	sangsa
trade law	통상법, 무역법	t'ongsangbeop, muyeokpeop
trade-off	교환	kyohwan
trademark	상표, 상호	sangp'yo, sangho
trader	상인, 무역 업자	sang-in, muyeogeopcha
trading company	무역 회사, 상사	muyeok hoesa, sangsa
trading limit	거래 제한	keorae jehan
trainee	연수생, 훈련생	yeonsusaeng, hullyeonsaeng

tranche	트랜슈	t'euraensyu
tranquilizer	신경 안정제	shin-gyeong anjeongje
transaction	거래(去來)	keorae
transfer	이전(移轉), 양도(讓渡)	ijeon, yangdo
transfer agent	(주식)대행(代行)	(chushik) taehaeng
transfer machine	자동 공작 기계	chadong gongjak kigye
transformer	변압기	pyeonapki
transit (in)	운송중	unsongjung
translator	번역자	peonyeokcha
transmission	변속 장치, 트랜스미션	pyeonsok changch'i, t'euraenseumisyeon
transmission loss	송전손(送電損)	songjeonson
transport equipment	수송기계	susong gigye
transportation	운수, 수송, 수송허가서	unsu, susong, susong heogaseo
traveler's check	여행자 수표	yeohaengja sup'yo
treasurer	금전 출납계	keumjeon ch'ullapkye
treasury bills	정부 단기 채권	cheongbu dan-gi ch'aekkweon
treasury bonds	회사 채권, 금고주(金庫株)	hoesa ch'aekkweon, keumgoju
treasury notes	재무성 증권	chaemuseong jeungkkweon
treasury stock	금고주(金庫株), 사내주(社內株)	keumgoju, sanaeju
treaty	조약, 협정	choyak, hyeopcheong
trend	동향, 추세	tonghyang, ch'use
trial balance	시산표(試算表)	shisanp'yo
tripod	삼각대	samgaktae
troubleshoot (v)	수리하다, 문제를 해결하다	suri-hada, munje-reul haegyeol-hada
truck load	전세 화물(專貰貨物)	cheonse hwamul
trust	신탁, 신용 대부(貸付)	shint'ak, shinyong daebu
trust company	신탁 회사	shint'ak hoesa
trust fund	신탁 자금	shint'ak chageum
trust receipt (finance)	수입 담보 하물 보관증	suip tamppo hamul bokwanjjeung
trustee	관재인(管財人), 수탁자(受託者)	kwanjaein, sut'akcha
tuner	동조기	tongjogi
tungsten	텅스텐	t'eongseut'en
turbo-charger	배기 터빈 과급기	paegi t'eobin gwageupki
turnkey	일괄 도급 방식	ilgwal dogeup pangshik
turnover, asset	자산 회전율(資産回轉率)	chasan hoejeonyul
turnover, inventory	재고품 회전율	chaegop'um hoejeonyul
turnover, sales	총매상고(總賣上高)	ch'ongmaesang-go
turnover, stock	주식 회전율	chushik hoejeonnyul
turret lathe	터릿 선반	t'eorit seonban
twin lens reflex camera	쌍렌즈 리프렉스 사진기(카메라)	ssang-renjeu rip'ureukseu sajinkki (k'amera)
two-name paper	2인 서명 어음	i-in seomyeong eo-eum
two-tiered market	두 계단식 시장	tu gyedanshik shijang

U

English	Korean	Romanization
ultrafine powder	분말(粉末)	*punmal*
ultra vires acts	월권 행위(越權行爲)	*weolkkweon haeng-wi*
unaccompanied goods	별도 수송 화물	*pyeoltto susong hwamul*
uncollectable accounts	수금 불가 계정 (收金不可計定)	*sugeum bulga gyejeong*
under-capitalized (adj)	자금 미달(未達)의, 투자 부족의	*chageum midal-eui, t'uja bujog-eui*
undercut (v)	절하(切下)하다, 내리다	*cheolha-hada, naerida*
underdeveloped nations	저개발국(低開發國)	*cheogaebalguk*
underestimate (v)	과소 평가하다	*kwaso p'yeongkka-hada*
underpaid (adj)	지불 부족의	*chibul bujog-eui*
undersigned	서명자	*seomyeongja*
understanding (agreement)	양해, 협정	*yanghae, hyeopcheong*
undertake (v)	인수(引受)하다	*insu-hada*
undervalue (v)	과소 평가하다	*kwaso p'yeongkka-hada*
underwater camera	수중 카메라	*sujung k'amera*
underwriter	보험 업자, 인수 업자	*poheom eopcha, insu eopcha*
undeveloped (adj)	미개발(未開發)의	*migaebal-eui*
unearned increment	자연 증가(自然增價)	*chayeon jeung-ga*
unearned revenue	자연 세입(歲入), 불로 수입(不勞收入)	*chayeon seip, pullo suip*
unemployment	실업(失業), 실직(失職)	*shireop, shiljjik*
unemployment compensation	실업 보상(失業補償)	*shireop posang*
unfair (adj)	불공평한, 불공정한	*pulgongp'yeong-han, pulgongjeong-han*
unfavorable (adj)	불리(不利)한, 역조(逆調)의	*pullihan, yeokcho-eui*
unfeasible (adj)	실행 불가능한	*shilhaeng bulganeunghan*
union contract	노조 계약	*nojo gyeyak*
union label	조합 부표(符標)	*chohap pup'yo*
union, labor	노동 조합	*nodong johap*
unisex	남녀 공동	*namnyeo gongdong*
unit cost	단위 원가	*tanwi weonkka*
unit load discount	단위 하중 할인	*tanwi hajung harin*
unit price	단가(單價)	*tankka*
universal grinder	자재 분쇄기	*chajae bunswaegi*
universal milling machine	자재(自在) 절삭 기계	*chajae jeolsak kigye*
unlead gasoline	무연 휘발유	*muyeon hwiballyu*
unlisted (adj)	미등록의, 비상장(非上場)의	*mideungnog-eui, pisangjang-eui*
unload (v)	매각하다, 짐을 부리다	*maegak-hada, chim-eul burida*
unsecured loan	무담보 대부(貸付)	*mudamppo daebu*
unskilled labor	미숙련 노동	*misungnyeon nodong*
up to our expectations	우리의 기대에 달 (達)하기까지	*uri-eui gidae-e dalhagi-kkaji*

upmarket	상향 시황(上向市況)	sanghyang shihwang
upturn	상승, 호전	sangseung, hojeon
urban renewal	도시 재개발	toshi jaegaebal
urban sprawl	도시 확대	toshi hwakttae
urea	요소(尿素)	yoso
urea resin	요소 수지(樹脂)	yoso suji
Uruguay Round (UR)	우루과이 라운드, 우루과이 협상	urugwai raundeu, urugwai hyeopsang
use tax	사용세, 이용세	sayongse, iyongse
useful life	유효 수명, 실용 수명	yuhyo sumyeong, siryong sumyeong
user	사용자	sayongja
user friendly	사용 편리한	sayong p'yeollihan
U.S. Trade Law 301	미 통상법 301조, 슈퍼 301조	mi t'ongsangbeop sambaek il cho, syup'eo sambaek il cho
usury	고리(高利), 고리 대금업	kori, kori-daegeumeop
utility	효용(效用), (전기, 수도)시설	hyoyong, (cheongi, sudo) shiseol

V

vaccine	우두종, 왁진	udujong, wakchin
valid (adj)	유효한, 확실한	yuhyohan, hwakshilhan
validate (v)	유효를 인정하다	yuhyo-reul injeong-hada
valuation	평가, 평가액, 가격 사정	p'yeongkka, p'yeongkka-aek, kagyeok sajeong
value	가치	kach'i
value, asset	자산가(資產價)	chasankka
value, book	장부 가격	changbu gagyeok
value engineering	가치 공학	kach'i gonghak
value, face	액면 가격	aengmyeon gagyeok
value for duty	세액 사정(稅額查定) 가격	se-aek sajeong gagyeok
value, market	시장 가격	shijang gagyeok
value-added tax	부가 가치세(附加價值稅)	puga gach'ise
valve	밸브	paelbeu
vanadium	바나듐	panadyum
variable annuity	가변 연금(可變年金)	kabyeon yeon-geum
variable costs	변동비(變動費)	pyeondongbi
variable import levy	가변 수입 과세 (可變輸入課稅)	kabyeon suip kwase
variable interest rate	변동 이자율	pyeondong ijayul
variable margin	가변 판매 수익(마진)	kabyeon p'anmae suik (majin)
variable rate	가변율, 변동율	kabyeon-nyul, pyeondong-nyul
variable rate mortgage	변동율 주택 융자	pyeondong-nyul jut'aek yungja
variable sequence robot	가변 연속 로보트	kabyeon yeonsok robot'eu
variance	상위(相違), 분산치(分散値)	sang-wi, punsanch'i
veil	면사포	myeonsap'o

velocity of money	통화 유통 속도	t'onghwa yut'ong sokto
vending machine	자판기	chap'an-gi
vendor	매주(買主), 양도인	maeju, yangdoin
vendor's lien	매주 유치권(賣主留置權)	maeju yuch'ikkweon
venture capital	위험 부담 자본	wiheom budam jabon
vertical boring mill	수직 천공기	sujik ch'eon-gong-gi
vertical integration	수직 통합(垂直統合)	sujik t'onghap
vertical milling machine	수직 절삭기	sujik jeolsakki
very large-scale integrated circuit	특대형 집적 회로	t'euktaehyeong jipcheok hoero
vest	조끼	chokki
vested interests	기득 이권(旣得利權)	kideuk ikkweon
vested rights	기득권	kideukkweon
veto	거부권(拒否權)	keobukkweon
vice-president	부회장, 부사장	puhoejang, pusajang
video cassette camera	비디오 카세트 카메라	pidio k'aset'eu k'amera
video cassette player	비디오 카세트 장치	pidio k'aset'eu jangch'i
video cassette recorder	비디오 카세트 녹음기	pidio k'aset'eu nogeumgi
video disc	비디오 디스크	pidio diseuk'eu
videOrche	비디오케, 영상음악 반주기	pidiok'e, yeongsang eumak panjugi
video tape recorder	비디오 테이프 녹음기	pidio t'eip'eu nogeumgi
view finder	파인더	p'aindeo
visible balance of trade	무역 수지 균형 (貿易收支均衡)	muyeok suji gyunhyeong
vitamin	비타민	pit'amin
voice-activated (adj)	음성 입력 작동 (音聲入力作動)의	eumseong imnyeok chaktong-eui
void (adj)	무효의	muhyo-eui
volatile market	휘발성 시황(市況)	hwibalseong shihwang
volume	거래량, 거래액	keoraeryang, keorae-aek
volume discount	거래량 할인	keoraeryang harin
volume, sales	판매량	p'anmaeryang
voting right	투표권	t'up'yokkweon
voucher	증표(證票), 증거 서류	cheungp'yo, cheung-geo seoryu

W

wafer	웨이퍼, 반도체박판	weip'eo, pandoch'e bakp'an
wage	임금(賃金)	imgeum
wage differential	임금 격차(格差)	imgeum gyeokch'a
wage dispute	임금 분쟁	imgeum bunjaeng
wage drift	임금 유동(流動)	imgeum yudong
wage earner	임금 생활자	imgeum saenghwalja
wage freeze	임금 동결(凍結)	imgeum dong-gyeol
wage level	임금 수준	imgeum sujun
wage scale	임금 폭, 임금 스케일	imgeump'ok, imgeum seuk'eil

English	Korean	Romanization
wage structure	임금(급여) 구조	imgeum (keubyeo) gujo
wage-price spiral	임금 및 물가의 악순환(惡循環)	imgeum mit mulkka-eui aksunhwan
wages	임금(賃金)	imgeum
waiver clause	기권 약관(棄權約款)	kikkweon yakkwan
walkout	파업, 항의 퇴장	p'a-eop, hang-eui t'oejang
want-ad	모집 광고, 구직 광고	mojip kwang-go, kujik kwang-go
warehouse	창고	ch'ang-go
warrant	보증장(保證狀), 영장(令狀)	pojeungjjang, yeongjjang
warranty	(품질)보증서	(p'umjil) pojeung-seo
wasting asset	소모성 자산	somoseong jasan
water-absorbing resin	흡수 수지	heupsu suji
waybill	화물 인환증(引換證)	hwamul inhwanjjeung
wealth	재산, 부(富)	chaesan, pu
wear and tear	마멸 소모(磨滅消耗)	mamyeol somo
weekly return	주보(週報)	chubo
weight	중량(重量)	chungnyang
weighted average	가중 평균(加重平均)	kajung p'yeong-gyun
wharfage charge	부두 사용료(埠頭使用料)	pudu sayongnyo
wheel	바퀴	pak'wi
when issued	발행 일자	palhaeng iljja
white collar worker	봉급 생활자, 사무직	pong-geup saenghwalja, samujik
wholesale market	도매 시장	tomae shijang
wholesale price	도매 가격	tomae gagyeok
wholesale trade	도매업	tomae-eop
wholesaler	도매 상인	tomae sang-in
wide-angle lens	광각 렌즈	kwang-gak renjeu
wildcat strike	무모(無謀)한 파업	mumohan p'a-eop
will	유언(遺言)	yueon
windfall profits	의외의 이윤, 우발적 이윤	eui-oe-eui iyun, ubaljeok iyun
window dressing (department store)	점두 장식(店頭裝飾)	cheomdu jangshik
(bank)	수식 결산(修飾決算)	sushik kyeolssan
windshield	바람막이 전면 유리	param-magi jeonmyeon yuri
wire	철사, 전선	ch'eolsa, cheonseon
wire telecommunication equipment	유선 통신 기기	yuseon t'ongshin gigi
wire transfer	전신환(電信換)	cheonshinhwan
wireless telecommunication equipment	무선 통신 기기	museon t'ongshin gigi
with average	단독 해손 담보(單獨海損擔保)	tandok haeson dambo
withholding tax	원천 과세(源泉課稅)	weonch'eon gwase
witness	증인(證人)	cheung-in
wool	양털, 모직물	yangt'eol, mojingmul
word processor	워드 프로세서	weodeu p'euroseseo
work (v)	작업하다, 근무하다	chageop-hada, keunmu-hada

work by contract	계약 근무	kyeyak keunmu
work cycle	작업 주기(週期)	chageop chugi
work day	근무일, 평일, 취업일(就業日)	keunmu-il, p'yeong-il, ch'wieobil
work in progress	진행중인 작업	chinhaengjung-in jageop
work order	작업 지시, 견적 지령서(見積指令書)	chageop chishi, kyeonjeok chiryeongseo
work station	작업장, 근무지	chageopchang, keunmuji
workforce	노동력, 인력	nodongnyeok, illyeok
working assets	운전 자산(運轉資産)	unjeon jasan
working balance	작업 균형	chageop kyunhyeong
working capital	운전(영업) 자본	unjeon(yeong-eop) jabon
working class	근로 계층	keullo gyech'eung
working contract	공사 청부	kongsa ch'eongbu
working funds	운전 자금	unjeon jageum
working hours	근무(노동) 시간	keunmu (nodong) shigan
working papers	노동 증명서, 감사 조서	nodong jeungmyeongseo, kamsa joseo
working tools	가동 장비(可動裝備)	kadong jangbi
workload	업무량, 작업 분량, 작업량	eommuryang, chageop pullyang, chageomnyang
workplace	작업장, 직장	chageopchang, chikchang
workshop	실습, 일터, 작업장	shilseup, ilt'eo, chageopchang
World Bank	세계 은행	segye eunhaeng
worth, net	정미(正味)가격, 순가치	cheongmi gagyeok, sun-gach'i
worthless (adj)	가치 없는	kach'i eomneun
writ	영장(令狀), 공문서	yeongjjang, kongmunseo
write off (v)	장부에서 말소하다	changbu-eseo malso-hada
write down (v)	기장(記帳)하다, 값을 내리다	kijang-hada, kaps-eul naerida
written agreement	계약서, 합의서	kyeyakseo, habeuiseo

X

xylene	크실렌	k'eushillen

Y

yardstick	표준, 척도, 판단 기준	p'yojun, ch'eokto, p'andan gijun
yarn	털실, 모사	t'eolshil, mosa
year	년(年)	nyeon
year, fiscal	회계 년도	hoegye nyeondo
year-end	연말(年末)	yeonmal
yield	생산액, 수익(收益), 이율(利率)	saengsanaek, suik, iyul
yield to maturity	만기 이율(滿期利率)	man-gi iyul

Z

zeolite	비석	*piseok*
zero coupon	영(零), 표면 이율없는 할인채, 무이자 할인 채권	*yeong, p'yomyeon iyuleomneun hanrinch'ae, muija harin ch'aekkweon*
zinc	아연	*ayeon*
zip code	우편 번호	*up'yeon beonho*
zone	구획(區劃), 지대(地帶), 지역(地域)	*kuhoek, chidae, chiyeok*
zoning law	구획 정리법(규정)	*kuhoek cheongnippeop (gyujeong)*
zoom lens	줌 렌즈	*chum renjeu*

KOREAN TO ENGLISH

A

abyeon-gi	rolling mill	압연기
ach'eol sanyeom	ferrite	아철 산염
aekch'e hellyum	liquid helium	액체헬륨
aekcheong	liquid crystal	액정(液晶)
aeksel	accelerator	액셀
aekseseori	accessory	액세서리
aengmyeon ch'ogwa-aek (cheungkkweon-eui) aengmyeon ch'ogwa-aek	bonus (premium) acceleration premium	액면 초과액 (증권의) 액면 초과액
aengmyeon gagyeog-euro	at par	액면 가격으로
aengmyeon gagyeok	par	액면 가격
aengmyeon gagyeok i-sang	above par	액면 가격 이상
aengmyeon iha-ro	below par	액면 이하로
aengmyeon isang-euro	above par (adv)	액면 이상으로
aengmyeon misang	no par value	액면 미상(額面未詳)
aengmyeonkka	face value	액면가(額面價)
a-jilsanyeom	nitrite	아질산염
alk'alliseong (yeomgaseong)	alkaline (adj)	알카리성(염가성)
allumina (sanhwa alminyum)	alumina	알루미나(산화 알미늄)
alluminyum	aluminum	알루미늄
amap'o	linen	아마포
amin	amine	아민
am-maeja	scalper	암매자(暗賣者)
ammonia	ammonia	암모니아
amnyu-hada	attach (v)	압류하다
amshijang	black market	암시장
ang-gora mojingmul	angora	앙고라 모직물
anjeon jangch'i	safeguard	안전 장치
anjeon yeoyu	margin of safety	안전 여유(安全餘裕)
anjeonhan imdae	leveraged lease	안전한 임대
ankkam	lining	안감
ankkeon	agenda	안건
annae t'ongji	advice note	안내 통지
ant'ena	antenna	안테나
allyak	pill	알약
ap'eut'eo sseobiseu	after-sales service	아프터 서비스
ap'yeon	opium	아편
aset'eu sanyeom	acetate	아세트 산염
aset'on	acetone	아세톤
aseup'irin	aspirin	아스피린
ayeon	zinc	아연

163 **chadong eungdap cheonhwagi**

B

baedang	allotment	배당
ba-i-eo	buyer	바이어
balsaeng	accrual	발생
(piyong-eul) budam-hada	bear (v)	(비용을)부담하다
(ija-ga) butta	accrue (v)	(이자가)붙다

C

chabaljeogin	autonomous	자발적인
chabon	capital	자본
chabon biyong	cost of capital	자본 비용
chabon gujo	capital structure	자본 구조
chabon gwa-ing	overcapitalized	자본 과잉
chabon gyejeong	capital account	자본 계정
chabon gyeongbi gamjeong (sajeong)	capital expenditure appraisal	자본 경비 감정(사정)
chabon ing-yeongeum	capital surplus	자본 잉여금
chabon jae-guseong	recapitalization	자본 재구성
chabon jeung-ga	capital increase	자본 증가
chabon jibyakjjeok	capital-intensive (adj)	자본 집약적(集約的)
chabon jich'ul	capital expenditure	자본 지출
chabon jich'ul yesan	capital budget	자본 지출 예산
chabon jodal	raising capital	자본 조달
chabon ju-eui	capitalism	자본 주의
chabon sanch'ullyul	capital-output ratio	자본 산출율(算出率)
chabon shijang	capital market	자본 시장
chabon such'ul	capital exports	자본 수출
chabon sudang	capital allowance	자본 수당
chabon su-ik	return on capital	자본 수익
chabon-geum	corpus	자본금
chabon-geum jich'ul p'yeongkka (gamjeong)	appraisal, capital expenditure	자본금 지출 평가(감정)
chabonhwa	capitalization	자본화
chabonjae	capital goods	자본재
chach'e gamjeong	self-appraisal	자체 감정
chach'e p'yeongkka josa	self-appraisal	자체 평가 조사
ch'adae beot'im jangch'i	suspension	차대 버팀 장치
chadong	automatic, automation	자동
chadong gigye	automatic	자동 기계
chadong byeonsok changch'i	automatic transmission	자동 변속 장치
chadong byeonsok kieo	automatic gearshift	자동 변속 기어
chadong ch'otcheom	automatic focusing	자동 촛점
chadong doegamkki	automatic rewinding	자동 되감기
chadong eungdap cheonhwagi	phone answering machine	자동 응답 전화기

chadong gaep'yegi	self-timer	자동 개폐기
chadong geomsagi	autochecker	자동 검사기
ch'adong gieo jangch'i	planetary gear train	차동 기어 장치
chadong gongjak kigye	transfer machine	자동 공작 기계
chadong gugyeong jojeol jangch'i	automatic aperture control device	자동 구경 조절 장치
chadong hyeonsang-gi	automatic developing machine	자동 현상기
chadong inhwagi	automatic printing machine	자동 인화기
chadong jangch'i	auto-loading	자동 장치
chadong jangjeon	auto-loading	자동 장전
chadong nasa gigye	automatic screw machine	자동 나사 기계
chadong noch'ul	automatic exposure	자동 노출
chadong p'aellit pyeon-gyeong-gi	automatic pallet changer	자동 팰릿 변경기
chadong np'anmaegi	slotting machine	자동 판매기
chadongch'a	automobile	자동차
chadongch'a bup'um	auto parts	자동차 부품
chadongch'a-yong jeonhwa	car telephone	자동차용 전화
chadongch'a-yong museon t'ongshin-gi	CB	자동차용 무선 통신기
chadong yeok-hoejeon	autoreverse	자동 역회전
chadong yeonjang byeong-gyeong-gi	automatic tool changer	자동 연장 변경기
chaebeol	financial clique, plutes	재벌(財閥)
chae-boheom gaipcha	reinsurer	재보험 가입자
chaebongt'eul	sewing machine	재봉틀
chae-ch'ungjeon ganeung-han	rechargeable	재충전 가능한
chaedansa	tailor	재단사
chaego yeong-eop yongp'um	stock-in-trade	재고(在庫) 영업 용품
chaegop'um gwalli	inventory control	재고품 관리
chaegop'um hoejeonnyul	inventory turnover	재고품 회전율
chaegop'um kwalli	inventory control	재고품 관리
chaegop'um mongnok	inventory	재고품 목록
chae-guseong	restructure	재구성
chae-gyoseop-hada	renegotiate (v)	재교섭하다
chaeha gwa-ing	overstock	재하 과잉(在荷過剩)
chaehae boheom	casualty insurance	재해 보험
chaeharinyul	rediscount rate	재할인율
chaehwa	goods	재화(財貨)
chaejeong bojeungseo	affidavit	재정 보증서
chaejeong bujang	financial director	재정 부장
chaejeong bunseok	financial analysis	재정 분석
chaejeong dong-gi	financial incentive	재정 동기
chaejeong gamjeong	financial appraisal	재정 감정(鑑定)
chaejeong gwalli	financial control	재정 관리
chaejeong gyehoek	financial planning	재정 계획
chaejeong jangnyeo	financial incentive	재정 장려
chaejeong jiyeon	fiscal drag	재정 지연(遲延)

chaejeong kwalli	financial management	재정 관리
chaejeong p'yeongkka	appraisal, financial	재정 평가
chaejeong samu	financial services	재정 사무
chaejeong t'ongje	financial control	재정 통제
chaejeongjeok chung-yojjeom	financial highlights	재정적 중요점
chae-jumun-hada	repeat order	재주문하다
ch'aek	book	책
ch'aek p'yoji	cover	책 표지
chae-maech'ul	secondary offering (securities)	재매출(再賣出)
chaemu bunseok	financial analysis	재무 분석
chaemu daeri-in	fiscal agent	재무 대리인
chaemu gwalli	financial management	재무 관리(財務管理)
chaemu gwan-gye seobiseu	financial services	재무 관계 서비스
chaemu isa	financial director	재무 이사
chaemu jep'yo	financial statement	재무 제표(財務諸表)
chaengban	tray	쟁반
chaeng-eui	dispute	쟁의(爭議)
chae-p'anmae	resale	재판매
chae-p'yeonseong	reorganization	재편성
chaeryang jumun	open order	재량 주문
chaeryo	materials	재료
chaeryo ch'wigeup robot'eu	material handling robot	재료 취급 로보트
chae-saengsan biyong	reproduction costs	재생산 비용
chaesan	property, wealth	재산
chae-such'ul	re-export	재수출
chae-t'uja-hada	plow back (earning) (v)	재투자하다
chaeweon-eui bongswae	blockage of funds	재원(財源)의 봉쇄
chae-yungja	refinancing	재융자(再融資)
chaga ch'wieopcha	self-employed	자가 취업자
chageomnyang	work load	작업량
chageop	labor	작업
chageop bunseok	job analysis	작업 분석
chageop chishi	work order	작업 지시
chageop chugi	work cycle	작업 주기(週期)
chageop kongjeongdo	flow chart	작업 공정도
chageop kyunhyeong	working balance	작업 균형
chageop pullyang	work load	작업 분량
chageop shigan mit tongjak	time and motion	작업(作業) 시간 및 동작(動作)
chageopchang	work station	작업장
chageop-hada	work (v)	작업하다
chageum	fund	자금
chageum bongswae	blockage of funds	자금 봉쇄
chageum midal-eui	undercapitalized (adj)	자금 미달(未達)의
chageun allyak	pellet	작은 알약
chageun ch'aekcha	pamphlet	작은 책자
chageun t'omni bak'wi	pinion	작은 톱니 바퀴
chageup chajok	autarky	자급 자족
chagi	china	자기
chagi ch'ukcheon-gi	ceramic condenser	자기 축전기

chagi diseuk'eu jangch'i	magnetic disc unit	자기 디스크 장치
chagi gich'o gieok changch'i	magnetic bubble memory	자기(磁器) 기초 기억 장치
chagi gieok changch'i	magnetic memory	자기(磁氣) 기억 장치
chagi t'eip'eu	magnetic tape	자기(磁氣) 테이프
chagi t'eip'eu jangch'i	magnetic tape unit	자기 테이프 장치
chagi-ap sup'yo	cashier's check	자기앞 수표
chagi yudongch'e	magnetic fluid	자기 유동체
chagiaek	magnetic fluid	자기액(磁器液)
chagyeok	qualifications	자격
chahoesa	subsidiary	자회사(子會社)
chajae bunswaegi	universal grinder	자재 분쇄기
chajae jeolsak kigye	universal milling machine	자재(自在) 절삭 기계
challa-naeda	corp (v)	잘라내다
chamjae shijang	market potential	잠재 시장
chamo	matrix	자모
chamshi	interim	잠시(暫時)
chamun gigeum	advisory funds	자문 기금
chamun-hada	advise	자문하다
chamun hoe-eui	advisory council	자문 회의
chamun samu (bongsa)	advisory service	자문 사무(봉사)
chamun wiweonhoe	advisory council	자문 위원회
chang-ae	handicap	장애
changbi	equipment	장비
changbi imdae	equipment leasing	장비 임대(裝備賃貸)
chang	chapter	장(章)
chang	sheet	장
changbu	journal	장부(帳簿)
changbu gagyeok	book value	장부 가격
changbu mongnok	book inventory	장부 목록
changbu-e namgiji aneun	off-the-books (adj)	장부에 남기지 않은
changbu-eseo malso-hada	write-off (v)	장부에서 말소하다
changbusang i-ik	paper profit	장부상 이익
changch'i	equipment	장치(裝置)
changdan	length	장단
chang-geori ch'otcheom renjeu	long-focus lens	장거리 촛점 렌즈
chang-gi buch'ae	long-term debt	장기 부채
chang-gi gyehoek	long-range planning	장기 계획
chang-gi jabon gyejeong	long-term capital account	장기 자본 계정
chang-gi yangdari geolch'igi	long hedge	장기 양다리 걸치기
changhwa	boots	장화
changmul	pilferage	장물(臟物)
changnae guje	save of the future	장래 구제(將來救濟)
changnae jung-gaein	rack jobber	장내 중개인
changnae jung-gaein-i such' wi-haneun ch'aikkeum	jobber's turn	장내 중개인이 수취하는 차익금(差益金)
changnyeogeum	subsidy	장려금
chang-oe	off board (stock market)	장외

chang-oe georae shise	over-the-counter quotation	장외 거래 시세
changshin-gu	jewel	장신구
chanjeokp'um	short shipment	잔적품(殘積品)
chaptongsani-eui	miscellaneous (adj)	잡동사니의
chareuda	cut (v)	자르다
ch'aryang	motor vehicles	차량
charyo	data	자료
charyo ch'wideuk	data acquisition	자료 취득
charyo seupteuk	data acquisition	자료 습득
chasan	asset	자산
chasan gach'i	asset value	자산 가치
chasan hoejeonnyul	asset turnover	자산 회전율
chasan maegak sodeuk/sonshil	capital gain/loss	자산 매각 소득/손실
chasan seont'aengnon	portfolio theory	자산 선택론
chasankka	asset value	자산가(資産價)
chaweon baebun	resource allocation	자원 배분
cha-yeon jeung-ga	accretion, unearned increment	자연 증가
chayeon seip	unearned revenue	자연 세입(歲入)
chayeong-in	self-employed	자영인(自營人)
chayu bang-im jueui	laissez-faire	자유 방임 주의
chayu gi-eop	free enterprise	자유 기업(自由企業)
chayu gyeyak-eui	freelance	자유 계약의
chayu muyeok chiyeok	free trade zone	자유 무역 지역
chayu shigan	free time	자유 시간
chayu shijang	free market	자유 시장(自由市場)
chayu shijang gi-eop	free market industry	자유 시장 기업
chayueop-eui	freelance	자유업의
chayuhang	free port	자유항(自由港)
chayureui	autonomous	자율의
che ilch'a jeongnipkeum	primary reserves	제1차 적립금
chebunso indo	ex mill	제분소 인도
chech'ul	tender	제출
chedong-gi	brake	제동기
ch'eje	format	체제
che-eui-hada	offer (v)	제의하다
chegangso	steel mill	제강소
chehan jumun	limit order (stock market)	제한 주문
chehanjeok nodong gwanseup	restrictive labor practices	제한적 노동 관습(慣習)
chehyu	affiliation	제휴
chehyu-hada	affiliate (v)	제휴하다
che-i-ch'a jeodang	second mortgage	제이차 저당(抵當)
cheil useonju	first preferred stock	제일 우선주(第一優先株)
cheiseun johang	Jason clause	제이슨 조항(條項)
chejakso indo	ex mill	제작소 인도
chejo eopcha	manufacturer	제조 업자(업체)
chejo eopcha daerijeom	manufacturer's agent	제조 업자 대리점

chejo eopch'e dae-ri	manufacturer's representative	제조 업체 대리
chejo gwalli	manufacturing control	제조 관리
chejo (saengsan) neungnyeok	manufacturing capacity	제조(생산) 능력
chejo t'ongje	manufacturing control	제조 통제
chejojang	factory	제조장
chemok	title	제목
cheoch'uk	savings	저축
cheoch'uk eunhaeng	savings bank	저축 은행(貯蓄銀行)
cheoch'uk kongch'ae	savings bond	저축 공채(公債)
cheoch'uk kujwa	savings account	저축 구좌
cheoch'uk kyejeong	savings account	저축 계정
cheodang	pledge	저당
cheodang-e deureo itchi-aneun	free and clear (adj)	저당에 들어 있지 않은
cheog-oeseon p'illeum	infrared film	적외선 필름
cheo-gaebalguk	underdeveloped nations	저개발국(低開發國)
cheogeum	savings	저금
cheogyong doen su-ik kyohwan	applied proceeds swap	적용된 수익 교환
cheojakkweon	copyright	저작권
cheojang	storage	저장
cheojang-hada	hoard (v), store	저장하다
cheokcha hyeon-geum yuch'ul	negative cash flow	적자 현금 유출 (赤字現金流出)
cheokcha-eui	in-the-red	적자의
cheokha	stowage (cargo)	적하(積荷)
cheokha biyong	stowage charges	적하 비용(積荷費用)
cheokha mongnok	manifest	적하 목록
cheokja	deficit	적자(赤字)
cheokja jaejeong	deficit financing	적자 재정(赤字財政)
cheokja jaejeong sobi	deficit spending	적자 재정 소비
cheokjae-yul	deficit spending	적자 재정 소비
cheokjae-yul	burden rate	적재율
cheokkeuk p'anmae	hard sell	적극 판매
cheokkeukcheok p'anmae	sell, hard	적극적 판매
cheokpeop sudo	good delivery (securities)	적법 수도(適法受渡)
cheoksong	shipment	적송(積送)
cheoksongbi	shipping expenses	적송비(積送費)
cheolbakhan byeonhwa	impending changes	절박한 변화
cheolch'a	method	절차
cheolha-hada	undercut (v)	절하(切下)하다
cheollyakp'um	strategic articles	전략품
cheollyun gudong jeondong jangch'i	front-wheel drive	전륜 구동 전동 장치
cheomdu jangshik	window dressing (department store)	점두 장식(店頭裝飾)
cheomgeom-hada	service (v)	점검하다
cheomgeomp'yo	checklist	점검표
cheonnaek chibul	payment in full	전액 지불

cheonaek nabip-hada	pay up (v)	전액 납입하다
cheonbiyong-eul deuryeo	all in cost	전 비용을 들여
cheonbu insu hogeun bubun insu	all or none	전부 인수 혹은 부분 인수
cheonbu weonkka gyesan	absorption costing	전부 원가 계산 (全部原價計算)
cheonch'eol susongnyo	switching charges	전철 수송료(轉轍輸送料)
cheondae	sublet	전대(轉貸)
cheondong jangch'i	gearing	전동 장치(傳動裝置)
cheongbak (se)	anchorage (dues)	정박(세)
cheongbak kigan	laydays	정박 기간(碇泊期間)
cheongbak shigan	lay time	정박 시간
cheongbo ch'eori	throughput	정보 처리
cheongbo (charyo) gijeo	date base	정보(자료) 기저(基底)
cheongbo hoekteuk	data acquisition	정보 획득
cheongbo sujip	data acquisition	정보 수집
cheongbo yuhyohwa gwajeong	data processing	정보 유효화 과정
cheongbon	script	정본(正本)
cheongbu	government	정부
cheongbu dan-gi ch'aekkweon	treasury bills	정부 단기 채권
cheongbu eunhaeng	government bank	정부 은행
cheongbu gigwan	government agency	정부 기관
cheongch'al gagyeok	fixed price	정찰 가격(正札價格)
cheongdon sangt'ae	deadlock	정돈(停頓) 상태
cheong-geum	authenticity (gold)	정금(正金)
cheong-gi	fixed term	정기(定期)
cheong-gi boheom	term insurance	정기 보험
cheong-gi ch'aekkweon	term bond	정기 채권
cheong-gi daebugeum	fixture (on balance sheet)	정기 대부금(定期貸付金)
cheong-gi jeomgeom gyeyak	service contract	정기 점검 계약
cheon-gi jeondoseong gomu	electrically conductive rubber	전기 전도성 고무
cheon-gi myeondo-gi	electric shaver	전기 면도기
cheon-gi nanbang-gi	electric heater	전기 난방기
cheon-gi yeon-gyeol gigye	electric interlocking machine	전기 연결 기계
cheon-gi-ro	electric furnace	전기로(電氣爐)
cheongji-gigi	static apparatus	정지기기(靜止機器)
cheong-gi yegeum	time deposit	정기 예금
cheong-gi yegeum jeungseo	certificate of deposit	정기 예금 증서
cheong-gwan	by-laws	정관(定款)
cheong-gyu ch'ang-kko	regular warehouse	정규 창고
cheong-gyo seomsehan dojagiryu	fine ceramics	정교 섬세한 도자기류
cheong-gyo seomsehan junghapch'e	fine polymer	정교 섬세한 중합체
cheonjagi bohomul	electro-magnetic shielding	전자기 보호물
cheonghwa junbi	gold reserves	정화 준비

cheon-gi gonghak	electrical engineering	전기 공학
cheongje	tablet	정제
cheongjoksu	quorum	정족수
cheongkka	fixed price	정가(定價)
cheongkka maegigi	price fixing	정가 매기기
cheongmi gagyeok	net worth	정미(正味) 가격
cheongmil geomsa biyul	acid-test ratio	정밀 검사 비율
cheongmil josaja	scanner	정밀 조사자
cheongmil gigye jangch'i	precision machinery	정밀 기계 장치
cheongni t'onghap	consolidation	정리 통합
cheongnipkeum	reserve	적립금
cheongnyang	tonnage	적량
ch'eongnyeok baneung jangch'i	audio response equipment	청력 반응 장치
cheongnyugi	rectifier	정류기
cheonja akki	electronic musical instruments	전자 악기(樂器)
cheongsanp'yo	spreadsheet	정산표(精算表)
cheongt'onghan soshikt'ong	reliable source	정통한 소식통
cheonhwan sach'ae	convertible debentures	전환 사채(社債)
cheonhwan useonju	convertible preferred stock	전환 우선주(株)
cheonja geumjeon deungnok-ki	electronic cash register	전자 금전 등록기
cheonja gineung hoero	microchip	전자 기능 회로
cheonja gonghak	electronics	전자 공학
cheonja gyesan-gi	computer	전자 계산기
cheonja hyeonmigyeong	electron microscope	전자 현미경
cheonja jaebongt'eul	electronic sewing machine	전자 재봉틀
cheonja obeun	microwave oven	전자 오븐
cheonja oreugan	electronic organ	전자 오르간
cheonja t'ajagi	electronic typewriter	전자 타자기
cheonja t'aksang-yong gyesan-gi	electronic desk calculator	전자 탁상용 계산기
cheonjach'ong	electron gun	전자총
cheonjaseok	electromagnet	전자석
cheonjaseon	electron beam	전자선
cheonji	battery	전지
cheonmae t'eukheokkweon yuhyo gigan	life of a patent	전매 특허권 유효 기간
cheonmae t'eukheop'un	patent	전매 특허품
cheonmu	executive director	전무(專務)
cheonmunjik	profession	전문직
cheonmyeonjeog-euro	down the line (adv)	전면적으로
cheonmyeonjeog-in	down the line (adj)	전면적인
cheomyukkweon	occupation	점유권
cheon-gi t'ongshin	telecommunications	전기 통신
cheonmae	monopoly	전매(專賣)
cheonmun-ga	specialist (stock exchange)	전문가

cheonmunp'um	specialty goods	전문품
cheonmyeon gwanse hyeopsang	across-the-board tariff negotiations	전면 관세 협상
cheonmyeonjeogin gyeolsan	across-the-board settlement	전면적인 결산
cheonp'a t'amjigi	radar	전파 탐지기
cheonsan such'i jojong	computerized numerical control	전산 수치 조종
cheonse hwamul	truck load	전세 화물(傳貰貨物)
cheonseon	electric cable	전선(電線)
cheonshin hoeseon	teleprocessing	전신 회선
cheonshinhwan	cable transfer	전신환
cheonsongshik t'ongshinmun	telex	전송식 통신문
cheopch'ok	liaison	접촉
cheopch'ok	contact	접촉
cheopshi	dish, plate	접시
cheopsokki	connector	접속기
cheori daebu	low-interest loans	저리 대부(低利貸付)
cheori jeungkkweon	low-yield bonds	저리 증권(低利證券)
cheosodeuk	low-income	저소득
chep'um	product	제품(製品)
chep'um bunseok	product analysis	제품 분석
chep'um chaego mongnok	finished goods inventory	제품 재고 목록
chep'um gaebal	product development	제품 개발
chep'um gwalli	product management	제품 관리
chep'um gyeyeol	product group	제품 계열
chep'um hwallyeok	product dynamics	제품 활력
chep'um jongmok	product line	제품 종목
chep'um seolgye	product design	제품 설계
chep'um sumyeong	life cycle (of a product)	제품 수명(壽命)
chep'um-eui su-ikseong	product profitability	제품의 수익성
cheryun-gi	pallet	제륜기
cheryun-gi susong	palletized freight	제륜기 수송(輸送)
chesam ch'ang-gu	third window	제3 창구
chesam such'ulja	third party exporter	제3 수출자
cheso-hada	prosecute (v)	제소하다
cheukseok eungdap pangshik	real time	즉석 응답 방식
cheung-aek	increase	증액
cheungbun-doen hyeon-geum yuch'ul	incremental cash flow	증분된 현금 유출
cheungdae (cheung-ga)-hada	increase (v)	증대(증가)하다
cheung-ga biyong	incremental cost, increased costs	증가 비용
cheung-gayul	rate of increase, accession rate	증가율
cheung-geo seoryu	voucher	증거 서류
cheung-geo-geum-euroseo	on account (adv)	증거금으로서
cheung-in	witness	증인(證人)
cheungkkweon	stock certificate (securities)	증권
cheungkkweon eopcha	dealer, operator	증권 업자

cheungkkweon-eui jangbu gagyeok	book value per share	증권의 장부 가격
ch-eungkkweon georae	stock exchange	증권 거래
cheungkkweon gu-ip yuji buch'ae-yul	maintenance margin	증권 구입 유지 부채율
cheungkkweon hoejeonnyul	stock turnover	증권 회전율(回轉率)
cheungkkweon shijang	stock market	증권 시장
cheungkkweon shise p'yoshi	tick, price	증권 시세 표시
cheungkkweon yongji	policyholder	증권 용지
cheungkkweon sang-eui jabon	instrumental capital	증권상의 자본
cheungmyeongseo	attestation, certificate (securities)	증명서
cheungp'okki	amplifier	증폭기
cheungp'yo	voucher	증표(證票)
cheungseo	letter, deed, bill	증서
cheungshik chasan	assets accrued	증식 자산
cheungnyu	distillation	증류(蒸溜)
chibae-in	manager	지배인
chibae juju	controlling interest	지배 주주(支配株主)
chibang segwan	local customs	지방 세관
chibangse	local taxes	지방세
chibul	payment, payout period	지불
chibul(geum)	disbursement	지불(금)
chibul bujog-eui	underpaid(adj)	지불 부족의
chibul bulneung-eui	insolvent(adj)	지불 불능의
chibul ch'eong-gukkweon	claim	지불 청구권
chibul geojeol	payment refused	지불 거절
chibul gihan gyeong-gwa	past due	지불기한 경과
chibul gyejeong (chultton)	accounts payable	지불 계정(줄돈)
chibul jeongji	moratorium	지불 정지
chibul jungji-hada	suspend payment (v)	지불 중지하다
chibul myeongnyeongseo	bank draft	지불 명령서
chibul neungnyeok	solvency	지불 능력
chibul yangdo	across-the-board settlement	지불 양도
chibul yejeong ch'ong-aek	amount due	지불 예정 총액
chibul-eul geojeol-hada	refuse payment (v)	지불을 거절하다
chibul-eul shimhi dokch'ok-hada	dun (v)	지불을 심히 독촉하다
chibulgye	paymaster	지불계
chibul-hada	reimburse, pay (v)	지불하다
chibureul sohori-hada	default (v)	지불을 소홀히 하다
chiburin	payer, drawee	지불인
chicheok soyukkweon	intellectual property right	지적(知的) 소유권
chich'amin	bearer	지참인
chich'amin-bul	payable to bearer	지참인불(持參人拂)
chich'e-eui	overdue(adj)	지체의
chich'ul	expenditure	지출
chich'ul gigan	payout period	지출 기간

chidae	zone	지대(地帶)
chidoja	leader	지도자
chiyeon sup'yo	stale check	지연 수표(遲延手票)
chigeop	profession	직업
chigeop anjeong bojang	job security	직업 안정 보장
chigeop ch'atkki	job shop	직업 찾기
chigeopsang-eui wiheom	occupational hazard	직업상의 위험
chigeup	air express	지급
chigweon	staff	직원
chihwi (myeongnyeong) gyet'ong	chain of command	지휘(명령) 계통
chijeom	branch office	지점
chijeong doch'ak chijeom	named point of destination	지정 도착 지점 (指定到着支店)
chijeong seonjeokhang	named port of shipment	지정 선적항
chijeong such'ul jijeom	named point of exportation	지정 수출 지점
chijeong suiphang	named port of importation	지정 수입항
chijeong weonsan jijeom	named point of origin	지정 원산(原産) 지점
chijeong yu-eon jiphaengja	executor	지정 유언 집행자
chijeongkka	price limit	지정가(指定價)
chiju	landowner, equity	지주(支柱)
chiju biyul jeoha	dilution of equity	지주 비율 저하 (持株比率低下)
chiju hoesa	holding company	지주(持株) 회사
chiju t'uja	equity investments	지주 투자(持株投資)
chiju t'uja suingnyul	return on equity	지주 투자 수익율 (持株投資收益率)
chikchang	workplace/foreman	직장
chikchang hullyeon	on-the-job training	직장 훈련
chikcheop cheopch'ok ki-eok changch'i	direct access storage	직접 접촉 기억 장치
chipcheop hoero	chip	집적 회로
chikcheop hwan-eo-eum	direct paper	직접 환어음
chikcheop hwanweon gwajeong	direct reduction process	직접 환원 과정
chikcheop kajeong baedal gwang-go	direct mail	직접 가정 배달 광고
chikcheop kyeongbi(chic-h'ul)	direct expenses	직접 경비(지출)
chikcheop nodong	direct labor(accounting)	직접 노동
chikcheop p'anmae	direct selling	직접 판매
chikcheop piyong	direct cost	직접 비용
chikcheop-pi	direct cost	직접비
chikcheop shisep'yo	direct quotation	직접 시세표
chikcheop t'uja	direct investment	직접 투자
chikchong	job description	직종
chikeop sogaeso	employment agency	직업 소개소
chikkong	journeyman	직공(職工)
chikkye ganbu yeokweon	line executive	직계 간부 역원

Korean Romanization	English	Korean
chikkyeoldoeji aneun	off line	직결되지 않은
chikseon-eui	linear	직선(直線)의
chikshi jeokchae	prompt (n)	직시 적재(直時積載)
ch'il	paint	칠
chilbyeong hyuga	sick leave	질병 휴가
chilsan	nitric acid	질산
chilsan k'allyum	nitrate	질산 칼륨
chilso	nitrogen	질소
chim-eul burida	unload (v)	짐을 부리다
chimkkalgae	dunnage	짐깔개
chimsitkki	stowage	짐싣기
chimyeon boksa	hard copy	지면 복사
chimyeong-hada	instruct (v)	지명하다
chindo-wa jiyeon	leads and lags	진도와 지연
chindong	pulse	진동
chingmae-hada	sell direct	직매하다
chingmu	job	직무
chingmu bunseok	job analysis	직무 분석
chingmu bunseok kirok	job description	직무 분석 기록
chingmu p'yeongkka	job evaluation	직무 평가
chingmu suhaeng seongjeok	job performance	직무 수행 성적
chingmul	fabric, textile	직물
chingmullyu	dry goods, soft goods	직물류
chingnyeol gi-eok changch'i	serial storage	직렬 기억 장치 (直列記憶裝置)
chingnyugye	DC machine	직류계
chingsu	expropriation	징수(徵收)
chingsu gigan	collection period	징수 기간
chinhaejeong	cough drop	진해정(鎭咳錠)
chinhae shireop	cough syrup	진해 시럽
chinhaengjung-in jageop	work in progress	진행중인 작업
chinjeong	barbiturate	진정
chinjeongje	sedative	진정제
chinp'ok pyeonjo	amplitude modulation	진폭 변조
chipcheok hoero	integrated circuit	집적 회로
chipchunghwa	centralization	집중화
chiphaeng-hada	enforce (v)	집행하다
chipkwang renjeu	condenser lens	집광 렌즈
chiptan gyejeong	group accounts	집단 계정
chiptan hoegye	group accounts	집단 회계
chiptan yeokhak	group dynamics	집단 역학
chip'ye	paper	지폐
ch'iryo	remedies	치료
chise	land tax	지세(地稅)
chishi-hada	instruct (v)	지시하다
chishi-in-bul	payable to order	지시인불(指示人拂)
chisu	index(indicator)	지수(指數)
chisuhwa	indexing	지수화
chiweon hwalttong	support activities	지원 활동(支援活動)
chiwi-reul bakt'al-hada	supersede (v)	지위를 박탈(剝奪)하다
chiyeok	zone	지역(地域)

chiyeok kwalli-in	area manager	지역 관리인
chiyeon	delay (n)	지연
chiyeon p'yoshigi	lagging indicator	지연(遲延) 표시기
chodal	procurement	조달(調達)
chodal gigan	lead time	조달 기간
cho-eon-hada	advise (v)	조언하다
cho-eop kaeshi biyong	start-up cost	조업 개시 비용 (操業開始費用)
cho-eop-pi	running expenses	조업비(操業費)
ch'o gyeokcha	super lattice	초 격자
chokkeon mit shigi-daero	as if and when	조건 및 시기대로
chokkeonbu narin jeungseo	escrow	조건부 날인 증서 (條件附捺印證書)
chohang	item	조항
chohap	partnership	조합
chohap pup'yo	union label	조합 부표(符標)
chohoe beonho	reference number	조회 번호
choin	signature	조인(調印)
chojang	foreman	조장(組長)
chojehag-eui	pharmaceutical	조제학의
chojeol deungkka	accommodation parity	조절 등가
chojeol eokchech'aek	adjustable peg	조절 억제책
chojeol gangnyeong	accommodation platform	조절 강령
chojeol jedong-gi	adjustment trigger	조절 제동기
chojeong	mediation, regulation	조정(調整)
chojeong biyul	adjusted rate	조정 비율
chojeong gi-ip sahang	adjusting entry	조정 기입 사항
chojeong gwajeong	adjustment process	조정 과정
chojeong su-ip	adjusted earned income	조정 수입
chojeong-hada	adjust (v)	조정하다
chojik	organization	조직(組織)
chojik bunseok	systes analysis	조직 분석
chojik konghak	systems engineering	조직 공학
chojik kwalli	management, systems	조직 관리
chojong-gan	joystick	조종간(操縱葭)
chojongsul	pilotage	조종술
chokkeonbu ch'oehyeguk	most-favored nation	조건부 최혜국
chokkeonbu eo-eum insu	conditional acceptance	조건부 어음 인수
chokkeonbu insu baeseo	qualified acceptance endorsement	조건부 인수 배서(背書)
chokkeonbu maemae gyeyak	conditional sales contract	조건부 매매 계약
chokkeonbu weonjo	tied aid	조건부 원조
chokki	vest	조끼
chomdoduk	pilferage	좀도둑
chong moyang-eui gokseon	bell-shaped curve	종 모양의 곡선
chong-eobweon	employee	종업원
chong-gase	duty ad valorem	종가세(從價稅)
chong-gyeolshik'ida	terminate (v)	종결(終結)시키다
chonghap chisu	composite index	종합 지수(指數)

chonghap kwanse

chonghap kwanse	combination duty	종합 관세
chongjang-e	at the close	종장(終場)에
chongkka-e sada	buy on close (v)	종가(終價)에 사다
chongnyangse	specific duty	종량세(從量稅)
chongnyo-il	expiry date	종료일
chongshin hoeweon	life member	종신 회원
chop'yeguk	mint	조폐국
chorip	assembly	조립
chorip kongjang	assembly factory	조립 공장
(chorip kongjang-eui) ilgwanjageopseon	assembly line	(조립공장의) 일관작업선(一貫作業線)
chorip piyong	set-up costs	조립 비용
chorip-hada	assemble (v)	조립하다
chorip-p'um	assembly	조립품
choripshik kaok pup'umjejo	prefabrication	조립식 가옥 부품 제조
chosa	research	조사
chose	tax	조세(租稅)
chosokhan shi-ilnae-e	as soon as possible (shipment)	조속한 시일 내에
chosu	assistant	조수
choyak	treaty	조약
chubo	weekly return	주보(週報)
chuda	allow (v)	주다
chudang sodeuk	earnings per share	주당(株當) 소득
chudoju	market-maker (securities)	주도주(主導株)
chugan muyeok	interstate commerce	주간 무역(州間貿易)
chugi seonha jeungseo jakseong	cycle billing	주기 선하 증서 작성
chugijeogin	seasonal (adj)	주기적인
chugijeok chaegop'um mongnok	periodic inventory	주기적 재고품 목록
chuin	holder (negotiable instruments)	주인
chuip	injection	주입
chujae gumaeweon	resident buyer	주재 구매원
chuji	publicity	주지(周知)
chuju	stockholder	주주(株主)
(chuju) ch'onghoe	general meeting	(주주) 총회
chuju hoe-eui	shareholders' meeting	주주 회의
chuju-eui sunkka	stockholders' equity	주주의 순가(純價)
chukka jisu opsyeon	index option	주가 지수(株價指數) 옵션
chukka su-ik piyul	p/e ratio	주가 수익 비율 (株價收益比率)
chukka su-ingnyul	price-earnings ratio	주가 수익률
chukkap'ok	spread	주가폭(株價幅)
chukkweon	stock certificate	주권(株券)
chukkweon yangdo wi-imjjang	stock power	주권 양도 위임장
chum renjeu	zoom lens	줌 렌즈
chumun	order	주문(注文)

chumun beonho	order number	주문 번호
chumun jan-go	backlog	주문 잔고
chumun yangshik	order form	주문 양식(注文樣式)
chumun-hada	place an order (v)	주문하다
chun amgeorae shijang	gray market	준 암거래 시장
chunbi	make-ready	준비
chunbigeum	primary reserves	준비금
chun-byeondong biyong	semi-variable costs	준 변동 비용(準變動費用)
chung-ang eunhaeng	central bank	중앙 은행
chung-ang yeonsan ch'eori jangch'i	central processing unit (computers)	중앙 연산 처리 장치
chung-anghwa	centralization	중앙화
chungbok	overlap	중복
chung-gae	mediation	중개(仲介)
chung-gae georae	arbitrage	중개 거래
chung-gae jojeongja	intermediary	중개 조정자
chung-gae-in	export middleman	중개인
chung-gaejeom	commission (agency)	중개점
chung-gae (taeri) kkweon	commission (agency)	중개(대리)권
chung-gaeryo	commission (fee)	중개료
chung-gan gyeong-yeong gwalli	middle management	중간 경영 관리
chung-gan gyeong-yeong kwalli	management, middle	중간 경영 관리
chung-gansang	middleman	중간상
chung-gi	medium term	중기(中期)
chung-gong-eop	heavy industry	중공업
chunghapch'e	polymer	중합체
chungjae	arbitration	중재(仲裁)
chungjae hyeopcheong	arbitration agreement	중재 협정
chungjae-in	arbitrator	중재인
chungji shigan (taun t'aim)	down time	중지 시간 (다운 타임)
chungnyang	weight	중량(重量)
chun-gongmo hoesa	quasi-public company	준(準) 공모 회사(公募會社)
chung-wisu	median	중위수(中位數)
chung-yeok	executive	중역(重役)
chung-yeok kanbu imweon	executive board	중역 간부 임원
chuseollyo	address commission	주선료
chu-seont'aekkweon	stock option	주(株) 선택권
chushik	stock	주식
chushik baedang t'ongjiseo	allotment letter	주식 배당 통지서
chushik chabon	capital stock, capitalization	주식 자본
chushik chip'yo	stock index	주식 지표
chushik chung-gae-in (beurok'eo)	stockbroker	주식 중개인 (仲介人)(브로커)
chushik hoejeonnyul	stock turnover	주식 회전율
chushik hoesa	domestic corporation	주식 회사
chushik in-gye insu	stock takeover	주식 인계 인수
chushik iyun	stock profit	주식 이윤(株式利潤)

chushik keorae	stock exchange	주식 거래
chushik kong-gae hoesa	public company	주식 공개 회사
chushik kong-gae maeip che-eui	tender offer	주식 공개 매입 제의
chushik kongmo hoesa	public company	주식 공모 회사
chushik kongsa	joint stock company	주식 공사(株式公社)
chushik kuip	stock purchase	주식 구입(購入)
chushik kwalli	stock control	주식 관리
chushik maemae jeungseo	deed of transfer	주식 매매 증서
chushik maesu seont'aekkweon	call option	주식 매수 선택권
chushik myeongseseo	stock protfolio	주식 명세서
chushik punhal	stock split	주식 분할(分割)
chushik sangjang p'yoshi t'eip'eu	ticker tape	주식 상장 표시 테이프
chushik shijang	stock market	주식 시장
chushik t'ongje	stock control	주식 통제
(chushik-eui) ch'uryeok cheung-geogeum	margin call	(주식의) 추력 증거금(追力證據金)
chushik-eul gong-gae-hada	go public (v)	주식을 공개하다
chut'aek tamdang buseo	housing authority	주택 담당 부서
chut'aek yungja	mortgage	주택 융자
chut'aek yungja eunhaeng	mortgage bank	주택 융자 은행
chuyo gyeongno bunseok	critical path analysis	주요 경로 분석 (主要經路分析)
chuyo jip'yo	major statistics	주요 지표
chuyo shigan	prime time	주요 시간
chuyo shijang	primary market	주요 시장
chuyo such'ulp'um	key exports	주요 수출품
ch'a-aeg-i eomneun daech'a gyejeong	closed account (accounting)	차액이 없는 대차 계정
ch'a-aek	spread	차액
ch'abyeol gwanse	tariff differential	차별 관세
ch'abyeol imgeum	wage differential	차별 임금
ch'abyeol seyul	tariff differential	차별 세율
ch'abyeon	debit	차변(借邊)
ch'abyeon gi-ip	charges, debit entry	차변 기입(借邊記入)
ch'abyeonp'yo	debit note	차변표
ch'aegim	accountability, liability	책임
ch'aegim boheom	liability insurance	책임 보험
ch'aegim bundam	allocation of responsibilities	책임 분담
ch'aegim halttang	allocation of responsibilities	책임 할당
ch'aekkweon	bond	채권
ch'aekkweon amnyu t'ong-go	garnishment	채권 압류 통고
ch'aekkweon balhaeng	bond issue	채권 발행
ch'aekkweon balhaeng-go	outstanding stock	채권 발행고
ch'aekkweon cheungseo	indenture	채권 증서
ch'aekkweon deung-geup	bond rating	채권 등급

ch'aekkweon hyoryeok	bond power	채권 효력
ch'aekkweonja	creditor	채권자
ch'aemu	encumbrance (liens, liabilities, commitments)	채무(債務)
ch'aengmu	accountability	책무
ch'aesan bunseok	analysis, breakeven	채산 분석
ch'aesanjjeom	breakeven point	채산점(採算點)
ch'aeweo neonneun mulgeon	stuffing	채워 넣는 물건
ch'aeyong	placement (personnel)	채용
ch'agam biyul	balance ratios	차감 비율(差減比率)
ch'agi-ro i-weol-hada	carry forward (v)	차기로 이월하다
ch'agwan	loan	차관
ch'ajang	assistant manager	차장
ch'akpok	embezzlement	착복
ch'amga daebu	participation loan	참가 대부(參加貸付)
ch'amga useonju	participating preferred stock	참가 우선주(參加優先株)
ch'amgabi	participation fee	참가비
ch'amjo beonho	reference number	참조 번호
ch'ammo	staff	참모
ch'ammo jikkyeshik	staff and line	참모 직계식(參謀直系式)
ch'o jeondo hyeonsang	superconductive phenomena	초 전도 현상
ch'ongmae	catalyst	촉매
ch'ammo jojik	staff organization	참모 조직
ch'amseok shigan	attended time	참석 시간
ch'amyeongje	borrowing name system	차명제(借名制)
ch'angkko	warehouse, storage	창고
ch'angkko indo	ex warehouse	창고 인도
ch'aryang	rolling stock	차량(車輛)
ch'aryang handaebun hwamul	carload	차량 한대분 화물
ch'arye	table of contents	차례
ch'aweol	outstanding debt	차월(借越)
ch'ayong-hada	borrow (v)	차용(借用)하다
ch'ebul	arrears	체불(滯拂)
ch'egye bunseok	systems analysis	체계 분석
ch'egyeolshi	at the close	체결시
ch'ehwa	back haul	체화(滯貨)
ch'ejae	format	체재
ch'enap kyejeong	delinquent account	체납 계정
ch'eokto	yardstick	척도
ch'eolmul	hardware	철물
ch'eoltto jeoksong	rail shipment	철도 적송(積送)
ch'eombu seoryu	rider (contracts)	첨부 서류
ch'eongbu susong-eopcha	contract carrier	청부 수송 업자
ch'eongbu-il	piecework	청부일
ch'eong-gu	claim	청구
ch'eong-gubul	payable on demand	청구불
ch'eong-gu-e ttara	on demand (adv)	청구(請求)에 따라
ch'eong-gu-haneundaero	at call	청구하는 대로
ch'eong-guseo	bill	청구서

ch'eongsajin	blueprint	청사진
ch'eongsan	full settlement	청산
ch'eongsan gyejeong	open account	청산 계정
ch'eongsanhae-beorida (kyesan ttawi-reul) ch'eongsan-hada	pay up (v) adjust (v)	청산해 버리다 (계산 따위를) 청산하다
ch'eongsanhae-beorida	pay up (v)	청산해 버리다
ch'eonyeon jaweon	natural resources	천연 자원
ch'eoreom	as if and when	처럼
ch'eseonryo	demurrage	체선료(滯船料)
ch'eukcheong-hada	measure (v)	측정하다
ch'imch'e	down turn	침체
ch'ingho	title	칭호
ch'ip	chip	칩
ch'o-an	rough draft	초안(草案)
ch'oech'o man-gi	original maturity	최초 만기(滿期)
ch'oedaehan hwallyong-hada	maximize (v)	최대한 활용하다
ch'oedaeryang buha	peak load	최대량 부하(負荷)
ch'oego gagyeok	top price	최고 가격
ch'oego gyeong-yeong-ch'eung (jin)	top management	최고 경영층(진)
ch'oego gyeong-yeong-in	chief executive	최고 경영인
ch'oego hando	ceiling	최고 한도
ch'oego ipch'aljja	highest bidder	최고 입찰자
ch'oegojo gigan	prime time	최고조 기간
ch'oego jokkeon-euro	at best (adv)	최고 조건으로
ch'oego p'umjil	top quality	최고 품질
ch'oego yurihan gagyeok-e sada	buy at best (v)	최고 유리한 가격에 사다
ch'oejeo hoegye	marginal account	최저 회계
ch'oejeo imgeum	minimum wage	최저 임금
ch'oejong saengsanp'um	end product	최종 생산품
ch'oejong yongdo jeungmyeongseo	end-use certificate	최종 용도 증명서
ch'oeseonch'aek kyeoljjeong	brainstorming	최선책 결정
ch'oesohan junbi	minimum reserves	최소한 준비
ch'o-gi-ip	original entry	초기입(初記入)
ch'ogo	rough draft	초고(草稿)
ch'ogwa balhaeng	overdraft	초과 발행
ch'ogwa ch'eong-gu	surcharge	초과 청구
ch'ogwa geunmu	overtime	초과 근무
ch'ogwa gyeongbi	out-of-pocket expense	초과 경비(經費)
ch'ogwa jaego	overstock	초과 재고(在庫)
ch'ogwa jeongbak	demurrage	초과 정박
ch'ogwa p'anmae	oversold	초과 판매
ch'ojang gagyeok	opening price	초장 가격(初場價格)
ch'ojang-e sada	buy on opening (v)	초장(初場)에 사다
ch'okchin	promotion	촉진
ch'okchin johang	acceleration clause	촉진 조항
ch'ong gagyeok	gross price	총 가격
ch'ong gapch'a-i	gross spread	총 값 차이

ch'ong (wanjeon) gyeolsan	full settlement	총(완전) 결산
ch'ong i-ik	gross profit	총 이익
ch'ong jibae-in	general manager	총 지배인
ch'ong jungnyang	gross weight	총 중량
ch'ong maesang-go	gross sales	총 매상고
ch'ong p'a-eop	general strike	총 파업
ch'ong p'anmae su-ik	gross margin	총 판매수익
ch'ong sodeuk	gross income	총 소득
ch'ong sonshil	gross loss	총 손실
ch'ong su-ik	gross yield	총 수익
ch'ong t'uja	gross investment	총 투자
ch'ong-aek	amount	총액
ch'ong daerijeom	sole agent	총 대리점
ch'ong gong-geup	aggregate supply	총 공급
ch'ong-gye	amount	총계
ch'ong-gye geumaek	lump sum	총계 금액
ch'onghoe	plenary meeting	총회(總會)
ch'ong-i-ik	gross profit	총 이익
ch'ongjae	president	총재
ch'ong jibae-in bojwa-yeok	assistant general manager	총 지배인 보좌역
ch'ongmaesang-go	sales turnover	총매상고(總賣上高)
ch'ongp'ankkweon	franchise	총판권(總販權)
ch'ongsonshil	gross loss	총손실
ch'ong suyo	aggregate demand	총 수요
ch'ong wiheom	agregate risk	총 위험
ch'oshimja	apprentice	초심자
ch'uga (sahang)	addendum	추가(사항)
ch'uga johang	rider (contracts)	추가 조항
ch'uga jumun-hada	reorder (v)	추가 주문하다
ch'uga yogeum	surcharge	추가 요금
ch'ugu jumun	follow-up order	추구 주문(追求注文)
ch'ugyung	milling	축융(縮絨)
ch'ujeong jeonson	actual total loss	추정 전손(推定全損)
ch'ujeongnyang	guesstimate	추정량(推定量)
ch'ukcheok gamkka sang-gak	accrued depreciation	축적 감가 상각
ch'ukso	cutback	축소
ch'ukso boksayong p'illeum	microfilm	축소 복사용(縮小複寫用) 필름
ch'ulbal yejeong shigan	estimated time of departure	출발 예정 시간
ch'uljjeong myeongnyeong	garnishment	출정 명령
ch'ullyeok cheongbo jishi t'eip'eu	printout	출력 정보 지시 테이프
ch'ulsan hyuga	maternity leave	출산 휴가
ch'ulso gihanppeop	statute of limitations	출소 기한법
ch'ungbok	man (gal) Friday	충복(忠僕)
ch'ungdang-geum	allowance	충당금
ch'ungdong gumae	impulse buying	충동 구매
ch'ung-go-hada	advise (v)	충고하다
ch'use	trend	추세

ch'wideuk	acquisition	취득
ch'wideuk ch'eungmyeon	acquisition profile	취득 측면
ch'wideuk weonkka	original cost	취득 원가(取得原價)
ch'wideuk yun-gwak	acquisition profile	취득 윤곽
ch'wideuk-hada	acquire (v)	취득하다
ch'wieobil	work day	취업일(就業日)
ch'wi-hada	phase in (v)	취하다
ch'wiso ganeung shint'ak	revocable trust	취소 가능 신탁
ch'wiso-hada	cancel	취소하다

D

daeri eunhaeng	agency bank	대리 은행
daeri-in	attorney, power of	대리인
daeri-in (jeom)	agent	대리인(점)
daerijeom	agency	대리점
daerijeom susu-ryo	agency fee	대리점 수수료
dalleo biyong p'yeong-gyunhwa	dollar cost averaging	달러 비용 평균화
(nosa-eui) danch'e kyoseop	bargaining, collective	(노사의)단체 교섭
(chushik-eui) dan-gi t'uja jageum	gogo fund	(주식의)단기 투자 자금
daun t'aim	time, down	다운 타임
deit'eo	data	데이터
deit'eo baengk'eu	data bank	데이터 뱅크
deureup'ut'eu	throughput	드르풋트
dibeogeu-hada	debug (v)	디버그하다
dijel gigwan	diesel	디젤 기관
dijit'al	digital	디지탈
dijit'al (gyesuhyeong)gyesan-gi	digital computer	디지탈(계수형) 계산기
di-raem	D-RAM	디-램
diseuk'et	diskette	디스켓
diseuk'eu	disk	디스크
diseuk'eu deuraibeu	disk drive	디스크 드라이브
doneot-hyeong p'andok cheonyong gieok changch'i	EP-ROM	도넛형 판독 전용 기억 장치
dop'yo	graph	도표
doshik	graph	도식

E

_____e dap-ha-yeo	reply, in_____ to	_____에 답하여
_____e gwanhae jungshi-hada	regard (with regard to)	_____에 관해 중시하다
enjin	engine	엔진
enuri	price cutting	에누리
eo-an renjeu	fish-eye lens	어안 렌즈
e-eobaek	air bag	에어백
e-eo-k'on	air conditioner	에어콘
eo-eum	balloon note	어음

eo-eum balhaeng-in	drawer	어음 발행인
eo-eum (cheung-kkweon) chung-gae-in	bill broker	어음(증권) 중개인
eo-eum gyohwanso	clearinghouse	어음 교환소
eo-eum insu eopcha	acceptance house	어음 인수 업자
eo-eum jijeong-in	drawee	어음 지정인
eo-eum naeipkeum	partial payment	어음 내입금(內入金)
eo-eum-eui insu	acceptance	어음의 인수
eo-eumnyu	paper	어음류
eokchehagi	pegging	억제하기
eokkae shim	shoulder pad	어깨심
eollon	mass communications	언론
eommu daehaeng eunhaeng	agent bank	업무 대행 은행
eommu gwalli	operations management	업무 관리
eommu (chingmu) p'yeongkka	evaluation, job	업무(직무) 평가
eommuryang	workload	업무량
eopchong gyeong-yeong ganbu	line executive	업종 경영 간부
eop'yo	logo	어표
eoreum-t'ong	ice bucket	얼음통
eseuk'euro	escrow	에스크로
eseup'eureseu k'eop	espresso cup	에스프레스컵
euibok	dress	의복
euimu	liability	의무
euimu bulihaeng	nonfeasance	의무 불이행
euimu-eui i-haeng	accord and satisfaction	의무의 이행
euimu-ga inneun	liable to (adj)	의무가 있는
weon-geum	principal	원금(元金)
euimun	problem	의문
eui-oe-eui iyun	windfall profits	의외의 이윤
euiroe	recourse	의뢰(依賴)
euiryu	apparel	의류
euisa	physician	의사
euisa iljeong	agenda	의사 일정
euisa jinhaeng-e gwanhankkeon	point of order	의사 진행에 관한 건
eumban suipcha	importer of record	음반 수입자
eumhyang yeon-gyeolgi	acoustic coupler	음향 연결기
eumseong imnyeok chaktong-eui	voice-activated	음성 입력 작동 (音聲入力作動)의
eumshik sutkkarak	serving spoon	음식 숟가락
eun-geunhan sangsul	soft sell	은근한 상술(商術)
eun-geup	pension fund	은급(銀給)
eun geureuseui	silverplate (adj)	은 그릇의
eungmo (shinip) ch'ogwa-eui	oversubscribed (adj)	응모(신입) 초과의
eunhaeng	bank	은행
eunhaeng bojeung eo-eum	bank acceptance	은행 보증 어음
eunhaeng bugwageum	bank charges	은행 부과금
eunhaeng daebu	bank loan	은행 대부
eunhaeng gamdokkwan	bank examiner	은행 감독관
eunhaeng harinnyul	bank rate	은행 할인율
eunhaeng heogajjeung	bank carnet	은행 허가증

eunhaeng hwan-eo-eum	bank draft	은행 환어음
eunhaeng hwanjeon	bank exchange	은행 환전
eunhaeng hyumu	bank holiday	은행 휴무
eunhaeng jan-go	bank balance	은행 잔고
eunhaeng myeongseseo (bogoseo)	bank statement	은행 명세서(보고서)
eunhaeng shinyongjjang	bank letter of credit	은행 신용장
eunhaeng sup'yo	bank check	은행 수표
eunhaeng yangdo jeungseo	bank release	은행 양도 증서
eunhaeng yegeum	bank deposit	은행 예금
eunhaeng-gan-eui	interbank	은행간의
eunhaenghwan	bank money order	은행환
eunhaenghwan (shise)	bank exchange	은행환(시세)
eunhaengkkweon	bank note	은행권
eunik chasan	hidden assets	은익 자산(隱匿資産)
eunt'oe	retirement	은퇴
(hoegye-reul) gamsa-hada	audit (v)	(회계를) 감사하다
ch'abyeonp'yo, maemae hwanp'yo	debit note	차변표, 매매환표
(taech'a daejop'yo jung-eui) geoch'i jasan	deferred assets	(대차 대조표중의) 거치 자산(据置資産)

G

gyeong-yeong dayanghwa (dagakhwa)	diversification	경영 다양화(多樣化) (다각화-多角化)
gwalli hoegye	accounting, management	관리 회계
(shinju halttang-eui) gweollirak	ex rights	(신주 할당-新株割當-의) 권리락(權利落)
(maemae) gyeyak	bargain	(매매)계약

H

habeui	agreement	합의
habeuiseo	written agreement	합의서
habu jojik	infrastructure	하부 조직
hach'eong gyeyak	subcontract	하청 계약(下請契約)
hach'eong-eopcha	subcontractor	하청 업자
hach'eong-in	subcontractor	하청인
hadae	pallet	하대
haego hyujik kigan	lay-off	해고 휴직 기간
haego-hada	fire (v)	해고(解雇)하다
haegyeol	resolution (legal document)	해결
haeje	exemption	해제
haejik sudang	severance pay	해직 수당
haek	nuclear	핵
haek sach'al	nuclear inspection	핵 사찰

haek shiseol	nuclear facility	핵 시설
haenan gujobi	salvage charges	해난 구조비(海難救助費)
haenan gujop'um gagyeok	salvage value	해난 구조품 가격
haendeubaek	handbag	핸드백
haeng	line	행
haengdong (hwalttong) eokche	disincentive	행동(활동) 억제(抑制)
haengjeong josa	executive search	행정 조사
haengjeong-gigwan	administration	행정 기관
haeng-wi	deed	행위
hae-oe hoesa	offshore company	해외 회사
hae-oe min-gan t'uja gongsa	overseas private investment corporation	해외 민간 투자 공사
hae-oe muyeok	foreign trade	해외 무역
haeri	knot (nautical)	해리(海里)
haesang boheom eopcha	marine underwriter	해상 보험 업자
haesang hwamul boheom	marine cargo insurance	해상 화물 보험
haeseok	analysis	해석
haeso t'eukkweon	put option	해소 특권(解消特權)
haeson	average	해손(海損)
haeun gyeyak	maritime contract	해운 계약
hagang	down swing	하강(下降)
haibeurideu jeonja gyesan-gi	hybrid computer	하이브리드 전자 계산기
haje	purgative	하제(下劑)
haju	shipper	하주(荷主)
hakseup kokseon	learning curve	학습 곡선
halttang	allotment	할당
halttang-aek	quota	할당액
halttang-hada	allot (v), assign	할당하다
halttangje	quota system	할당제
hamch'uk	implication	함축
hammyeong hoesa	general partnership	합명 회사
hamnihwa-hada	streamline (v)	합리화하다
hamnyu-ryang	content	함유량
hamu-reul yangnyuk-hada	discharge (v)	하물(荷物)을 양륙(揚陸)하다
han t'eureok miman jeokchae hwamul	less-than-truckload	한 트럭 미만 적재 화물
hanbeol	lot	한 벌
hang-eui t'oejang	walkout	항의 퇴장
hang-gong hwamul	air freight	항공 화물
hang-gong jeokha	air shipments	항공 적하
hang-gong sajin k'amera	aerial photographic camera	항공 사진 카메라
hang-gong soktal	air express	항공 속달
hang hyeorap kanghaje	anticholinergic	항 혈압 강하제
hangmokpyeol-lo gijang-hada	itemize	항목별로 기장(記帳)하다
hangse	harbor dues	항세(港稅)
hang yeomjjeung-eui	anti-inflammatory (adj)	항 염증의
hangsaeng-eui	antibiotic	항생의
han-gye biyong	marginal cost	한계(限界) 비용
han-gye gagyeok	marginal pricing	한계 가격

han-gye gyejeong	marginal account	한계 계정
han-gye saengsannyeok	marginal productivity	한계 생산력
han-gye suip	marginal revenue	한계 수입(收入)
hapcha hoesa	limited partnership	합자 회사(合資會社)
hapchak hoesa	joint venture	합작 회사
hapkeum	alloy	합금(合金)
hapkeumch'eol	ferroalloys	합금철
hapkeumgang	alloy steel	합금강(合金鋼)
hapkye	footing (accounting)	합계
hapkyeok p'anjeong shi-heom	acceptance test	합격 판정 시험
hapkyeok p'umjil su-jun	acceptable quality level	합격 품질 수준
happyeong	consolidation	합병(合倂)
hapseongmul	compounds	합성물
hapseong suedeu	synthetic suede	합성 수에드
hapseong-eui	synthetic (adj)	합성의
hap-tong	amalgamation	합동
harakse	bear market	하락세
harin	discounting	할인
harin yukka jeungkkweon	discount securities	할인 유가 증권
harinaek	discount	할인액
harinnyul	discount rate	할인율
hasuin	consignee	하수인(荷受人)
heoga	permit	허가
heogadoen hwamul	freight allowed	허가된 화물
heoga-hada	authorize (v)	허가하다
heoyong-hada	allow	허용하다
heukpaek p'illeum	black and white film	흑백 필름
hoegyekkwa	accounting department	회계과
hoesu gigan	payback period	회수(回收) 기간
heukcha	favorable balance	흑자
heukcha hyeon-geum yuch'ul	positive cash flow	흑자 현금 유출
(sang-eop) heungshinso	credit bureau	(상업) 홍신소
heungbunje	stimulant	홍분제
heyon-geum p'anmae	cash-and-carry	현금 판매
hobaktan	taffeta	호박단(琥珀緞)
hobyeol bangmun p'anmae	door-to-door (sales)	호별 방문 판매
hoebok	repossession	회복(回復)
hoedam	interview	회담
hoedap-hada	reply (v)	회답하다
hoe-eui	meeting	회의
hoe-euishil	conference room	회의실
hoegwi bunseok	regression analysis	회귀 분석(回歸分析)
hoegye bangbeop	accounting method	회계 방법
hoegye bi-yul	accounting ratio	회계 비율
hoegye gamsagwan	auditor, comptroller	회계 감사관
hoegye gigan	financial period	회계 기간
hoegye jeonp'yo	check	회계 전표
hoegye juim	chief accountant	회계 주임
hoegye nyeondo	fiscal year	회계 년도
hoegye juim	paymaster	회계 주임
hoegyeon	interview	회견

hoegyesa	accountant	회계사
hoejang	president	회장
hoejeon gigeum	revolving fund	회전 기금
hoejeon sokto	tachometer	회전 속도
hoekchi	lot	획지(劃地)
hoengnyeong	enbezzlement	횡령
hoep'i ganeung biyong	avoidable costs	회피 가능 비용
hoep'i-hada	go around	회피하다
hoeram	memorandum	회람(回覽)
hoesa	company	회사
hoesa ch'aekkweon	treasury bonds	회사 채권
hoesa ch'aryang boheom ga-ip jeungseo	fleet policy	회사 차량 보험 가입 증서
hoesa insu shinch'eong	takeover bid	회사 인수 신청
hoesa jeongch'aek	company policy	회사 정책
hoesa mokp'yo	company goal	회사 목표
hoesa seongjang	growth, corporate	회사 성장
hoesaweon	member of firm	회사원
hoesu	recovery (acct. receivable)	회수(回收)
hoesu biyong	salvage charges	회수 비용(回收費用)
hoesu gach'i	salvage value	회수 가치(回收假値)
hoesu-hada	salvage (v)	회수(回收)하다
hoeweonsa	member firm	회원사(會員社)
hohwang	boom	호황
hohye yeonsu	reciprocal training	호혜 연수(互惠研修)
hojeon	upturn	호전
hongbo	public relations	홍보
honhap muljjil	composite materials	혼합 물질
honhap piyong	mixed cost	혼합 비용
honhaptoen geyonbon jeokch'ul	mixed sampling	혼합된 견본 적출
honseong muljjil	hybrid materials	혼성 물질
horeumon	hormone	호르몬
hubul-hada	afterdate (v)	후불하다
huch'u jebun-gi	pepper mill	후추 제분기
huch'ut karu-t'ong	pepper shaker	후춧가루통
hu-ip seonch'ulbeop	last in-first out	후입 선출법(後入先出法)
hullyeon jiptan (tanch'e)	group, training	훈련 집단(단체)
hullyeonsaeng	trainee	훈련생
hushing-yong geureut	dessert plate	후식용(後食用) 그릇
husunwi dong-eopcha	junior partner	후순위 동업자
husunwi yukka jeungkkweon	junior security	후순위 유가 증권
huweonja	sponsor (of fund, partnership)	후원자
hwach'ado	free on rail	화차도(貨車渡)
hwahak chep'um	chemical	화학 제품
hwahak piryo	chemical fertilizer	화학 비료
hwakcheong buch'ae	fixed charges	확정 부채(確定負債)
hwakcheong ch'aegullyo	dead rent	확정 채굴료(確定採掘料)
hwakcheong jokkeon	fixed term	확정 조건(確定條件)

hwakshilhan	valid (adj)	확실한
hwakttae-hada	enlarge (v)	확대하다
hwakttae	blowup	확대
hwaljja	font	활자
hwalp'an inswaegi	letterpress	활판 인쇄기
hwalttong do-p'yo	activity chart	활동 도표
hwalttong gyehoek	action plan	활동 계획
hwalttong jungji	moratorium	활동 중지
hwalttong yeon-gu	action research	활동 연구
hwamul	freight	화물
hwamul indo t'ongjiseo	delivery notice	화물 인도 통지서
hwamul inhwanjjeung	waybill	화물 인환증(引換證)
hwamul jeokha	bale cargo	화물 적하(貨物積荷)
hwamul (unim) p'oham	freight included	화물(운임) 포함
hwamul suyongnyang	bale capacity	화물 수용량
hwamul unsong	freight	화물 운송
hwamul yangnyukpi	landing charges	화물 양륙비(揚陸費)
hwamulch'a	flat car	화물차(貨物車)
hwanbu	feedback	환부(還付)
hwanbul	rebate	환불
hwanbul ija gyesan	factoring	환불 이자 계산
hwanbulse	drawback	환불세(還拂稅)
hwan-eoeum	bill of exchange	환어음
hwan-eoeum-eui hwagin	confirmation of order	환어음의 확인
hwangsan	sulfuric acid	황산
hwangsanyeom	sulfate	황산염
hwan-harin	exchange discount	환할인(換割引)
hwankka ganeung jeungkkweon	marketable securities	환가 가능 증권 (換價可能證券)
hwan-p'yeongkka	par value	환 평가
hwanse jeungmyeongseo	debentures	환세 증명서(還稅證明書)
hwan-shise	exchange rate	환시세(換時勢)
hwan-sonsil	exchange loss	환손실(換損失)
hwan-t'uja	divestment	환투자(換投資)
hwanweonppeop	reduction	환원법
hwan-wiheom	exchange risk	환위험(換危險)
hwap'ye	currency	화폐
hwap'ye (t'onghwa) baendeu	currency band	화폐(통화) 밴드
hwap'ye ch'ahwan	currency conversion	화폐 차환(借換)
hwap'ye gyohwan	currency exchange	화폐 교환
hwap'ye johang	currency clause	화폐 조항
hwap'ye jung-gae-in	money broker	화폐 중개인
hwap'ye shinyong	monetary credits	화폐 신용
hwap'yesang	money shop	화폐상
hwasalp'yo-eui hwalttong	activity on arrow	화살표의 활동
hwiballyu	gasoline	휘발류
hwiballyu gong-geup palp'an, p'aedal	gas pedal	휘발류 공급 발판, 패달
hwiballyu t'ong	gasoline tank	휘발류 통
hwibalseong shihwang	volatile market	휘발성 시황(市況)
hyeobeop hyeopcheong	cooperation agreement	협업 협정(協業協定)

hyeokshin	innovation	혁신
hyeoktae	belt	혁대
hyeolch'eong	serum	혈청
hyeonch'al	cash	현찰
hyeonch'al kwalli	cash management	현찰 관리
hyeondae	modern	현대
hyeong	format	형(型)
hyeon-geum	cash	현금
hyeon-geum ch'ulnappu	cash book	현금 출납부
hyeon-geum gijang	cash entry	현금 기장(記帳)
hyeong gieok hapkeum	shape-memory alloy	형(型) 기억 합금
hyeon-geum gijun	cash basis	현금 기준
hyeon-geum gwallija	money manager	현금 관리자
hyeon-geum harin	cash discount	현금 할인
hyeon-geum i-ik paedang	cash dividend	현금 이익 배당
hyeon-geum indo	cash delivery	현금 인도
hyeon-geum jagukseon susongju-eui	cash-and-carry	현금 자국선 수송 주의
hyeon-geum jan-go	cash balance	현금 잔고
hyeon-geum jeukshibul	ready cash	현금 즉시불
hyeon-geum ju-eui weonch'ik	cash basis	현금 주의 원칙
hyeon-geum jungdo haeyak hwan-geupkeum	cash surrender value	현금 중도 해약 환급금(還給金)
hyeon-geum suji harin	discounted cash flow	현금 수지(收支) 할인
hyeon-geum yesan	cash budget	현금 예산
hyeon-geum yuch'urip	cash flow	현금 유출입(流出入)
hyeon-geum yuch'urip myeongseseo	cash flow statement	현금 유출입 명세서
hyeon-geum yuip	positive cash flow	현금 유입(現金流入)
hyeon-geumbul	payment in kind	현금불
hyeon-geumbul jueui	pay as you go	현금불 주의
hyeongp'yeong gagyeok	accommodation parity	형평 가격
hyeongse	outlook	형세
hyeonhaeng biyul	current ratio	현행 비율
hyeonhaeng sanch'ulgo	current yield	현행 산출고
hyeonhaeng yoyul	going rate (or price)	현행 요율
hyeonjang indo	ex works	현장 인도
hyeonjang indo	spot delivery	현장 인도
hyeonji nongsanmul	native produce	현지 농산물
hyeonmul shijang	spot market	현물 시장
hyeonsangt'ae mulp'um	as is goods	현상태 물품
hyeonsujun hogeun geu-isang	at or better	현수준 혹은 그 이상
hyeopcheong	agreement	협정
hyeopcheong-gwa (pij-eui) byeonje	accord and satisfaction	협정과 (빚의) 변제
hyeophoe	consortium	협회
hyeoppak	duress	협박
hyeopsang	negotiation	협상
hyeopsang ganeung-han	negotiable	협상 가능한
hyeopsang-hada	negotiate (v)	협상하다

hyeoptong gwang-go	cooperative advertising	협동 광고
hyeoptong johap	cooperative	협동 조합
hyeoraek	blood	혈액
hyoso	enzyme	효소(酵素)
hyoyong	utility	효용(效用)
hyoyul	efficiency	효율
hyudaep'um	accompanied goods	휴대품
hyudae-yong diseuk'eu yeonju jangch'i	compact disc player	휴대용 디스크 연주 장치
hyudae-yong jeonhwagi	mobile phone	휴대용 전화기
hyudae-yong t'erebi	portable TV	휴대용 테레비
hyuga	leave of absence	휴가
hyuge shigan	coffee break	휴게 시간
hyuhang	lay up	휴항(休航)
hyushik shigan	coffee break	휴식 시간

I

ich'a shijang	fringe market	이차(二次) 시장
idong deungkka	moving parity	이동 등가(移動等價)
idong p'yeong-gyunppeop	moving average	이동 평균법
iril daech'ul	day loan	일일 대출(貸出)
ieo batta	takeover	이어 받다
ieui-reul jegi-hada	protest (banking, law) (v)	이의(異議)를 제기(提起)하다
ieummae eomneun gangch'eolgwan	seamless steel tube	이음매 없는 강철관
igeuk chin-gong-gwan	diode	이극 전공관
ihae sangban (ch'ungdol)	conflict of interest	이해 상반(충돌)
i-ik	perks	이익
i-ik ch'wideuk	profit-taking	이익 취득
i-ik keorae	arms length	이익 거래
i-ik paedang	bonus (premium)	이익 배당
i-ik bunbae	profit sharing, pay off	이익 분배(分配)
i-ik p'yeonseung georae	pyramiding	이익 편승 거래
i-ikkeum	profit	이익금
i-in seomyeong eo-eum	two-name paper	2인 서명 어음
i-injeom	duopoly	이인점(二人占)
ija	interest	이자
ija biyong	interest expenses	이자 비용
ija gigan	interest period	이자 기간
ija jaejeong	interest arbitrage	이자 재정(利子裁定)
ija p'yeonghyeong (p'yeongkka)	interest parity	이자 평형(평가)
ija sodeuk	interest income	이자 소득
ijayul	rate of interest	이자율
ijayul-eul gojeong-hada	lock in (rate of interest) (v)	이자율을 고정하다
ijeon	transfer	이전(移轉)
ijeonbi	moving expenses	이전비
ijik	separation	이직(離職)

ijinppeop	binary notation	2진법
ijung gagyeok	double pricing	이중 가격
ijung georae	double dealing	이중 거래
ijung gwase	double taxation	이중 과세(課稅)
ijung shigan	double time	이중 시간
ikkweon	interest	이권
ikkweonbu ch'aekkweon	coupon (bond interest)	이권부(利權付) 채권
ilbag-eui	overnight (adj)	일박(一泊)의
ilban ch'uga johang	codicil	일반 추가 조항
ilban muyeok kwanse hyeopcheong	GATT	일반 무역 관세 협정
ilban saweon	junior partner	일반 사원
ilban shijang	open market	일반 시장
ilban unsong eopcha (hoesa)	common carrier	일반 운송 업자(회사)
ilgwal ch'eo-ri	batch processing	일괄 처리
ilgwal ch'wigeup (georae)	deal, package	일괄 취급(거래)
ilgwal dogeup pangshik	turnkey	일괄 도급 방식
ilgwal georae	package deal	일괄(一括) 거래
ilgwal saengsan	batch production	일괄 생산
ilgwan jageop	production line	일관 작업(一貫作業)
ilhoebun	dose	1회분
iljjeong	order of the day	일정(日程)
iljudang	per share	일주당(一株當)
illambul	at sight	일람불(一覽拂)
illambul eo-eum	sight draft	일람불(一覽拂) 어음
illamp'yo	schedule	일람표
illyang	load, work	일량
illyeok	manpower	인력
illyeok chaweon	human resources	인력 자원
ilnyeonmada-eui	annual	1년마다의
ilp'eni jushik	penny stock	1페니 주식
ilsang samu	routine	일상 사무(日常事務)
ilshi ch'a-ipkeum	floating debt	일시 차입금
ilshibul	lump sum	일시불
ilshihaego	lay-off	일시 해고
ilt'eo	workshop	일터
ilttang	per diem	일당(日當)
imch'ain	lessee	임차인(賃借人)
imdae	rent	임대
imdaech'a gyeyak	lease	임대차 계약(賃貸借契約)
imdae-hada	lease (v)	임대(賃貸)하다
imdaehan bumun	leased department	임대한 부문
imdaein	lessor	임대인(賃貸人)
imeui chumun	discretionary order	임의 주문
(chushig-eui) imeui chumun	discretionary account	(주식의) 임의 주문 (任意注文)
imeui-eui	optional	임의의
imgeum	wage	임금(賃金)
imgeum budam	payload	임금 부담
imgeum bunjaeng	wage dispute	임금 분쟁
imgeum dong-gyeol	wage freeze	임금 동결(凍結)

Korean (romanized)	English	Korean
imgeum (keubyeo) gujo	wage structure	임금(급여) 구조
imgeum gyeokch'a	wage differential	임금 격차(格差)
imgeum mit mulkka-eui aksunhwan	wage-price spiral	임금 및 물가의 악순환(惡循環)
imgeum saenghwalja	wage earner	임금 생활자
imgeum seuk'eil	wage scale	임금 스케일
imgeum sujun	wage level	임금 수준
imgeum yudong	wage drift	임금 유동(流動)
imgeump'ok	wage scale	임금폭
immyeong	appointment	임명
imnyeok	input	입력
imshi buch'ae	contingent liability	임시 부채(臨時負債)
imshi gigeum	contingent fund	임시 기금
imshi gyesanseo	interim statement	임시 계산서
imshi yangnyuk shin-goseo	bill of sight	임시 양륙 신고서
imshi yesan	interim budget	임시 예산
imshibi	incidental expenses	임시비
imshi byeont'ong sudan	makeshift	임시 변통 수단
inbeo-eot'eo	inverter	인버어터
inbu	laborer	인부(人夫)
inch'e gonghak	ergonomics	인체 공학(人體工學)
indo	delivery	인도(引渡)
indo gagyeok	delivery price	인도 가격
indo-hada	abandon (v)	인도(引渡)하다
indojeon hyeonch'al jibul	cash before delivery	인도전 현찰 지불
indop'um bujok	short delivery	인도품 부족(引渡品不足)
in-ga	approval	인가
in-gong dunoe	artificial intelligence	인공 두뇌
inhwa	printing	인화
injo gyeonsa	rayon	인조 견사
immyeong	appointment	임명
in-ga-doen yangdo shiseol	approved delivery facility	인가된 양도 시설
in-ga-hada	approve (v)	인가하다
in-gajjang	investment letter	인가장
in-gaseo	license	인가서
ingmyeong saweon	silent partner	익명 사원(匿名社員)
in-gu t'ong-gyehaksang-eui	demographic (adj)	인구 통계 학상의
ing-yeo jabon	surplus capital	잉여 자본(剩餘資本)
ing-yeo sangp'um	surplus goods	잉여 상품
ing-yeop'um	surplus goods	잉여품
inha	abatement	인하(引下)
inhwankkweon	rain check	인환권(引換券)
inja (yoin) bunseok	factor analysis	인자(因子), 요인(要因), 분석(分析)
injae seonbal damdangja	headhunter	인재 선발 담당자
injo-eui	synthetic (adj)	인조의
injo seomyu	manmade fibers	인조 섬유
inki-inneun jushik	leader	인기있는 주식
inp'eure	inflation	인프레
inp'eureseong	inflationary (adj)	인프레싱

insa gwalli	personnel management	인사 관리
insa haengjeong	personnel administration	인사 행정
insa kwalli	management, personnel	인사 관리
insakkwa	personnel department	인사과
inshi	man hours	인시(人時)
insu	guarantee	인수
insu ch'aegimaek	assumed liability	인수 책임액
insu ch'aemu	liability, assumed	인수 채무(引受債務)
insu eo-eum	acceptance bill	인수 어음
insu eopcha	underwriter	인수 업자
insu gagyeok	delivered price	인수(引受) 가격
insu geojeol	dishonor (as a check)	인수 거절
insu gyeonbon ch'uch'ul	acceptance sampling	인수 견본 추출(抽出)
insu seung-nak	acceptance agreement	인수 승낙
insu shinyong	acceptance credit	인수 신용
insu-hada	takeover	인수(引受)하다
(eo-eum-eul) insu-hada	accept (v)	(어음을) 인수하다
insu-in	acceptor	인수인(引受人)
insuja	acceptance house	인수자
insu-reul geojeol-hada	refuse acceptance (v)	인수를 거절하다
inswaegi	printer	인쇄기
inswae	printout	인쇄
inswaemul	printed matter	인쇄물
insyullin	insulin	인슐린
inyoje	diuretic	이뇨제
ipch'al	bid (takeover)	입찰
ipch'al gweonyu (ch'odae)	invitation to bid	입찰(入札) 권유(초대)
ipch'al mit ch'eong-gu	bid and asked	입찰 및 청구
ipch'al shinch'eong	request for bid	입찰 신청
ipch'al-e buch'ida	put in a bid (v)	입찰에 붙이다
ipch'e eumhyang jangch'i-eui	stereophonic (adj)	입체 음향 장치의
ipha mit seonjeokchi	at and from	입하 및 선적지
(cheungkkweon georaeso-eui) iphoejang	board room	(증권 거래소의) 입회장
iphoejang	floor (of exchange)	입회장(立會場)
ipkeum sup'yo	cancelled check	입금 수표
ipsagak	angle of incidence	입사각(入射角)
ipsu kaneung-hada	make available (v)	입수 가능하다
ipsuhu baedal	pick up and delivery	입수 후 배달
ireumsun-euro nayeoldoeji aneun	not otherwise indexed by name	이름 순으로 나열되지 않은
iril daebu	day loan	일일 대부(貸付)
iril suju	day order (stock market)	일일 수주(受注)
irindang	per capita	일인당
iryeok (seo)	curriculum vitae	이력(서)
iryeokseo	resume	이력서
iryongp'um	commodity	일용품
isa	director	이사(理事)
isa hoe-eui	board meeting	이사 회의
isabi	moving expense	이사비

isahoe	board of directors	이사회
isa hoe-euishil	board room	이사 회의실
i-sahoe hoejang	chairman of the board	이사회 회장
isajang	chairman of the board	이사장
isanhwa t'anso reijeo	carbon dioxide laser	이산화탄소 레이저
iweol	carryover	이월(移越)
iweol jan-go	opening balance	이월 잔고(移越殘高)
iweolgeum	carryover	이월금
iyong ganeung jokkeonha-e	subject to availability	이용 가능 조건하에
iyong neungnyeok	capacity, utilization	이용 능력
iyongse	use tax	이용세
iyul	yield	이율
iyun	profit	이윤
iyun biyul	percentage of profit	이윤 비율
iyun hyokkwa	profit impact	이윤 효과
iyun ma-ajin	profit margin	이윤 마아진
iyun-nyul	rate of return	이윤율
iyun yech'euk	profit projection	이윤 예측(豫測)
iyun yoso	profit factor	이윤 요소
iyunp'ok	profit margin	이윤폭

J

jageopcho gwalli	team management	작업조 관리
jangshing-yong bach'im	place mat	장식용 받침
(kumaeryeog-i) jeohahan	cheap (adj)	(구매력이) 저하한
(yakso-gi p'agidoen) jeokharyo	broken stowage	(약속이 파기된) 적하료
(muyeogeopcha-eui) jeongwich'i	net position (of a trader)	(무역 업자의) 정위치(正位置)
jeungjin	promotion	증진
jibul yujagyeok kae-nyeom	ability-pay concept	지불 유자격 개념
jich'im	guidelines	지침(指針)
(chaesan-eui) jijeong	appointment	(재산의) 지정
jjalbeun somae	short sleeves	짧은 소매
(ch'uljja) johabweon	partner	(출자) 조합원
(eunhaeng-eui) junbigeum han-gyeseon	deadlin	(은행의) 준비금 한계선

K

kabyeon p'anmae suik (majin)	variable margin	가변 판매 수익(마진)
kabyeon suip kwase	variable import levy	가변 수입 과세 (可變輸入課稅)
kabyeon yeon-geum	variable annuity	가변 연금(可變年金)
kabyeon-nyul	variable rate	가변율
kach'eobun sodeuk	disposable income	가처분 소득(假處分所得)
kach'i	value	가치
kach'i eomneun	worthless (adj)	가치없는

kach'i gonghak	value engineering	가치 공학
kach'i jeogam	depreciation	가치 저감(價値低減)
kach'i jeung-ga	appreciation	가치 증가
kadong jangbi	working tools	가동 장비(稼動裝備)
kadong jungji shigan	downtime	가동 중지 시간
kaebangjeok kongjang	open shop	개방적 공장
kaehyeok	reform	개혁(改革)
kaein baech'i	private placement (finance)	개인 배치
kaein euimu	personal liability	개인 의무
kaein gongje	personal deduction	개인 공제(控除)
kaein sangp'yo	private label (or brand)	개인 상표
kaein seondan	private fleet	개인 선단(船團)
kaein sodeukse	personal income tax	개인 소득세
kaein jeomju	sole proprietorship	개인 점주(個人店主)
kaein-yong ipch'e eumhyang radio	personal stereo radio	개인용 입체 음향 라디오
kaein-yong k'aset'eu jeonch'uk	personal cassette player	개인용 카세트 전축
kaein-yong k'eomp'yut'eo	personal computer	개인용 컴퓨터
kaein-yong t'erebi	personal TV	개인용 테레비
kaeip-hada	intervene	개입(介入)하다
kaejangshi	at the opening	개장시(開場時)
kaejo	alteration	개조(改組)
kaejeong	amendment	개정
kaejeong-hada	amend (v)	개정하다
kaengshin-hada	renew (v)	갱신하다
kaeryak kyeonjeokseo	rough estimate	개략 견적서(概略見積書)
kaeseon	improvements	개선
kaeseon-hada	improve upon (v)	개선하다
kaeseu reijeo	gas laser	개스 레이저
k'aeswimieo	cashmere	캐쉬미어
kagong ch'eori-hada	process (v)	가공 처리(加工處理)하다
kagong oryu	processing error	가공 오류(加工誤謬)
kagyeogi matta	meet the price (v)	가격이 맞다
kagyeok	price	가격
kagyeok ch'a (kyeokch'a)	price differential	가격차(격차)
kagyeok ch'ai	spread	가격 차이
kagyeok cheomgeom	price tick	가격 점검
kagyeok cheonjaeng	price war	가격 전쟁
kagyeok chojak	price fixing	가격 조작
kagyeok inha	markdown	가격 인하
kagyeok insang	markup	가격 인상
kagyeok peomwi	price range	가격 범위
kagyeok sajeong	valuation	가격 사정
kagyeok t'allyeokseong	price elasticity	가격 탄력성
kagyeok yuji	price support	가격 유지
kagyeokp'yo	price list	가격표
kagyeyak	binder	가계약
kajae	chattel	가재(家財)
kajangjari jangshik	lace	가장자리 장식

kajok kyeong-yeong sa-eop	family-run business	가족 경영 사업
kajuk-kkeun	strapping	가죽끈
kajung p'yeong-gyun	weighted average	가중 평균(加重平均)
kakchong wiheom-e banhaeseo	against all risks (adv)	각종 위험에 반해서
kak k'eot'eo	angular cutter	각(角) 커터
k'aldishian jojeong robot'eu	cartesian coordinates robot	칼디시안 조정 로보트
kamch'ae gigeum	sinking fund	감채 기금(減債基金)
kamch'imjil	hem	감침질
kamdokcha	supervisor	감독자
kamgeum	duress	감금
kamgwang dogye	sensitometer	감광 도계
kamjeong	appraisal	감정
kamjeong gagyeok	assessed valuation	감정 가격
kamji jangch'i	sensor	감지 장치
kamkka	discounting	감가
kamkka sang-gak	depreciation	감가 상각(減價償却)
kamkka sang-gak ch'ungdang	depreciation allowance	감가 상각 충당
kamkka sang-gak ch'ungdang-geum	accumulated depreciation	감가 상각 충당금
kamneun gigan	payback period	갚는 기간
kamsa	inspection	감사(監査)
kamsa ch'ujeok	audit trail	감사 추적
kamsa daech'a daejop'yo	auditing balance sheet	감사 대차 대조표
kamsa joseo	working papers	감사 조서
kamse sudan	tax shelter	감세 수단(減稅手段)
kamso	abatement	감소(減少)
kamshi jangch'i	monitor	감시 장치
kamyeongje	false name system	가명제(假名制)
kanbu yeogweon bosu	executive compensation	간부 역원 보수
kaneunghanhan	as soon as possible (shipment)	가능한한
kangch'eol bakp'yeon	steel foil	강철 박편
kangdeung	demotion	강등
kangje hyu-eop	lay-off	강제 휴업
kangje myeognyeong	injunction	강제 명령
kangje sanghwan	mandatory redemption	강제 상환
kangjjeom	competitive edge	강점
kangse shijang	bull market	강세 시장
kangsech'euk	long interest	강세측
kanhaeng	edition	간행
kanjeop ch'eong-gu	indirect claim	간접 청구
kanjeop gyeongbi	overhead	간접 경비
kanjeop nodong	indirect labor	간접 노동
kanjeop piyong	indirect cost	간접 비용
kanjeop-pi	indirect expenses	간접비
kanjeoppi-ro	on cost (adv)	간접비로
kanjeopse	indirect tax	간접세
kaok mit taeji	premises	가옥 및 대지

kaps-eul kkakta	take off (v)	값을 깍다
kapseul maegida	price (v)	값을 매기다 (정하다)
(jeong-hada)		
kapseul naerida	writedown (v)	값을 내리다
kapta	repay (v)	갚다
karu-ro mandeun	ground(adj)	가루로 만든
kasan p'anmae	add-on sales	가산 판매
kasok changch'i	accelerator	가속 장치
kasok haljjeung-geum	acceleration premium	가속 할증금
kasok kamkka sang-gak	accelerated depreciation	가속 감가 상각
kasok poheomnyo	acceleration premium	가속 보험료
kasok pun-hwal sang-hwan	accelerated amortization	가속 분할 상환
kasok-hada	speed up (v)	가속(加速)하다
kasollin	gasoline	가솔린
kasollin t'aengk'eu	gasoline tank	가솔린 탱크
keobukkweon	veto	거부권(拒否權)
keoch'i biyong	deferred charges	거치 비용(据置費用)
keoch'i gyobu	deferred deliveries	거치 교부
keoch'i insu	deferred deliveries	거치 인수
keoch'i jasan	deferred assets	거치 자산
keoch'i segeum	deferred tax	거치 세금
keoch'i su-ik	deferred income	거치 수익
keoch'i yeon-geum	deferred annuities	거치(据置) 연금
keomnyeolgwan	inspector	검열관
keomsa	inspection	검사(檢查)
keomsagwan	inspector	검사관
keonban	keyboard	건반
keonhwa	dry cargo	건화(乾貨)
keonhyeon	freeboard	건현(乾舷)
keorae	transaction, trade, deal	거래(去來)
keorae eunhaeng	correspondent bank	거래 은행
keorae gigan	account period	거래 기간
keorae han-gye	position limit	거래 한계
keorae jehan	trading limit	거래 제한
keorae jokkeon	bargain	거래 조건
keorae-aek	volume	거래액
keoraeyang	volume	거래량
keoraeyang harin	volume discount	거래량 할인
keoraeso	exchange (n) (stock) commodity	거래소
keorigye	rangefinder	거리계
keoshi gyeongjehak	macroeconomics	거시 경제학(巨視經濟學)
keship'an	billboard	게시판
keuktaehwa-hada	maximize (v)	극대화하다
keullo gyech'eung	working class	근로계층
keumaek	amount	금액
keumbak	gilt (British govt. security)	금박(金嚙)
k'eugi	size	크기
keukchwap'yo robot'eu	polar coordinates robot	극좌표 로보트

keum dogeum-doen	goldplated (adj)	금 도금된
keum-eun-goe	ingot	금은괴
keumgo	depository	금고
keumgoju	trasury bonds	금고주(金庫株)
keumgoju	treasury stock	금고주(金庫株)
keumgoju, sanaeju	treasury stock	금고주(金庫株), 사내주(社內株)
keumjeon	money	금전
keumjeon ch'ullapkye	treasurer	금전 출납계
keumjeon deungnok-ki	cash register	금전 등록기
(suip) keumjip'um	prohibited goods	(수입) 금지품
keumkka	gold price	금가(金價)
keumni	interest rate	금리
kimyeong jeungkkwon	registered security	기명 증권(記名證券)
keumnyo	remuneration	급료
keumnyo jibul	pay off	급료 지불
keumnyo jibulbu	payroll	급료지불부
keumnyo jibulse	payroll tax	급료지불세
keumnyung	money	금융
keumnyung bunseok	financial analysis	금융 분석
keumnyung hoesa	money shop	금융 회사
keumnyung jeongch'aek	monetary policy	금융 정책
keumnyung shijang	money market	금융 시장
keumsok	metals	금속(金屬)
keumsu	embargo	금수(禁輸)
keumyakkwan	gold clause	금약관(金約款)
keumnyung (chaejeong) t'ongje	financial control	금융(재정) 통제
keumsok cheolsak-ki	milling machine	금속 절삭기
keumsok susohwamul	metal hydride	금속 수소화물
keumul p'an-yuri	screen	그물 판유리
keunch'eo-eui	around (exchange term)	근처의
keunjeop keori renjeu	close-up lens	근접 거리 렌즈
keunmu (nodong)-shigan	working hours	근무(노동) 시간
keunmu-hada	work (v)	근무하다
keunmu-il	work day	근무일
keunmuji	work station	근무지
keunsa t'onghwa	near money	근사 통화(近似通貨)
keup-chumun	rush order	급주문(急注文)
keupsok hwankka jasan	quick assets	급속 환가 자산
keupsu ch'egambeop	sum-of-the-years digits	급수 체감법(給水遞減法)
keureut	bowl	그릇
keurim mulkkam	pigment	그림 물감
kibon yogeum	base rate	기본 요금
kibon-geum	down payment	기본금
kibu	endowment	기부(寄附)
kich'o gongje	personal exemption	기초 공제
kich'imnyak (deurop)	cough drop	기침약(드롭)
kich'imnyak (shireop)	cough syrup	기침약(시럽)
kideuk ikkwon	vested interests	기득 이권(旣得利權)
kideukkwon	acquired rights	기득권
kideukkwon	vested rights	기득권

kieo	gearshift	기어
ki-eop	enterprise	기업
ki-eop kihoek	corporate planning	기업 기획(企業企劃)
kieop kwang-go	institutional advertising	기업 광고
ki-eop kyeolhap	combination	기업 결합
ki-eop yeonhap	cartel	기업 연합
ki-eopkka	entrepreneur	기업가
ki-eopkka haptong	syndicate	기업가 합동
kigeum	fund	기금
kigeum	pension fund	기금(基金)
kigu	organization	기구(機構)
kigu	instrument	기구
kigu	tools	기구
kigwan	organization	기관
kigwan t'ujaga	institutional investor	기관 투자가(機關投資家)
kigye	hardware	기계
kigye	instrument	기계
kigye apch'akki	mechanical press	기계 압착기
kigye gong-gu	machine tools	기계 공구
kigye gonghak	mechanical engineering	기계 공학
kigye gongjakso	machining center	기계 공작소(工作所)
kigyegong yuch'ikkweon	mechanics' lien	기계공 유치권(機械工留置權)
kigyejeogin	mechanical	기계적인
kigyeryu	machinery	기계류
kihanbu hwaneo-eum	time bill (of exchange)	기한부 환어음
kihanbu yungja	term loan	기한부 융자
kihan gyeong-gwa-eui	overdue (adj)	기한 경과의
kihoe biyong	opportunity costs	기회 비용
kihoek	project (n)	기획
kihoek-hada	project (v)	기획하다
kihwagi	carburetor	기화기
kijang-hada	writedown (v)	기장(記帳)하다
kijeong (kiseong) p'yeonji	form letter	기정(旣定)
		(기성-旣成) 편지
kijun	norm	기준
kijunch'i	basis point (1/100%)	기준치
kijun dankka	base price	기준 단가
kijun hwap'ye (t'onghwa)	base currency	기준 화폐(통화)
kijun ijayul	prime rate	기준 이자율
kijunkka	base price	기준가
kijun nyeondo	base year	기준 년도
kijun-nyul	rate, base	기준율
kikkweon yakkwan	waiver clause	기권 약관(棄權約款)
kimal	end of period	기말(期末)
kimireui	confidential (adj)	기밀의
kimyeong jeungkkweon	registered security	기명 증권(記名證券)
kimyeong sup'yo	resistered check	기명 수표(記名手票)
kinch'uk shijang	tight market	긴축 시장
kineung bunseok	functional analysis	기능 분석
kineung bunseok	analysis, functional	기능 분석
kireum	oil	기름

kireum p'eomp'eu	oil pump	기름 펌프
kirogil	record date	기록일
kiseongbok	apparel	기성복
kiso	litigation	기소
kiso-hada	prosecute	기소하다
kit'a jasan (mit puch'ae)	other assets (and liabilities)	기타 자산(및 부채)
kit'a-eui	miscellaneous (adj)	기타의
kit'ak kyejeong	escrow account	기탁 계정(寄託計定)
koch'e reijeo	solid-state laser	고체 레이저
kogaek	customer	고객
kogaek pongsa	customer service	고객 봉사
kogi gungmul geureut	gravy boat	고기 국물 그릇
kogi sseoneun k'al	carving knife	고기 써는 칼
kojangbu seonha jeungkkweon	foul bill of lading	고장부 선하 증권 (故障附船荷證券)
kojeong ch'otcheom k'amera	fixed-focus camera	고정 촛점 카메라
kojeong biyong	fixed costs	고정 비용
kojeong buch'ae	liability, fixed	고정 부채(固定負債)
kojeong gagyeok	pegged price	고정 가격(固定價格)
kojeong gyeongbi	standing charges	고정 경비
kojeong hwannyul	fixed rate of exchange	고정 환율(固定換率)
kojeong jabon	fixed capital	고정 자본(固定資本)
kojeong jasan	fixed assets, capital asset	고정 자산(固定資産)
kojeong jich'ul	fixed expenses	고정 지출
kojeong su-ip pojang	fixed income security	고정 수입 보장
kojeong t'uja	fixed investment	고정 투자
kojeongbi	fixed charges	고정비(固定費)
kojeongbi budam biyul	cover ratio	고정비 부담 비율
kojeonghagi	pegging	고정하기
kokka-reul maegida	outbid (v)	고가(高價)를 매기다
kokson	bends	곡손(曲損)
kolttongp'um gamjeong jeungmyeongseo	antique authenticity certificate	골동품 감정 증명서
k'omp'aekdiseuk'eu	compact disc (CD)	콤팩 디스크
komun	management consultant	고문
kongch'ae	public funds	공채
kongch'aebit	funded debt	공채빚
kongch'ae-reul balhaeng-hada	float (v) (issue stock)	공채(公債)를 발행하다
kongdong	sinus	공동(空洞)
kongdong biyong	joint cost	공동 비용
kongdong boheom	coinsurance	공동 보험
kongdong ch'aegim	joint liability	공동 책임
kongdong ch'uljashik happyeongppeop	pooling of interests	공동 출자식 합병법 (共同出資式合併法)
kongdong ch'uljja	pool (of funds)	공동 출자
kongdong ch'uljja-hada	pool (v)	공동 출자하다
kongdong euimu	joint liability	공동 의무
kongdong gujwa	joint account	공동 구좌

kongdong haeson bunshil	general average loss	공동 해손 분실
kongdong jasan	joint estate	공동 자산
kongdong jikch'aek	combination duty	공동 직책
kongdong sa-eopch'e	joint venture	공동 사업체
kongdong shijang	common market	공동 시장
kongdong soyu	joint owner	공동 소유
kongdong soyuji	joint estate	공동 소유지
kongdong soyukkweon	co-ownership	공동 소유권
kong-eop chong-eopweon boheom	industrial insurance	공업 종업원 보험
kong-gae shijang	open market	공개 시장
kong-gae shijang jojak	open market operations (money policy)	공개 시장 조작
kong-geum	public funds	공금
kong-geum sut'akso	depository	공금 수탁소
kong-geumnyul	feed ratio	공급율
kong-geup kwada (kwaing)	glut	공급과다(과잉)
kong-geup kwa-ing	oversupply	공급과잉
kong-geup pujok	short supply	공급 부족(供給不足)
kong-geup tokcheom	monopoly	공급 독점
kong-geupcha	supplier	공급자
kong-geup-hada	allow (v)	공급하다
kong-gong bumun	public sector	공공 부문
kong-gong gigeum	funds, public	공공 기금
kong-gong t'omok sa-eop	public works	공공 토목 사업
kong-gu	tools	공구
konghak	engineering	공학(工學)
konghak hapseong suji	engineering plastic	공학 합성 수지
konghak seolgyekkwa	engineering and design department	공학 설계과
kong-ik sa-eop	public utility	공익 사업
kong-in eopcha	authorized dealer	공인 업자
kong-in hoegyesa	certified public accountant	공인 회계사
kong-in (in-ga) jeungkkweon eopcha	authorized dealer	공인(인가) 증권 업자
kong-in yukka jeungkkweon	approved securities	공인 유가 증권
kong-in (in-ga) doen seomyeong	authorized signature	공인(인가)된 서명
kongjang	factory	공장
kongjang ch'ong-gyeongbi	factory overhead	공장 총경비(工場總經費)
kongjang gwallija	plant manager	공장 관리자
kongjang indo	ex factory	공장 인도
kongjang p'yeswae	lock out	공장 폐쇄
kongjang p'yeswae gigan	down period	공장 폐쇄 기간
kongjang saengsan neungnyeok	plant capacity	공장 생산 능력
kongjang wich'i	plant location	공장 위치
kongjangjang	plant manager	공장장
kongje (aek)	deduction	공제(액)
kongje daesang-eui	deductible (adj)	공제 대상(控除對象)의

kongjeong geumni	central rate	공정 금리
kongjeong gwalli	production control	공정 관리(工程管理)
kongjeong sijangkka	fair market value	공정 시장가(公正市場價)
kongjeong su-ik	fair return	공정 수익(公正收益)
kongjeong-georae	fair trade	공정 거래(公正去來)
kongjeung-in	notary	공증인(公證人)
kongmae	public sale	공매
kongmae sangt'ae	short position	공매 상태(空賣狀態)
kongmo	public offering	공모(公募)
kongmul	grain	곡물
kongmunseo	writ	공문서
kongnyu	dry goods	곡류
kongp'yeong	equity	공평(公平)
kongsa ch'eongbu	working contract	공사 청부
kongt'akkeum	trust fund	공탁금(供託金)
kong-yu jaesan	public property	공유 재산
kong-yu yeong-yeok	interface	공유 영역
kong-yuji	public domain	공유지
kong-yukkweon	co-ownership	공유권
kori	usury	고리(高利)
kori daegeumeop	usury	고리 대금업
koso	lawsuit	고소
koyak	ointment	고약
koyong	placement (personnel)	고용
koyong ch'abyeol sujeong joch'i	affirmative action	고용 차별 수정 조치
koyong-in	employee	고용인
koyong-in gwan-gye	employee relations	고용인 관계
koyong-in sangdam	employee counseling	고용인 상담
koyu gach'i	intrinsic value	고유 가치
kuch'ul-hada	salvage (v)	구출(救出)하다
kudu	shoe	구두
kudu yaksok	binder	구두(口頭) 약속
keumbun	gilt (British govt. security)	금분(金粉)
kugyeong	nationalization	국영
kugyuhwa	nationalization	국유화
kuhoek	zone	구획(區劃)
kuhoek cheongni-ppeop (gyujeong)	zoning law	구획 정리법(규정)
kuin	classified ad	구인 구직 광고
kuip-hada	purchase (v)	구입하다
kuip weonkka	prime costs	구입 원가
ku-ip yejeongja	potential buyer	구입 예정자
kuje	remedy (law)	구제
kujik kwang-go	want-ad	구직 광고
kujik kwang-go	classified ad	구직 광고
kuju jeungkkweon	Eurobond	구주 증권
kujwa beonho	account number	구좌 번호
kujwa damdang	account executive	구좌 담당
kujwa, kyejeong	account	구좌, 계정(計定)

kwallibi

kukch'ae	government bonds	국채(國債)
kukch'ae	public funds	국채
kukche gyeongjaengnyeok	global competitiveness	국제 경쟁력
kukche hoe-eui	international conference	국제 회의
kukche naljja byeon-gyeongseon	International Date Line	국제 날짜 변경선
kukche suji	balance of payments	국제 수지(國際收支)
kukchegan dan-gi jageum	hot money	국제간 단기 자금
kukka ch'aemu	national debt	국가 채무(債務)
kukkajueui	nationalism	국가 주의
kukkyeong	border	국경
kukkyeong segeum jojeong	border tax adjustment	국경 세금 조정
kukpyeol wiheomdo	country of risk	국별 위험도
kuksan-p'um	domestic product	국산품
kumae ch'aegimja	buyer, chief	구매 책임자
kumae daerijeom	purchasing agent	구매 대리점
kumae gagyeok	purchase price	구매 가격
kumae gwallija	purchasing manager	구매 관리자
kumae juim	chief buyer	구매 주임
kumaeja	buyer	구매자
kumaeja shijang	buyer's market	구매자 시장
kumaegwan	chief buyer	구매관
kumaeryeok	purchasing power	구매력
kumae-weon	purchasing agent	구매원
kumeong gage	mom-and-pop store	구멍가게
kunae	premises	구내(構內)
kunbi	armaments	군비
kungmin ch'ongsaengsan	gross national product	국민 총생산
kungnae beobin	domestic corporation	국내 법인
kungnae ch'ong saengsan	gross domestic product	국내 총 생산
kungnae eoeum	domestic bill	국내 어음
kungnae-eui	internal	국내의
kungnae saengsan-p'um	domestic product	국내 생산품
kungnae shijang	home market	국내 시장
kungnae sobise	excise tax	국내 소비세
kungnae sobise	tax, excise	국내 소비세
kungnae unsong jeokha jeungkkweon	inland bill of lading	국내 운송 적하 증권
kungnip eunhaeng	national bank	국립 은행
kusang muyeok	compensation trade	구상(求償) 무역
kuseong yoso	component	구성 요소
kusok taebu	tied loan	구속 대부(拘束貸付)
kwabul-eui	overpaid (adj)	과불(過拂)의
kwadae p'yeongkkadoen	overvalued (adj)	과대 평가된
kwa-ing	overhang	과잉
kwa-ing ch'eong-gu	overcharge	과잉 청구
kwajeom	oligopoly	과점(寡占)
kwalli	management, maintenance	관리
kwallibi	management fee, managed costs	관리비

kwalli biyong	administrative expense, managed costs	관리 비용
kwalli budong jeunkkweon	managed float	관리 부동 증권 (管理浮動證券)
kwalli dop'yo	management chart	관리 도표
kwalli (kyeong-yeong)-eui	administrative	관리(경영)의
kwalli (chojong) ganeung biyong	controllable costs	관리(조종) 가능 비용
kwalli hoegye	management accounting	관리 회계
kwalli jasan su-ik	return on assets managed	관리 자산 수익(收益)
kwallidan	management group	관리단
kwalli-hada	manage (v)	관리하다
kwalli-in	manager	관리인
kwallija	administrator	관리자
kwallyeon hoesa	associate company	관련 회사
kwallyo	bureaucrat	관료
kwallyo ju-euija	bureaucrat	관료주의자
kwamaeip	overbought	과매입(過買入)
kwanch'eongshik beonjaphan susok	red tape	관청식 번잡한 수속
kwang	godown	광
kwang diseuk'eu	optical disc	광 디스크
kwang gieok changch'i	optical memory	광 기억 장치
kwang jagi gieok changch'i	optical magnetic memory	광 자기 기억 장치
kwang jeonsong jangch'i	optical transmission	광 전송장치(光電送裝置)
kwang jipcheok hoero	optical integrated circuit	광 집적 회로
kwang k'eibeul	optical cable	광(光) 케이블
kwang k'eomp'yut'eo	optical computer	광 컴퓨터
kwang-eopso indo	ex mine	광업소 인도
kwang-eul naen jong-i	coated paper	광을 낸 종이
kwang-go	advertising, publictity	광고
kwang-go biyong	advertising expenses	광고 비용
kwang-go bujang	advertising manager	광고 부장
kwang-go daehaeng eop (cha)	advertising agency	광고 대행업(자)
kwang-go hyokkwa josa	copy testing	광고 효과 조사
kwang-go maegae	advertising media	광고 매개
kwang-go munan	copy (text)	광고 문안(文案)
kwang-go seonjeon	advertising campaign	광고 선전
kwang-go yeon-gu	advertising research	광고 연구
kwang-go yesan	advertising budget	광고 예산
kwang-gojeon	campaign, advertising	광고전
kwang-gop'an	billboard	광고판
kwanghak cheonjahak	opto-electronics	광학 전자학
kwanghak kiho p'andokki	optical mark reader	광학 기호 판독기
kwanhalkkweon	jurisdiction	관할권(管轄權)
kwanjae-in	assignee	관재인(管財人)
kwanjae-in	trustee	관재인(管財人)
kwanse	tariff	관세

kwanse biyong	tariff charge	관세 비용
kwanse deung-geup pullyu	tariff classification	관세 등급 분류
kwanse dongmaeng	customs union	관세 동맹
kwanse jangbyeok	tariff barriers	관세 장벽
kwanse jedo	customs duty	관세 제도
kwanse jeonjaeng (bunjaeng)	tariff war	관세 전쟁(분쟁)
kwanse jingsu-weon	collector of customs	관세 징수원
kwanse sangp'um	tariff commodity	관세 상품
kwanseyul gyeokch'a	tariff differential	관세율 격차(格差)
kwaryo	fine (penalty)	과료(科料, 過料)
kwase	taxation	과세
kwase gijun	tax base	과세 기준
kwase-hada	assess (v)	과세하다
kwaso p'yeongkka-hada	undervalue (v), understimate	과소 평가하다
kweolli jeungseo yo-yakseo	abstract of title	권리 증서 요약서
kweolli p'ogi jeungseo	quit claim deed	권리 포기 증서
kweolli somyeol sangt'ae	public domain	권리 소멸 상태
kweonik	interest	권익
kwihwan	feedback	귀환(歸還)
kwijungp'um bogwanham	safe deposit box	귀중품 보관함
kwisok	escheat	귀속(歸屬)
kwisok-toen	imputed (adj)	귀속된
kyehoeg-eul se-uda	program (v)	계획을 세우다
kyehoek	plan (n)	계획
kyehoekcheok p'yegi (nohuhwa)	planned obsolescense	계획적 폐기 (노후화-老朽化)
kyehoekseo	prospectus	계획서
kyejeoljeogin	seasonal (adj)	계절적인
kyejeong gigan	accounting period	계정 기간
kyejeong jan-go	account balance	계정 잔고
kyejeong-hada	account for (v)	계정하다
kyeokcha	grid	격자(格子)
kyeokha	demotion	격하
kyeol	grain	결
kyeolham inneun	defective (adj)	결함있는
kyeoljae	approval	결재
kyeoljae-hada	approve (v)	결재하다
kyeolmal	end of period	결말(結末)
kyeolmal-eul jitta	finalize (v)	결말을 짓다
kyeolsan	settlement	결산
kyeolsanil	account day	결산일(決算日)
kyeolson	deficit	결손(缺損)
kyeolssan gijae	closing entry (accounting)	결산 기재(決算記載)
kyeomim jungyeokhoe	interlocking directorate	겸임 중역회
kyeongbi	outlay	경비
kyeongbi halttang	costs, allocation of	경비 할당
kyeonbon	dummy	견본
kyeonbon	pattern	견본

kyeonbon jongmok	sample line	견본 종목
kyeonbon k'eugi	sample size	견본 크기
kyeonbon-eul mandeulda	sample (v)	견본을 만들다
kyeong-gae	novation	경개(更改)
kyeong-gam gwanse	remission duty	경감 관세(輕減關稅)
kyeong-gi	business activity	경기(景氣)
kyeong-gi ch'imch'e	slump	경기 침체(景氣沈滯)
kyeong-gi hut'oe	recession	경기 후퇴
kyeong-gi sunhwan	business cycle	경기 순환
kyeong-gwa	accrual	경과(經過)
kyeonghapcha bunseok	competitor analysis	경합자 분석
kyeongheom gokseon	learning curve	경험 곡선
kyeonghwa	hard currency	경화(硬貨)
kyeongjaeng	competition	경쟁
kyeongjaeng gagyeok	competitive price	경쟁 가격
kyeongjaeng jeollyak	competitive strategy	경쟁 전략
kyeongjaeng sangdae	competitor	경쟁 상대
kyeongjaeng sangdae bunseok	competitor analysis	경쟁 상대 분석
kyeongjaengjeok u-se	competitive edge	경쟁적 우세
kyeongjaengnyeok	competitiveness	경쟁력
kyeongjaengsang-eui it-jeom	advantage, competitive	경쟁상의 이점
kyeongjaengsang-eui yuri (ijjeom)	competitive advantage	경쟁상의 유리(이점)
kyeongje baljuryang	economic order quantity (EOQ)	경제 발주량(發注量)
kyeongje buheung ch'okchin	pump priming	경제 부흥 촉진
kyeongje jip'yo	economic indicators	경제 지표
kyeongje saenghwal	economic life	경제 생활
kyeongje (sang)-eui	economic (adj)	경제(상)의
kyeongjehak	economics	경제학
kyeongjehak-eui	economic (adj)	경제학의
kyeongmae	public sale, public auction	경매
kyeongmae gagyeok sin-go	bid (takeover)	경매 가격 신고
kyeongmae-e igida	outbid (v)	경매(競賣)에 이기다
kyeongnae	premises	경내(境內)
kyeongni	bookkeeping	경리
kyeongni bujang	comptroller	경리 부장
kyeongnikkwa	accounting department	경리과
kyeongsang gyejeong	current account	경상 계정(經常計定)
kyeongsang jabon	ordinary capital	경상 자본(經常資本)
kyeongsangbi	running expenses	경상비(經常費)
kyeong-yeong	management	경영
kyeong-yeong bonbu	operations headquarters	경영 본부
kyeong-yeong ganbu	executive	경영 간부
kyeong-yeong gomun	management consultant	경영 고문
kyeong-yeong gyehoek	business plan	경영 계획
kyeong-yeong jamun	management consultant	경영 자문
kyeong-yeong jeongbo eunhaeng	data bank	경영 정보 은행
kyeong-yeong kwalli	business management	경영 관리

kyeong-yeong-hada	manage (v)	경영하다
kyeong-yeong-in	manager	경영인
kyeong-yeongja	proprietor	경영자
kyeonjeok	estimate	견적
kyeonjeok chiryeongseo	work order	견적 지령서(見積指令書)
kyeonjeok isang saengsanaek	overage	견적 이상 생산액
kyeonjeok gagyeok	estimated, price	견적 가격
kyeonjeok kyesanseo	pro-forma statement	견적 계산서
kyeonjeok myeongseseo	pro-forma statement	견적 명세서
kyeonjeok songjjang	pro-forma invoice	견적 송장
kyeonjeok-hada	assess (v)	견적하다
kyeopch'im	overlap	겹침
kyeoreui	resolution (legal document)	결의
kyerisa	accountant	계리사
kyeryang gyeongjehak	econometrics	계량 경제학
kyesan-gi	calculator	계산기
kyesanseo	statement of account	계산서
kyesok p'anmae jumun	standing order	계속 판매 주문
kyesok yeong-eop kach'i	going concern value	계속 영업 가치
kyesuhyeong	digital	계수형(計數形)
kyesuhyeong (dijit'al) jeonja gyesan-gi	digital computer	계수형(디지탈) 전자 계산기
kyeyagweol	contract month	계약월
kyeyak	covenant (promises)	계약
kyeyak keunmu	work by contract	계약 근무
kyeyak pojeung	performance bond	계약 보증
kyeyak (cheonsok) susong-eopcha	contract carrier	계약(전속) 수송 업자
kyeyakkeum-euroseo	on account (adv)	계약금으로서
kyeyak-kwon	bargaining, power	계약권
kyeyakseo	written agreement	계약서
kyeyeol hoesa	affiliates	계열회사
kyoch'ak sangt'ae	deadlock	교착 상태
kyoch'e bup'um	replacement parts	교체 부품
kyodae shigan	shift (labor)	교대 시간(交代時間)
kyohwan	trade-off	교환
kyohwan gach'i	exchange value	교환 가치
kyohwan ganeung t'onghwa	hard currency	교환 가능 통화
kyohwan sudan (chung-gaemul)	medium of exchange	교환 수단(중개물)
kyohwan-hada	exchange (v), trade	교환하다
kyojebi	expense account	교제비(交際費)
kyojeong	proofreading	교정
kyojeongswae	galley proof	교정쇄(校正刷)
kyoryugi	alternator	교류기
kyoseop	negotiation	교섭
kyoseop sangdae	customer	교섭 상대
kyoseop-hada	negotiate (v)	교섭하다
kyoseopkweon	bargaining power	교섭권
kyoyeok	trade	교역(交易)

kyoyeok chokkeon	terms of trade	교역 조건
kyubeom	norm	규범
kyuch'ik	regulation	규칙
kyugyeok (p'yojun) iha	substandard	규격(表準) 이하
kyuje	regulation	규제
kyumo gyeongje	economy of scale	규모 경제
kyunbun-hada	averaging	균분하다
kyundeung jakeop kyundeung imgeum	equal pay for equal work	균등 작업 균등 임금
kyunhyeongse	countervailing duty	균형세
kyunil iyun	flat yield	균일 이윤(均一利潤)
kyunil yogeum	flat rate	균일 요금(均一料金)
k'adarogeu	catalog	카다로그
k'aset'eu (t'e-i-p'eu)	cassette	카세트(테이프)
k'einjeu gyeongjehak	Keynesian economics	케인즈 경제학
k'eomp'yut'eo	computer	컴퓨터
k'eomp'yut'eo ch'ullyeok	computer output	컴퓨터 출력(出力)
k'eomp'yut'eo eoneo	computer language	컴퓨터 언어
k'eomp'yut'eo eunhaeng	computer bank	컴퓨터 은행
k'eomp'yut'eo gi-eok changch'i (yongnyang)	computer memory	컴퓨터 기억 장치(용량)
k'eomp'yut'eo imnyeok	computer input	컴퓨터 입력(入力)
k'eomp'yut'eo jeojang jangch'i	computer storage	컴퓨터 저장 장치
k'eomp'yut'eo p'eurogeuraem	computer program	컴퓨터 프로그램
k'eomp'yut'eo sent'eo	computer center	컴퓨터 센터
k'eomp'yut'eo seuk'eurin	monitor	컴퓨터 스크린
k'eomp'yut'eo t'eominal	computer terminal	컴퓨터 터미날
k'eont'eineo	container	컨테이너
k'eont'eineo seonbak susong seobiseu	fishy-back service (container)	컨테이너 선박 수송 서비스
keumnyung shilmyeongje	real name financial system	금융실명제(金融實名制)
k'euraedit pa-i-eo (shinyong gumaeja)	credit buyer	크레딧 바이어 (신용 구매자)
k'euredit k'a-deu	credit card	크레딧 카-드
k'ip'eonch'i	keypunch	키펀치
kkeonaeda	take out (v)	꺼내다
kkeun	strapping	끈

M

mach'wi-eui	anaesthetic	마취의
mach'wiseong-eui	narcotic	마취성의
maech'ul gagyeok	issue price	매출 가격
maedo mit imdae	sell and lease back	매도(賣渡) 및 임대(賃貸)
maedoin	payer	매도인(賣渡人)
maedojjeung	bill of sale	매도증
maegae sangp'um	intermediary goods	매개 상품(媒介商品)
maegak-hada	unload (v)	매각하다
maegwago	overage	매과고(買過高)

maei	daily	매일
maeil-eui	daily (adj)	매일의
mae-ip (kumae) jumun	purchase order	매입(구매) 주문
maeip kyeonjeok songjjang	invoice, pro forma	매입 견적 송장
mae-ip taegeum jeodang	purchase money mortgage	매입 대금 저당
mae-ipseo	invoice	매입서(買入書)
maejeom	buyout	매점(買占)
maeju	vendor	매주(賣主)
maeju ch'aegim	buyer's responsibility	매주 책임
maeju seont'aek	buyer's option	매주(買主) 선택
maeju shijang	buyer's market	매주(買主) 시장
maeju yuch'ikkweon	vendor's lien	매주 유치권(買主留置權)
maeju-eui haljeung-geum	buyer's premium	매주의 할증금
maek'euro renju	macro lens	매크로 렌즈
(keoraeso-eui) maemae gyeyak	commitment	(거래소의) 매매 계약
maemae hwanp'yo	debit note	매매환표
maemae p'yeongkka	sales estimate	매매 평가
maemae-hada	trade (v)	매매하다
maen	sewn (adj)	맨
maesang-go	sales	매상고
maesangse	sales tax	매상세
maeseu midieo	mass media	매스 미디어
maeseuk'om	mass communications	매스콤
maet'eu	matt	매트
maet'eurikseu gwalli	matrix management	매트릭스 관리
maeyak cheungseo	deed of sale	매약 증서(賣約證書)
maik'euro ch'eori jangch'i	micro processor	마이크로 처리 장치
maik'euro k'aset'eu nogeumgi	micro cassette recorder	마이크로 카세트 녹음기
maik'euro k'eomp'yut'eo	micro computer	마이크로 컴퓨터
maik'euro-weibeu	microwave	마이크로 웨이브
maik'euro (ch'uk-sa) p'illeum	microfilm	마이크로(축사) 필름
magam	deadline	마감
maik'euro p'illeum	microfilm	마이크로 필름
mail-su	mileage	마일수
majin	margin	마진
majin-yul	margin rate	마진율
mak'et'ing	marketing	마케팅
mak'et'ing yesan	marketing budget	마케팅 예산
makttaehyeong dop'yo	bar chart	막대형 도표
mamuri	topping up	마무리
mamyeol somo	wear and tear	마멸 소모(磨滅消耗)
man-gi	maturity	만기(滿期)
man-gi iyul	yield to maturity	만기 이율(滿期利率)
man-gi-il	maturity date	만기일
mang-weon renju	telephoto lens	망원 렌즈
maryeok	horsepower	마력
mason	attrition	마손
mat-ton	down payment	맞돈
mein p'eureim k'eomp'yut'eo	mainframe computer	메인 프레임 컴퓨터

meori-e eonjeun jim	headload	머리에 얹은 짐
meorijim	headload	머리짐
mi t'ongsangbeop sambaek iljo	U.S. Trade Law, 301	미 통상법 301조
mibongch'aek	makeshift	미봉책
mideungnog-eui	unlisted (adj)	미등록의
migaebal-eui	undeveloped (adj)	미개발(未開發)의
miguk kyugyeok hyeophoe sokto	ASA speed	미국 규격 협회 속도
migyeolje jaegop'um	outstanding stock	미결제 재고품
mihaegyeol gyeyak	outstanding contract	미해결 계약
mi-jigeup ija	accrued interest	미지급 이자(未支給利子)
mi-jigeup piyong	accrued expenses	미지급 비용(未支給費用)
mi-jigeupse	accrued taxes	미지급세(未支給稅)
mijong-gyeol ija	inchoate interest	미종결 이자
miljjip sangt'ae	density	밀집 상태
milyak	deal	밀약(密約)
minjokchueui	nationalism	민족주의
minsa sosong	civil action	민사 소송
miri shitki	forward shipment	미리싣기
misu ija	accrued interest	미수 이자(未收利子)
misu su-ip	accrued revenue	미수 수입(未收收入)
misungnyeon nodong	unskilled labor	미숙련 노동
mit'eohwa	metrification	미터화
mobang	imitation	모방
model	model	모델
mo-eui shilheom-hada	simulate (v)	모의 실험(模擬實驗)하다
mogae heungjeong	round lot	모개 흥정
moheom	risk	모험
moheom jabon	capital risk	모험 자본
mohoesa	holding company	모회사(母會社)
mohyeong	pattern	모형
mojingmul	wool	모직물
mojip kwang-go	want-ad	모집 광고
mojo	imitation	모조
mojop'um	counterfeit	모조품
mok	equity share	몫
mok	quota	몫
mokch'a	table of contents	목차
mok-kin gudu	boots	목긴 구두
mokp'yo gagyeok	target price	목표 가격
mokp'yo-e euihan kwalli	management by objectives	목표에 의한 관리
moktori	scarf	목도리
molsu	escheat	몰수(沒收)
mongnok ki-ip	listing	목록 기입(目錄記入)
mont'e k'allobeop	Monte Carlo technique	몬테 칼로법
moreup'in	morphine	모르핀
mosa	yarn	모사
mot'eo deuraibeo	motor drive	모터 드라이버
mu euigyeolkkweon jushik	nonvoting stock	무 의결권 주식

moyok	libel	모욕(侮辱)
mudambo ch'aemu	unsecured liability	무담보 채무
mudampo daebu	unsecured loan	무담보 대부(貸付)
mudeogi-ro p'aneun yeomkkap'um	job lot	무더기로 파는 염가품(廉價品)
muganseopchueui	laissez-faire	무간섭주의
mugimyeong ch'aekkweon	bearer bond	무기명 채권
mugimyeong jeungkkweon	bearer security	무기명 증권
mugojang seonha jeungkkweon	letter of indemnity	무고장 선하 증권 (無故障船荷證券)
mugwanse t'eukpyeol heogajjeung	carnet	무관세 특별 허가증
muhajung t'uja shint'ak kigeum	no load fund	무하중(無荷重) 투자 신탁 기금
muhyeoyng jasan	intangible assets	무형 자산
muhyo	null and void	무효
muhyoro-hada	nullify (v)	무효로 하다
muija harin ch'aekkweon	zero coupon	무이자 할인 채권
mu-ishik kongch'ae	flat bond	무이식 공채(無利息公債)
mujagwi ch'uch'ul	random sample	무작위 추출
mujeondong jangch'i-eui	gearless	무전동 장치의
mujunbi balhaeng	fiduciary issue	무준비 발행
mukkye	implied agreement	묵계(默契)
mukshijeok tongeui	implied agreement	묵시적 동의
mul-jujeonja	pitcher	물주전자
mulkka anjeong	price stability	물가 안정
mulkka gyeongjaeng	price war	물가 경쟁
mulkka harak	deflation	물가 하락
mulkka inha jeongch'aek	rollback	물가 인하 정책
mulkka jisu	price index	물가 지수
mulkka sangseung	inflation	물가 상승
mulkkam	color	물감
mulkkyeol muni otkkam-eui iljjong	moire	물결 무늬 옷감의 일종
mulmul kyohwan-hada	barter (v)	물물 교환하다
mulp'um p'anmaese	sales tax	물품 판매세
mulp'umse	excise duty	물품세
mumohan p'a-eop	wildcat strike	무모(無謀)한 파업
munho gaebang jeongch'aek	open door policy	문호 개방 정책
munhwajae	cultural property	문화재
munhwajae such'ul heogaseo	cultural export permit	문화재 수출 허가서
munje	problem	문제
munje bunseok	problem analysis	문제 분석
munje eomneun	no problem	문제없는
munje eopseum	no problem	문제없음
munje haegyeol	problem solving	문제 해결
munseo myeong-ye hweson	libel	문서 명예 훼손 (文書名譽毀損)
musang t'oji bulha	land grant	무상 토지 불하
muse	dutyfree	무세(無稅)

musep'ump'yo	free list (commodities without duty)	무세품표(無稅品表)
mut'ongseong-eui	analgesic	무통성의
muyeogeopcha	trader	무역 업자
muyeogoe suji	invisible	무역외 수지(貿易外 收支)
muyeok	trade	무역
muyeok changbyeok	trade barrier	무역 장벽(障壁)
muyeok hoesa	trading company	무역 회사
muyeok hyeophoe	trade association	무역 협회
muyeok iljja	trade date	무역 일자
muyeok insu eo-eum	trade acceptance	무역 인수 어음
muyeok keorae jokkeon hyeopcheongseo	agreement	무역 거래 조건 협정서
muyeokpeop	trade law	무역법
muyeok shinyongjjang	trade credit	무역 신용장
muyeok suji	balance of trade	무역 수지(收支)
muyeok suji gyunhyeong	visible balance of trade	무역 수지 균형 (貿易收支均衡)
muyeok wiweonhoe	trade commission	무역 위원회
muyueon samangja	intestate	무유언 사망자 (無遺言死亡者)
myeon	cotton	면
myeonch'aek	indemnity	면책(免責)
myeonch'aek yakkwan	escape clause	면책 약관
myeongham	business card	명함
myeongmoksang gagyeok	nominal price	명목상 가격
myeongmoksang suik	nominal yield	명목상 수익
myeongnyeong	injunction	명령
myeongnyeong shinch'eong	motion	명령 신청
myeongse jeongsanseo	itemized account	명세 정산서(明細精算書)
myeonheo	license	면허
myeonheojjang	charter	면허장
myeonje	exemption	면제
myeonjeok halttang	acreage allotment	면적 할당
myeonjese	remission duty	면제세
myeonjingmul	cotton	면직물
myeonse	dutyfree	면세(免稅)
myeonse sodeuk	tax-free income	면세 소득
myobi	tombstone	묘비(墓碑)
myoseok	tombstone	묘석(墓石)

N

nabi nekt'ai	bow tie	나비 넥타이
naebu bunsawegi	internal grinder	내부 분쇄기
naebu gamsa	internal audit	내부 감사(監査)
naebu jageum jodal	internal funding	내부 자금 조달
naebu jeongbo	tip (inside information)	내부 정보(內部情報)
naebu suingnyul	internal rate of return	내부 수익율
naebu-eui	internal	내부의

nomu jaehae

naegujae	durable goods	내구재(耐久財)
naegukse	internal revenue tax	내국세
naehwa byeoktol	refractories	내화 벽돌
naejang muyeok sangp'um	packaging	내장(內裝) 무역 상품
naeng-gan-abyeon	cold rolling	냉간압연(冷間壓延)
naep'o	implication	내포
naerida	undercut (v)	내리다
naeyeol dojagiryu	heat-resistant ceramics	내열(耐熱) 도자기류
naeyeol k'oil	hot strip coil	내열(耐熱) 코일
naillon	nylon	나일론
nakt'a t'eol	camel's hair	낙타 털
nal	bit	날
nalyeom-hada	print	날염하다
namnyeo gongdong	unisex	남녀 공동
nangbi-hada	lash (v)	낭비하다
nangnong jep'um	dairy products	낙농 제품(酪農製品)
nap'euk'in	napkin	나프킨
nappu	payment	납부
napsehu shilje baedang-yul	after-tax real rate of return	납세 후 실제 배당율
nasa jeolttan seonban	screw cutting lathe	나사 절단 선반
naseon-hyeong gangch'eol-gwan	spiral tube	나선형 강철관
nekt'ai	tie	넥타이
neungnyeok	capacity	능력
neungnyul	efficiency	능률
neungnyuljeog-euro hada	streamline (v)	능률적으로 하다
nik'elch'eol	ferronickel	니켈철
nodong	labor	노동
nodong beopcheon	labor code	노동법전
nodong gadongseong (yudongseong)	mobility of labor	노동 가동성(유동성)
nodong gyegeup	working class	노동 계급
nodong heuiseok	dilution of labor	노동 희석(稀釋)
nodong idong	labor turnover	노동 이동
nodong jaeng-eui	labor dispute	노동 쟁의
nodong jeoryak-eui	labor-saving (adj)	노동 절약의
nodong jeungmyeongseo	working papers	노동 증명서
nodong jibyak-hyeong-eui	labor-intensive (adj)	노동 집약형의
nodong jidoja	labor leader	노동 지도자
nodong johap	labor union	노동 조합
nodong shigan	man hours	노동 시간
nodong shijang	labor market	노동 시장
nodongja	laborer	노동자
nodongyeok	labor force, manpower, work force	노동력
nodongpeop	labor law	노동법
nogeum jangch'i robot'eu	playback robot	녹음 장치 로보트
no-hau	know-how	노-하우
nojo gyeyak	union contract	노조 계약
nomu jaehae	industrial accident	노무 재해

nonbak-hada	dispute (v)	논박하다
nong-eop	agriculture	농업
nong-eop eo-eum	agricultural paper	농업 어음
nongsanmul	agricultural products	농산물
nonjaeng	dispute	논쟁(論爭)
nonjaeng-hada	dispute (v)	논쟁하다
nosa gwan-gye	labor relations	노사 관계
noseon (eopchong) gyeong-yeong	line management	노선(업종) 경영
not'eu	knot (nautical)	노트
not'eubuk k'eomp'yut'eo	notebook computer	노트북 컴퓨터
nugajeok	cumulative (adj)	누가적(累加的)
nugamse	regressive tax	누감세(累減稅)
nujeok kamkka sangkak	accumulated depreciation	누적 감가 상각
nujeok useonju	cumulative preferred stock	누적 우선주
nujeokhaneun	cumulative (adj)	누적(累積)하는
nuson	leakage	누손(漏損)
nyeon	year	년(年)

O

obeohedeu	overhead	오버 헤드
odo	misleading	오도(誤導)
(chageop-eul) oebu-e matkkida	farm out (v)	(작업을) 외부에 맡기다
oebyeon (puga) shijang	fringe market	외변(外邊) (부가-附加) 시장
oech'ae	foreign debt	외채(外債)
oeguk cheonbo	cable (n)	외국 전보
oeguk hoesa	alien corporation	외국 회사
oeguk hoesa (peobin)	foreign corporation	외국 회사(법인)
oeguk hwap'ye	foreign currency	외국 화폐
oeguk muyeok	foreign trade	외국 무역
oeguk sanp'um	foreign product	외국 산품
oeguk yukka jeungkkeon	foreign securities	외국 유가 증권
oegukhwan	foreign exchange	외국환
oegukhwan gwalli	exchange control	외국환 관리
oegukhwan eo-eum	foreign bill of exchange	외국환 어음
oegukse gammyeon	foreign tax credit	외국세 감면(外國稅減免)
oehwa	foreign currency	외화
oehwa jokkeon bojeungseo	letter of guaranty	외화 조건 보증서
oeje	foreign product	외제(外製)
oejep'um	foreign product	외제품(外製品)
oesang georae gyejeong	charge account	외상 거래 계정
oesang georae-hada	credit (v)	외상 거래하다
oesang jangbu	passbook	외상 장부
oesang p'anmae-hada	credit (v)	외상 판매하다
oesang-euro	on account (adv)	외상으로

oeshin	cable (n)	외신
ogyangmok	muslin	옥양목
ohae	misunderstanding	오해(誤解)
okso	iodine	옥소(沃素)
oksusu	maize	옥수수
ondo jojeol jangch'i	thermostat	온도 조절 장치
o-om	ohm	오옴
onrain	on line	온 라인
op'euset inswae	offset printing	오프셋 인쇄
oryu	error	오류(誤謬)
oryureul sujeong-hada	debug (v)	오류를 수정하다
osan	miscalculation, error	오산(誤算)
o-sedae k'eomp'yut'eo	fifth-generation computer	5세대 컴퓨터
ot'omeisyeon	automation	오토메이션

P

paech'i	layout	배치
paedal	delivery	배달
paedal bongsa (p'yeon-eui)	courier service	배달 봉사(편의)
paedal iljja	delivery date	배달 일자
pach'im jeopshi	saucer	받침 접시
p'adong	pulse	파동
paedal jijeom	delivery points	배달 지점
paedang	passed dividend	배당
paedangbu	cum dividend	배당부(配當附)
paedang-hada	assign (v)	배당하다
paedang-geum	dividend	배당금
paedang-geum su-ik	dividend yield	배당금 수익
paedangnak	ex dividend	배당락(配當落)
paedangyul	dividend	배당율
(pae-ga) iphang-hada	put into	(배가) 입항하다
paegeup	rationing	배급(配給)
paegeup eopcha	distributor	배급 업자
paekhwajeom	department store	백화점
p'aekshimilli	facsimile	팩시밀리
paelleoseut'eu boneoseu	ballast bonus	밸러스트 보너스
paesu	multiples	배수(倍數)
paesang	compensation	배상
paeseo	endorsement	배서(背書)
paeseo eo-eum	backed note	배서 어음
paeseo mit poch'ung	backing and filling	배서 및 보충
p'aet'eon inshik	pattern recognition	패턴 인식
paejim	cargo	뱃짐
paguni	basket	바구니
paji	slacks	바지
pa-i-t'eu (p'al bi-t'eu)	byte	바이트(8비트)
pakche	stuffing	박제(剝製)
pakp'an bong-gang	sheet bar	박판 봉강(棒鋼)

Korean (romanized)	English	Korean
pakp'an deomi	sheet pile	박판더미
pak'wi-dallin jaengban	coaster	바퀴달린 쟁반
palhaeng	issue (stock)	발행
palhaeng iljja	when issued	발행 일자
palhaeng-in	publisher	발행인
palhaeng jushik	issued shares	발행 주식
paljjeon-gi	dynamo, generator	발전기
paljju-hada	place an order (v)	발주(發注)하다
palsaeng-hada	accrue (v)	발생하다
palhaeng-hada	issue (v)	발행하다
palsaeng-ju-eui weonch'ik	accrual method	발생주의 원칙
palsong	dispatch	발송
panbok robot'eu	repeatable robot	반복 로보트
pan deomp'ing gwanse	anti-dumping duty	반덤핑 관세
pandeung	rally	반등(反騰)
pandoch'e	semiconductor	반도체
pandoch'e bakp'an	wafer	반도체 박판
pandoch'e ch'ukcheon-gi	chip condenser	반도체 축전기
pandoch'e reijeo	semiconductor laser	반도체 레이저
paneujil-hada	sew	바느질하다
pangbu-eui	antiseptic	방부(防腐)의
pangch'im	policy	방침
pan-gam (cheung-kkweon)	half-life (bonds)	반감(反減)(증권)
pangbeop	mode, method	방법
pangsa igeuk chin-gong-gwan	light-emitting diode	방사 이극 진공관
pangsasang ch'eon-gong-gi	radial-drilling machine	방사상 천공기
pangshik	mode	방식
pang-yeolgi	radiator	방열기
panhwan	kickback	반환
panhwan	rollover	반환(反還)
panhwan	fair return	반환(反還)
panhwanmul	refund (n)	반환물
panhyang hyokkwa	backwash effect	반향 효과
param-magi jeonmyeon yuri	windshield	바람막이 전면 유리
pansa jeungp'ok jangch'i k'amera	reflex camera	반사 증폭 장치 카메라
pan-yangjangbon	paperback	반 양장본
patteri	battery	밧데리
peobin	corporation	법인
peobin gujo (hyeongt'ae)	corporate structure	법인 구조(형태)
peobin (ki-eop) imiji	corporate image	법인(기업) 이미지
peobin seollip in-gajjeung	certificate of incorporation	법인 설립 인가증
peobin (ki-eop) seongjang	corporate growth	법인(기업) 성장
peobinse	corporation tax	법인세
peo-geu	bug (defect in computer program)	버그
peolgeum	fine (penalty)	벌금
peomnyeong	statute	법령
peomnyul	law	**법률**
peomnyulga	lawyer	**법률가**

peomnyulsang-eui jabon-geum	legal capital	법률상의 자본금
peomnyulsang-eui shilch'emul	legal entity	법률상의 실체물
peomp'eo	bumper	범퍼
peopcheong dokcheom	legal monopoly	법정 독점
peopcheong hyuil	legal holiday	법정 휴일
peopcheong jagyeok	capacity	법정 자격
peopcheong t'onghwa	legal tender	법정 통화
peophwa	legal tender	법화(法貨)
peopkyu	law	법규
peonyeokcha	translator	번역자
peoseu t'eomjeu jokkeon	berth terms	버스 텀즈 조건
peot'eo jeopshi	butter dish	버터 접시
peot'eo naip'eu	butter knife	버터 나이프
peullauseu	blouse	블라우스
peullejieo	blazer	블레지어
peuraun gwan	Braun tube	브라운관
peureik'eu	brake	브레이크
peurogeuraem	program	프로그램
peurouch'ing meoshi-in	broaching machine	브로우칭 머시인
ph'yojun iha-eui hangmok	below the line	표준 이하의 항목
pi	ratio	비
pi yeongni	nonprofit	비영리
pibeop	know-how	비법(秘法)
pidan	silk	비단
pidio diseuk'eu	video disc	비디오 디스크
pidio k'aset'eu jangch'i	video cassette player	비디오 카세트 장치
pidio k'aset'eu k'amera	video cassette camera	비디오 카세트 카메라
pidio k'aset'eu nogeumgi	video cassette recorder	비디오 카세트 녹음기
pidiok'e	VideOrche	비디오케
pidio t'eip'eu nogeumgi	video tape recorder	비디오 테이프 녹음기
pi geojuja	nonresident	비거주자
pigeumsok kwangmul	non-metallic mineral	비금속 광물
pi-gyeoljjeong gyuso	amorphous silicon	비결정 규소
pi-gong-gae hoesa	closely held corporation	비공개 회사
pi hoeweon	nonmember	비회원
pijageum	secret fund	비자금(秘資金)
pijeongjil bandoch'e	amorphous semiconductor	비정질(非定質) 반도체
pillida	borrow (v)	빌리다
pi naegujae	nondurable goods	비 내구재(非耐久財)
pindo gokseon	frequency curve	빈도 곡선
pineungnyulcheok	inefficient (adj)	비능률적(非能率的)
pinireui	vinyl (adj)	비닐의
pi-ot	raincoat	비옷
pip'um	logistics	비품
pirye junghang	mean (average)	비례 중항
pisangjang-eui	unlisted (adj)	비상장(非上場)의
piseo	secretary	비서
pit'amin	vitamin	비타민

pit	debt	빚
pit'allyeokseong suyo gong-geup	inelastic demand or supply	비탄력성 수요 공급
pit pangsa igeuk chin-gong-gwan	light-emitting diode	빛 방사 이극 진공관
pityeu	bit	비트
piyong	outlay, expenses	비용
piyong gwalli	cost control	비용 관리
piyong hyokkwa bunseok	analysis, cost-benefit	비용 효과 분석
piyong hyokkwajeogin	cost effective (adj)	비용 효과적인
piyong-hyokkwa bunseok	cost-benefit analysis	비용-효과 분석
piyong jeolgam	cost reduction	비용 절감
piyong manhoe	recovery of expenses	비용 만회
piyong mit hwamul susong	cost and freight	비용 및 화물 수송
piyong yoso	cost factor	비용 요소
piyong-eui halttang	allocation of costs	비용의 할당
pi yudong jasan	noncurrent assets	비 유동 자산
piyul	ratio, rate, loss-loss ratio	비율
piyul su-ikko	percentage earnings	비율 수익고
podo	report	보도
pogo	report	보고
pogwan-hada	store (v)	보관하다
poheom	insurance	보험(保險)
poheom	indemnity	보험
poheom beomwi jehan geumaek	coverage (insurance)	보험 범위 제한 금액
poheom eopcha	underwriter	보험 업자
poheom gyeyak peomwi	coverage (insurance)	보험 계약 범위
poheom gyeyakjja	policyholder	보험 계약자
poheom hoegyesa	actuary	보험 회계사
poheom hoesa	insurance company	보험 회사
poheom insu eopcha	insurance underwriter	보험 인수 업자
poheom jageum	insurance fund	보험 자금
poheom jeungkkwon	insurance policy	보험 증권
poheom jung-gaein	insurance broker	보험 중개인
poheomnyo	insurance premium	보험료
poheomnyo burip	premium payment	보험료 불입
poheomnyo p'yeongkka	premium pricing	보험료 평가
poho	safeguard	보호
poho muyeokchu-eui	protectionism	보호 무역 주의
poik'ot	boycott	보이콧
poilleo gangp'an	boiler plate	보일러 강(鋼)판
pojeung	security, guarantee	보증
pojeung-geum biyul	cover ratio	보증금 비율
pojeung-geum suyo	margin requirements	보증금 수요
pojeung gyeyak	bond	보증 계약
pojeung hoesa	surety company	보증 회사
pojeung hoesa	quaranty company	보증 회사
pojeung-in	sponsor (of fund, partnership)	보증인

pojeung seoryu	backing support	보증 서류
pojeung sup'yo	cashier's check	보증 수표
pojeung sup'yo	certified check	보증 수표
pojeungjjang	warrant	보증장(保證狀)
(p'umjil) pojeungseo	warranty	(품질) 보증서
pojeungseo	guaranty bond	보증서
pojo gongch'ae jeungseo	back-up bonds	보조 공채 증서
pojo hyokkwa	ancillary operations	보조 효과
pojo renjeu	auxiliary lens	보조 렌즈
pojogeum	subsidy	보조금
pojwa ch'ammo	staff assistant	보좌 참모
pojwa-yeok	assistant	보좌역
pokcheom	duopoly	복점(複占)
pokhap ki-eop	conglomerate	복합 기업
poksa	copy	복사
pokshik hwannyul	multiple exchange rate	복식 환률
pokshik kijangbeop pugi	double-entry bookkeeping	복식 기장법 부기 (複式記帳法簿記)
pokshik kwase	multiple taxation	복식 과세(複式課稅)
poksu bangch'u ch'eon-gong-gi	multispindle drilling machine	복수 방추 천공기
poksu jeolttan seonban	multicut lathe	복수 절단 선반
poksu t'onghwa	multicurrency	복수 통화(複數通貨)
polliseut'illen	polystyrene	폴리스틸렌
p'olliuret'an	polyurethane	폴리우레탄
pon	pattern	본
pong-geup	salary	봉급(俸給)
pong-geup saenghwalja	white collar worker	봉급 생활자
pongham ipch'al	sealed bid	봉함 입찰(封緘入札)
pongjae-hada	saw	봉재하다
pongni	compound interest	복리(複利)
pongsa gyeyak	service contract	봉사 계약
pongsa-hada	service (v)	봉사(奉仕)하다
pongswae t'onghwa	blocked currency	봉쇄 통화
ponhoe-eui	plenary meeting	본회의(本會議)
ponjeom	head office	본점(本店)
ponjeon-ida	breakeven (v)	본전이다
ponsa	head office, headquarters	본사(本社)
ponseondo	free on board	본선도(本船渡)
po-oring meoshin	boring machine	보오링 머신
poryu	passed dividend	보류
posang	remuneration	보상
posang	indemnity	보상
posang	compensation	보상
posang yegeum	compensating balance	보상 예금
pose ch'angkko	bonded warehouse	보세 창고
pose guyeok	bond areas	보세 구역(保稅區域)
pose hwamul	bonded goods	보세 화물
pose hwamul unsong-in	bonded carrier	보세 화물 운송인
posep'um	bonded goods	보세품

posu	remuneration	보수
posu	gratuity	보수
posu	compensation	보수
pot'ong insu	general acceptance	보통 인수
pot'ong jushik	common stock	보통 주식
pot'ong su-ip shin-go	entry, cash	**보통 수입 신고**
poyu gigan	holding period	보유 기간
(keum-eul jung-ang eunhang-eui boyugeum-eseo) ppaenaeda	earmark (v)	(금을 중앙은행의 보유금에서) 빼내다
pu	wealth	부(富)
pu	department (company)	**부(部)**
pubu byeolgeo	separation	부부별거(夫婦別居)
pubun hamul (paetchim)	part cargo	부분 하물(部分荷物)(뗏짐)
puch'ae	debt	부채
puch'ae	debit	부채(負債)
puch'ae eomneun	free and clear (adj)	부채없는
puch'ae sayong	leverage	부채 사용
puch'aeaek	indebtedness	부채액
puch'ak-hada	attach (v)	부착하다
pudam	encumbrance (liens, liabilities, commitments)	부담(負擔)
pudam shi-k'ida	absorb (v)	부담시키다
pudang yeommae daehangse	duty, anti-dumping	부당 염매 대항세 (不當廉賣對抗稅)
pudo	dishonor (as a check)	부도
pudong jeungkkweon	float (outstanding checks, stock)	부동 증권(浮動證券)
pudongsan	real estate	부동산
pudongsan yungja susuryo	point (percentage) (mortgage term)	부동산 융자 수수료
pudu sayongnyo	wharfage charge	부두 사용료(埠頭使用料)
pu-eop	moonlighting	부업(副業)
puga gach'ise	value-added tax	부가 가치세(附加價値稅)
puga jeodang	collateral	부가 저당(附加抵當)
puga shijang	fringe market	부가 시장
pugageup	fringe benefits	부가급(附加給)
pugaryo	load (sales charge)	부가료(附加料)
pugase	surtax	부가세(附加稅)
pugi	bookkeeping	부기
pugi gyesanp'yo	spreadsheet	부기 계산표
pu-gwalli-in	assistant manager	부관리인
puhayul	load factor	부하율(負荷率)
puhayul	factor, load	부하율(負荷率)
puhoejang	vice-president	부회장
puhoejang	deputy chairman	부회장
pujae jiju	ownership, absentee	부재 지주
pujae jiju jedo	absenteeism	부재 지주 제도
pujaeja soyukkkweon	absentee ownership	부재자 소유권
pujeongjeok eonjil	negative pledge	부정적 언질(否定的言質)

pujeonji	allonge	부전지(附箋紙)
pujeok unim	dead freight	부적 운임(不積運賃)
pujibae-in	assistant manager	부지배인
pujibae-in	deputy manager	부지배인
pujogaek	shortage	부족액
pujok	shortage	부족
pulbeop haeng-wi	tort	불법 행위
pulbeop-eui	illegal (adj)	불법의
pulbeop seonjeok	illegal shipments	불법 선적
pulch'ukcheok paedang (ju)	noncumulative preferred stock	불축적 배당(주)
pulch'ungbunhan	inadequate (adj)	불충분한
pulgahangnyeok	force majeure	불가항력(不可抗力)
pulgahangnyeok	act of God	불가항력
pulgongjeonghan	unfair (adj)	불공정한
pulgongp'yeonghan	unfair (adj)	불공평한
pulgyeong-gi	depression	불경기
pulhwang	depression	불황(不況)
pulihaeng	failure	불이행
pulip ing-yeogeum	paid-in surplus	불입 잉여금
pulip-p'il jabon-geum	paid up capital	불입필(拂入畢) 자본금
pulip-p'ilju	paid up shares	불입필주(拂入畢株)
pulli	handicap	불리
pulli shinseol-hada	spin off (v)	분리 신설(分離新設) 하다
pullihan	unfavorable (adj)	불리(不利)한
pullo suip	unearned revenue	불로수입(不勞收入)
pullyang	quantity	분량
pullyang buch'ae	bad debt	불량 부채
pulmae undong	boycott	불매 운동
pulp'yeong ch'eori jeolch'a	grievance procedure	불평 처리 절차
punbae gyeongno	channel of distribution	분배 경로
puneop	division of labor	분업(分業)
punhae jangch'i	take down	분해 장치(分解裝置)
punhal buripkeum	partial payment	분할 불입금
punhal gyehoek	installment plan	분할 계획
punhal sanghwan	amortization	분할 상환
punhal shinyongdae	installment credit	분할 신용대(分割信用貸)
punjeom	office, branch	분점
punjeom	branch office	분점
punsanch'i	variance	분산치(分散値)
punseok	assay	분석
punshil	office, branch	분실
punshil	loss	분실
pup'um	parts	부품
puranjeong	instability	불안정
puripkeum jijeong	assessment	불입금 지정
purok	codicil	부록
pusajang	vice-president	부사장
pusanmul	by-product	부산물(副產物)
punseok	analysis	분석
punseokcha (ka)	analyst	분석자(가)

puseon unban	lighterage	부선 운반(假船運搬)
pusu jangch'i	peripherals	부수 장치(附隨裝置)
pusu sangp'um	accompanied goods	부수 상품
pusu unyong	ancillary operations	부수 운용
puweon	mint	부원(富源)
pyeol munje eomneun	no problem	별 문제없는
pyeoltto susong hamul	unaccompanied goods	별도 수송 하물
pyeondongbi	variable costs	변동비(變動費)
pyeondong deungkka	sliding parity	변동 등가(變動等價)
pyeondong hwannyul	floating exchange rate	변동 환율
pyeondong ijayul	variable interest rate	변동 이자율
pyeondong-nyul	variable rate	변동율
pyeondong-nyul jut'aek yungja	variable rate mortgage	변동율 주택 융자
pyeondong shise	floating rate	변동 시세
pyeondongbi	costs, variable	변동비(變動費)
pyeongch'amp'um	logistics	병참품
pyeong-ga	sick leave	병가(病暇)
pyeon-gyeong	alteration	변경
pyeonhosa	lawyer, attorney	변호사
pyeonje	liquidation	변제
pyeonje gach'i	liquidation value	변제 가치
pyeonjo	forgery	변조(變造)
pyeonjogi saengsan	modular production	변조기 생산
pyeonsang	remedy (law)	변상
pyeonsang-hada	reimburse	변상하다
p'a-eop	walkout	파업
p'a-eop	picket line	파업
p'a-eop p'agi	strikebreaker	파업 파기(罷業破棄)
p'a-eop shiwi	picket line	파업 시위(罷業示威)
p'aerit'i gagyeok	parity price	패러티 가격
p'a-i-hyeong dop'yo	pie chart	파이형 도표
p'ajang shise	closing price	파장 시세(罷場時勢)
p'alda	sell (to) (v)	팔다
p'allo	outlet	판로(販路)
p'allo (shijang) josa	market research	판로(시장) 조사
p'amyeon-hada	fire (v)	파면(罷免)하다
p'andan	appreciation	판단
p'andan gijun	yardstick	판단 기준
p'aneunjjok	bear	파는 쪽
p'anjeong-hada	adjudge (v)	판정하다
p'ankkweon	copyright	판권
p'anmae bunseok	analysis, sales	판매 분석
p'anmae bunseok	sales analysis	판매 분석
p'anmae ch'okchin	sales promotion	판매 촉진
p'anmae-aek	sales	판매액
p'anmae gaenyeom	marketing concept	판매 개념
p'anmae ganeungseong	potential sales	판매 가능성
p'anmae gwalli	sales management	판매 관리
p'anmae gyehoek	market plan	판매 계획
p'anmae gyehoek	marketing plan	판매 계획

p'anmae gyeongno (t'ongno)	distribution, channel of	판매 경로(통로)
p'anmae halttang	quota, sales	판매 할당
p'anmae halttang-aek	sales quota	판매 할당액
p'anmae-hada	sell (to) (v)	판매하다
p'anmae je-eui gagyeok	offer for sale	판매 제의 가격
p'anmae jeongch'aek	distribution policy	판매 정책
p'anmae jeungjin (ch'okchin)	promotion, sales	판매 증진(촉진)
p'anmae jokkeon	terms of sale	판매 조건
p'anmae kwalli	management, sales	판매 관리
p'anmae sangp'um biyong	cost of goods sold	판매 상품 비용
p'anmae shijang	market	판매 시장
p'anmae shijang ch'imt'u	market penetration	판매 시장 침투
p'anmae shijang kwalli	market management	판매 시장 관리
p'anmae shijang kwalli	management, market	판매 시장 관리
p'anmae shijang p'yeongkka	market appraisal	판매 시장 평가
p'anmae shijjeom	point of sale	판매 시점(販賣時點)
p'anmae su-ik	return on sales	판매 수익
p'anmae yech'euk	forecast, sales	판매 예측
p'anmae yeong-yeok	sales territory	판매 영역(領域)
p'anmae yesan	sales budget	판매 예산
p'anmae yesan	budget, sales	판매 예산
p'anmae yesang-go	sales estimate	판매 예상고(豫想高)
p'anmaebi	distribution costs	판매비
p'anmae-hada	market (v)	판매하다
p'anmae-in	distributor	판매인
p'anmaekkweon	dealership	판매권
p'anmaemang	distribution network	판매망
p'anmaeryang	volume, sales	판매량
p'anmaese	tax, sales	판매세
p'anmaeweon	sales force	판매원
p'asan	bankruptcy	파산
p'asan	failure	파산
p'asan-hada	fail (v)	파산하다
p'eonch'i k'adeu	punch card	펀치 카드
p'eulop'i diseuk'eu	floppy disk	플로피 디스크
p'eullow ch'aat'eu	flow chart	플로우 차아트
p'eurojekt'eu gihoek	project planning	프로젝트 기획
p'i-ideubaek	feedback	피이드 백
p'ilsu	requirement	필수(必須)
p'ilsup'um bunseok	needs analysis	필수품 분석
p'iramit-shik p'anmae	pyramid selling	피라밋식 판매
p'iryodo bunseok	analysis, needs	필요도 분석
p'iryo mulgeon	requirements	필요 물건
p'ogi-hada	abandon (v)	포기하다
p'ojang	packaging	포장(包裝)
p'ojang georae	package deal	포장 거래
p'ojang myeongseseo	packing list	포장 명세서
p'ojang sangja	packing case	포장 상자
p'oktteung	boom	폭등
p'ongnak	slump	폭락(暴落)
p'o-om ret'eo	form letter	포옴 레터

p'umjil ch'aegimja	brand manager	품질 책임자
p'umjil gwalli	quality control	품질 관리
p'umjil gwalli	control, quality	품질 관리
p'umjil gyeong-yeong	quality management	품질 경영
p'umjil insu	brand acceptance	품질 인수
p'ummok	item	품목
p'ummok kwalli	management, line	품목 관리
p'ungseon jeungkkweon	balloon note	풍선 증권
p'ungseon jibulgeum	balloon (payment)	풍선 지불금
p'yegi	obsolescence	폐기
p'yejang shise	closing price	폐장(廢場) 시세
p'yeong-gyun	average	평균
p'yeong-gyun danwi biyong	average unit cost	평균 단위 비용
p'yeong-gyun gagyeok	average price	평균 가격
p'yeong-gyun-hada	averaging	평균하다
p'yeong-gyun sumyeong	average life	평균 수명
p'yeong-gyun weonkka	average cost	평균 원가
p'yeong-gyunch'i	mean (average)	평균치
p'yeonghyeong gagyeok	parity	평형(平衡)가격
p'yeonghyeong sodeungnyul	parity income ratio	평형 소득율
p'yeong-gyun weonkka (biyong)	cost, average	평균 원가(비용)
p'yeong-il	work day	평일
p'yeongkka-aek	valuation	평가액
p'yeongkka	valuation	평가
p'yeongkka	evaluation, estimate, assay, appraisal, appreciation	평가
p'yeongkka gonghak	engineering, value	평가 공학
p'yeongkka jeolha	devaluation	평가 절하
p'yeongkka-eui sop'ok chojeong	crawling peg	평가(評價)의 소폭 조정
p'yeongkka-hada	estimate (v)	평가하다
p'yeongp'yeonghi hada	level out (v)	평평히 하다
p'yeongweonban	disk	평원반(平圓盤)
p'yeongkka jeolsang	revaluation	평가 절상(評價切上)
p'yoji seohan	cover letter	표지 서한
p'yojun	yardstick	표준
p'yojun biyong	standard costs	표준 비용
p'yojun gwallye	standard practice	표준 관례(標準慣例)
p'yojunhwa	standardization	표준화
p'yojun i-sang-eui	above-the-line	표준 이상의
p'yojun nomu shigan	standard time	표준 노무 시간
p'yojun p'yeonch'a	standard deviation	표준 편차(標準偏差)
p'yojunshi	standard time	표준시
p'yojun weonkka	costs, standard	표준 원가
p'yomyeon iyul-eomneun harinch'ae	zero coupon	표면 이율 없는 할인채
p'yoshi gagyeok	list price	표시 가격

R

radio	radio	라디오
radio k'aset'eu jeonch'uk	radio cassette player	라디오 카세트 전축
raem	RAM	램
rajiet'a	radiator	라지에타
reida	radar	레이다
reidieol t'aieo	radial tire	레이디얼 타이어
reijeo	laser	레이저
reijeo ch'eori	laser processing	레이저 처리
reijeo-gwang inswaegi	laser beam printer	레이저광 인쇄기
reijeo haeng-yunghap	laser fusion	레이저 핵융합
reijeo sajinsul gieok changch'i	holographic memory	레이저 사진술 기억 장치
renjeu	lens	렌즈
rideu t'aim	time, lead	리드 타임
rimok'on	remote control	리모콘
rinnereu	linen	린네르
rinnereuje-eui	linen (adj)	린네르 제(製)의
robi hwalttong	lobbying	로비 활동
rom	ROM	롬

S

sabal	bowl	사발
sabimmul	insert	삽입물
sabipki	insert machine	삽입기
sabon	copy	사본
sach'ae	debentures	사채(社債)
sach'i p'ummokse	luxury tax	사치 품목세
sach'ip'um	luxury goods	사치품(奢侈品)
sadan beobin	corporation	사단 법인
sae hwap'ye	new money	새 화폐
saegida	engrave (v)	새기다
saegin mongnok	catalog	색인 목록
saegin-eul dalda	index (v)	색인을 달다
sae jaeryo	new materials	새 재료(材料)
sae jedosul	new ceramics	새 제도술(製陶術)
saek	color	색
saek punhae	color separation	색 분해
saelleodeu jeopshi	salad plate	샐러드 접시
saelleodeu-yong jeopshi	salad bowl	샐러드용 접시
saeng-hwahak	biochemistry	생화학
saeng yo-eop	bio-ceramics	생(生) 요업(窯業)
saeng-k'eomp'yut'eo	bio-computer	생 컴퓨터
saeng-gyebi	cost of living	생계비
saenghwal sujun	standard of living	생활 수준
saenghwalbi	cost of living	생활비
saengjon shint'ak	living trust	생존 신탁(生存信託)
saengmyong boheom bojeungkkwon	life insurance policy	생명 보험 보증권

saengnyak-hada	omit (v)	생략하다
saengsan	production	생산
saengsan guip kyeolcheong	make-or-buy decision	생산 구입 결정
saengsan gwajeong	production process	생산 과정
saengsan gwalli	engineering, industrial, production control	생산 관리
saengsan hwalgi	dynamics, product	생산 활기
saengsan jiptan (tanch'e)	group, product	생산 집단(단체)
saengsan (chejo) neungnyeok	capacity, manufacturing	생산(제조) 능력
saengsan yejeongp'yo	production schedule	생산 예정표
saengsanaek	yield	생산액
saengsanbi	production costs	생산비
saengsaneop	industry	생산업
saengsan-go	outturn	생산고
saengsanja jiksong	drop shipment	생산자 직송(直送)
saengsanp'um	product	생산품
saengsanp'um bunseok	analysis, product	생산품 분석
saengsanp'um p'anmae ch'okchin undong	campaign, productivity	생산품 판매 촉진 운동
saengsanseon	production line	생산선
saengsanseong	productivity	생산성
saengsan-yeok ch'ujin undong	productivity campaign	생산력 추진 운동
sa-eop	project, enterprise	사업
sa-eop hwalttong	business activity	사업 활동
sa-eop (kyeong-yeong) jeollyak	business strategy	사업(경영) 전략
sa-eop kyehoek	business plan	사업 계획
sa-eop kyeong-yeong	business management	사업 경영
sa-eop noseon	line of business	사업 노선
sa-eop pangch'im	business policy	사업 방침
sa-eopkka	entrepreneur	사업가
sa-eopkka boheom	key man insurance	사업가 보험
sagi	morale, fraud	사기(士氣, 詐欺)
sagi haeng-wi beolgeum joch'i	penalty-fraud action	사기 행위 벌금 조치
sahoe ganjeop chabon	infrastructure	사회 간접 자본
sahu geomt'o-hada	follow-up (v)	사후(事後) 검토(檢討)하다
sahu ilbu	postdated (adj)	사후 일부(事後日附)
sajang	president	사장
sajeon t'ong-go	advance notice	사전 통고
sajeong gagyeok	assessed valuation	사정(査定) 가격
sajeong-aek	assessment	사정액
sajin jeondo muljjil	photo-conductive materials	사진 전도 물질
sajin jeondoryeok	photo-conductivity	사진 전도력
sajiin jeonjagi hyokkwa	photo electro-magnetic effect	사진 전자기 효과
sajinkki	camera	사진기
sajinkki momch'e	camera body	사진기 몸체
sajjeok paech'i	private placement (finance)	사적 배치
sak'arin	saccharin	사카린
sakje-hada	cancel (v)	삭제하다

sanghwan jeongnipkeum

sakkam	cutback, drawdown	삭감
salsaram	buyer, potential	살 사람
samgaktae	tripod	삼각대
samshibo milli sajinkki (k'amera)	35mm camera	35밀리 사진기(카메라)
samu gwalli	office management	사무 관리
samu kwalli	management, office	사무 관리
samujik	white collar worker	사무직
samushil	office	사무실
sanaeju	treasury stock	사내주(社內株)
sanch'ulgo	output	산출고
sanch'ullyang	output	산출량
sanch'ulaek	outturn	산출액
saneop	industry	산업
saneop cheonch'e-eui	industry-wide (adj)	산업 전체의
saneop chungjae	industrial arbitration	산업 중재
saneop konghak	industrial engineering	산업 공학
saneop kyehoek	industrial planning	산업 계획
saneop sangp'um	industrial goods	산업 상품
saneop-p'um	goods, industrial	산업품
saneoppyeol nodong johap	industrial union	산업별 노동 조합
san-eui	acid (adj)	산(酸)의
(shise sangseung-eul yesang) saneun-jjok	bull	(시세 상승을 예상) 사는 쪽
sangdamdoen p'anmae	negotiated sale	상담(相談)된 판매
sangdamnyeok	consultant	상담역
sangdanghan ju-eui	reasonable care	상당(相當)한 주의(注意)
sang-eop	mercantile	상업
sang-eop eunhaeng	commercial bank	상업 은행
sang-eop heungshinso	mercantile agency	상업 흥신소
sang-eop (muyeok) songjjang	commercial invoice	상업(무역) 송장(送狀)
sang-eopchi	place of business	상업지
sang-eop (muyeok) sang deung-geup	commercial grade	상업(무역)상 등급
sang-geum	gratuity	상금
sang-gi-eui	above-mentioned	상기의
sang-gong hoe-euiso	chamber of commerce	상공 회의소
sanghanseon	ceiling	상한선
sangho	trademark	상호
sangho baeje johang	mutually exclusive classes	상호 배제 조항
sangho jagyong-hada	interact (v)	상호 작용하다
sangho jeoch'uk eunhaeng	mutual savings bank	상호 저축 은행
sangho t'eukheo sayong heoga	crosslicensing	상호 특허 사용 허가
sanghwan ch'eong-gu	recourse	상환 청구
sanghwan ch'eong-gukkweon	right of recourse	상환 청구권
sanghwan geubyeo	redemption allowance	상환 급여
sanghwan-geum	refund (n)	상환금
sanghwan haljjeung-geum	redemption premium	상환 할증금
sanghwan jeongnipkeum	redemption fund	상환 적립금

sanghwan kasok chohang	acceleration clause	상환 가속 조항
sanghwan susuryo	redemption premium	상환 수수료
sanghyang shihwang	upmarket	상향 시황(上向市況)
sang-im isahoe	executive board	상임 이사회
sang-in	mercantile	상인
sang-in johap	merchant guild	상인 조합
sangjangju	listed securities	상장주(上場株)
sangjeom	firm	상점
sangnap	kickback	상납(上納)
sangnil	piecework	삯 일
sangppeop	mercantile law	상법
sangp'um	merchandise, commodity	상품
sangp'um donghyang	movement of goods	상품 동향(動向)
sangp'um georaeso	commodity exchange	상품 거래소
sangp'um mongnok kwalli	control, inventory	상품 목록 관리
sangp'umhwa jeongch'aek (kyehoek)	merchandising	상품화 정책(계획)
sangp'yo	trademark, brand	상표
sangp'yo damdang-in	brand manager	상표 담당인
sangp'yo injeong	brand acceptance	상표 인정
sangp'yo inshik	brand recognition	상표 인식
sangp'yo moyang	brand image	상표 모양
sangp'yo seonho	brand loyalty	상표 선호(商標選好)
sangsa	trade house, trading company	상사(商社)
sangsahyeong (anarogeu) jeonja gyesan-gi	computer, analog	상사형(아나로그) 전자 계산기
sangseung	upturn	상승
sangseup cheonjikcha	job hopper	상습 전직자(常習轉職者)
sangseupcheok kyeol-geun	absenteeism	상습적 결근
sangsokse	inheritance tax	상속세
sansul p'yeong-gyun	arithmetic mean	산술 평균
sangsul-han	above-mentioned	상술한
sangswae gwanse	countervailing duty	상쇄 관세(相殺關稅)
sang-wi	variance	상위(相違)
sang-wi jushik	senior issue	상위 주식(上位株式)
sanhwa	oxidation	산화(酸化)
saphwa, tohae	illustration	삽화, 도해
sanji ipko	field warehousing	산지 입고(産地入庫)
sanseong geomsa biyul	acid-test ratio	산성 검사 비율 (酸性檢査比率)
saryun gudong jeondong jangch'i	four-wheel drive	4륜 구동 전동 장치
saseol bose ch'angkko	licensed warehouse	사설 보세 창고
saweon	member of firm	사원
sayong p'yeollihan	user friendly	사용 편리한
sayong-in	employee	사용인
sayongja	user	사용자
sayongnyo	rent	사용료
sayongse	use tax	사용세

se	duty	세
se-aek sajeong gagyeok	value for duty	세액 사정(稅額査定)가격
sech'ik	by-laws	세칙
segeum (chose) budam	tax burden	세금(조세) 부담
segeum gongje	tax allowance	세금 공제(控除)
segeum gongje (aek)	tax deduction	세금 공제(액)
segeum jibul euimu	liable for tax	세금 지불 의무
segeum myeonje	remission of a tax	세금 면제
segeum t'alp'ich'eo	tax haven	세금 탈피처
segeum-eul gwa-hada	levy taxes (v)	세금을 과하다
segwan	customs	세관
segwan hwamul ch'wigeubin	customs broker	세관 화물 취급인
segye eunhaeng	World Bank	세계 은행
se-ip	revenue	세입(歲入)
selp'eu seobiseu	self-service	셀프 서비스
seobiseu-ryo	cover charge	서비스료
seoboe	public relations	섭외
seo-eon	introduction	서언
seogigwan	secretary	서기관
seogyu dalleo	petrodollars	석유 달러
seogyu hwahak	petrochemical	석유 화학
seohan	letter	서한
seokhoeseok	limestone	석회석
seokki	stoneware	석기
seokt'ansan	phenol	석탄산
seokt'an	coal	석탄
seolbi	facilities	설비
seolbi biyong	set-up costs	설비 비용
seolch'ibi	costs, set-up	설치비
seolgyeja	designer	설계자
seolgye	plan (n)	설계
seolgye gonghak	design engineering	설계 공학
seolgyedo	blueprint	설계도
seollip ch'wijiseo	prospectus	설립 취지서
seollipi	costs, set-up	설립비
seolp'aje	sulphamide	설파제
seolt'ang geureut	sugar bowl	설탕 그릇
seomgwang jeon-gu	flash bulb	섬광 전구
seomgwang jeon-gu balgwang jangch'i	flash cube	섬광 전구 발광 장치
seomyeong	signature	서명(署名)
seomyeongja	undersigned	서명자
seomyu bogang hapseong suji	fiber-reinforced plastics	섬유 보강 합성 수지
seonban	lathe	선반(旋盤)
seonbul	cash in advance	선불(先拂)
seonbul biyong	prepaid expenses (balance sheet), front-end fee	선불 비용(先拂費用)
seonbul jaejeong	front-end financing	선불 재정
seonbul unim	advance freight	선불 운임
seonbul-hada	prepay (v)	선불하다

seonbul k'adeu	prepaid credit card	선불 카드
seong	department (U.S. government)	성(省)
seonch'eol	pig iron	선철
seonch'eug-e	alongside	선측(船側)에
seonch'eukto	free alongside ship	선측도(船側渡)
seonch'wikkweon	priority	선취권
seonch'wi t'eukkweon	lien	선취 특권(先取特權)
seondae	private fleet	선대(船隊)
seondae-hada	advance (v)	선대하다
seondo sanghwan	advance refunding	선도 상환
seongbun	component	성분(成分)
seon-geo hasujjeung	dock(ship's receipt)	선거 하수증(船渠荷受證)
seon-geo sayongryo	dock handling charges	선거 사용료(船渠使用料)
seon-geup chasan	accrued assets	선급 자산(先給資產)
seongjang	growth	성장
seongjang jamjaeryeok	growth potential	성장 잠재력
seongjang jisu	growth index	성장 지수(指數)
seongjang jushik	growth stock	성장 주식
seongjang saneop	growth industry	성장 산업
seongjangnyul	growth rate	성장율
seongkkyeok keomsa	personality test	성격 검사
seongmyeongseo	statement	성명서
seon-go	adjudication	선고
seongsil gyeyak	fidelity bond	성실 계약
seongsil jeungkkweon	fidelity bond	성실 증권
seon-gwang-gi	jig (production)	선광기(選鑛機)
seonha jeungkkweon	bill of lading	선하(船荷) 증권
seonhaeng jip'yo	leading indicator	선행 지표(先行指標)
seonhyeong gyehoek-peop	linear programming	선형 계획법(線形計劃法)
seonhyeong-hyeong	linear terms	선형형(線形型)
seonhyeongshik kyeonjeok	linear estimation	선형식 견적
seonimkkweon	seniority	선임권(先任權)
seonip seonch'ulppeop	first in-first out	선입 선출법(先入先出法)
seonjeok	shipment	선적
seonjeok chishiseo	shipping instructions	선적 지시서
seonjeok piyong	shipping expenses	선적 비용
seonjeok seoryu	document	선적 서류
seonjeok taehaeng eopjja	shipping agent	선적 대행 업자
seonjeokpi	shipping charges	선적비
seonjeoksong	forward shipment	선적송(先積送)
seonjeon	publicity	선전(宣傳)
seonweon-eui bihaeng	barratry	선원의 비행(非行)
seonjeong-hada	adjudge (v)	선정하다
seonju-eui sunkka	owner's equity	선주의 순가(純價)
seonmaekkweon	pre-emptive right	선매권(先買權)
seonmul	futures	선물(先物)
seonmul gu-ip	forward purchase	선물 구입(先物購入)
seonmul gyeyak	forward contract	선물 계약
seonmul jibul	forward cover	선물 지불(先物支拂)
seonmul majin	forward margin	선물(先物) 마진

seonmul seont'aek	futures option	선물(先物) 선택
seonmul shijang	forward market	선물 시장(先物市場)
seonmul su-ik	forward margin	선물 수익(先物收益)
seonsang-eui	linear	선상(線上)의
seonseo-seo	affidavit	선서서(宣誓書)
seont'aekkweon	option	선택권
seoryu	document	서류
seoryu gabang	briefcase	서류 가방
seoryuch'eol	file	서류철
seoshin wangnae	correspondence	서신 왕래
seoyak	covenant (promises)	서약
seoyeol	seniority	서열(序列)
sesu	taxation	세수(稅收)
seuk'ai renjeu	sky lens	스카이 렌즈
seuk'eurin	screen	스크린
seullaideu	slide	슬라이드
seullaideu yeongsagi	slide projector	슬라이드 영사기
seung-in	approval	승인
seung-in-hada, (su-ryeong-eul) t'ongji-hada	acknowledge (v), acknowledge receipt of (v)	승인하다, (수령을), 통지하다
seungjin	promotion	승진
seungsu	multiplier	승수(乘數)
seup'onji	sponge	스폰지
seupteuk	acquisition	습득
seut'aegeu-p'euleisyeon	stagflation	스태그플레이션
seut'enreseu-gang	stainless steel	스텐레스 강(鋼)
seut'ereo (ipch'e eumhyang) t'erebi	stereo TV	스테레오(입체음향) 테레비
seut'eureseu gwalli	stress management	스트레스 관리
seuwich'i	switch	스위치
seyul	tariff	세율
shi bunhal jedo	time sharing	시분할 제도(時分割制度)
shich'aekkweon	municipal bond	시채권(市債券)
shich'a-ro inhan p'iro	jet lag	시차로 인한 피로
shigandae	time zone	시간대(時間帶)
shigandang suip	hourly earnings	시간당 수입
shiganp'yo	timetable	시간표
shihan jumun	time order	시한 주문(時限注文)
shihwang	long interest	시황(市況)
shihwang bogo	market report	시황 보고
shijang	marektplace	시장(市場)
shijang bunbae	market share	시장 분배
shijang deung-geup	rating, market	시장 등급
shijang eo-eum balhaeng-in	market-maker (securities)	시장 어음 발행인
shijang gaech'eokpi	budget, marketing	시장 개척비
shijang gagyeog-euro	at the market	시장 가격으로
shijang gagyeok	market value	시장 가격
shijang gamjeong	appraisal, market	시장 감정
shijang gyehoek	plan, market	시장 계획
shijang hwalgi	dynamics, market	시장 활기(活氣)

shijang hwalseong	market dynamics	시장 활성(活盛)
shijang jeopkeun	market access	시장 접근
shijang jipchung	market concentration	시장 집중
shijang jip'yo (jisu)	market index	시장 지표(지수)
shijang josa	market survey	시장 조사
shijang josa yesan	budget, marketing	시장 조사 예산
shijang kagyeok	price, market	시장 가격
shijang p'ohwa sangt'ae	market saturation	시장 포화 상태
shijang sanghwang	market position	시장 상황
shijang wich'i	market position	시장 위치
shijang yech'euk	market forecast	시장 예측
shijang-yul	market rating	시장율
shijangnyeok	market forces	시장력(市場力)
shiljejeogin	practical	실제적인
shikka	market price	시가(市價)
shikka-eui ch'use	market trends	시가(市價)의 추세(趨勢)
shikki hanbeol	place setting	식기 한벌
shikkiryu	plate	식기류
shikp'um gagong-gi	food processor	식품 가공기
shikt'akpo	tablecloth	식탁보
shikt'ang-yong ch'eoljep'um (k'al, p'ok'eu deung)	cutlery	식탁용 철제품(칼, 포크 등)
shikt'ang-yong eun-jep'um	silverware	식탁용 은제품
shikt'ang-yong k'eun sutkkarak	tablespoon	식탁용 큰 숟가락
shikt'ang-yong magae- inneun yuribyeong	decanter	식탁용 마개있는 유리병
shilgeumnyo	take-home pay	실급료(實給料)
shilhaeng bulganeunhan	unfeasible (adj)	실행 불가능한
shilhaeng (chip-haeng) wiweonhoe	executive committee	실행(집행) 위원회
shilje	actuals	실제
shilje biyong	actual cost	실제 비용
shilje buch'ae	actual liability	실제 부채
shilje hyeon-geum gach'i	actual cash value	실제 현금 가치
shilje shiijang georae-ryang	actual market volume	실제 시장 거래량
shilje sodeuk	actual income	실제 소득
shiljjae gach'i	intrinsic value	실재 가치
shiljje gagyeok	real price	실제 가격
shiljje t'uja	real investment	실제 투자
shiljji jaego	inventory, physical	실지 재고
shiljji mullyang jaego josappeop	physical inventory	실지 물량 재고 조사법
shiljjik	unemployment	실직(失職)
shiljjil	actuals	실질
shiljjil ch'aemu	liability, actual	실질 채무
shiljjil imgeum	real wages	실질 임금
shiljjil iyun	effective yield	실질 이윤(實質利潤)
shiljjil jasan	real assets	실질 자산
shiljjil sodeuk	real income	실질 소득

shillindeo ch'eon-gong-gi	cylinder boring machine	실린더 천공기
shilmul k'eugi mohyeong	mock-up	실물 크기 모형
shilp'ae	failure	실패
shilp'ae-hada	fail (v)	실패하다
shilseup	workshop	실습
shilsuip	actual income	실수입
shimbok	man (gal) Friday	심복
shimch'eung bunseok	analysis, depth	심층 분석
shimdo bunseok	depth analysis	심도 분석(深度分析)
shinch'eong gagyeok	offered price	신청 가격
shinch'eong yongji	application form	신청 용지
shinch'eong-hada	offer (v)	신청하다
shinch'eongseo	application form	신청서
shinch'eong-yul	offered rate	신청율
shinch'uk chohang	escalator clause	신축 조항(伸縮條項)
shinch'ukpeop	sliding scale	신축법(伸縮法)
shinch'ukseong gwanseyul	flexible tariff	신축성 관세율 (伸縮性關稅率)
shindik'eit'eu	syndicate	신디케이트
shingmul (hag)-eui	botanic	식물(학)의
shingmul wisaeng gyuch'ik	phytosanitary regulations	식물 위생 규칙
shingnyang	foodstuffs	식량
shingnyop'um	foodstuffs	식료품
shin-gyeong anjeongje	tranquilizer	신경 안정제
shin-gyu balhaeng	new issue	신규 발행
shinheung saneop	infant industry	신흥 산업(新興産業)
shinjep'um gaebal	new product development	신제품 개발
shinjunghan t'uja gyuch'ik	prudent man rule	신중한 투자 규칙
shinmun	paper	신문
shinmun yongji	newsprint	신문 용지
shinp'um gyoch'ebi	replacement cost	신품 교체비
shinsa hyeopcheong	gentlemen's agreement	신사 협정
shinsokhan	prompt (adj)	신속한
shint'ak	trust	신탁
shint'ak chageum	trust fund	신탁 자금
shint'ak cheungseo	deed of trust	신탁 증서
shint'ak hoesa	investment company	신탁 회사
shint'ak-eui	fiduciary (adj)	신탁의
shinyong	credit	신용
shinyong	jawbone	신용
shinyong balhaeng	fiduciary issue	신용 발행
shinyong boheom	credit insurance	신용 보험
shinyong daebu	fiduciary loan, trust	신용 대부(信用貸付)
shinyong daebu eunhaeng	credit bank	신용 대부 은행
shinyong daebu jan-go	credit balance	신용 대부 잔고 (信用貸付殘高)
shinyong daebu t'ongje	credit control	신용 대부 통제
shinyong deung-geup	rating, credit	신용 등급

shinyong guipkkweon	credit card	신용 구입권
shinyong gwalli	credit management	신용 관리
shinyong johap	credit union	신용 조합
shinyong johoe (ch'eo)	credit reference	신용 조회(처)
shinyong johoech'eo	reference, credit	신용 조회처
shinyong josaso	credit bureau	신용 조사소
shinyong jokkeon	credit terms	신용 조건
shinyong kwalli	management, business	신용 관리
shinyong p'yeongkka	credit rating	신용 평가
shinyong yogu hando	demand line of credit	신용 요구 한도
shinyongdo	credit rating	신용도
shinyongjjang	letter of credit	신용장
shinyongsang-eui	fiduciary (adj)	신용상의
shinyongsang-eui t'uja	legal list (fiduciary investments)	신용상의 투자
shireop	unemployment	실업(失業)
shireop posang	unemployment compensation	실업 보상(失業補償)
shiryongjeogin	practical	실용적인
shisanp'yo	trial balance	시산표(試算表)
shise	quotation	시세(時勢)
shiseol	facilities	시설
shisep'yo	quotation	시세표
shiseut'em dijain (seolgye)	systems design	시스템 디자인(설계)
shikka-ro	at the market	싯가로
shyup'eo sambaek iljo	U.S. Trade Law, 301	슈퍼 301조
siryong sumyeong	useful life	실용 수명
siseut'em bunseok	systems analysis	시스템 분석
siseut'em (chojik) konghak	systems engineering	시스템(조직) 공학
siseut'em (chojik) kwalli	systems management	시스템(조직) 관리
sobija	consumer	소비자
sobija josa	consumer research	소비자 조사
sobija mulkka jisu	consumer price index	소비자 물가 지수
sobija manjok	consumer satisfaction	소비자 만족
sobija seung-in	consumer acceptance	소비자 승인
sobija shinyong	consumer credit	소비자 신용
sobijae	consumer goods	소비재(消費財)
sobise myeonheo	excise license	소비세 면허
sodeuk	income	소득
sodeuk kyech'eung	income bracket	소득 계층
sodeuk kyesanseo	income statement	소득 계산서
sodeuk suik	income yield	소득 수익
sodeukse	income tax	소득세
sodun	annealing	소둔(燒鈍)
soe buseureogi	scrap	쇠 부스러기
soe damgeumjil-hada	quench (v)	쇠 담금질하다
sogaejjang	letter of introduction	소개장(紹介狀)
sogeukcheok p'anmae	sell, soft	소극적 판매
sogeum garu-t'ong	salt shaker	소금 가루통
sogieop	small business	소기업(小企業)
sogeuphaneun	retroactive (adj)	소급하는

sohyeong gujo siseut'em	mini component system	소형 구조 시스템
sohyeong jung-ang ch'eori jangch'i	micro processor	소형 중앙 처리 장치
sohyeong k'eomp'yut'eo	mini computer	소형 컴퓨터
sohyeong k'eomp'yut'eo	micro computer	소형 컴퓨터
sohyeong p'ileum k'adeu	microfiche	소형 필름 카드
soji-in	bearer	소지인(所持人)
soktoreul naeda	speed up (v)	속도를 내다
sok'uri	basket	소쿠리
somae	retail	소매(小賣)
somae-eop	retail trade	소매업
somae eunhaeng	retail bank	소매 은행
somae mulkka	retail price	소매 물가
somae p'allo	retail outlet	소매 판로(販路)
somae p'anmaese	retail sales tax	소매 판매세
somae sangp'um	retail merchandise	소매 상품
somaejeom	retail outlet	소매점
somo	attrition	소모
somo (kamso) gyejeong	depletion accounting	소모(감소) 계정
somo (kamso) t'ongje	depletion control	소모(감소) 통제
somoseong jasan	wasting asset	소모성 자산
somunjja	lower case	소문자
son	loss	손(損)
son-euro bup'ullyeo mandeun yuri jep'um	handblown glass	손으로 부풀려 만든 유리제품
son-euro ch'ilhan	handpainted (adj)	손으로 칠한
son-euro jjan	hand-knit (adj)	손으로 짠
son-euro kkwemaen	hand-sewn (adj)	손으로 꿰맨
son-euro tteun	hand-woven (adj)	손으로 뜬
songdal	delivery	송달
songjeonson	transmission loss	송전손(送電損)
songjjang	invocie	송장(送狀)
songjjang biyong	invoice cost	송장 비용
sonhae	damage	손해
sonhae baesang ch'eong-guseo	claim	손해 배상 청구서
sonhae jeungmyeong	proof of loss	손해 증명
sonhae-reul pudam-hada	absorb the loss	손해를 부담하다
sonig-i eopta	breakeven (v)	손익(損益)이 없다
sonik kyejeong	profit-and-loss account	손익 계정
sonik kyesanseo	profit-and-loss statement	손익 계산서
sonik pun-gi bunseok	analysis, breakeven	손익 분기 분석
sonik pun-gijjeom	breakeven point	손익 분기점
sonik pun-gijjeom bunseok	breakeven analysis	손익 분기점 분석
sonsang	damage	손상(損傷)
sonsangp'um	spoilage	손상품(損傷品)
sonshil	loss	손실
sonshil bangji jumun	stop-loss order	손실 방지 주문
sonshil gongje	charge-off	손실 공제
sop'eut'eu we-eo	software	소프트 웨어
sop'eut'eu we-eo burok'eo	broker, software	소프트 웨어 브로커

sop'eut'eu we-eo jung-gae-in (beurok'eo)	software broker	소프트 웨어 중개인(仲介人)(브로커)
sop'o up'yeon	parcel post	소포 우편
soryang	drop	소량
soryang ch'wigeup hwamul	less-than-carload	소량 취급 화물
sosong	lawsuit, litigation	소송
sosu dokcheom	oligopoly	소수 독점
sosu gumae dokcheom	oligopsony	소수 구매 독점
sosu juju soyubun	minority interest	소수 주주 소유분 (小數株主所有分)
soyo gyeongbi	expense account	소요 경비(所要經費)
soyo shigan	time, lead	소요 시간
soyo yokkeon	requirements	소요 요건
soyu-eui	proprietary	소유의
soyuja	proprietor, owner	소유자
soyuji	estate	소유지
soyukkweon	ownership, title	소유권
soyukkweon boheom	title insurance	소유권 보험
soyumul	property	소유물
soyu-kkweon p'ogi	abandonment	소유권 포기
ssaijeu	size	싸이즈
ssan	cheap (adj)	싼
ssang-renjeu rip'eurekseu sajinkki (k'amera)	twin lens reflex camera	쌍렌즈 리프렉스 사진기(카메라)
such'i je-eo	numerical control	수치 제어(數値制御)
such'i je-eo robot'eu	numerical control robot	수치 제어 로보트
such'i je-eogi	numerical control machine	수치 제어기
such'uk p'ojang	shrink-wrapped	수축 포장(收縮包裝)
such'ul bujang	export manager	수출 부장
such'ul daerijeom	export agent	수출 대리점
such'ul geumji	embargo	수출 금지
such'ul gwanse	duty, export	수출 관세
such'ul gyuch'ik	export regulation	수출 규칙
such'ul gyujeong	export regulation	수출 규정
such'ul halttang	quota, export	수출 할당
such'ul halttang (k'weot'eo)	export quota	수출 할당(쿼터)
such'ul heoga (seo)	export permit	수출 허가(서)
such'ul jehan	restrictions on export	수출 제한
such'ul jung-gansang	export middleman	수출 중간상
such'ul maemae gyeyak	export sales contract	수출 매매 계약
such'ul sangsa	export house	수출 상사
such'ul shinyongjjang	export credit	수출 신용장
such'ul t'ong-gwan susok	export entry	수출 통관 수속
such'ul-hada	export (v)	수출하다
such'ulp'umse	export taxes	수출 품세
such'ulse	export duty	수출세
such'ulyong	for export	수출용
such'urip euhaeng	export-import bank	수출입 은행
such'wi gyejeong (padeultton)	accounts receivable	수취 계정(받을 돈)
such'wi yaksok eo-eum	note receivable	수취 약속 어음

such'wi-in	beneficiary, payee	수취인
sudang	perks	수당
(maemae hwamul-eui) sudo iljja	date of delivery	(매매 화물의) 수도 일자(受渡日字)
sudo yuye	backwardation	수도 유예(受渡猶豫)
suedeu	suede	수에드
su-eui-eui	optional	수의의
sugeum bulga gyejeong	uncollectable accounts	수금 불가 계정 (收金不可計定)
sugeum gigan	collection period	수금 기간
suhakcheok mohyeong	mathematical model	수학적 모형(模型)
suhoe	graft	수회(收賄)
suhyeja	beneficiary	수혜자
su-ik	yield	수익(收益)
su-ik chabon	capital, return on	수익 자본
su-ik chageop	earnings performance	수익 작업
su-ik chasan	earnings of assets	수익 자산(受益資産)
su-ik cheomgam beopch'ik	law of diminishing returns	수익 점감 법칙
su-ik chukka biyul	earnings/price ratio	수익 주가 비율 (收益株價比率)
su-ik ch'aekkweon	income bonds	수익(收益) 채권
su-ik ihaeng	earnings performance	수익 이행
su-ik iyul	earnings yield	수익 이율(利率)
su-ik pogo	earnings report	수익 보고
su-ikko	earnings	수익고(收益高)
su-ikseong	profitability	수익성
su-ikseong bunseok	profitability analysis	수익성 분석
suing-nyul	rate of return	수익률
suip	import, revenue	수입
suip-hada	import (v)	수입하다
suip halttang	import quota	수입 할당
suip kwanse	import duty	수입 관세
suip kyejeong	income account	수입 계정(收入計定)
suip kyujeong	import regulations	수입 규정
suip seung-injjeung	import license	수입 승인증
suip seyul	import tariff	수입 세율
suip shin-go	import declaration	수입 신고
suip susok	import entry	수입 수속
suip tambo ch'aekkweon	revenue bond	수입 담보(收入擔保) 채권(債權)
suip tamppo hamul bogwanjjeung	trust receipt (finance)	수입 담보 하물 보관증
suip yech'i	import deposits	수입 예치
suiphang bonseon indo	ex ship	수입항 본선 인도 (輸入港本船引渡)
suiphang bududo	ex dock	수입항 부두도 (輸入港埠頭渡)
suipkungnae jijeong jijeom	named inland point in country of importation	수입국내 지정 지점
suipse	tax, import	수입세

sujeong	amendment	수정
sujeong geuraeseu	crystal glass	수정 그래스
sujeonghada	amend (v)	수정하다
suji-eui shiganjeok ch'ajil	leads and lags	수지의 시간적 차질
sujik ch'eon-gong-gi	vertical boring mill	수직 천공기
sujik jeolsakki	vertical milling machine	수직 절삭기
sujik t'onghap	vertical integration	수직 통합(垂直統合)
sujip'um	collections	수집품
suju hwagin	confirmation of order	수주(受注) 확인
sujung k'amera	underwater camera	수중 카메라
sukkweon jushik (jeungkkweon)	authorized shares	수권 주식(증권)
sukkweon seomyeong	authorized signature	수권 서명
sukkweonseo	authority (to have)	수권서(授權書)
sumyeonje	barbiturate, sleeping pill	수면제
sun	net (adj)	순(純)
sun byeonhwa	net change	순 변화
sunch'a jojeol	sequential control	순차 조절
sun ch'ayong junbigeum	net borrowed reserves	순 차용(借用) 준비금
sungach'i	worth, net	순 가치
sun hyeon-geum yuch'ul	net cash flow	순 현금 유출
sun hyeongp'yeong jasan	net equity assets	순 형평 자산(純衡平資産)
sun i-ik	net profit, net margin	순 이익
sun jasan	net assets	순 자산
sun jasan	net worth	순 자산(純資産)
sun jasan gach'i	net asset worth	순 자산 가치
sun jasankka	net asset value	순 자산가(純資産價)
sun maesang-go	net sales	순 매상고
sun sodeuk	net income	순 소득
sun sodeuk	income, net	순 소득
sun son	net loss	순 손(純損)
sun sonshil	loss, net	순 손실
sun t'uja	net investment	순 투자
sun unjeon jabon	net working capital	순 운전 자본
sun yeong-eop chabon	net working capital	순 영업 자본
suneung-nyul	sliding scale	순응률(順應率)
sungnyeon nodong	skilled labor	숙련 노동
sunhwan gigeum	revolving fund	순환 기금
sunhwan shinyong	revolving credit	순환 신용(循環信用)
sunhwan shinyongjjang	revolving letter of credit	순환 신용장
sunig-eui	net (adj)	순익의
sunkka	equity	순가(純價)
sunkka halttang	equity share	순가 할당(純價割當)
sunkka su-ik	return on equity	순가 수익(純價收益)
sunseodo	chart, flow	순서도
sunsu hyeonjae gach'i (hyeonkka)	net present value	순수 현재 가치 (현가-現價)
sunsu jasan	assets, net	순수 자산
sup'eu jeopshi	soup dish	수프 접시
sup'euyong sutkkarak	soup spoon	수프용 숟가락
sup'yo	check	수표

surak	acceptance	수락
suri-hada	troubleshoot (v)	수리하다
suro annae	pilotage	수로 안내(水路案內)
suryang	quantity	수량
suryang harin	quantity discount	수량 할인
suryeong	receipt	수령(受領)
suseri	tax collector	수세리(收稅吏)
susegong-eui	handmade (adj)	수세공(手細工)의
sushi sanghwan gongch'ae	redeemable bond	수시 상환 공채
sushik kyeolssan	window dressing (bank)	수식 결산(修飾決算)
susong	transportation	수송
susong heogaseo	transportation	수송 허가서
susong-gwan	pipage	수송관
susongnyo	pipage	수송료
susuryo	commission (fee)	수수료
susuryo je-eui shinch'eong	premium offer	수수료 제의 신청
sut'ak p'anmaeja	consignee	수탁 판매자
sut'akcha	assignee, trustee	수탁자
suyo dokcheom	monopsony	수요 독점(需要獨占)
suyo gong-geup	supply and demand	수요 공급
suyoja	consumer	수요자
suyong	expropriation	수용(收用)

T

tabyeon hyeopcheong	multilateral agreement	다변 협정
tabyeon muyeok	multilateral trade	다변 무역
taebu	loan	대부(貸付)
taebyeon gi-ip	credit	대변 기입(貸邊記入)
taebyeon janaek	balance, credit	대변 잔액
taebyeon jeonp'yo	credit note	대변 전표
taebyeonp'yo	note, credit	대변표(貸邊表)
taech'a	flat car	대차(臺車)
taech'adaejop'yo	balance sheet	대차 대조표
taech'aek ponbu	task force	대책 본부
taech'e biyong	cost, replacement	대체(代替) 비용
taech'e ganeung sangp'um	fungible goods	대체 가능 상품
taech'ul ch'oejeo suikkeum	lending margin	대출 최저 수익금
taech'ul hando-aek	credit line	대출 한도액
taedaejeog-in p'anmae	advertising drive	대대적인 판매
taedeung muyeok	trade, fair	대등 무역
tae-eung gyeonbon	matched samples	대응 견본
taegeum	price	대금
taegeum gyohwan indo	collect on delivery	대금 교환 인도(引渡)
taegeum sanghwan indo	cash on delivery	대금 상환 인도
taegyumo-eui	large-scale (adj)	대규모의
(chushik) taehaeng	transfer agent	(주식) 대행(代行)
taehoe	rally	대회(大會)
taehyeong chipcheok hoero	large-scale integrated circuit	대형 집적 회로

Korean (romanized)	English	Korean
taejang	ledger	대장(臺帳)
taejang gi-ip	entry, ledger	대장(臺帳) 기입
taeji	lot	대지(垈地)
taejop'yo	checklist	대조표
taejung maech'e	mass media	대중 매체(大衆媒體)
taekka	consideration (bus. law)	대가(對價)
taemul renjeu	objective lens	대물 렌즈
taemunjja	capital	대문자
taep'okcheog-euro	down the line (adv)	대폭적으로
taep'okcheog-in	down the line (adj)	대폭적인
taep'yo	representative	대표
taeri	representative	대리(代理)
taeri (kweon)	proxy	대리(권)
taeri-in	attorney	대리인
taeri-in myeongseseo	proxy statement	대리인 명세서
taerijeom	factor	대리점
taeryang mak'et'ing	mass marketing	대량 마케팅
taeryang saengsan	mass production	대량 생산
taeseonjeon	advertising drive	대선전
taeweolbun	carryback	대월분(貸越分)
taeyeo-hada	farm out (v)	대여(貸與)하다
taeyeo jushik	loan stock	대여 주식
tagukcheok hoesa	multinational corporation	다국적 회사
ta-gyeoljjeong gyuso	poly-crystal silicon	다결정 규소
ta-i	die	다이
tajong-eui hwamul	freight all kinds	다종의 화물
tajung p'eurogeuraeming	multiprogramming	다중 프로그래밍
tambo	guarantee	담보
tambo ch'aemu	liability, secured	담보(擔保) 채무
tambo gyeyak	hypothecation	담보 계약
tambo jeungseo	mortgage certificate	담보 증서
tambo sach'aekkweon	mortgage debenture	담보 사채권(社債權)
tambobu ch'aekkweon	mortgage bond	담보부 채권(擔保附債權)
tampo	security	담보
tampo gyejeong	accounts, secured	담보 계정
tampobu-gyejeong	secured accounts	담보부 계정(擔保附計定)
tampomul	pledge	담보물
tanch'e boheom	group insurance	단체 보험
tanch'e gyoseop	collective bargaining	단체 교섭
tanch'e haengdong	combination	단체 행동
tanch'e hyeobyak	collective agreement	단체 협약
tandok haeson	particular average loss	단독 해손(單獨海損)
tandok haeson budambo	free of particular average	단독 해손 부담보 (單獨海損不擔保)
tandok haeson dambo	with average	단독 해손 담보 (單獨海損擔保)
tan-gi buch'ae	short-term debt	단기 부채(負債)
tan-gi jabon gyejeong	short-term capital account	단기 자본 계정
tan-gi yech'euk maegak	short sale	단기 예측 매각

tan-gi yungja	short sale	단기 융자
tan-gi yungja	short-term financing	단기 융자
tang-il gyeoljje	cash delivery	당일 결제
tangjwa biyul	acid-test ratio	당좌 비율
tangjwa buch'ae	liability, current	당좌 부채(當座負債)
tangjwa daeweol	overdraft	당좌 대월
tangjwa gyejeong	open account	당좌 계정
tangjwa yegeum	bank account	당좌 예금
tangjwa yegeum gujwa	checking account	당좌 예금 구좌
tangnyoppyeong	diabetes	당뇨병
tan-gyejeog-euro jegeo-hada	phase out (v)	단계적으로 제거(除去)하다
tan-gyejeog-euro t'u-ip-hada	phase in (v)	단계적으로 투입하다
tanju	broken lot, odd lot	단주(端株)
tanju jung-gae-in	odd lot broker	단주 중개인
tankka	unit price	단가(單價)
tanmal jangch'i	terminal	단말 장치
tansaeg-eui	black and white (adj)	단색의
t'anso seomyu	carbon fiber	탄소 섬유
t'eolshil	yarn	털실
tanwi hajung harin	unit load discount	단위 하중 할인
tanwi weonkka	unit cost	단위 원가
tappyeon-hada	reply (v)	답변하다
tasu i-ik	majority interest	다수 이익
teomp'ing	dumping (goods in foreign market)	덤핑
t'eorit seonban	turret lathe	터릿 선반
teung-euro nareuneun il	piggyback service	등으로 나르는 일
teung-gi up'yeon	registered mail	등기 우편
teungjjim seobiseu	piggyback service	등짐 서비스
teungnogil	record date	등록일
teungnok sangp'yo	registered trademark	등록 상표
teungnoktoen daeri-in	registered representative	등록된 대리인
teungsok hoch'ul gieok changch'i	random access memory	등속 호출 기억 장치
teureseu	dress	드레스
tijaineo	designer	디자이너
tip'eure	deflation	디프레
toan	pattern	도안
toan-hada	design (v)	도안하다
toch'ak yejeong shigan	estimated time of arrival	도착 예정 시간
toech'ajeum	repossession	되찾음
toe-sada	buy back (v)	되사다
togani	crucible	도가니
togi	pottery, earthenware	도기
togi enjin	ceramic engine	도기(陶器) 엔진
togi gamji jangch'i	ceramic sensor	도기 감지 장치(感知裝置)
togi seomyu	ceramic fiber	도기 섬유
togi yeogwagi	ceramic filter	도기 여과기(濾過器)
tojagi	china	도자기

toje	apprentice	도제
tojeonnyul	conductivity	도전율
tokcheom	monopoly	독점
tokcheom geumjibeop	antitrust laws	독점 금지법
tokcheom-eui	proprietary	독점의
tokcheomkkweon	sole rights	독점권
tokchik	graft	독직(瀆職)
tokso	toxin	독소
tolgeureut	stoneware	돌그릇
tomae-eop	wholesale trade	도매업
tomae gagyeok	wholesale price	도매 가격
tomae sang-in	wholesaler	도매 상인
tomae shijang	wholesale market	도매 시장
tomaesang	jobber, factor	도매상
tong	copper	동(銅)
tong-eop	partnership	동업
tong-eop chohap	trade association	동업 조합
tong-eopcha	partner	동업자
tong-eopcha harin	trade discount	동업자 할인
tong-eopja	colleague	동업자
tong-eopsa	associate company	동업사
tong-gi	incentive	동기
tong-gi josa	motivation study	동기 조사
tong-gyeol jasan	frozen assets	동결 자산
tonghyang	trend	동향
tongkka	parity	동가(東價)
tongmaeng p'a-eop-hada	strike (v)	동맹 파업하다
tongmulhak	toxicology	독물학
tongniphyeong jageopchang	stand-alone workstation	독립형 작업장
tongniphyeong weonmun p'euroseseo	stand-alone text processor	독립형 원문 프로세서
tongnyeok chot'a jangch'i	power steering	동력 조타 장치
tongnyo	colleague	동료
tongsan	chattel	동산(動産)
tongsan yangdo jeodang	chattel mortgage	동산 양도 저당
tongshi balhaeng daebu	back-to-back loan	동시 발행 대부
tongshi balhaeng shinyongjjang	back-to-back credit	동시 발행 신용장
top'an	plate	도판
toseong hapkeum	cement	도성(陶性) 합금
toshi hwakttae	urban sprawl	도시 확대
toshi jaegaebal	urban renewal	도시 재개발
tu gyedanshik shijang	two-tiered market	두 계단식 시장
tu-beon-jjae wich'i	second position	두 번째 위치
t'aekchi	lot	택지(宅地)
t'aeman	nonfeasance	태만
t'aemanhan	negligent (adj)	태만(怠慢)한
t'aengk'eo	tanker	탱커
t'aksong	cosignment	탁송
(suyo-na gong-geup-eui) t'allyeokseong	elasticity (of supply or demand)	(수요나 공급의) 탄력성

t'alse	tax evasion	탈세(脫稅)
t'elle mak'et'ing	telemarketing	텔레 마케팅
t'ellep'eurosesing	teleprocessing	텔레 프로세싱
t'eomineol	terminal	터미널
t'eukchep'um	specialty goods	특제품
t'eukheo ch'urweon	patent application	특허 출원
t'eukheo ch'urweonjung	patent pending	특허 출원중
t'eukheo sayong gyohwan	crosslicensing	특허 사용 교환
t'eukheobeop	patent law	특허법
t'eukheojjang	charter	특허장
t'eukheokkweon	patent	특허권
t'eukheokkweon sayongnyo	patent royalty (payment)	특허권 사용료
t'eukheokkweon-i inneun saengsan gwajeong	patented process	특허권이 있는 생산 과정
t'eukkweonbu maemae	put and call	특권부 매매
t'eukpyeol baedang-geum	extra dividend	특별 배당금
t'eukpyeol jeonmun wiweonhoe	task force	특별 전문 위원회
t'eukpyeol jungnyang hwamul yangyungnyo	heavy lift charges	특별 중량 화물 양육료
t'eukp'a	dispatch	특파
t'euktaehyeong sangp'um	outsized articles	특대형 상품
t'euraensyu	tranche	트랜슈
t'im gwalli	team management	팀 관리
t'ip	perks	팁
t'oehwa	obsolescence	퇴화
t'oejik	retirement	퇴직
t'oejikkeum	severance pay	퇴직금
t'oji	land	토지
t'oji gaehyeok	land reform	토지 개혁
t'oji gwalli-in	estate agent	토지 관리인
t'omok konghak	civil engineering	토목 공학
t'ong-gwan myeonheo	entry permit	통관 면허
t'ong-gwan shin-go	customs entry	통관 신고
t'ong-gwansa	customs broker	통관사
t'ong-gye	statistics	통계
t'ong-gye jeonmun-ga	analyst	통계 전문가
t'onghaengkkweon	right of way	통행권
t'onghap unyeong ch'egye	integrated management system	통합 운영 체계
t'onghwa	currency	통화
t'onghwa gach'i harak	depreciation of currency	통화 가치 하락
t'onghwa gijun	monetary base	통화 기준
t'onghwa gong-geumnyang	money supply	통화 공급량
t'onghwa jaep'aengch'ang	reflation	통화 재팽창
t'onghwa p'aengch'ang	inflation	통화 팽창
t'onghwa p'aengch'ang-eui	inflationary (adj)	통화 팽창의
t'onghwa such'uk	deflation	통화 수축
t'onghwa yut'ong-aek	currency	통화 유통액
t'onghwa yut'ong sokto	velocity of money	통화 유통 속도

t'ongje gyeongje	managed economy	통제 경제
t'ongjidaero	as per advice	통지대로
t'ongji-e euihayeo	as per advice	통지에 의하여
t'ongsang	trade, commerce	통상
t'ongsangbeop	trade law	통상법
t'ongsang (muyeok) hyeopcheong	trade agreement	통상(무역) 협정
t'ongsang wiweonhoe	trade commission	통상 위원회
t'ongshin	correspondence	통신
t'ongshin p'anmae	mail order	통신 판매
t'ong-yong seonha jeungkkweon	through bill of lading	통용 선하 증권
t'ugi jungmaein	operator	투기 중매인
t'ugija	speculator	투기자
t'ugikkun	speculator	투기꾼
t'uip	input	투입
t'uip sanch'ul bunseok	input-output analysis	투입 산출 분석
t'uja	investment	투자
t'uja bujog-eui	under-capitalized (adj)	투자 부족의
t'uja bunseok	investment analysis	투자 분석
t'uja deung-geup	investment grade	투자 등급
t'uja eunhaeng	investment bank	투자 은행
t'uja gamjeong	appraisal, investment	투자 감정
t'uja gijun	investment criteria	투자 기준
t'uja gomun	investment adviser	투자 고문
t'uja gyehoek	investment program	투자 계획
t'uja iyun	investment, return on	투자 이윤
t'uja jabon	investment capital	투자 자본
t'uja jeollyak	investment strategy	투자 전략
t'uja jeongch'aek	investment policy	투자 정책
t'uja p'yeongkka gamjeong	investment appraisal	투자 평가 감정
t'uja seoryu	investment letter	투자 서류
t'uja shint'ak	mutual fund, investment trust	투자 신탁
t'uja shinyong	investment credit	투자 신용
t'uja su-ik	return on investment	투자 수익
t'uja yesan	investment budget	투자 예산
t'ujageum	investment	투자금
t'uja-hada	invest (v)	투자하다
t'ujaja ihae	investor relations	투자자 이해(利害)
t'umae	dumping (goods in foreign market)	투매(投賣)
t'up'yokkweon	voting right	투표권

U

ubal ch'aemu	contingent liability	우발 채무
ubal daebi jageum	contingent fund	우발 대비 자금
ubal sago	contingencies	우발 사고(偶發事故)
ubaljeok iyun	windfall profits	우발적 이윤

ubaljeok sonhae	accidental damage	우발적 손해
udujong	vaccine	우두종
uhoe-hada	go around	우회하다
unbanbi	drayage	운반비
undong	motion	운동
undong-bok	sportswear	운동복
unim	drayage	운임
unim boheomnyo p'oham jojeong gagyeok	adjusted CIF price	운임 보험료 포함 조정 가격
unim doch'ak chibul	freight collect	운임 도착 지불
unim seonbul	freight prepaid	운임 선불
unjeon (yeong-eop) jabon	working capital	운전(영업) 자본
unjeon jasan	working assets	운전 자산(運轉資產)
unsong daerijeom (eopcha)	forwarding agent	운송 대리점(업자)
unsong eopcha	freight forwarder	운송업자
unsong eopja	carrier	운송업자
unsong eopja wiheom	carrier's risk	운송업자 위험
unsongjung	in transit	운송중
unsu	transportation	운수
unyeong dop'yo	chart, management	운영 도표
unyeong jabon	capital, working	운영 자본
unyeong jageum	working funds	운영 자금
unyeong jageum	funds, working	운영 자금
unyeongjin	management team	운영진
up'yeon beonho	zip code	우편 번호
up'yeon jumun	mail order	우편 주문
up'yeon sangdae myeongbu	mailing list	우편 상대 명부
up'yeonhwan	money order	우편환(郵便換)
uri-eui gidae-e bueung-haneun	expectations, up to our	우리의 기대에 부응하는
uri-eui gidae-e dalhagi-kkaji	up to our expectations	우리의 기대에 달(達)하기까지
urugwai hyeopsang	Uruguay Round (UR)	우루과이 협상
urugwai raundeu	Uruguay Round (UR)	우루과이 라운드
uryang jushik (jeungkkweon)	blue chip stock	우량 주식(증권)
uryangp'um	quality goods	우량품(優良品)
useon ch'aemu	preferential debts	우선 채무(優先債務)
useon gwanse	preferred tariff	우선 관세
useon seonjeok	front-end loading	우선 선적
useon seyul	preferred tariff	우선 세율
useonju	preferred stock	우선주(優先株)
useonkkweon	priority	우선권

W

wakchin	vaccine	왁진
wanbul	paid in full	완불(完拂)
wanch'ung-gi	bumper	완충기
wanch'ung gieok changch'i	buffer memory	완충 기억 장치
wanch'ung jangch'i	shock absorber	완충 장치

wanjeon gwangseok keomp'a jangch'i gisul	perfect crystal device technology	완전 광석 검파 장치 기술
wanjeon gyeolsan	full settlement	완전 결산
wanseong	topping up	완성
weodeu p'euroseseo	word processor	워드 프로세서
weip'eo	wafer	웨이퍼
weolbu p'anmae haljjeung-geum	carrying charge	월부 판매 할증금
weolkkweon haeng-wi	ultra vires acts	월권 행위(越權行爲)
weolli hapkye	amount	원리 합계
weollyo	raw materials	원료
weonbon	script	원본
weonbu	ledger	원부(原簿)
weonch'eon gwase	withholding tax	원천 과세(源泉課稅)
weon-geum	principal	원금(元金)
weon-geum gyejeong	principal	원금 계정
weonjajae	raw materials	원자재(原資材)
weonjang	entry, ledger	원장(原帳)
weonjang-euro omgyeo sseuda	post (bookkeeping) (v)	원장(原帳)으로 옮겨 쓰다
weonjang gi-ip	ledger entry	원장 기입
weonjang gyejeong	ledger account	원장 계정(原帳計定)
weonkka	cost	원가
weonkka baedang	costs, allocation of	원가 배당
weonkka bunseok	cost analysis	원가 분석
weonkka gwalli	control, cost	원가 관리
weonkka hoegye	cost accounting	원가 회계
weonkka t'ongje	control, cost	원가 통제
weonkka yoso	factor, cost	원가 요소(原價要素)
weonkka-gagyeok imun	cost-price squeeze	원가-가격 이문
weonkka-gasan gyeyak	cost-plus contract	원가-가산 계약
weonkka-reul gyesan-hada	cost (v)	원가를 계산하다
weonkkyeok chojong jangch'i	remote control	원격 조종 장치
weonoe undong	lobbying	원외 운동
weonp'an	negative	원판
weonp'an jedong jangch'i	disc brake	원판 제동 장치
weonsan-guk	country of origin	원산국
weonsanji	country of origin	원산지
weonsanji jeungmyeongseo	certificate of origin	원산지 증명서
weont'onghyeong bunswaegi	cylindrical grinder	원통형 분쇄기
weont'onghyeong ch'atchan	mug	원통형 찻잔
weont'onghyeong jojeong robot'eu	cylindrical coordinates robot	원통형 조정 로보트
wibeop-eui	illegal (adj)	위법의
wibu	abandonment	위부(委付)
wibu-hada	abandon (v)	위부(委付)하다
wiheom	risk	위험
wiheom budam	pure risk	위험 부담
wiheom budam jabon	venture capital	위험 부담 자본
wiheom jabon	risk capital	위험 자본

wiheom muljjil ch'wigeup changch'i	manipulator	위험 물질 취급 장치
wiheom p'yeongkka (sajeong)	risk assessment	위험 평가(사정－查定)
wiheomdo bunseok	risk analysis	위험도 분석
wiheomguk	country of risk	위험국
wi-im	mandate	위임(委任)
wi-im-hada	authorize (v)	위임하다
wi-imjjang	proxy statement	위임장
wi-imkkweon	attorney	위임권
wijo	forgery	위조(偽造)
wijop'um	counterfeit	위조품
wit'ak hwamul songjjang	consignment note	위탁 화물 송장(送狀)
wit'ak p'anmae	consignment	위탁 판매
wit'ak p'anmae (kyeyak) -(eu)ro	on consignment (adv)	위탁 판매(계약)(으)로
wit'akkeum-eul sobi-hada	default (v)	위탁금을 소비하다
wiyak chohang	penalty clause	위약 조항(違約條項)
wiyak paesang-geum	dead freight	위약 배상금

Y

yagan bogwanso	night depository	야간 보관소
yagyong-yeom	salts	약용염
yak	around (exchange term)	약
yak	medicine	약
yakche	drug	약제
yakcheong	currency clause, credit terms, commitment	약정
yakchesa	pharmacist	약제사
yakho	logo	약호
yakse	bear market	약세
yakse shihwang	thin market	약세 시황(弱勢市況)
yaksok eo-eum	promissory note	약속 어음
yaksok eo-eum balhaeng-in	maker (of a check, draft, etc.)	약속 어음 발행인
yalbeun diseuk'eu	floppy disk	얇은 디스크
yang	quantity	양
yangbok	suite	양복
yangdari geolch'ida	hedge (v)	양다리 걸치다
yangdo	transfer	양도(讓渡)
yangdohal su inneun	negotiable	양도할 수 있는
yangdo-in	assignor	양도인(讓渡人)
yanghae	understanding (agreement)	양해
yanghwa	positive	양화
yangjangbon	hardcover	양장본
yangja t'aegil-eui jumunseo	alternative order	양자 택일의 주문서
yangmul ch'iryo	medication	약물치료
yangnip	straddle	양립(兩立)
yangnyuk cheungmyeongseo	landing certificate	양륙(揚陸) 증명서

yangnyukpi	landing costs	양륙비(揚陸費)
yangnyukpi p'oham weonkka	landed cost	양륙비(揚陸費) 포함 원가
yangsu-in	assignee	양수인
yangt'eol	wool	양털
yebang yujibi	preventive maintenance	예방 유지비
yebi sa-eop kyehoek yogang	preliminary prospectus	예비 사업 계획 요강
yebo	forecast	예보
yebo-hada	forecast (v)	예보하다
yech'euk	forecast	예측
yech'euk-hada	forecast (v)	예측하다
yech'i jageum	impound	예치 자금
yegeum	deposit, savings	예금
yegeum gyejeong	deposit account	예금 계정
yegeum t'ongjang	passbook	예금 통장
yegich'i-aneun jalmot	bug (defect in computer program)	예기치 않은 잘못
yejeong	schedule	예정(豫定)
yeobun-eui gyeong-gwa ija	plus accrued interest	여분의 경과 이자
ye-oe gyujeong	escape clause	예외 규정
yeohaengja sup'yo	traveler's check	여행자 수표
yeok-chushik punhal	reverse stock split	역주식 분할(逆株式分割)
yeokhal	job	역할
yeokjo-eui	unfavorable (adj)	역조(逆調)의
yeokshijang	inverted market	역(逆) 시장
yeoksuch'ul	re-export	역수출
yeoksuji	adverse balance	역수지(逆收支)
yeol hoejeon	hot rolling	열 회전
yeollak	liaison	연락
yeollamhu	after-sight	열람 후
yeollangmang	network (to)	연락망
yeollye bogoseo	annual report	연례 보고서
yeollye-eui	annual	연례의
yeollye gyejeong	annual accounts	연례 계정
yeollye hoegye gamsa	annual audit	연례 회계 감사
yeollyo bunsa ch'egye	fuel injection system	연료 분사 체계
yeollyo sobi	fuel consumption	연료 소비
yeon (chong-i obaengmae)	ream	연(連:종이 500매)
yeon ch'otcheom renjeu	soft focus lens	연 촛점 렌즈
yeon-go	ointment	연고
yeonjeop-pong	connecting rod	연접봉
yeongsagi	projector	영사기
yeonan hoesa	offshore company	연안 회사
yeonch'e hwamul	back haul	연체(延滯) 화물
yeonch'e-il	back date	연체일(延滯日)
yeonch'e jumun	back order	연체 주문
yeonch'e p'anmae	back selling	연체 판매
yeonch'e segeum	back taxes	연체 세금
yeong	zero coupon	영(零)
yeong-eop changso	place of business	영업 장소
yeong-eop iyun	operating profit	영업 이윤
yeong-eop kamsa	operations audit	영업 감사(監査)

yeong-eop p'ummok	line of business	영업 품목
yeong-eop shigan oe-eui muyeok	after-hours trading	영업 시간 외의 무역
yeong-eop sodeuk	operating income	영업 소득
yeong-eop sonik kyesanseo	operating statement	영업 손익 계산서
yeong-eop yesan	operating budget	영업 예산
yeong-eopkkweon	good will	영업권
yeong-eoppi	operating expenses	영업비
yeon-geum	pension fund	연금(年金)
yeon-geum suryeong-in	annuitant	연금 수령인
yeon-geum (suryeongkkweon)	annuity	연금(수령권)
yeonghae	territorial waters	영해
yeonghyang (ch'ung-gyeok)-eul juda	impact on (v)	영향(충격)을 주다
yeon-gi	delay (n)	연기
yeon-gi-hada	postpone (v)	연기하다
yeongjjang	warrant	영장(令狀)
yeongsa jeungmyeong songjjang	consular invoice	영사 증명 송장
yeongsa songjjang	invoice, consular	영사 송장
yeongsokcheok chaego gwalli	perpetual inventory	영속적 재고 관리
yeongsujeung	receipt	영수증
yeongt'o	territory	영토
yeongt'on	long ton	영톤(英톤)
yeon-gu	research	연구
yeon-gu gaebal	research and development	연구 개발
yeon-gyeol jaejeong gyeolsanseo	consolidated financial statement	연결 재정 결산서
yeonhap	combination	연합
yeonhwa	soft currency	연화(軟貨)
yeonhwa ch'agwan	soft loan	연화 차관
yeonjang-hada	renew (v)	연장하다
yeonmal	year-end	연말(年末)
yeonsan bangshik	algorithm	연산(演算) 방식
yeonsan eoneo	algorithmic language	연산 언어
yeonsok chinhaeng robot'eu	sequence robot	연속 진행 로보트
yeonsok sach'ae	serial bonds	연속 사채(連續社債)
yeonsusaeng	trainee	연수생
yeonswaejeom	chain store, network (to)	연쇄점
yeonswaejeomgun	chain store group	연쇄점 군(群)
yeonswaemang	chain store group	연쇄망
yeoron josa	public opinion poll	여론 조사
yeoseong gwalli (kwanje)-in	administratrix	여성 관리(관재)인
yesan	budget	예산
yesan jich'ulgeum	budget appropriation	예산 지출금
yesan yech'euk	budget forecast	예산 예측
yesan geumaek	appropriation	예산 금액
yesang gumaeja	buyer, potential	예상 구매자
yesang gyeolgwa	expected results	예상 결과
yesang i-ik	expected results	예상 이익

yeyak	forward contract	예약(豫約)
yeyak kagyeok	subscription price	예약 가격
yogeum	charges	요금
yogu	demand	요구
yogu gagyeok	asking price	요구 가격
yogubul	payable on demand	요구불
yogubul biyul	call rate	요구불 비율
yogubul boho	call protection	요구불 보호
yogubul dan-gi ch'aipkeum	call money	요구불 단기 차입금
yogubul dan-gi daebugeum	call loan	요구불 단기 대부금
yogubul gagyeok	call price	요구불 가격
yogubul kyujeong	calll rule	요구불 규정
yogubul seong	call feature	요구불성(要求拂性)
yogubul soeng-kkyeog-eul jinin	call feature	요구불 성격을 지닌
yogubul yegeum	demand deposit	요구불 예금
yogu (ch'eong-gu)-hada	demand (v)	요구(청구)하다
yong-gwangno	blast steel	용광로
yongjeok t'onsu	tonnage	용적 톤수
yongseollo	cupola	용선로(溶銑爐)
yongseon	affreightment	용선(傭船)
yongseon	charter (shipping)	용선(傭船)
yongseon gyeyak	bareboat charter	용선(傭船) 계약
yongseon gyeyak taehaengja (jeom)	charterparty agent	용선 계약 대행자(점)
yongtton	allowance	용돈
yoryeong	know-how	요령
yoso (inja)	factor rating	요소(인자)
yubo i-ik	retained profits	유보 이익(留保利益)
yubo sodeuk	retained earnings	유보 소득(留保所得)
yubo su-ik	earnings, retained	유보 수익(留保收益)
yuch'e jasan	tangible assets	유체 자산(有體資産)
yudo	flow chart	유도(流圖)
yudo jip'yo	guidelines	유도 지표
yudong biyul	liquidity ratio, current yield	유동 비율
yudong buch'ae	floating debt	유동 부채
yudong dambo	floating charge	유동 담보(流動擔保)
yudong jasan	liquid assets, current or floating assets	유동 자산
yudongseong	liquidity	유동성
yudongseong seonho	liquidity preference (economics)	유동성 선호(選好)
yu-eon	will	유언(遺言)
yu-eon bojokseo	codicil	유언 보족서(補足書)
yu-eon geomjeung	probate	유언 검증(遺言檢證)
yugaek (yuinyong) sangp'um	loss leader	유객(誘引用) 상품(誘客商品)
yugeup hyuga	paid holiday	유급 휴가
yuhan ch'aegim	limited liability	유한 책임
yuhan ch'aegim hoesa-ro deungnok-hada	incorporate (v)	유한 책임 회사로 등록하다

yuhyeong jasan	tangible assets	유형 자산(有形資産)
yuhyo ch'aemu	active debt	유효 채무
yuhyo gyejeong	active account	유효 계정
yuhyo jasan	active assets	유효 자산
yuhyo oesang (p'anmae)	active trust	유효 외상(판매)
yuhyo sumyeong	useful life	유효 수명
yuhyo-han	valid (adj)	유효한
yuhyo-reul injeong-hada	validate (v)	유효를 인정하다
yuhyu neungnyeok	idle capacity	유휴 능력
yuin	incentive	유인(誘因)
yujeung	legacy, bequest	유증(遺贈)
yuji	maintenance	유지(維持)
yuji gwalli gyeyak	maintenance contract	유지 관리 계약
yujibi	carrying charge	유지비(維持費)
yujich'i	carrying value	유지치(維持値)
yujoseon	tanker	유조선(油槽船)
yukch'e nodongja	manual workers, blue collar workers	육체 노동자
yukka jeungkkweon	securities	유가 증권
yukka jeungkkweon gwalli	portfolio management	유가 증권 관리
yukka jeungkkweon myeongseseo	portfolio	유가 증권 명세서
yumul	bequest	유물(遺物)
yumyeong sangp'um	brand	유명 상품
yungja (keumyung) hoesa	finance company	융자(금융) 회사
yungja-hada	finance (v)	융자하다
yungt'ong bae-seo	accommodation endorsement	융통 배서
yungt'ong bo-jeung	accommodation endorsement	융통 보증
yungt'ong eo-eum	accommodation paper	융통 어음
yungt'ong eo-eum balhaeng	kiting (banking)	융통 어음 발행
yungt'ong shin-yong	accommodation credit	융통 신용
yungt'ong su-p'yo	accommodation bill	융통 수표(融通手票)
yuro dalleo	Eurodollar	유로 달러
yuro t'onghwa	Eurocurrency	유로 통화
yuryo hajung	payload	유료 하중(荷重)
yusahyeong jeon-ja gyesan-gi	analogue computer	유사형 전자 계산기
yusan	bequest	유산
yusang soyuin	holder in due course	유상 소유인(有償所有人)
yusan-gwalli	administration	유산 관리
yusanse	estate tax	유산세(遺産税)
yut'ong	negotiation	유통
yut'ong gyeongno	channel of distribution	유통 경로
yut'ong jeongch'aek	distribution policy	유통 정책
yut'ong shijang	secondary market (securities)	유통 시장(流通市場)
yut'ong yukka jeungkkweon	negotiable securities	유통 유가 증권
yut'ongbi	distribution costs	유통비
yut'ongdoeneun	negotiable	유통되는
yut'ong-hayeo	afloat	유통하여

yut'ongmang	distribution network	유통망
yut'ongshik'ida	negotiate (v)	유통시키다
yuye gigan	grace period	유예 기간(猶豫期間)

KEY WORDS FOR KEY INDUSTRIES

The dictionary that forms the centerpiece of *Korean for the Business Traveler* is a compendium of some 6000 words (English-Korean, Korean-English) that you are likely to use or encounter as you do business abroad. It will greatly facilitate fact-finding about the business possibilities that interest you, and will help guide you through negotiations as well as reading documents. To supplement the dictionary, we have added a special feature-grouping of key terms about eleven industries. As you explore any of these industries, you'll want to have this book at your fingertips to help make sure you don't misunderstand or overlook an aspect that could have a material effect on the outcome of your business decision. The industries covered in the vocabulary lists are the following:

- *advanced technology*
- *chemicals*
- *chinaware and tableware*
- *electronics and electricity*
- *fashion and textiles*
- *machine tools*
- *metalworks*
- *motor vehicles*
- *pharmaceuticals*
- *photography*
- *printing and publishing*

Key Words for Key Industries   254

ADVANCED TECHNOLOGY

English to Korean

English	Korean	Romanization
absolute temperature	절대 온도	*cheolttae ondo*
advanced technology	첨단 기술	*ch'eomdan gisul*
amorphous semiconductor	비정질(非定質) 반도체	*pijeongjil bandoch'e*
amorphous silicon	비결정 규소	*pi-gyeoljjeong gyuso*
artificial intelligence	인공 두뇌	*in-gong dunoe*
bio-ceramics	생(生)요업(窯業)	*saeng yo-eop*
bio-computer	생 컴퓨터	*saeng-k'eomp'yut'eo*
carbon dioxide laser	이산화 탄소 레이저	*isanhwa t'anso reijeo*
carbon fiber	탄소 섬유	*t'anso seomyu*
ceramic engine	도기(陶器) 엔진	*togi enjin*
ceramic fiber	도기 섬유	*togi seomyu*
ceramic filter	도기 여과기(濾過器)	*togi yeogwagi*
ceramic sensor	도기 감지장치 (感知裝置)	*togi gamji jangch'i*
composite materials	혼합 물질	*honhap muljjil*
compound semiconductor	복합 반도체 (複合半導體)	*pokhap pandoch'e*
electrical resistance	전기 저항	*cheon-gi jeohang*
electrically conductive rubber	전기 전도성 고무	*cheon-gi jeondoseong gomu*
electro-conductive glass	전기 전도 유리	*cheon-gi jeondo yuri*
electro-conductive polymer	전기 전도 중합체	*cheon-gi jeondo junghapch'e*
electro-magnetic shielding	전자기 보호물	*cheonjagi bohomul*
engineering plastic	공학 합성 수지	*konghak hapseong suji*
fiber-optic communication	광학 섬유 통신	*kwanghak seomyu t'ongshin*
fiber-reinforced plastics	섬유 보강 합성 수지	*seomyu bogang hapseong suji*
fifth-generation computer	5세대 컴퓨터	*o-sedae k'eomp'yut'eo*
fine ceramics	정교 섬세한 도자기류	*cheong-gyo seomsehan dojagiryu*
fine polymer	정교 섬세한 중합체	*cheong-gyo seomsehan junghapch'e*
gas laser	개스 레이저	*gaeseu reijeo*
glass fiber	유리 섬유	*yuri seomyu*
glass laser	유리 레이저	*yuri reijeo*
glass-reinforced cement	유리 보강 시멘트	*yuri bogang simemd*
glassy semiconductor	유리질 반도체	*yurijil bandoch'e*
heat-resistant ceramics	내열(耐熱) 도자기류	*naeyeol dojagiryu*
holographic memory	레이저 사진술 기억 장치	*reijeo sajinsul gieok changch'i*
hybrid materials	혼성 물질	*honseong muljjil*
intelligent robot	지능 로보트	*chi-neung robot'eu*
Josephson device	죠셉슨 장치	*chyosepseun jangch'i*
laser	레이저	*reijeo*
laser fusion	레이저 핵융합	*reijeo haengyunghap*
laser processing	레이저 처리	*reijeo ch'eori*

light-emitting diode	빛 방사 이극 진공관	pit pangsa igeuk chin-gong-gwan
liquid crystal	액정(液晶)	aekcheong
liquid helium	액체 헬륨	aekch'e hellyum
magnetic fluid	자기액(磁器液)	chagiaek
new ceramics	새 제도술(製陶術)	sae jedosul
new materials	새 재료(材料)	sae jaeryo
nuclear	핵(核)	haek
nuclear facility	핵 시설	haek shiseol
nuclear inspection	핵 사찰	haek sach'al
optical cable	광(光) 케이블	kwang k'eibeul
optical computer	광 컴퓨터	kwang k'eomp'yut'eu
optical disc	광 디스크	kwang diseuk'eu
optical fiber	광 섬유	kwang seomyu
optical integrated circuit	광 집적 회로	kwang jipcheok hoero
optical magnetic memory	광 자기 기억 장치	kwangjagi gieok changch'i
optical transmission	광 전송장치 (光電送裝置)	kwang jeonsong jangch'i
opto-electronics	광학 전자학	kwanghak cheonjahak
opto-electronics industry	광학 전자 산업	kwanghak cheonja saneop
pattern recognition	패턴 인식	p'aeteon inshik
perfect crystal device technology	완전 광석 검파 장치 기술	wanjeon gwangseok keomp'a jangch'i gisul
photo conductive materials	사진 전도 물질	sajin jeondo muljjil
photo conductivity	사진 전도력	sajin jeondoryeok
photo electromagnetic effect	사진 전자기 효과	sajin jeonjagi hwyokkwa
pulse	파동, 진동(振動)	p'adong, chindong
semiconductor laser	반도체 레이저	pandoch'e reijeo
solid-state laser	고체 레이저	koch'e reijeo
superconduction ceramics	초 전도체 제도술	ch'o jeondoch'e jedosul
superconductive coil	초 전도 코일	ch'o jeondo k'oil
superconductive materials	초 전도 물질	ch'o jeondo muljjil
superconductive phenomena	초 전도 현상	ch'o jeondo hyeonsang
superconductor	초 전도체	ch'o jeondoch'e
super lattice	초 격자	ch'o gyeokcha
transmission loss	송전손(送電損)	songjeonson

Korean to English

aekch'e hellyum	liquid helium	액체 헬륨
aekcheong	liquid crystal	액정(液晶)
chagiaek	magnetic fluid	자기액(磁器液)
cheolttae ondo	absolute temperature	절대 온도
ch'eomdan gisul	advanced technology	첨단 기술
cheon-gi jeohang	eceltrical resistance	전기 저항
cheon-gi jeondo junghapch'e	electro-conductive polymer	전기 전도 중합체
cheon-gi jeondo yuri	electro-conductive glass	전기 전도 유리
cheon-gi jeondoseong gomu	electrically conductive rubber	전기 전도성 고무

cheong-gyo seomsehan dojagiryu	fine ceramics	정교 섬세한 도자기류
cheong-gyo seomsehan junghapch'e	fine polymer	정교 섬세한 중합체
cheonjagi bohomul	electro-magnetic shielding	전자기 보호물
chindong	pulse	진동
chi-neung robot'eu	intelligent robot	지능 로보트
ch'o gyeokcha	super lattice	초 격자
ch'o jeondo hyeonsang	superconductive phenomena	초 전도 현상
ch'o jeondo k'oil	superconductive coil	초 전도 코일
ch'o jeondo muljjil	superconductive materials	초 전도 물질
ch'o jeondoch'e	superconductor	초 전도체
ch'o jeondoch'e jedosul	superconducting ceramics	초 전도체 제도술
chyosepseun jangch'i	Josephson device	죠셉슨 장치
haek	nuclear	핵
haek sach'al	nuclear inspection	핵 사찰
haek shiseol	nuclear facility	핵 시설
honhap muljjil	composite materials	혼합 물질
honseong muljjil	hybrid materials	혼성 물질
in-gong dunoe	artificial intelligence	인공 두뇌
isanhwa t'anso reijeo	carbon dioxide laser	이산화탄소 레이저
kaeseu reijeo	gas laser	개스 레이저
koch'e reijeo	solid-state laser	고체 레이저
konghak hapseong suji	engineering plastic	공학 합성 수지
kwang diseuk'eu	optical disc	광 디스크
kwang gieok changch'i	optical memory	광 기억 장치
kwang jagi gieok changch'i	optical magnetic memory	광 자기 기억 장치
kwang jeonsong jangch'i	optical transmission	광 전송장치(光電送裝置)
kwang jipcheok hoero	optical integrated circuit	광 집적 회로
kwang k'eibeul	optical cable	광(光) 케이블
kwang k'eomp'yut'eo	optical computer	광 컴퓨터
kwang seomyu	optical fiber	광섬유
kwanghak cheonja saneop	opto-electronics industry	광학 전자 산업
kwanghak cheonjahak	opto-electronics	광학 전자학
kwanghak seomyu t'ongshin	fiber-optic communication	광학 섬유 통신
naeyeol dojagiryu	heat-resistant ceramics	내열(耐熱) 도자기류
o-sedae k'eomp'yut'eo	fifth-generation computer	5세대 컴퓨터
p'adong	pulse	파동
p'aet'eon inshik	pattern recognition	패턴 인식
pandoch'e reijeo	semiconductor laser	반도체 레이저
pi-gyeoljjeong gyuso	amorphous silicon	비결정 규소

Advanced Technology

pijeongjil bandoch'e	amorphous semiconductor	비정질(非定質) 반도체
pit pangsa igeuk chin-gong-gwan	light-emitting diode	빛 방사 이극 진공관
pokhap pandoch'e	compound semiconductor	복합 반도체(複合半導體)
reijeo	laser	레이저
reijeo ch'eori	laser processing	레이저 처리
reijeo haeng-yunghap	laser fusion	레이저 핵융합
reijeo sajinsul gieok changch'i	holographic memory	레이저 사진술 기억 장치
sae jaeryo	new materials	새 재료(材料)
sae jedosul	new ceramics	새 제도술(製陶術)
saeng yo-eop	bio-ceramics	생(生) 요업(窯業)
saeng-k'eomp'yut'eo	bio-computer	생 컴퓨터
sajin jeondo muljjil	photo conductive materials	사진 전도 물질
sajin jeondoryeok	photo conductivity	사진 전도력
sajin jeonjagi hyokkwa	photo electromagnetic effect	사진 전자기 효과
seomyu bogang hapseong suji	fiber-reinforced plastics	섬유 보강 합성 수지
songjeonson	transmission loss	송전손(送電損)
t'anso seomyu	carbon fiber	탄소 섬유
togi enjin	ceramic engine	도기(陶器) 엔진
togi gamji jangch'i	ceramic sensor	도기 감지 장치(感知裝置)
togi seomyu	ceramic fiber	도기 섬유
togi yeogwagi	ceramic filter	도기 여과기(濾過器)
wanjeon gwangseok keomp'a jangch'i gisul	perfect crystal device technology	완전 광석 검파 장치 기술
yuri bogang siment'eu	glass-reinforced cement	유리 보강 시멘트
yuri reijeo	glass laser	유리 레이저
yuri seomyu	glass fiber	유리 섬유
yurijil bando-ch'e	glassy semiconductor	유리질 반도체

Key Words for Key Industries

CHEMICALS

English to Korean

acetaldehyde	흡반(吸盤)	heuppan
acetate	아세트 산염	aset'eu sanyeom
acetic acid	아세트 산(酸)	aset'eu san
acetone	아세톤	aset'on
acid (adj)	산(酸)의	san-eui
alkaline (adj)	알카리성(염기성)	alk'ariseong (yeomgiseong)
amine	아민	amin
ammonia	암모니아	ammonia
base	염기(鹽基)	yeomgi
benzene	벤젠	penjen
biochemistry	생화학	saeng-hwahak
butanol	부타놀	put'anol
catalyst	촉매(觸媒)	ch'ongmae
chemical fertilizer	화학 비료	hwahak piryo
chemicals	화학제품	hwahak chep'um
chloride	염화물	yeomhwamul
chloroform	클로로 포름	k'eulloro p'oreum
compound	배합 원료	paehap weollyo
distillation	증류(蒸溜)	cheungnyu
dyes	염료(染料)	yeomnyo
electrolysis	전기 분해	cheon-gi bunhae
enzyme	효소(酵素)	hyoso
ethane	에탄	et'an
ether	에테르	e'tereu
ethylene	에틸렌	et'illen
ethylene dichloride	에틸렌 이염화물	et'illen iyeomhwamul
ethylene glycol	에틸렌 그리콜	et'illen geurik'ol
ethylene oxide	에틸렌 옥시드	et'illen okshideu
formaline	포르말린	p'oreumallin
hydrocarbon	탄화수소	t'anhwa suso
hydrochloric acid	염산	yeomsan
hydrolysis	가수분해	kasu bunhae
inorganic chemicals	무기 화학물	mugi hwahakmul
latex	고무유액	komu yuaek
methane	메탄	met'an
methanol	메탄놀	met'anol
naphtha	나프타	nap'eut'a
neutral (adj)	중성(中性)의	chungseong-eui
nitrite	질산염	chilsanyeom
nitric acid	질산	chilsan
nitrite	아질산염	a-jilsanyeom
organic chemicals	유기(有機) 화학품	yugi hwahakp'um
oxidation	산화(酸化)	sanhwa
petrochemicals	석유 화학 제품	seogyu hwahak chep'um
petroleum	석유	seogyu
phosphate	인산염	insanyeom
plastic	플라스틱	p'eullaseut'ik
polymer	중합체	chunghapch'e

Chemicals

polystyrene	폴리스틸렌	*polliseut'illen*
polyurethane	폴리우레탄	*p'olliuret'an*
propylene	프로필렌	*p'europ'illen*
pulp	펄프	*p'eolp'eu*
reduction	환원법	*hwanweonppeop*
rubber	고무	*komu*
salt	염(鹽), 소금	*yeom, sogeum*
saponification	비누화	*pinuhwa*
solubility	용해도	*yonghaedo*
solute	용질	*yongjil*
solution	용액	*yong-aek*
solvent	용매	*yongmae*
sulfate	황산염	*hwangsanyeom*
sulfuric acid	황산	*hwangsan*
synthetic rubber	합성고무	*hapseong gomu*
toluene	톨루엔	*t'olluen*
urea	요소(尿素)	*yoso*
urea resin	요소 수지(樹脂)	*yoso suji*
water-absorbing resin	흡수 수지	*heupsu suji*
xylene	크실렌	*k'eushillen*
zeolite	비석	*piseok*

Korean to English

a-jilsanyeom	nitrite	아질산염
alk'ariseong (yeomgiseong)	alkaline (adj)	알카리성(염기성)
amin	amine	아민
ammonia	ammonia	암모니아
aset'eu san	acetic acid	아세트 산(酸)
aset'eu sanyeom	acetate	아세트 산염
aset'on	acetone	아세톤
cheon-gi bunhae	electrolysis	전기 분해
cheungyu	distillation	증류(蒸溜)
chilsan	nitric acid	질산
chilsanyeom	nitrate	질산염
ch'ongmae	catalyst	촉매
chunghapch'e	polymer	중합체
chungseong-eui	neutral (adj)	중성(中性)의
et'an	ethane	에탄
e'tereu	ether	에테르
et'illen	ethylene	에틸렌
et'illen geurik'ol	ethylene glycol	에틸렌 그리콜
et'illen iyeomhwamul	ethylene dichloride	에틸렌 이염화물
et'illen okshideu	ethylene oxide	에틸렌 옥시드
hapseong gomu	synthetic rubber	합성 고무
heuppan	acetaldehyde	흡반(吸盤)
heupsu suji	water-absorbing resin	흡수 수지
hwahak chep'um	chemicals	화학 제품
hwahak piryo	chemical fertilizer	화학 비료
hwangsan	sulfuric acid	황산
hwangsanyeom	sulfate	황산염

Key Words for Key Industries

hwanweonppeop	reduction	환원법
hyoso	enzyme	효소(酵素)
insanyeom	phosphate	인산염
kasu bunhae	hydrolysis	가수 분해
komu	rubber	고무
k'eulloro p'oreum	chloroform	클로로 포름
k'eushillen	xylene	크실렌
komu yuaek	latex	고무 유액
met'an	methane	메탄
met'anol	methanol	메타놀
mugi hwahakmul	inorganic chemicals	무기 화학물
nap'eut'a	naphtha	나프타
paehap weollyo	compound	배합 원료
penjen	benzene	벤젠
p'eolp'eu	pulp	펄프
p'eulaseut'ik	plastic	플라스틱
p'europ'illen	propylene	프로필렌
pinuhwa	saponification	비누화
piseok	zeolite	비석(沸石)
polliseut'illen	polystyrene	폴리스틸렌
p'olliuret'an	polyurethane	폴리우레탄
p'oreumallin	formaline	포르말린
put'anol	butanol	부타놀
saeng-hwahak	biochemistry	생화학
san-eui	acid (adj)	산(酸)의
sanhwa	oxidation	산화(酸化)
seogyu	petroleum	석유
seogyu hwahak chep'um	petrochemicals	석유 화학 제품
sogeum	salt	소금
t'anhwa suso	hydrocarbon	탄화 수소
t'olluen	toluene	톨루엔
yeom	salt	염(鹽)
yeomgi	base	염기(鹽基)
yeomhwamul	chloride	염화물
yeomnyo	dyes	염료(染料)
yeomsan	hydrochloric acid	염산
yong-aek	solution	용액
yonghaedo	solubility	용해도
yongjil	solute	용질
yongmae	solvent	용매
yoso	urea	요소
yoso suji	urea resin	요소 수지
yugi hwahakp'um	organic chemicals	유기 화학품

CHINAWARE AND TABLEWARE

English to Korean

basket	바구니, 소쿠리	*paguni, sok'uri*
bone china	골제(骨製) 그릇	*koljje geureut*
bowl	그릇, 사발	*keureut, sabal*
breadbasket	빵 바구니	*ppang baguni*
butter dish	버터 접시	*peot'eo jeopshi*
butter knife	버터 나이프	*peot'eo naip'eu*
candlestick	촛대	*ch'ottae*
carving knife	고기 써는 칼	*kogi sseoneun k'al*
champagne glass	샴페인 잔	*syamp'ein jan*
cheese tray	치즈 쟁반	*ch'ijeu jaengban*
china	도자기, 자기	*tojagi, chagi*
coaster	바퀴달린 쟁반	*pak'wi-dallin jaengban*
coffeepot	커피 주전자	*k'eop'i jujeonja*
crystal glass	수정 그래스	*sujeong geuraeseu*
cup	컵	*k'eop*
cutlery	식탁용 철제품 (칼, 포크 등)	*shikt'ang-yong ch'eoljep'um (k'al, p'ok'eu deung)*
decanter	식탁용 마개 있는 유리병	*shit'ang-yong magae-inneun yuribyeong*
dessert plate	후식용(後食用) 그릇	*hushing-yong geureut*
dish	접시	*cheopshi*
earthenware	토기, 질그릇	*t'ogi, chil-geureut*
egg cup	계란용 컵	*kyeran-yong k'eop*
espresso cup	에스프레스 컵	*eseup'eureseu k'eop*
flute	긴 술잔	*kin suljjan*
fork	포크	*p'ok'eu*
glass	유리잔	*yuri-jan*
goldplated (adj)	금 도금된	*keum dogeum-doen*
gravy boat	고기 국물 그릇	*kogi gungmul geureut*
handblown glass	손으로 부풀려 만든 유리 제품	*son-euro bup'ullyeo mandeun yuri jep'um*
handmade (adj)	수세공(手細工)의	*susegong-eui*
handpainted (adj)	손으로 칠한	*son-euro ch'ilhan*
ice bucket	얼음통	*eoreum-t'ong*
knife	칼	*k'al*
ladle	국자	*kukcha*
lace	가장자리 장식	*kajangjari jangshik*
linen (adj)	린네르제(製)의	*rinnereuje-eui*
mug	원통형 찻잔	*weont'onghyeong ch'atchan*
napkin	냅킨	*nap'euk'in*
pastry server	과자 쟁반	*kwaja jaengban*
pattern	도안	*toan*
pepper mill	후추 제분기	*huch'u jebun-gi*
pepper shaker	후춧가루통	*huch'ut karu-t'ong*
pitcher	물주전자	*mul-jujeonja*
place mat	(접시) 장식용 받침	*(cheopshi) jangshing-yong bach'im*

place setting	식기 한벌	shikki hanbeol
plate	접시, 식기류	cheopshi, shikkiryu
platter	큰 접시	k'eun jeopshi
pottery	도기	togi
salad bowl	샐러드용 접시	saelleodeu-yong jeopshi
salad plate	샐러드 접시	saelleodeu jeopshi
salt shaker	소금 가루통	sogeum garu-t'ong
saucer	받침 접시	pach'im jeopshi
serving spoon	음식 숟가락	eumshik sutkkarak
set	한 벌	han beol
silverplate (adj)	은 그릇의	eun geureuseui
silverware	식탁용 은제품	shikt'ang-yong eun-jep'um
soup dish	수프 접시	sup'eu jeopshi
soup spoon	수프용 숟가락	sup'euyong sutkkarak
spoon	숟가락	sutkkarak
stainless steel	스텐레스	seut'enreseu
stoneware	석기(石器), 돌그릇	seokki, tol geureut
sugar bowl	설탕 그릇	seolt'ang geureut
tablecloth	식탁보	shikt'akpo
tablespoon	식탁용 큰 숟가락	shikt'ang-yong k'eun sutkkarak
teapot	찻주전자	ch'at-chujeonja
teaspoon	찻숟가락	ch'at-sutkkarak
tray	쟁반	chaengban
trivet	삼각대	samgaktae
tureen	뚜껑달린 그릇	ttukkeong-dallin geureut
vinyl (adj)	비닐의	pinireui
wine glass	포도주 잔	p'odoju jan

Korean to English

chaengban	tray	쟁반
chagi	china	자기
cheopshi	dish, plate	접시
ch'ijeu jaengban	cheese tray	치즈 쟁반
chil-geureut	earthenware	질그릇
ch'at-chujeonja	teapot	찻주전자
ch'at-sutkkarak	teaspoon	찻숟가락
ch'ottae	candlestick	촛대
eoreum-t'ong	ice bucket	얼음통
eseup'eureseu k'eop	espresso cup	에스프레스컵
eumshik sutkkarak	serving spoon	음식 숟가락
eun geureuseui	silverplate (adj)	은 그릇의
han beol	set	한 벌
huch'u jebun-gi	pepper mill	후추 제분기
huch'ut karu-t'ong	pepper shaker	후춧가루통
hushing-yong geureut	dessert plate	후식용(後食用) 그릇
jangshing-yong bach'im	place mat	장식용 받침
kajangjari jangshik	lace	가장자리 장식
keum dogeum-doen	goldplated (adj)	금 도금된
keureut	bowl	그릇

Chinaware and Tableware

kin suljjan	flute	긴 술잔
kogi gungmul geureut	gravy boat	고기 국물 그릇
kogi sseoneun k'al	carving knife	고기써는 칼
koljje geureut	bone china	골제(骨製) 그릇
kukcha	ladle	국자
kwaja jaengban	pastry server	과자 쟁반
kyeran-yong k'eop	egg cup	계란용 컵
k'al	knife	칼
k'eop	cup	컵
k'eop'i jujeonja	coffeepot	커피 주전자
k'eun jeopshi	platter	큰 접시
mul-jujeonja	pitcher	물주전자
nap'euk'in	napkin	나프킨
pach'im jeopshi	saucer	받침 접시
paguni	basket	바구니
pak'wi-dallin jaengban	coaster	바퀴달린 쟁반
peot'eo jeopshi	butter dish	버터 접시
peot'eo naip'eu	butter knife	버터 나이프
pinireui	vinyl (adj)	비닐의
ppang baguni	breadbasket	빵 바구니
p'odoju jan	wine glass	포도주 잔
p'ok'eu	fork	포크
rinnereuje-eui	linen (adj)	린네르 제(製)의
sabal	bowl	사발
saelleodeu jeopshi	salad plate	샐러드 접시
saelleodeu-yong jeopshi	salad bowl	샐러드용 접시
samgaktae	trivet	삼각대
seokki	stoneware	석기
seolt'ang geureut	sugar bowl	설탕 그릇
seut'enreseu	stainless steel	스텐레스
shikki hanbeol	place setting	식기 한벌
shikkiryu	plate	식기류
shikt'akpo	tablecloth	식탁보
shikt'ang-yong ch'eoljep'um	cutlery	식탁용 철제품(칼, 포크 등)
shikt'ang-yong eun-jep'um	silverware	식탁용 은제품
shikt'ang-yong k'eun sutkkarak	tablespoon	식탁용 큰 숟가락
shit'ang-yong magae-inneun yuribyeong	decanter	식탁용 마개 있는 유리병
sogeum garu-t'ong	salt shaker	소금 가루통
sok'uri	basket	소쿠리
son-euro bup'ullyeo mandeun yuri jep'um	handblown glass	손으로 부풀려 만든 유리제품
son-euro ch'ilhan	handpainted (adj)	손으로 칠한
sujeong geuraeseu	crystal glass	수정 그래스
sup'eu jeopshi	soup dish	수프 접시
sup'euyong sutkkarak	soup spoon	수프용 숟가락
susegong-eui	handmade (adj)	수세공(手細工)의
sutkkarak	spoon	숟가락
syamp'ein jan	champagne glass	샴페인 잔
toan	pattern	도안

Key Words for Key Industries

togi	pottery, earthenware	도기
tojagi	china	도자기
tolgeureut	stoneware	돌그릇
ttukkeong-dallin geureut	tureen	뚜껑달린 그릇
weont'onghyeong ch'atchan	mug	원통형 찻잔
yuri-jan	glass	유리잔

Electronics and Electricity

ELECTRONICS AND ELECTRICITY

English to Korean

alternating current	교류	kyoryu
amplifier	증폭기	cheungp'okki
amplitude modulation	진폭 변조	chinp'ok pyeonjo
audio component system	오디오 전축 시스템	odio jeonch'uk siseut'em
audio response equipment	청력 반응 장치	ch'eongnyeok baneung jangch'i
automatic teller machine (ATM)	현금 자동 출납기	hyeon-geum jadong ch'ulnapki
autoreverse	자동 역회전	chadong yeok-hoejeon
bit	비트	pit'eu
black and white TV	흑백 테레비	heukpaek t'erebi
Brown tube	브라운관	peuraun gwan
buffer memory	완충 기억 장치	wanch'ung gieok changch'i
calculator	계산기	kyesan-gi
car telephone	자동차용 전화, 카폰	chadongch'a-yong jeonhwa, ko-p'on
cash register	금전 등록기	keumjeon deungnok-ki
cassette	카세트	k'aset'eu
CB	자동차용 무선 통신기	chadongch'a-yong museon t'ongshin-gi
ceramic condenser	자기 축전기	chagi ch'ukcheon-gi
chip condenser	반도체 축전기	pandoch'e ch'ukcheon-gi
circuit breaker	회로 차단기	hoero ch'adan-gi
color liquid crystal	색무늬 수정	saengmuni sujeong
color TV	컬러 테레비	k'eolleo t'erebi
compact disc (CD)	콤팩 디스크	k'omp'aek diseuk'eu
compact disc player	휴대용 디스크 연주장치	hyudae-yong diseuk'eu yeonju jangch'i
component	부품(部品)	pup'um
computer	컴퓨터	k'eomp'yut'eo
condenser	축전기	ch'ukcheon-gi
conductivity	도전율	tojeonnyul
connector	접속기	cheopsokki
contact	접촉	cheopch'ok
converter	전로(轉爐), 컨버터	cheollo, k'eonbeot'eo
cordless phone	무선 전화기	museon jeonhwagi
DC machine	직류계	chingnyugye
desk-top calculator	탁상용 계산기	t'aksang-yong gyesan-gi
digital (adj)	계수형의, 디지탈의	kyesu-hyeong-eui, dijit'areui
digital audio disc	계수형 가청 디스크	kyesu-hyeong gach'eong diseuk'eu
digital audio tape recorder	계수형 청취 테이프 녹음기	kyesu-hyeong ch'eongch'wi t'eip'eu nogeumgi
diode	이극 진공관	igeuk chin-gong-gwan
diskette	디스켓	diseuk'et
display unit	표시 단위	p'yoshi danwi
dynamic memory	역학 기억 장치	yeokhak kieok changch'i

Key Words for Key Industries

dynamo	발전기	paljeon-gi
electric cable	전선(電線)	cheonseon
electric circuit	전기 회로	cheon-gi hoero
electric furnace	전기로(電氣爐)	cheon-gi-ro
electric heater	전기 난방기	cheon-gi nanbang-gi
electric interlocking machine	전기 연결 기계	cheon-gi yeon-gyeol gigye
electric line telephone	유선 전화기	yuseon jeonhwagi
electric resistance	전기 저항	cheon-gi jeohang
electric shaver	전기 면도기	cheon-gi myeondo-gi
electric tools	전기 공구	cheon-gi gong-gu
electrode	전극	cheon-geuk
electromagnet	전자석	cheonjaseok
electron beam	전자선	cheonjaseon
electron gun	전자총	cheonjach'ong
electron microscope	전자 현미경	cheonja hyeonmigyeong
electronic cash register	전자 금전 등록기	cheonja geumjeon deungnok-ki
electronic desk calculator	전자 탁상용 계산기	cheonja t'aksang-yong gyesan-gi
electronic home appliance	가정용 전자	kajeong-yong jeonja
electronic musical instruments	전자 악기(樂器)	cheonja akki
electronic organ	전자 오르간	cheonja oreugan
electronic sewing machine	전자 재봉틀	cheonja jaebongt'eul
electronic typewriter	전자 타자기	cheonja t'ajagi
electronics	전자 공학	cheonja gonghak
EP ROM	도넛형 판독 전용 기억장치	doneot-hyeong p'andok cheonyong gieok changch'i
equalizer	균압선, 균형 장치	kyunapseon, kyunhyeong jangch'i
facsimile	팩시밀리, 팩스	p'aekshimilli, p'aekseu
fixed resistor	고정 정보 기억 사용 장치	kojeong jeongbo gieok sayong jangch'i
food processor	식품 가공기	shikp'um gagong-gi
frequency modulation	주파수 변조	chup'asu byeonjo
fun music player	노래 반주기	norae banjugi
generator	발전기, 제네레타	paljjeon-gi, cheneret'a
heavy-electric equipment	중전기기(重電機器)	chungjeon gigi
high fidelity	최고 음질(音質)	ch'oego eumjil
humidifier	가습기	kaseupki
industrial electronics	산업용 전자	saneop-yong jeonja
industrial robot	산업용 로보트	saneop-yong robot'eu
integrated circuit	집적 회로	chipcheok hoero
inverter	인버어터	inbeo-eo'teo
KaraOrche	노래반주기, 가라오케	norae banjugi, karaok'e
keyboard	건반, 키보드	keonban, k'ibodeu
large-scale interated circuit	대형 집적 회로	taehyeong chipcheok hoero
laser beam printer	레이저 광 인쇄기	reijeo-gwang inswaegi
light-emitting diode	방사 이극 진공관	pangsa igeuk chin-gong-gwan
line printer	행(行) 인쇄기	haeng inswaegi
liquid crystal	투명 수정	t'umyeong sujeong

Electronics and Electricity

machine tools	공구	kong-gu
magnetic bubble memory	자기(磁器) 기포 기억 장치	chagi gip'o gieok changch'i
magnetic disc unit	자기 디스크 장치	chagi diseuk'eu janghch'i
magnetic tape unit	자기 테이프 장치	chagi t'eip'eu jangch'i
micro cassette recorder	마이크로 카세트 녹음기	maik'euro k'aset'eu nogeumgi
micro computer	마이크로 컴퓨터	maik'euro k'eomp'yut'eo
micro processor	마이크로 처리 장치	maik'euro ch'eori jangch'i
microwave	마이크로 웨이브	maik'euro-weibeu
microwave oven	전자 오븐, 전자 렌지	cheonja obeun, cheonja renji
mini component system	소형 구조 시스템	sohyeong gujo siseut'em
mobile phone	휴대용 전화기	hyudaeyong jeonhwagi
multi bit memory cell	초 고밀도 기억 소자	ch'o gomildo gieok soja
ohm	오옴, 전기 저항 단위	o-om, cheon-gi jeohang danwi
optical character reader	광학 문자 판독기	kwanghak munjja p'andokki
optical mark reader	광학 기호 판독기	kwanghak kiho p'andokki
opto-electronics	광학 전자학	kwanghak cheonjahak
parts	부품, 부분품	pup'um, pubunp'um
peripheral equipment	주변 장치	chubyeon jangch'i
personal cassette player	개인용 카세트 전축	kaein-yong k'aset'eu jeonch'uk
personal computer	개인용 컴퓨터, 퍼스컴	kaein-yong k'eomp'yut'eo, p'eoseuk'eom
personal stereo radio	개인용 입체 음향 라디오	kaein-yong ipch'e eumhyang radio
personal TV	개인용 테레비	kaein-yong t'erebi
phone-answering machine	자동 응답 전화기	chadong eungdap cheonhwagi
plasma etching	플라즈마 부식동판술	p'eullajeuma bushik tongp'ansul
pocket-sized TV	포켓용 소형 테레비	p'ok'ennyong sohyeong t'erebi
poly-crystal silicon	다결정 규소	ta-gyeoljjeong gyuso
portable TV	휴대용 테레비	hyudae-yong t'erebi
precision machinery	정밀 기계 장치	cheongmil gigye jangch'i
printer	인쇄기, 프린터	inswaegi, p'eurint'eo
radar	레이다, 전파 탐지기	reida, cheonp'a t'amjigi
radio	라디오	radio
radio cassette player	라디오 카세트 전축	radio k'aset'eu jeonch'uk
RAM	등속 호출 기억 장치, 램	teungsok hoch'ul gieok changch'i, raem
rechargeable (adj)	재충전 가능한	chae-ch'ungjeon ganeung-han
record player	전축	cheonch'uk
rectifier	정류기	cheongnyugi
refrigerater	냉장고	naengjang-go
remote control	원격 조종 장치, 리모콘	weonkkyeok chojong jangch'i, rimok'on
ROM	판독 전용 기억 장치, 롬	p'andok cheonyong gieok changch'i, rom

Key Words for Key Industries

semiconductor	반도체	pandoch'e
sensor	감지 장치	kamji jangch'i
serial printer	연속 인쇄기	yeonsok inswaegi
sound equipment	음향기기	eumhyang gigi
sound recorder	녹음기	nogeumgi
speaker	확성기, 스피커	hwakseong-gi, seup'ik'eo
static apparatus	정지기기(靜止機器)	cheongji-gigi
stereophonic (adj)	입체 음향 장치의	ipch'e eumhyang jangch'i-eui
stereo TV	스테레오(입체 음향) 테레비	seut'ereo(ipch'e eumhyang) t'erebi
switch	스위치	seuwich'i
tape recorder	녹음기	nogeumgi
television	테레비	t'erebi
telex	텔렉스, 전송식 통신문	t'ellekseu, cheonsongshik t'ongshinmun
terminal	단말 장치, 터미널	tanmal jangch'i, t'eomineol
thermostat	온도 조절 장치	ondo jojeol jangch'i
transformer	변압기	pyeonapki
tuner	동조기	tongjogi
very large-scale integrated circuit	특대형 집적 회로	t'euktaehyeong jipcheok hoero
video cassette camera	비디오 카세트 카메라	pidio k'aset'eu k'amera
video cassette player	비디오 카세트 장치	pidio k'aset'eu jangch'i
video cassette recorder	비디오 카세트 녹음기	pidio k'aset'eu nogeumgi
video disc	비디오 디스크	pidio diseuk'eu
video music player	영상 음악 반주기	yeongsang eumak panjugi
videOrche	비디오케, 영상음악 반주기	pidiok'e, yeongsang eumak panjugi
video tape recorder	비디오 테이프 녹음기	pidio t'eip'eu nogeumgi
wafer	웨이퍼, 반도체 박판	weip'eo, pandoch'e bakp'an
wire telecommunication equipment	유선 통신 기기	yuseon t'ongshin gigi
wireless telecommunication equipment	무선 통신 기기	museon t'ongshin gigi
word processor	워드 프로세서	weodeu p'euroseseo

Korean to English

ant'ena	antenna	안테나
chadong eungdap cheonhwagi	phone-answering machine	자동 응답 전화기
chadong yeok-hoejeon	autoreverse	자동 역회전
chadongch'a-yong jeonhwa	car telephone	자동차용 전화
chadongch'a-yong museon t'ongshin-gi	CB	자동차용 무선 통신기
chae-ch'ungjeon ganeung-han	rechargeable	재충전 가능한
chagi ch'ukcheon-gi	ceramic condenser	자기 축전기
chagi diseuk'eu jangch'i	magnetic disc unit	자기 디스크 장치
chagi gich'o gieok changch'i	magnetic bubble memory	자기(磁器) 기초 기억 장치

Electronics and Electricity

chagi t'eip'eu jangch'i	magnetic tape unit	자기 테이프 장치
cheneret'a	generator	제네레타
cheollo	converter	전로(轉爐)
cheonch'uk	record player	전축
cheon-geuk	electrode	전극
cheon-gi gong-gu	electric tools	전기 공구
cheon-gi hoero	electric circuit	전기 회로
cheon-gi jeohang	electric resistance	전기 저항
cheon-gi jeohang danwi	optical character reader	전기 저항 단위
cheon-gi myeondo-gi	electric shaver	전기 면도기
cheon-gi nanbang-gi	electric heater	전기 난방기
cheon-gi yeon-gyeol gigye	electric interlocking machine	전기 연결 기계
cheon-gi-ro	electric furnace	전기로(電氣爐)
cheongji-gigi	static apparatus	정지기기(靜止機器)
cheongmil gigye jangch'i	precision machinery	정밀 기계 장치
cheonja renji	microwave oven	전자 렌지
ch'eongnyeok baneung jangch'i	audio response equipment	청력 반응 장치
cheongnyugi	rectifier	정류기
cheonja akki	electronic musical instruments	전자 악기(樂器)
cheonja geumjeon deungnok-ki	electronic cash register	전자 금전 등록기
cheonja gonghak	electronics	전자 공학
cheonja hyeonmigyeong	electron microscope	전자 현미경
cheonja jaebongt'eul	electronic sewing machine	전자 재봉틀
cheonja obeun	microwave oven	전자 오븐
cheonja oreugan	electronic organ	전자 오르간
cheonja t'ajagi	electronic typewriter	전자 타자기
cheonja t'aksang-yong gyesan-gi	electronic desk calculator	전자 탁상용 계산기
cheonjach'ong	electron gun	전자총
cheonjaseok	electromagnet	전자석
cheonjaseon	electron beam	전자선
cheonp'a t'amjigi	radar	전파 탐지기
cheonseon	electric cable	전선(電線)
cheonsongshik t'ongshinmun	telex	전송식 통신문
cheopch'ok	contact	접촉
cheopsokki	connector	접속기
cheungp'okki	amplifier	증폭기
chingnyugye	DC machine	직류계
chinp'ok pyeonjo	amplitude modulation	진폭 변조
chipcheok hoero	integrated circuit	집적 회로
chubyeon jangch'i	peripheral equipment	주변 장치
chungjeon-gigi	heavy-electric equipment	중전기기(重電機器)
chup'asu byeonjo	frequency modulation	주파수 변조
ch'oego eumjil	high fidelity	최고 음질(音質)
ch'o gomildo gieok soja	multi bit memory cell	초 고밀도 기억 소자

Key Words for Key Industries

ch'ukcheon-gi	condenser	축전기
dijit'areui	digital (adj)	디지탈의
di-raem	D-RAM	디-램
diseuk'et	diskette	디스켓
doneot-hyeong p'andok cheonyong gieok changch'i	EP ROM	도넛형 판독 전용 기억 장치
eumhyang gigi	sound equipment	음향 기기
haeng inswaegi	line printer	행(行) 인쇄기
hereuch'eu	hertz	헤르츠
heukpaek t'erebi	black and white TV	흑백 테레비
hoero ch'adan-gi	circuit breaker	회로 차단기
hyeon-geum jadong ch'ulnapki	automatic teller machine (ATM)	현금 자동 출납기
hwakseong-gi	speaker	확성기
hyudae-yong diseuk'eu	compact disc	휴대용 디스크
hyudae-yong diseuk'eu yeonju jangch'i	compact disc player	휴대용 디스크 연주 장치
hyudae-yong jeonhwagi	mobile phone	휴대용 전화기
hyudae-yong t'erebi	portable TV	휴대용 테레비
igeuk chin-gong-gwan	diode	이극 진공관
inbeo-eot'eo	inverter	인버어터
inswaegi	printer	인쇄기
ipch'e eumhyang jangch'i-eui	stereophonic (adj)	입체 음향 장치의
kaein-yong ipch'e eumhyang radio	personal stereo radio	개인용 입체 음향 라디오
kaein-yong k'aset'eu jeonch'uk	personal cassette player	개인용 카세트 전축
kaein-yong k'eomp'yut'eo	personal computer	개인용 컴퓨터
kaein-yong t'erebi	personal TV	개인용 테레비
kajeong-yong jeonja	electronic home appliance	가정용 전자
kamji jangch'i	sensor	감지 장치
karaok'e	KaraOrche	가라오케
kaseupki	humidifier	가습기
keonban	keyboard	건반
keumjeon deungnok-ki	cash register	금전 등록기
kojeong jeongbo gieok sayong jangch'i	fixed resistor	고정 정보 기억 사용 장치
kong-gu	machine tools	공구
kwanghak cheonjahak	opto-electronics	광학 전자학
kwanghak kiho p'andokki	optical mark reader	광학 기호 판독기
kwanghak munjja p'andokki	optical character reader	광학 문자 판독기
kyesan-gi	calculator	계산기
kyesu-hyeong ch'eongch'wi t'eip'eu nogeumgi	digital audio tape recorder	계수형 청취 테이프 녹음기
kyesu-hyeong gach'eong diseuk'eu	digital audio disc	계수형 가청 디스크
kyesuhyeong-eui	digital (adj)	계수형의
kyoryu	alternating current	교류
kyunapseon	equalizer	균압선
kyunhyeong jangch'i	equalizer	균형 장치

Electronics and Electricity

k'a-p'on	car telephone	카폰
k'aset'eu	cassette	카세트
k'eolleo t'erebi	color TV	컬러 테레비
k'eomp'yut'eo	computer	컴퓨터
k'eonbeot'eo	converter	컨버터
k'ibodeu	keyboard	키보드
k'omp'aek diseuk'eu	compact disc (CD)	콤팩 디스크
maik'euro ch'eori jangch'i	micro processor	마이크로 처리 장치
maik'euro k'aset'eu nogeumgi	micro cassette recorder	마이크로 카세트 녹음기
maik'euro k'eomp'yut'eo	micro computer	마이크로 컴퓨터
maik'euro-weibeu	microwave	마이크로 웨이브
museon jeonhwagi	cordless phone	무선 전화기
museon t'ongshin gigi	wireless telecommunication equipment	무선 통신 기기
naengjang-go	refrigerater	냉장고
nogeumgi	tape recorder, sound recorder	녹음기
norae banjugi	fun music player	노래 반주기
norae banjugi	KaraOrche	노래 반주기
odio jeonch'uk siseut'em	audio component system	오디오 전축 시스템
ondo jojeol jangch'i	thermostat	온도 조절 장치
o-om	ohm	오옴
p'aekshimilli	facsimile	팩시밀리
paljjeon-gi	dynamo	발전기
paljjeon-gi	generator	발전기
pandoch'e	semiconductor	반도체
pandoch'e bakp'an	wafer	반도체 박판
pandoch'e ch'ukcheon-gi	chip condenser	반도체 축전기
pangsa igeuk chin-gong-gwan	light-emitting diode	방사 이극 진공관
peuraun gwan	Brown tube	브라운관
pidio diseuk'eu	video disc	비디오 디스크
pidio k'aset'eu jangch'i	video cassette player	비디오 카세트 장치
pidio k'aset'eu k'amera	video cassette camera	비디오 카세트 카메라
pidio k'aset'eu nogeumgi	video cassette recorder	비디오 카세트 녹음기
pidiok'e	videOrche	비디오케
pidio t'eip'eu nogeumgi	video tape recorder	비디오 테이프 녹음기
pit'eu	bit	비트
poksa jeonsong jangch'i	facsimile	복사 전송 장치
pubunp'um	parts	부분품
pup'um	component, parts	부품(部品)
pyeonapki	transformer	변압기
p'aekseu	facsimile	팩스
p'andok cheonyong gieok changch'i	ROM	판독 전용 기억 장치
p'eoseuk'eom	personal computer	퍼스컴
p'eullajeuma bushik tongp'ansul	plasma etching	플라즈마 부식 동판술
p'eurint'eo	printer	프린터
p'ok'ennyong sohyeong t'erebi	pocket-sized TV	포켓용 소형 테레비

Key Words for Key Industries

p'yoshi danwi	display unit	표시 단위
radio	radio	라디오
radio k'aset'eu jeonch'uk	radio cassette player	라디오 카세트 전축
raem	RAM	램
reida	radar	레이다
reijeo-gwang inswaegi	laser beam printer	레이저광 인쇄기
rimok'on	remote control	리모콘
rom	ROM	롬
saengmuni sujeong	color liquid crystal	색무늬 수정
saneop-yong jeonja	industrial electronics	산업용 전자
saneop-yong robot'eu	industrial robot	산업용 로보트
seup'ik'eo	speaker	스피커
seut'ereo (ipch'e eumhyang) t'erebi	stereo TV	스테레오(입체음향) 테레비
seuwich'i	switch	스위치
shikp'um gagong-gi	food processor	식품 가공기
sohyeong gujo siseut'em	mini component system	소형 구조 시스템
taehyeong chipcheok hoero	large-scale integrated circuit	대형 집적 회로
ta-gyeoljjeong gyuso	poly-crystal silicon	다결정 규소
tanmal jangch'i	terminal	단말 장치
teungsok hoch'ul gieok changch'i	RAM	등속 호출 기억 장치
tojeonnyul	conductivity	도전율
tongjogi	tuner	동조기
toshik kyunhyeong jangch'i	graphic equalizer	도식 균형 장치
t'aksang-yong gyesan-gi	desk-top calculator	탁상용 계산기
t'ellekseu	telex	텔렉스
t'eomineol	terminal	터미널
t'erebi	television	테레비
t'euktaehyeong jipcheok hoero	wafer	특대형 집적 회로
t'umyeong sujeong	liquid crystal	투명 수정
wanch'ung gieok changch'i	buffer memory	완충 기억 장치
weip'eo	wafer	웨이퍼
weodeu p'euroseseo	word processor	워드 프로세서
weonkkyeok chojong jangch'i	remote control	원격 조종 장치
yeokhak kieok changch'i	dynamic memory	역학 기억 장치
yeongsang eumak panjugi	video music player	영상 음악 반주기
yeongsang eumak panjugi	VideOrche	영상 음악 반주기
yeonsok inswaegi	serial printer	연속 인쇄기
yuseon jeonhwagi	electric line telephone	유선 전화기
yuseon t'ongshin gigi	wire telecommunication equipment	유선 통신 기기

FASHION AND TEXTILES

English to Korean

accessory	액세서리	*aekseseori*
angora	앙고라 모직물	*ang-gora mojingmul*
belt	혁대	*hyeoktae*
blazer	블레지어	*peullejieo*
blouse	블라우스	*peullauseu*
boots	목긴 구두, 장화	*mok-kin gudu, changhwa*
bow tie	나비 넥타이, 보우 타이	*nabi nekt'ai, pou t'ai*
camel's hair	낙타 털	*nakt'a t'eol*
cashmere	캐쉬미어	*k'aeswimieo*
coat	코트	*k'ot'eu*
collar	깃	*kit*
color	물감, 색	*mulkkam, saek*
collections	수집품, 소장품	*sujip'um, sojangp'um*
cotton	면, 면직물	*myeon, myeonjingmul*
cufflink	소맷부리 단추	*somaetpuri danch'u*
cut (v)	자르다	*chareuda*
design (v)	도안하다	*toan-hada*
designer	디자이너	*tijaineo*
dress	의복, 드레스	*euibok, teureseu*
fabric	직물	*chingmul*
fashion	유행	*yuhaeng*
flannel	면 플란넬	*myeon p'eullannel*
French cuff	샤쓰 꺾어 접는 커프스	*syasseu kkeokkeo jeomneun k'eop'euseu*
handbag	핸드백	*haendeubaek*
hand-knit (adj)	손으로 짠, 뜨게질 한	*son-euro jjan, tteugejil-han*
hand-sewn (adj)	손으로 꿰맨	*son-euro kkwemaen*
hand-woven (adj)	손으로 뜬	*son-euro tteun*
hem	감침질	*kamch'imjil*
jewel	보석, 장신구	*poseok, changshin-gu*
length	길이, 장단	*kiri, changdan*
linen	린네르, 아마포	*rinnereu, amap'o*
lining	안감	*ankkam*
long sleeves	긴 소매	*kin somae*
moire	물결 무늬 옷감의 일종	*mulkkyeol muni otkkam-eui iljong*
muslin	옥양목	*ogyangmok*
nylon	나일론	*naillon*
pattern	본, 패턴	*pon, p'aet'eon*
pleat	주름	*chureum*
polyester	폴리에스테르 섬유	*p'ollieseutereu seomyu*
poplin	포프린	*p'op'eurin*
print	날염하다, 프린트하다	*nalyeom-hada, p'eurint'eu-hada*
raincoat	비옷	*pi-ot*
rayon	인조 견사	*injo gyeonsa*
ready-to-wear	기성복	*kiseongbok*
scarf	목도리, 스카프	*moktori, seuk'ap'eu*

Key Words for Key Industries

sew	바느질하다, 봉재하다	paneujil-hada, pongjae-hada
shirt	셔쓰	syeosseu
shoe	구두	kudu
short sleeves	짧은 소매	jjalbeun somae
shoulder pad	어깨심	eokkae shim
silk	비단	pidan
size	싸이즈, 크기	ssaijeu, k'eugi
skirt	스커트, 치마	seuk'eot'eu, ch'ima
slacks	바지	paji
sportswear	운동복	undong-bok
style	유행(형)	yuhaeng (hyeong)
suede	**수에드**	suedeu
suit	양복	yangbok
sweater	스웨터	seuwet'eo
synthetic (adj)	합성의, 인조의	hapseong-eui, injo-eui
synthetic suede	합성 수에드	hapseong suedeu
taffeta	호박단(琥珀緞)	hobaktan
tailor	재단사	chaedansa
textile	직물, 섬유	chingmul, seomyu
tie	넥타이, 타이	nekt'ai, t'ai
unisex	남녀 공동	namnyeo gongdong
veil	면사포	myeonsap'o chokki
wool	양털, 모직물	yangt'eol, mojingmul
yarn	털실, 모사	t'eolshil, mosa

Korean to English

aekseseori	accessory	액세서리
amap'o	linen	아마포
ang-gora mojingmul	angora	앙고라 모직물
ankkam	lining	안감
chaedansa	tailor	재단사
changdan	length	장단
changhwa	boots	장화
changshin-gu	jewel	장신구
chareuda	cut (v)	자르다
chingmul	fabric, textile	직물
chokki	vest	조끼
chureum	pleat	주름
ch'ima	skirt	치마
eokkae shim	shoulder pad	어깨심
euibok	dress	의복
haendeubaek	handbag	핸드백
hapseong suedeu	synthetic suede	합성 수에드
hapseong-eui	synthetic (adj)	합성의
hobaktan	taffeta	호박단(琥珀緞)
hyeoktae	belt	혁대
injo gyeonsa	rayon	인조 견사
injo-eui	synthetic (adj)	인조의
jjalbeun somae	short sleeves	짧은 소매
kamch'imjil	hem	감침질

Fashion and Textiles

k'aeswimieo	cashmere	캐쉬미어
kin somae	long sleeves	긴 소매
k'eugi	size	크기
kiri	length	길이
kiseongbok	ready-to-wear	기성복
kit	collar	깃
kudu	shoe	구두
k'ot'eu	coat	코트
mojingmul	wool	모직물
mok-kin gudu	boots	목긴 구두
moktori	scarf	목도리
mosa	yarn	모사
mulkkam	color	물감
mulkkyeol muni otkkam-eui iljjong	moire	물결 무늬 옷감의 일종
myeon	cotton	면
myeon p'eullannel	flannel	면 플란넬
myeonjingmul	cotton	면직물
myeonsap'o	veil	면사포
nabi nekt'ai	bow tie	나비 넥타이
naillon	nylon	나일론
nakt'a t'eol	camel's hair	낙타 털
nalyeom-hada	print	날염하다
namnyeo gongdong	unisex	남녀 공동
nekt'ai	tie	넥타이
ogyangmok	muslin	옥양목
paji	slacks	바지
paneujil-hada	sew	바느질하다
peullauseu	blouse	블라우스
peullejieo	blazer	블레지어
pidan	silk	비단
pi-ot	raincoat	비옷
pon	pattern	본
pongjae-hada	sew	봉재하다
poseok	jewel	보석
pou t'ai	bow tie	보우 타이
p'aet'eon	pattern	패턴
p'eurint'eu-hada	print	프린트하다
p'ollieseutereu seomyu	polyester	폴리에스테르 섬유
p'op'eurin	poplin	포프린
rinnereu	linen	린네르
saek	color	색
seomyu	textile	섬유
seuk'ap'eu	scarf	스카프
seuk'eot'eu	skirt	스커트
seuwet'eo	sweater	스웨터
sojangp'um	collections	소장품
somaetpuri danch'u	cufflink	소맷부리 단추
son-euro jjan	hand-kint (adj)	손으로 짠
son-euro kkwemaen	hand-sewn (adj)	손으로 꿰맨
son-euro tteun	hand-woven (adj)	손으로 뜬

Key Words for Key Industries

ssaijeu	size	싸이즈
suedeu	suede	수에드
sujip'um	collections	수집품
syasseu kkeokkeo jeomneun k'eop'euseu	French cuff	샤쓰 꺾어 접는 커프스
syeosseu	shirt	셔쓰
t'ai	tie	타이
t'eolshil	yarn	털실
teureseu	dress	드레스
tijaineo	designer	디자이너
toan-hada	design (v)	도안하다
tteugejil-han	hand-knit (adj)	뜨게질 한
undong-bok	sportswear	운동복
yangbok	suit	양복
yangt'eol	wool	양털
yuhaeng	fashion	유행
yuhaeng (hyeong)	style	유행(형)

MACHINE TOOLS

English to Korean

English	Korean	Romanization
angular cutter	각(角) 커터	kak k'eot'eo
articulated robot	정교한 로보트	cheong-gyo-han robot'eu
autochecker	자동 검사기	chadong geomsagi
automatic pallet changer	자동 팰릿 변경기	chadong p'aellit pyeon-gyeong-gi
automatic screw machine	자동 나사 기계	chadong nasa gigye
automatic tool changer	자동 연장 변경기	chadong yeonjang byeon-gyeong-gi
bit	날	nal
boring machine	보오링 머신, 천공기(穿孔機)	po-oring meoshiin, ch'eon-gong-gi
broaching machine	브로우칭 머신	peurouch'ing meoshiin
cartesian coordinates robot	칼디시안 조정 로보트	k'aldishian jojeong robot'eu
centerless grinder	무중심 분쇄기	mu-jungshim bunswaegi
computerized numerical control	전산 수치 조종	cheonsan such'i jojong
cutting tool	깎는 연장	kkangneun yeonjang
cylinder boring machine	실린더 천공기	shillindeo ch'eon-gong-gi
cylindrical coordinates robot	원통형 조정 로보트	weont'ong-hyeong jojeong robot'eu
cylindrical grinder	원통형 분쇄기	weont'onghyeong bunswaegi
die	다이	ta-i
drilling machiner	천공기	ch'eon-gong-gi
end mill	말단부 제작 기계	malttanbu jejak kigye
fixed sequence robot	고정 반복 진행 로보트	kojeong banbok chinhaeng robot'eu
friction press	마찰 압착기	mach'al apch'akki
gear cutting machine	톱니 바퀴 깎는 기계	t'omni bak'wi kkangneun gigye
grinder	분쇄기	punswaegi
injection molding machine	분사틀 기계	punsa-t'eul gigye
insert machine	삽입기	sabipki
internal grinder	내부 분쇄기	naebu bunswaegi
jet condenser	분출 축전기	punch'ul ch'ukcheon-gi
jig	선광기(選鑛機)	seon-gwang-gi
knurling tool	마디 공구	madi gong-gu
lapping machine	접는 기계	cheomneun gigye
lathe	선반(旋盤)	seonban
machine tools	기계 공구	kigye gong-gu
machining center	기계 공작소(工作所)	kigye gongjakso
manipulator	위험 물질 취급 장치	wiheom muljjil ch'wigeup changch'i
material handling robot	재료 취급 로보트	chaeryo ch'wigeup robot'eu
mechanical press	기계 압착기	kigye apch'akki
metal processing machine	금속 공작 기계	keumsok kongjak kigye
milling machine	금속 절삭기	keumsok cheolsak-ki
molding machine	주조기	chujo-gi
multicut lathe	복수 절단 선반	poksu jeolttan seonban

Key Words for Key Industries

English	Korean	Romanization
multispindle drilling machine	복수 방추 천공기	poksu bangch'u ch'eon-gong-gi
numerical control machine	수치 제어기	such'i je-eogi
numerical control robot	수치 제어 로보트	such'i je-eo robot'eu
paper machine	제지 기계	cheji gigye
planetary gear train	차동 기어 장치	ch'adong gieo janghch'i
plasma cutting machine	플라즈마 절단기	p'eullajeuma jeolttan-gi
playback robot	녹음 장치 로보트	nogeum jangch'i robot'eu
polar coordinates robot	극좌표 로보트	keukchwap'yo robot'eu
precision machinery	정밀 기계류	cheongmil gigyeryu
prime mover	원동기(原動機)	weondong-gi
printing machine	인쇄 기계	inswae gigye
profiler	측도도, 프로파일러	ch'eungmyeondo, p'europ'ailleo
punch press	구멍 뚫는 기구	kumeong ttulneun gigu
radial drilling machine	방사상 천공기	pangsasang ch'eon-gong-gi
reamer	확공기(擴孔機)	hwakkong-gi
repeatable robot	반복 로보트	panbok robot'eu
roll turning lathe	회전 세공 선반	hoejeon segong seonban
sewing machine	재봉틀	chaebongt'eul
screw cutting lathe	나사 절단 선반	nasa jeolttan seonban
sequence robot	연속 진행 로보트	yeonsok chinhaeng robot'eu
sequential control	순차 조절	sunch'a jojeol
shaft lather	샤프트 선반공	syap'eut'eu seonban-gong
shaping machine	형삭반(形削盤)	hyeongsakpan
shearing machine	전단기(剪斷機)	cheondan-gi
slotting machine	자동 판매기	chadong p'anmaegi
spline milling machine	키홈 절삭 기계	k'ihom jeolsak kigye
surface grinder	표면 분쇄기	p'yomyeon bunswaegi
tool	공구(工具)	kong-gu
transfer machine	자동 공작 기계	chadong gongjak kigye
turret lathe	터릿 선반	t'eorit seonban
universal grinder	자재 분쇄기	chajae bunswaegi
universal milling machine	자재(自在) 절삭 기계	chajae jeolsak kigye
variable sequence robot	가변 연속 로보트	kabyeon yeonsok robot'eu
vending machine	자판기	chap'an-gi
vertical boring mill	수직 천공기	sujik ch'eon-gong-gi
vertical milling machine	수직 절삭기	sujik jeolsakki

Korean to English

chadong geomsagi	autochecker	자동 검사기
chadong gongjak kigye	transfer machine	자동 공작 기계
chadong nasa gigye	automatic screw machine	자동 나사 기계
chadong p'aellit pyeon-gyeong-gi	automatic pallet changer	자동 팰릿 변경기
chadong p'anmaegi	slotting machine	자동 판매기
chadong yeonjang byeon-gyeong-gi	automatic tool changer	자동 연장 변경기

Machine Tools

chaebongt'eul	sewing machine	재봉틀
chaeryo ch'wigeup robot'eu	material handling robot	재료 취급 로보트
chajae bunswaegi	universal grinder	자재 분쇄기
chajae jeolsak kigye	universal milling machine	자재(自在) 절삭 기계
chap'an-gi	vending machine	자판기
ch'adong gieo jangch'i	planetary gear train	차동 기어 장치
cheji gigye	paper machine	제지 기계
cheomneun gigye	lapping machine	접는 기계
cheondan-gi	shearing machine	전단기(剪斷機)
cheong-gyo-han robot'eu	articulated robot	정교한 로보트
cheongmil gigyeryu	precision machinery	정밀 기계류
cheonsan such'i jojong	computerized numerical control	전산 수치 조종
chujo-gi	molding machine	주조기
ch'eon-gong-gi	drilling machine	천공기(穿孔機)
ch'eungmyeondo	profiler	측면도
hoejeon segong seonban	roll turning lathe	회전 세공 선반
hwakkong-gi	reamer	확공기(擴孔機)
hyeongsakpan	shaping machine	형삭반(形削盤)
inswae gigye	printing machine	인쇄 기계
kabyeon yeonsok robot'eu	variable sequence robot	가변 연속 로보트
kak k'eot'eo	angular cutter	각(角) 커터
k'aldishian jojeong robot'eu	cartesian coordinates robot	칼디시안 조정 로보트
keukchwap'yo robot'eu	polar coordinates robot	극좌표 로보트
keumsok cheolsak-ki	milling machine	금속 절삭기
keumsok kongjak kigye	metal processing machine	금속 공작 기계
kigye apch'akki	mechanical press	기계 압착기
kigye gong-gu	machine tools	기계 공구
kigye gongjakso	machining center	기계 공작소(工作所)
kkangneun yeonjang	cutting tool	깎는 연장
kojeong banbok chinhaeng robot'eu	fixed sequence robot	고정 반복 진행 로보트
kong-gu	tool	공구(工具)
kumeong ttulneun gigu	punch press	구멍 뚫는 기구
k'ihom jeolsak kigye	spline milling machine	키홈 절삭 기계
mach'al apch'akki	friction press	마찰 압착기
madi gong-gu	knurling tool	마디 공구
malttanbu jejak kigye	end mill	말단부 제작 기계
mu-jungshim bunswaegi	centerless grinder	무중심 분쇄기
naebu bunswaegi	internal grinder	내부 분쇄기
nal	bit	날
nasa jeolttan seonban	screw cutting lathe	나사 절단 선반
nogeum jangch'i robot'eu	playback robot	녹음 장치 로보트
panbok robot'eu	repeatable robot	반복 로보트
pangsasang ch'eon-gong-gi	radial drilling machine	방사상 천공기
peurouch'ing meoshiin	broaching machine	브로우칭 머신
p'eullajeuma jeolttan-gi	plasma cutting machine	플라즈마 절단기
p'europ'ailleo	profiler	프로파일러

Key Words for Key Industries

poksu bangch'u ch'eon-gong-gi	multispindle drilling machine	복수 방추 천공기
poksu jeolttan seonban	multicut lathe	복수 절단 선반
po-oring meoshin	boring machine	보오링 머신
punch'ul ch'ukcheon-gi	jet condenser	분출 축전기
punsa-t'eul gigye	injection molding machine	분사틀 기계
punswaegi	grinder	분쇄기
p'yomyeon bunswaegi	surface grinder	표면 분쇄기
sabipki	insert machine	삽입기
seonban	lathe	선반(旋盤)
seon-gwang-gi	jig	선광기(選鑛機)
shillindeo ch'eon-gong-gi	cylinder boring machine	실린더 천공기
such'i je-eo robot'eu	numerical control robot	수치 제어 로보트
such'i je-eogi	numerical control machine	수치 제어기
sujik ch'eon-gong-gi	vertical boring mill	수직 천공기
sujik jeolsakki	vertical milling machine	수직 절삭기
sunch'a jojeol	sequential control	순차 조절
syap'eut'eu seonban-gong	shaft lather	샤프트 선반공
ta-i	die	다이
t'eorit seonban	turret lathe	터릿 선반
t'omni bak'wi kkangneun gigye	gear cutting machine	톱니 바퀴 깍는 기계
weondong-gi	prime mover	원동기(原動機)
weont'onghyeong bunswaegi	cylindrical grinder	원통형 분쇄기
weont'ong-hyeong jojeong robot'eu	cylindrical coordinates robot	원통형 조정 로보트
wiheom muljjil ch'wigeup changch'i	manipulator	위험 물질 취급 장치
yeonsok chinhaeng robot'eu	sequence robot	연속 진행 로보트

METALWORKS

English to Korean

alloy	합금(合金)	hapkeum
alloy steel	합금강(合金鋼)	hapkeumgang
alumina	알루미나(산화알미늄)	allumina (sanhwa alminyum)
aluminum	알루미늄	alluminyum
annealing	소둔(燒鈍)	sodun
bars	봉강(棒鋼)	pong-gang
billets	철봉	ch'eolbong
blast furnace	용광로	yong-gwangno
carbon steel	탄소강	t'ansogang
cast iron	주철, 무쇠	chuch'eol, musoe
cast steel	주강(鑄鋼)	chugang
cement	도성(陶性)합금	toseong hapkeum
chromium	크롬	k-eurom
coil	코일(螺管:나관)	k'oil (nagwan)
cold rolling	냉간압연(冷間壓延)	naeng-gan-abyeon
continuous caster	부단한 주조자	pudan-han jujoja
copper	구리, 동(銅)	kuri, tong
crucible	도가니	togani
cupola	용선로(溶銑爐)	yongseollo
die casting	주조	chujo
direct reduction process	직접 환원 과정	chikcheop hwanweon gwajeong
electric arc furnace	전기 호(弧)형 화로	cheon-gi ho-hyeong hwaro
electrolytic process	전기 분해 과정	cheon-gi bunhae gwajeong
ferrite	아철 산염	ach'eol sanyeom
ferroalloys	합금철	hapkeumch'eol
ferrochromium	철과 크롬의 합금	ch'eol-gwa k'eurom-eui hapkeum
ferromanganese	망간철	mang-gan-ch'eol
ferronickel	니켈철	nik'elch'eol
ferrosilicon	규소철	kyusoch'eol
foundry	주조 공장	chujo gongjang
furnace	용광로	yong-gwangno
hot rolling	열회전	yeol hoejeon
hot strip coil	내열(耐熱) 코일	naeyeol k'oil
induction furnace	유도 전기로	yudo jeon-giro
ingot	금은괴	keum-eun-goe
iron ore	철광석	ch'eolgwangseok
limestone	석회석	seokhoeseok
magnetic fluid	자기 유동체	chagi yudongch'e
manganese ore	망간 광석	mang-gan gwangseok
manganese steel	망간강	mang-gan-gang
metal alloys for hydrogen storage	수소 저장을 위한 금속 합금	suso jeojang-eul wi-han geumsok hapkeum
metal hydride	금속 수소 화물	keumsok suso hwamul
metallic fiber	금속질 섬유	keumsokchil seomyu
mineral	광물(鑛物)	kwangmul
molybdenum	몰리브덴	mollibeuden

Key Words for Key Industries

mould	금형(金型)	keumhyeong
nitrogen	질소	chilso
non-metallic mineral	비금속 광물	pigeumsok kwangmul
pickling	묽은 산 용액으로 닦음	mulgeun san yong-aegeuro dakkeum
pig iron	선철	seonch'eol
plate	판금	p'angeum
powder metallurgy	분말 야금	punmal yageum
quench (v)	쇠 담금질하다	soe damgeumjil-hada
refractories	내화 벽돌	naehwa byeoktol
rod	측량간	ch'eungnyang-gan
rolling mill	압연기	abyeon-gi
scrap	쇠 부스러기	soe buseureogi
seamless steel tube	이음매 없는 강철관	ieummae eomneun gangch'eol-gwan
shape-memory alloy	형(型) 기억 합금	hyeong gieok hapkeum
sheet bar	박판 봉강(棒鋼)	pakp'an bong-gang
sheet pile	박판 더미	pakp'an deomi
spiral tube	나선형 강철관	naseon-hyeong gangch'eol-gwan
sponge	스폰지	seup'onji
stainless steel	스텐레스강(鋼)	seut'enreseu-gang
steel foil	강철박편	kangch'eol bakp'yeon
steel mill	제강소	chegangso
super alloys	초 합금(超合金)	ch'o hapkeum
titanium	티타늄	t'it'anyum
titanium metal	티타늄 금속	t'it'anyum geumsok
tungsten	텅스텐	t'eongseut'en
ultrafine powder	분말(粉末)	punmal
vanadium	바나듐	panadyum
wire	철사, 전선	ch'eolsa, cheonseon

Korean to English

abyeon-gi	rolling mill	압연기
ach'eol sanyeom	ferrite	아철산염
allumina (sanhwa alminyum)	alumina	알루미나(산화 알미늄)
alluminyum	aluminum	알루미늄
chagi yudongch'e	magnetic fluid	자기 유동체
chegangso	steel mill	제강소
cheon-gi bunhae gwajeong	electrolytic process	전기 분해 과정
cheon-gi ho-hyeong hwaro	electric arc furnace	전기 호(弧)형 화로
cheonseon	wire	전선
chikcheop hwanweon gwajeong	direct reduction process	직접 환원 과정
chilso	nitrogen	질소
chuch'eol	cast steel	주철
chugang	cast steel	주강(鑄鋼)
chujo	die casting	주조
chujo gongjang	foundry	주조 공장

Metalworks

ch'eol-gwa k'eurom-eui hapkeum	ferrochromium	철과 크롬의 합금
ch'eolgwangseok	iron ore	철광석
ch'eolsa	wire	철사
ch'eolbong	billets	철봉
ch'eungnyang-gan	rod	측량간
ch'o hapkeum	super alloys	초합금(超合金)
hapkeum	alloy	합금(合金)
hapkeumch'eol	ferroalloys	합금철
hapkeumgang	alloy steel	합금강(合金鋼)
hyeong gieok hapkeum	shape-memory alloy	형(型) 기억 합금
ieummae eomneun gangch'eol-gwan	seamless steel tube	이음매 없는 강철관
kangch'eol bakp'yeon	steel foil	강철 박편
keum-eun-goe	ingot	금은괴
keumhyeong	mould	금형(金型)
keumsok suso hwamul	metal hydride	금속 수소 화물
keumsokchil seomyu	metallic fiber	금속질 섬유
kuri	copper	구리
kwangmul	mineral	광물(鑛物)
kyusoch'eol	ferrosilicon	규소철
k'eurom	chromium	크롬
k'oil (nagwan)	coil	코일(螺管:나관)
mang-gan gwangseok	manganese ore	망간 광석
mang-gan-ch'eol	ferromanganese	망간철
mang-gan-gang	manganese steel	망간강
mollibeuden	molybdenum	몰리브덴
mulgeun san yong-aegeuro dakkeum	pickling	묽은 산 용액으로 닦음
musoe	cast iron	무쇠
naehwa byeoktol	refractories	내화 벽돌
naeng-gan-abyeon	cold rolling	냉간압연(冷間壓延)
naeyeol k'oil	hot strip coil	내열(耐熱) 코일
naseon-hyeong gangch'eol-gwan	spiral tube	나선형 강철관
nik'elch'eol	ferronickel	니켈철
pakp'an bong-gang	sheet bar	박판 봉강(棒鋼)
pakp'an deomi	sheet pile	박판더미
pigeumsok kwangmul	non-metallic mineral	비금속 광물
panadyum	vanadium	바나듐
pong-gang	bars	봉강(棒鋼)
pudan-han jujoja	continuous caster	부단한 주조자
punmal	ultrafine powder	분말(粉末)
punmal yageum	powder metallurgy	분말 야금
p'angeum	plate	판금
seokhoeseok	limestone	석회석
seonch'eol	pig iron	선철
seup'onji	sponge	스폰지
seut'enreseu-gang	stainless steel	스텐레스 강(鋼)
sodun	annealing	소둔(燒鈍)
soe buseureogi	scrap	쇠 부스러기

Key Words for Key Industries

soe damgeumjil-hada	quench (v)	쇠 담금질하다
suso jeojang-eul wi-han geumsok hapkeum	metal alloys for hydrogen storage	수소 저장을 위한 금속 합금
togani	crucible	도가니
tong	copper	동(銅)
toseong hapkeum	cement	도성(陶性) 합금
t'ansogang	carbon steel	탄소강
t'eongseut'en	tungsten	텅스텐
t'it'anyum	titanium	티타늄
t'it'anyum geumsok	titanium metal	티타늄 금속
yeol hoejeon	hot rolling	열 회전
yong-gwangno	blast steel	용광로
yongseollo	cupola	용선로(溶銑爐)
yudo jeon-giro	induction furnace	유도 전기로

MOTOR VEHICLES

English to Korean

accelerator	가속장치, 액셀	kasok changch'i, aeksel
air bag	에어백	e-eobaek
air conditioner	에어콘	e-eo-k'on
alternator	교류기	kyoryugi
assembly factory	조립 공장	chorip kongjang
automatic gearshift	자동 변속 기어	chadong byeonsok kieo
automobile	자동차	chadongch'a
auto parts	자동차 부품	chadongch'a bup'um
axle	차축	ch'ach'uk
battery	밧데리	patteri
body	차체	ch'ach'e
brake	제동기, 브레이크	chedong-gi, peureik'eu
bumper	완충기, 범퍼	wanch'ung-gi, peomp'eo
camshaft	캠축	k'aemch'uk
car	자동차	chadongch'a
carburetor	기화기, 캬부레터	kihwagi, k'yaburet'eo
chassis	차대	ch'adae
clutch	전동 장치, 클러치	cheondong jangch'i, k'euleoch'i
condenser	축전기	ch'ukcheon-gi
connecting rod	연접봉	yeonjeop-pong
crankshaft	크랭크축	k'euraengk'eu ch'uk
cylinder	실린더	shillindeo
defroster	서리 제거 장치	seori jegeo jangch'i
designer	설계자	seolgyeja
diesel	디젤 기관	dijel gigwan
disc brake	원판 제동 장치	weonp'an jedong jangch'i
distributor	배전기	paejeon-gi
electric car	전기 자동차	cheon-gi jadongch'a
engine	엔진	enjin
fender	바퀴 덮개	pak'wi deopkkae
four-wheel drive	4륜 구동 전동 장치	saryun gudong jeondong jangch'i
front-wheel drive	전륜 구동 전동 장치	cheollyun gudong jeondong jangch'i
fuel consumption	연료 소비	yeollyo sobi
fuel injection system	연료 분사 체계	yeollyo bunsa ch'egye
gas pedal	휘발류 공급 발판, 패달	hwiballyu gong-geup palp'an, p'aedal
gasoline	휘발류, 가솔린	hwiballyu, kasollin
gasoline tank	휘발류 통, 가솔린 탱크	hwiballyu t'ong, kasollin t'aengk'eu
gearshift	기어, 변속지레	kieo, pyeonsok chire
generator	발전기	paljjeon-gi
horsepower	마력	maryeok
ignition	점화	cheomhwa
independent suspension	독립 차대 버팀 장치	tongnip ch'adae beot'im jangch'i

Key Words for Key Industries

injection pump	분사 펌프	punsa p'eomp'eu
lead gasoline	유연 휘발유	yuyeon hwiballyu
mileage	마일수	mail-su
model	모형, 모델	mohyeong, model
motor vehicles	차량	ch'aryang
odometer	주행 거리계	chuhaeng geori-gye
oil	오일(기름)	oil(kireum)
oil pump	기름(오일)펌프	kireum (oil) p'eomp'eu
optional equipment	선택 장치	seont'aek changch'i
paint	칠	ch'il
passenger car	승용차	seung-yong-ch'a
pinion	작은 톱니바퀴	chageun t'omni bak'wi
piston	피스톤	p'iseut'on
power steering	동력 조타 장치	tongnyeok chot'a jangch'i
radial tire	레이디얼 타이어	reidieol t'aieo
radiator	방열기, 라지에타	pang-yeolgi, rajiet'a
rear axle	뒤 차축	twi ch'ach'uk
seat	좌석	chwaseok
seatbelt	좌석벨트	chwaseok pelt'eu
shock absorber	완충 장치	wanch'ung jangch'i
spark plug	스파크 플러그, 발화 장치 마개	seup'ak'eu p'eulleogeu, palhwa jangch'i magae
speedometer	속도계	soktogye
standard equipment	표준 장치	p'yojun jangch'i
steering wheel	타륜 핸들	t'aryun haendeul
suspension	차대 버팀 장치	ch'adae beot'im jangch'i
tachometer	회전 속도	hoejeon sokto
tire	바퀴, 타이어	pak'wi, t'aieo
torque	비트는 힘	pit'euneun him
traction control system	트랙션 콘트롤 시스템	t'euraekyeon k'ont'eurol siseut'em
transmission	변속 장치, 트랜스미션	pyeonsok changch'i, t'euraenseumisyeon
transport equipment	수송 기계	susong gigye
turbo-charger	배기 터빈 과급기	paegi t'eobin gwageupki
unlead gasoline	무연 휘발유	muyeon hwiballyu
valve	밸브	paelbeu
wheel	바퀴	pak'wi
windshield	바람막이 전면 유리	param-magi jeonmyeon yuri

Korean to English

aeksel	accelerator	액셀
chadong byeonsok changch'i	automatic transmission	자동 변속 장치
chadong byeonsok kieo	automatic gearshift	자동 변속 기어
chadongch'a	automobile	자동차
chadongch'a	car	자동차
chadongch'a bup'um	auto parts	자동차 부품
chageun t'omni bak'wi	pinion	작은 톱니 바퀴
chedong-gi	brake	제동기

Motor Vehicles

cheollyun gudong jeondong jangch'i	front-wheel drive	전륜 구동 전동 장치
cheon-gi jadongch'a	electric car	전기 자동차
saryun gudong jeondong jangch'i	four-wheel drive	4륜 구동 전동 장치
cheomhwa	ignition	점화
cheondong jangch'i	clutch	전동 장치
cheonji	battery	전지
chorip kongjang	assembly factory	조립 공장
chuhaeng geori-gye	odometer	주행거리계
chwaseok	seat	좌석
chwaseok pelt'eu	seatbelt	좌석 벤트
ch'ach'e	body	차체
ch'ach'uk	axle	차축
ch'adae	chassis	차대
ch'adae beot'im jangch'i	suspension	차대 버팀 장치
ch'aryang	motor vehicles	차량
ch'il	paint	칠
ch'ukcheon-gi	condenser	축전기
dijel gigwan	diesel	디젤 기관
e-eobaek	air bag	에어백
e-eo-k'on	air conditioner	에어콘
enjin	engine	엔진
hoejeon sokto	tachometer	회전 속도
hwiballyu	gasoline	휘발류
hwiballyu gong-geup palp'an, p'aedal	gas pedal	휘발류 공급 발판, 패달
hwiballyu t'ong	gasoline tank	휘발류 통
kasok changch'i	accelerator	가속 장치
kasollin	gasoline	가솔린
kasollin t'aengk'eu	gasoline tank	가솔린 탱크
kieo	gearshift	기어
kihwagi	carburetor	기화기
kireum	oil	기름
kireum p'eomp'eu	oil pump	기름 펌프
kyoryugi	alternator	교류기
k'aemch'uk	camshaft	캠축
k'eulleoch'i	clutch	클러치
k'yaburet'eo	carburetor	카뷰레터
mail-su	mileage	마일수
maryeok	horsepower	마력
model	model	모델
mohyeong	model	모형
muyeon hwiballyu	unlead gasoline	무연 휘발유
oil	oil	오일
paegi t'eobin gwageupki	turbo-charger	배기 터빈 과급기
paejeon-gi	distributor	배전기
paelbeu	valve	밸브
pak'wi	tire, wheel	바퀴
pak'wi deopkkae	fender	바퀴 덮개
palhwa jangch'i magae	spark plug	발화 장치 마개

paljeon-gi	generator	발전기
pang-yeolgi	radiator	방열기
param-magi jeonmyeon yuri	windshield	바람막이 전면 유리
patteri	battery	밧데리
peomp'eo	bumper	범퍼
peureik'eu	brake	브레이크
punsa p'eomp'eu	injection pump	분사 펌프
pyeonsok changch'i	transmission	변속 장치
pyeonsok chire	gearshift	변속 지레
pit'euneun him	torque	비트는 힘
p'iseut'on	piston	피스톤
p'yojun jangch'i	standard equipment	표준 장치
rajiet'a	radial tire	라지에타
reidieol t'aieo	radiator	레이디얼 타이어
saryun gudong jeondong jangch'i	four-wheel drive	4륜 구동 전동 장치
seolgyeja	designer	설계자
seont'aek changch'i	optional equipment	선택 장치
seori jegeo jangch'i	defroster	서리 제거 장치
seung-yong-ch'a	passenger car	승용차
seup'ak'eu p'eulleogeu	spark plug	스파크 플러그
shillindeo	cylinder	실린더
soktogye	speedometer	속도계
susong gigye	transport equipment	수송기계
tongnip ch'adae beot'im jangch'i	independent suspension	독립 차대 버팀 장치
tongnyeok chot'a jangch'i	power steering	동력 조타 장치
twi ch'ach'uk	rear axle	뒤 차축
t'aieo	tire	타이어
t'aryun haendeul	steering wheel	타륜 핸들
t'euraenseumisyeon	transmission	트랜스미션
wanch'ung jangch'i	shock absorber	완충 장치
wanch'ung-gi	bumper	완충기
weonp'an jedong jangch'i	disc brake	원판 제동 장치
yeollyo bunsa ch'egye	fuel injection system	연료 분사 체계
yeollyo sobi	fuel consumption	연료 소비
yeonjeop-pong	connecting rod	연접봉
yuyeon hwiballyu	lead gasoline	유연 휘발유

PHARMACEUTICALS

English to Korean

anaesthetic (adj)	마취의	mach'wi-eui
analgesic (adj)	무통성의	mut'ongseong-eui
antacid (adj)	제산성의	chesanseong-eui
anti-inflammatory (adj)	항 염증의	hang yeomjjeung-eui
antibiotic (adj)	항생의	hangsaeng-eui
anticholinergic	항 혈압 강하제	hang hyeolap kanghaje
antiseptic (adj)	방부(防腐)의	pangbu-eui
aspirin	아스피린	aseup'irin
barbiturate	진정, 수면제	chinjeong, sumyeonje
bleed (v)	출혈하다	ch'ulhyeol-hada
blood	혈액, 피	hyeoraek, p'i
botanic (adj)	식물(학)의	shingmul (hag)-eui
calcium	칼슘	k'alsyum
capsule	캡슐	k'aepsyul
compounds	합성물	hapseongmul
content	함유량	hamnyu-ryang
cortisone	코티손	k'ot'ison
cough drop	기침약(드롭), 진해정(鎭咳錠)	kich'imnyak (deurop), chinhaejeong
cough syrup	기침약(시럽), 진해시럽	kich'imnyak (shireop), chinhae shireop
density	밀집 상태	miljjip sangt'ae
diabetes	당뇨병	tangnyoppyeong
diuretic	이뇨제	inyoje
dose	1회분	ilhoebun
drop	소량	soryang
drug	약제	yakche
ground (adj)	가루로 만든	karu-ro mandeun
hexachlorophene	6가 엽록소	yukka yeomnokso
hormone	호르몬	horeumon
injection	주입	chuip
insulin	인슐린	insyullin
iodine	옥소(沃素)	okso
iron	철제	ch'eolche
medication	약물치료	yangmul ch'iryo
medicine	약	yak
morphine	모르핀	moreup'in
narcotic	마취성의	mach'wiseong-eui
nitrate	질산 칼륨	chilsan k'allyum
nitrite	아질산염	ajilsanyeom
ointment	연고, 고약	yeon-go, koyak
opium	아편	ap'yeon
pellet	작은 알약	chageun allyak
penicillin	페니실린	p'enishillin
pharmaceutical (adj)	조제학의	chojehag-eui
pharmacist	약제사	yakchesa
phenol	석탄산	seokt'ansan
physician	의사	euisa

pill	알약	allyak
prescription	처방	ch'eobang
purgative	하제(下劑)	haje
remedies	치료	ch'iryo
saccharin	사카린	sak'arin
salts	약용염	yagyong-yeom
salve	연고	yeon-go
sedative	진정제	chinjeongje
serum	혈청	hyeolch'eong
sinus	공동(空洞)	kongdong
sleeping pill	수면제	sumyeonje
starch	전분	cheonbun
stimulant	흥분제	heungbunje
sulphamide	설파제	seolp'aje
synthesis	접골	cheopkol
syringe	관장기	kwanjang-gi
tablet	정제	cheongje
toxicology	독물학	tongmulhak
toxin	독소	tokso
tranquilizer	신경 안정제	shin-gyeong anjeongje
vaccine	우두종, 왁진	udujong, wakchin
vitamin	비타민	pit'amin
zinc	아연	ayeon

Korean to English

ajilsanyeom	nitrite	아질산염
allyak	pill	알약
ap'yeon	opium	아편
aseup'irin	aspirin	아스피린
ayeon	zinc	아연
chageun allyak	pellet	작은 알약
cheonbun	starch	전분
cheongje	tablet	정제
cheopkol	synthesis	접골
chesanseong cui	antacid (adj)	제산성의
chilsan k'allyum	nitrate	질산 칼륨
chinhae shireop	cough syrup	진해시럽
chinhaejeong	cough drop	진해정(鎭咳錠)
chinjeong	barbiturate	진정
chinjeongje	sedative	진정제
ch'iryo	remedies	치료
chojehag-eui	pharmaceutical (adj)	조제학의
chuip	injection	주입
ch'eobang	prescription	처방
ch'eolche	iron	철제
ch'ulhyeol-hada	bleed (v)	출혈하다
euisa	physician	의사
haje	purgative	하제(下劑)
hamnyu-ryang	content	함유량
hang hyeorap kanghaje	anticholinergic	항 혈압 강하제

Pharmaceuticals

hang yeomjjeung-eui	anti-inflammatory (adj)	항 염증의
hangsaeng-eui	antibiotic (adj)	항생의
hapseongmul	compounds	합성물
heungbunje	stimulant	흥분제
horeumon	hormone	호르몬
hyeolch'eong	serum	혈청
hyeoraek	blood	혈액
ilhoebun	dose	1회분
insyullin	insulin	인슐린
inyoje	diuretic	이뇨제
karu-ro mandeun	ground (adj)	가루로 만든
kich'imnyak (deurop)	cough drop	기침약(드롭)
kich'imnyak (shireop)	cough syrup	기침약(시럽)
kongdong	sinus	공동(空洞)
koyak	ointment	고약
kwanjang-gi	syringe	관장기
k'aepsyul	capsule	캡슐
k'alsyum	calcium	칼슘
k'oti'son	cortisone	코티손
mach'wi-eui (adj)	anaesthetic (adj)	마취의
mach'wiseong-eui (adj)	narcotic (adj)	마취성의
miljjip sangt'ae	density	밀집 상태
moreup'in	morphine	모르핀
mut'ongseong-eui	analgesic (adj)	무통성의
okso	iodine	옥소(沃素)
pangbu-eui (adj)	antiseptic (adj)	방부(防腐)의
pit'amin	vitamin	비타민
p'enishillin	penicillin	페니실린
p'i	blood	피
sak'arin	saccharin	사카린
seokt'ansan	phenol	석탄산
seolp'aje	sulphamide	설파제
shingmul (hag)-eui	botanic (adj)	식물(학)의
shin-gyeong anjeongje	tranquilizer	신경 안정제
soryang	drop	소량
sumyeonje	barbiturate, sleeping pill	수면제
tangnyoppyeong	diabetes	당뇨병
tokso	toxin	독소
tongmulhak	toxicology	독물학
udujong	vaccine	우두종
wakchin	vaccine	왁진
yagyong-yeom	salts	약용염
yak	medicine	약
yakche	drug	약제
yakchesa	pharmacist	약제사
yangmul ch'iryo	medication	약물치료
yeon-go	ointment	연고
yukka yeomnokso	hexachlorophene	6가 엽록소

Key Words for Key Industries
PHOTOGRAPHY

English to Korean

English	Korean	Romanization
accessory	액세서리, 부속품	aekseseori, pusokp'um
aerial photographic camera	항공 사진 카메라	hang-gong sajin k'amera
all-weather camera	전천후 카메라	cheonch'eonhu k'amera
aperture	구경	kugyeong
ASA speed	미국 규격 협회 속도	miguk kyugyeok hyeophoe sokto
auto-loading	자동 장치, 자동 장전	chadong jangch'i, chadong jangjeon
automatic aperture control device	자동 구경 조절 장치	chadong gugyeong jojeol jangch'i
automatic developing machine	자동 현상기	chadong hyeonsang-gi
automatic exposure	자동 노출	chadong noch'ul
automatic focusing	자동 촛점	chadong ch'otcheom
automatic printing machine	자동 인화기	chadong inhwagi
automatic rewinding	자동 되감기	chadong doegamkki
auxiliary lens	보조 렌즈	pojo renjeu
black and white film	흑백 필름	heukpaek p'illeum
cable release	유선 이완	yuseon iwan
camera	사진기, 카메라	sajinkki, k'amera
camera body	사진기 몸체	sajinkki momch'e
cartridge	필름통	p'illeumt'ong
close-up lens	근접 거리 렌즈	keunjeop keori renjeu
color film	천연색(컬러) 필름	ch'eonyeonsaek (k'eolleo) p'illeum
color print	천연색(컬러) 인화(印畵)	ch'eonyeonsaek(k'eolleo) inhwa
color slide	천연색 슬라이드	ch'eonyeonsaek seullaideu
condenser lens	집광 렌즈	chipkwang renjeu
develop (v)	현상하다	hyeonsang-hada
EE camera	광전관 사진기	kwangjeon-gwan sajinkki
enlargement	확대	hwakttae
enlarger	확대기	hwakttaegi
exposure	노출	noch'ul
exposure meter	노출계	noch'ulgye
film	필름	p'illeum
filter	필터	p'ilt'eo
fish-eye lens	어안 렌즈	eo-an renjeu
fixed focus camera	고정 촛점 카메라	kojeong ch'otcheom k'amera
flash bulb	섬광 전구	seomgwang jeon-gu
flash cube	섬광 전구 발광 장치	seomgwang jeon-gu balgwang jangch'i
focus	촛점	ch'otcheom
infrared film	적외선 필름	cheog-oeseon p'illeum
interchangeable lens	교환 가능 렌즈	kyohwan ganeung renjeu
lens	렌즈	renjeu
long-focus lens	장거리 촛점 렌즈	chang-geori ch'otcheom renjeu

Photography

macro lens	매크로 렌즈	*maek'euro renjeu*
micro camera	현미경 사진용 카메라	*hyeonmigyeong sajinyong k'amera*
microfilm	마이크로(축사) 필름	*maik'euro (ch'uksa) p'illeum*
motor drive	모터 드라이브	*mot'eo deuraibeu*
nickel-cadmium battery	니켈 카드뮴 전지	*nik'el k'adeumyum jeonji*
objective lens	대물 렌즈	*taemul renjeu*
printing	인화	*inhwa*
projector	영사기	*yeongsagi*
range finder	거리계	*keorigye*
reflex camera	반사 증폭 장치 카메라	*pansa jeungp'ok jangch'i k'amera*
screen	스크린	*seuk'eurin*
self-timer	자동 개폐기	*chadong gaep'yegi*
sensitometer	감광 도계	*kamgwang dogye*
shutter	셔터	*syeot'eo*
shutter speed	셔터 속도	*syeot'eo sokto*
sky lens	스카이 렌즈	*seuk'ai renjeu*
slide	슬라이드	*seullaideu*
slide projector	슬라이드 영사기	*seullaideu yeongsagi*
soft focus lens	연 촛점 렌즈	*yeon ch'otcheom renjeu*
standard lens	표준 렌즈	*p'yojun renjeu*
strobe	섬광 전구	*seomgwang jeon-gu*
telephoto lens	망원 렌즈	*mang-weon renjeu*
35mm camera	35밀리 사진기(카메라)	*samshibo milli sajinkki (k'amera)*
tripod	삼각대	*samgaktae*
twin lens reflex camera	쌍렌즈 리프렉스 사진기(카메라)	*ssang-renjeu rip'eurekseu sajinkki (k'amera)*
underwater camera	수중 카메라	*sujung k'amera*
view finder	파인더	*p'aindeo*
wide angle lens	광각 렌즈	*kwang-gak renjeu*
zoom lens	줌 렌즈	*chum renjeu*

Korean to English

aekseseori	accessory	액세서리
chadong ch'otcheom	automatic focusing	자동 촛점
chadong doegamkki	automatic rewinding	자동 되감기
chadong gaep'yegi	self-timer	자동 개폐기
chadong gugyeong jojeol janghch'i	automatic aperture control device	자동 구경 조절 장치
chadong hyeonsang-gi	automatic developing machine	자동 현상기
chadong inhwagi	automatic printing machine	자동 인화기
chadong jangch'i	auto-loading	자동 장치
chadong jangjeon	auto-loading	자동 장전
chadong noch'ul	automatic exposure	자동 노출
chang-geori ch'otcheom renjeu	long-focus lens	장거리 촛점 렌즈
cheog-oeseon p'illeum	infrared film	적외선 필름

Key Words for Key Industries

cheonch'eonhu k'amera	all-weather camera	전천후 카메라
chipkwang renjeu	condenser lens	집광 렌즈
chum renjeu	zoom lens	줌 렌즈
ch'eonyeonsaek (k'eolleo) inhwa	color print	천연색(컬러) 인화(印畵)
ch'eonyeonsaek (k'eolleo) p'illeum	color film	천연색(컬러) 필름
ch'eonyeonsaek seullaideu	color slide	천연색 슬라이드
ch'otcheom	focus	촛점
eo-an renjeu	fish-eye lens	어안 렌즈
hang-gong sajin k'amera	aerial photographic camera	항공 사진 카메라
heukpaek p'illeum	black and white film	흑백 필름
hwakttae	enlargement	확대
hwakttaegi	enlarger	확대기
hyeonmigyeong sajinyong k'amera	micro camera	현미경 사진용 카메라
hyeonsang-hada	develop (v)	현상하다
inhwa	printing	인화
kamgwang dogye	sensitometer	감광 도계
keorigye	range finder	거리계
keunjeop keori renjeu	close-up lens	근접 거리 렌즈
kojeong ch'otcheom k'amera	fixed focus camera	고정 촛점 카메라
kugyeong	aperture	구경
kwang-gak renjeu	wide-angle lens	광각 렌즈
kwangjeon-gwan sajinkki	EE camera	광전관 사진기
kyohwan ganeung renjeu	interchangeable lens	교환 가능 렌즈
k'amera	camera	카메라
maek'euro renjeu	macro lens	매크로 렌즈
maik'euro (ch'uksa) p'illeum	microfilm	마이크로(축사) 필름
mang-weon renjeu	telephoto lens	망원 렌즈
miguk kyugyeok hyeophoe sokto	ASA speed	미국 규격 협회 속도
mot'eo deuraibeu	motor drive	모터 드라이브
nik'el k'adeumyum jeonji	nickel-cadmium battery	니켈 카드뮴 전지
noch'ul	exposure	노출
noch'ulgye	exposure meter	노출계
pansa jeungp'ok jangch'i k'amera	reflex camera	반사 증폭 장치 카메라
pojo renjeu	auxiliary lens	보조 렌즈
pusokp'um	accessory	부속품
p'aindeo	view finder	파인더
p'illeum	film	필름
p'illeumt'ong	cartridge	필름통
p'ilt'eo	filter	필터
p'yojun renjeu	standard lens	표준 렌즈
renjeu	lens	렌즈
sajinkki	camera	사진기
sajinkki momch'e	camera body	사진기 몸체
samgaktae	tripod	삼각대

Photography

samshibo milli sajinkki (k'amera)	35mm camera	35밀리 사진기(카메라)
seomgwang jeon-gu	flash bulb	섬광 전구
seomgwang jeon-gu balgwang jangch'i	flash cube	섬광 전구 발광 장치
seuk'ai renjeu	sky lens	스카이 렌즈
seuk'eurin	screen	스크린
seullaideu	slide	슬라이드
seullaideu yeongsagi	slide projector	슬라이드 영사기
ssang-renjeu rip'eurekseu sajinkki (k'amera)	twin lens reflex camera	쌍렌즈 리프렉스 사진기(카메라)
sujung k'amera	underwater camera	수중 카메라
syeot'eo	shutter	셔터
syeot'eo sokto	shutter speed	셔터 속도
taemul renjeu	objective lens	대물 렌즈
yeon ch'otcheom renjeu	soft focus lens	연 촛점 렌즈
yeongsagi	projector	영사기
yuseon iwan	cable release	유선 이완

Key Words for Key Industries

PRINTING AND PUBLISHING

English to Korean

appendix	부록	*purok*
black and white (adj)	단색의	*tansaeg-eui*
bleed	절단된 페이지	*cheolttandoen p'eiji*
blowup	확대	*hwakttae*
boldface	굵은 활자	*kulgeun hwaljja*
book	책, 서적	*ch'aek, seojeok*
capital	대문자	*taemunjja*
chapter	장(章)	*chang*
coated paper	광을 낸 종이	*kwang-eul naen jong-i*
color separation	색 분해	*saek punhae*
copy	사본, 복사	*sabon, poksa*
copyright	저작권, 판권	*cheojakkweon, p'ankkweon*
cover	책 표지	*ch'aek p'yoji*
crop (v)	잘라내다	*challa-naeda*
dummy	견본	*kyeonbon*
edit (v)	편집하다	*p'yeonjip-hada*
edition	판, 간행	*p'an, kanhaeng*
editor	편집자	*p'yeonjipcha*
engrave (v)	파다, 새기다	*p'ada, saegida*
font	활자	*hwaljja*
form	조판	*chop'an*
format	체제, 판	*ch'eje, p'an*
four colors	4색	*sa-saek*
galley proof	교정쇄(校正刷)	*kyojeongswae*
glossy (adj)	광택있는	*kwangt'aeginneun*
grain	결	*kyeol*
grid	격자(格子)	*kyeokcha*
hardcover	양장본	*yangjangbon*
headline	표제	*p'yoje*
illustration	삽화, 도해	*saphwa, tohae*
ink	잉크	*ingk'eu*
insert	삽입물	*sabimmul*
introduction	서언, 서문	*seo-eon, seomun*
italic	이탤릭체	*it'aellik-ch'e*
jacket	(가제본의) 표지	*(ka-jebon-eui) p'yoji*
justify (v)	(-의 행을) 가지런히 하다	*(-eui haeng-eul) gajireonhi-hada*
layout	페이지 배정	*p'eiji baejeong*
letterpress	인쇄 자구, 활판 인쇄기	*inswae jagu, hwalp'an inswaegi*
line	행	*haeng*
line drawing	선화	*seonhwa*
lower case	소문자	*somunjja*
matrix	자모, 모형	*chamo, mohyeong*
matt	매트	*maet'eu*
mechanical (adj)	기계적인	*kigyejeogin*
negative	원판	*weonp'an*
newsprint	신문 용지	*shinmun yongji*

Printing and Publishing

page	페이지	p'eiji
page makeup	페이지 조판	p'eiji jop'an
pagination	페이지 매김	p'eiji maegim
pamphlet	팜플렛, 작은 책자	p'amp'eullet, chageun ch'aekcha
paper	종이, 신문	chong-i, shinmun
paperback	반양장본	pan-yangjangbon
pigment	그림 물감	keurim mulkkam
plate	도판	top'an
point	포인트	p'oint'eu
positive	양화	yanghwa
preface	서문, 서언	seomun, seo-eon
printed matter	인쇄물	inswaemul
printing	인쇄, 인쇄술	inswae, inswaesul
printing machine	인쇄 기계	inswae gigye
printing shop	인쇄소	inswaeso
proofreading	교정	kyojeong
publisher	발행인, 출판인	palhaeng-in, ch'ulp'an-in
ream	연(連: 종이 500매)	yeon (chong-i obaengmae)
register	인쇄 지면의 안팎의 일치	inswae jimyeon-eui anp'ak-eui ilch'i
scanner	정밀 조사자	cheongmil josaja
screen	그물 판유리	keumul p'an-yuri
sewn (adj)	철한, 맨	ch'eol-han, maen
sheet	장	chang
size	크기	k'eugi
soft cover	종이 표지	chong-i p'yoji
spine	(책의) 등	(ch'aeg-eui) deung
table of contents	목차	mokch'a
title	표제, 제목	p'yoje, chemok

Korean to English

chaek	book	책
ch'aek p'yoji	cover	책 표지
chageun ch'aekcha	pamphlet	작은 책자
challa-naeda	crop (v)	잘라내다
chamo	matrix	자모
chang	chapter	장(章)
chang	sheet	장
ch'eje	format	체제
chemok	title	제목
cheojakkweon	copyright	저작권
ch'eol-han	sewn (adj)	철한
cheolttandoen p'eiji	bleed	절단된 페이지
cheongmil josaja	scanner	정밀 조사자
chong-i	paper	종이
chong-i p'yoji	soft cover	종이 표지
chop'an	form	조판
ch'ulp'an-in	publisher	출판인
(ch'aeg-eui) deung	spine	(책의) 등

(-eui haeng-eul) gajireonhi-hada	justify (v)	(—의 행을) 가지런히 하다
haeng	line	행
hwakttae	blowup	확대
hwaljja	font	활자
hwalp'an inswaegi	letterpress	활판 인쇄기
ingk'eu	ink	잉크
inswae	printing	인쇄
inswae gigye	printing machine	인쇄 기계
inswae jagu	letterpress	인쇄 자구
inswae jimyeon-eui anp'ak-eui ilch'i	register	인쇄 지면의 안팎의 일치
inswaemul	printed matter	인쇄물
inswaeso	printing shop	인쇄소
inswaesul	printing	인쇄술
it'aellik-ch'e	italic	이탤릭체
kanhaeng	edition	간행
k'eugi	size	크기
keumul p'an-yuri	screen	그물 판유리
keurim mulkkam	pigment	그림물감
kigyejeogin	mechanical (adj)	기계적인
kulgeun hwaljja	boldface	굵은 활자
kwang-eul naen jong-i	coated paper	광을 낸 종이
kwangt'aeginneun	glossy (adj)	광택있는
kyeokcha	grid	격자(格子)
kyeol	grain	결
kyeonbon	dummy	견본
kyojeong	proofreading	교정
kyojeongswae	galley proof	교정쇄(校正刷)
maen	sewn (adj)	맨
maet'eu	matt	매트
mohyeong	matrix	모형
mokch'a	table of contents	목차
palhaeng-in	publisher	발행인
pan-yangjangbon	paperback	반양장본
poksa	copy	복사
purok	appendix	부록
p'ada	engrave (v)	파다
p'amp'eullet	pamphlet	팜플렛
p'an	edition, format	판
p'ankkweon	copyright	판권
p'eiji	page	페이지
p'eiji baejeong	layout	페이지 배정
p'eiji jop'an	page makeup	페이지 조판
p'eiji maegim	pagination	페이지 매김
p'oint'eu	point	포인트
p'yeonjipcha	editor	편집자
p'yeonjip-hada	edit (v)	편집하다
p'yoje	headline, title	표제
(ka-jebon-eui) p'yoji	jacket	(가제본의) 표지
sabimmul	insert	삽입물

Printing and Publishing

sabon	copy	사본
saegida	engrave (v)	새기다
saek punhae	color separation	색 분해
saphwa, tohae	illustration	삽화, 도해
sa-saek	four colors	4색
seo-eon	introduction	서언
seojeok	book	서적
seomun	introduction	서문
seonhwa	line drawing	선화
shinmun	paper	신문
shinmun yongji	newsprint	신문 용지
somunjja	lower case	소문자
taemunjja	capital	대문자
tansaeg-eui	black and white (adj)	단색의
top'an	plate	도판
weonp'an	negative	원판
yanghwa	positive	양화
yangjangbon	hardcover	양장본
yeon (chong-i obaengmae)	ream	연(連 : 종이 500매)

V. GENERAL INFORMATION

ABBREVIATIONS

a.a. always afloat
a.a.r. against all risks
a/c account
A/C account current
acct. account
a.c.v. actual cash value
a.d. after date
a.f.b. air freight bill
agcy. agency
agt. agent
a.m.t. air mail transfer
a/o account of
A.P. accounts payable
A/P authority to pay
approx. approximately
A.R. accounts receivable
a/r all risks
A/S, A.S. account sales
a/s at sight
at.wt. atomic weight
av. average
avdp. avoirdupois
a/w actual weight
a.w.b. air waybill
bal. balance
bar. barrel
bbl. barrel
b/d brought down
B/E, b/e bill of exchange
b/f brought forward
B.H. bill of health
bk. bank
bkge. brokerage
B/L bill of landing
b/o brought over
B.P. bills payable
b.p. by procuration
B.R. bills receivable
B/S balance sheet
b.t. berth terms
bu. bushel
B/V book value
ca. circa; centaire
C.A. chartered accountant
c.a. current account
C.A.D. cash against documents

C.B. cash book
C.B.D. cash before delivery
c.c. carbon copy
c/d carried down
c.d. cum dividend
c/f carried forward
cf. compare
c & f cost and freight
C/H clearing house
C.H. custom house
ch.fwd. charges forward
ch.pd. charges paid
ch.ppd. charges prepaid
chq. check, cheque
c.i.f. cost, insurance, freight
c.i.f & c. cost, insurance, freight, and commission
c.i.f & e. cost, insurance, freight, and exchange
c.i.f & i. cost, insurance, freight, and interest
c.l. car load
c/m call of more
C/N credit note
c/o care of
co. company
C.O.D. cash on delivery
comm. commission
corp. corporation
C.O.S. cash on shipment
C.P. carriage paid
C/P charter party
c.p.d. charters pay duties
cpn. corporation
cr. credit; creditor
C/T cable transfer
c.t.l. constructive total loss
c.t.l.o. constructive total loss only
cum. cumulative
cum div. cum dividend
cum. pref. cumulative preference
c/w commercial weight
C.W.O. cash with order
cwt. hundredweight
D/A documents againt acceptance; deposit account
DAP documents against payment
db. debenture
DCF discounted cash flow
d/d days after date; delivered
deb. debenture
def. deferred
dept. department
d.f. dead freight
dft. draft

dft/a. draft attached
dft/c. clean draft
disc. discount
div. dividend
DL dayletter
DLT daily letter telegram
D/N debit note
D/O delivery order
do. ditto
doz. dozen
D/P documents against payment
dr. debtor
Dr. Doctor
d/s, d.s. days after sight
d.w. deadweight
D/W dock warrant
dwt. pennyweight
dz. dozen
ECU European Currency Unit
E.E.T. East European Time
e.g. for example
encl. enclosure
end. endorsement
E. & O.E. errors and omissions excepted
e.o.m. end of month
e.o.h.p. except otherwise herein provided
esp. especially
Esq. Esquire
est. established
ex out
ex cp. ex coupon
ex div. ex dividend
ex int. ex interest
ex h. ex new (shares)
ex stre. ex store
ex whf. ex wharf
f.a.a. free of all average
f.a.c. fast as can
f.a.k. freight all kinds
f.a.q. fair average quality; free alongside quay
f.a.s. free alongside ship
f/c for cash
f.c. & s. free of capture and seizure
f.c.s.r. & c.c. free of capture, seizure, riots, and civil commotion
F.D. free delivery to dock
f.d. free discharge
ff. following; folios
f.g.a. free of general average
f.i.b. free in bunker
f.i.o. free in and out
f.i.t. free in truck

General Information

f.o.b. free on board
f.o.c. free on charge
f.o.d. free of damage
fol. following; folio
f.o.q. free on quay
f.o.r. free on rail
f.o.s. free on steamer
f.o.t. free on truck(s)
f.o.w. free on wagons; free on wharf
F.P. floating policy
f.p. fully paid
f.p.a. free of particular average
frt. freight
frt.fwd. freight forward
frt.pd. freight paid
frt.ppd. freight prepaid
ft. foot
fwd. forward
f.x. foreign exchange
g.a. general average
GATT General Agreement on Tariffs and Trade
g.b.o. goods in bad order
g.m.b. good merchantable brand
g.m.q. good merchantable quality
G.M.T. Greenwich Mean Time
GNP gross national product
g.o.b. good ordinary brand
gr. gross
GRT gross register ton
gr.wt. gross weight
GT gross tonnage
h.c. home consumption
hgt. height
hhd. hogshead
H.O. head office
H.P. hire purchase
HP horsepower
ht. height
IAEA International Atomic Energy Agency
IDP integrated data processing
i.e. that is
I/F insufficient funds
i.h.p. indicated horse power
imp. import
Inc. incorporated
incl. inclusive
ins. insurance
int. interest
inv. invoice
I.O.U. I owe you
J/A, j.a. joint account

Jr. junior
KV kilovolt
KW kilowatt
KWh kilowatt hour
L/C, l.c. letter of credit
LCD telegram in the language of the country of destination
LCO telegram in the language of the country of origin
ldg. landing; loading
l.t. long ton
Ltd. limited
l.tn. long ton
m. month
m/a my account
max. maximum
M.D. memorandum of deposit
M/D, m.d. months after date
memo. memorandum
Messrs. plural of Mr.
mfr. manufacturer
min. minimum
MLR minimum lending rate
M.O. money order
m.o. my order
mortg. mortgage
M/P, m.p. months after payment
M/R mate's receipt
M/S, m.s. months' sight
M.T. mail transfer
M/U making up price
n. name; nominal
n/a no account
N/A no advice
n.c.v. no commercial value
n.d. no date
n.e.s. not elsewhere specified
N/F no funds
NL night letter
N/N no noting
N/O no orders
no. number
n.o.e. not otherwise enumerated
n.o.s. not otherwise stated
nos. numbers
NPV no par value
nr. number
n.r.t. net register ton
N/S net sufficient
NSF not sufficient funds
n.wt. net weight
o/a on account
OCP overseas common point

O/D, o/d on demand; overdraft
o.e. omissions excepted
o/h overhead
ono. or nearest offer
O/o order of
O.P. open policy
o.p. out of print; overproof
O/R, o.r. owner; ordinary
O.S., o/s out of stock
OT overtime
p. page; per; premium
P.A., p.a. particular average; per annum
P/A power of attorney; private account
PAL phase alternation line
pat. pend. patent pending
PAYE pay as you earn
p/c petty cash
p.c. percent; price current
pcl. parcel
pd. paid
pf. preferred
pfd. preferred
pkg. package
P/L profit and loss
p.l. partial loss
P/N promissory note
P.O. post office; postal order
P.O.B. post office box
P.O.O. post office order
p.o.r. pay on return
pp. pages
p & p postage and packing
p.pro per procuration
ppd. prepaid
ppt. prompt
pref. preference
prox. proximo
P.S. postscript
pt. payment
P.T.O., p.t.o please turn over
ptly.pd. partly paid
p.v. par value
qlty. quality
qty. quantity
r. & c.c. riot and civil commotions
R/D refer to drawer
R.D.C. running down clause
re in regard to
rec. received; receipt
recd. received
red. redeemable

ref. reference
reg. registered
retd. returned
rev. revenue
R.O.D. refused on delivery
R.P. reply paid
r.p.s. revolutions per second
RSVP please reply
R.S.W.C. right side up with care
Ry railway
s.a.e. stamped addressed envelope
S.A.V. stock at valuation
S/D sea damaged
S/D, s.d. sight draft
s.d. short delivery
SDR special drawing rights
sgd. signed
s. & h.ex Sundays and holidays excepted
shipt. shipment
sig. signature
S/LC, s. & l.c. sue and labor clause
S/N shipping note
s.o. seller's option
s.o.p. standard operating procedure
spt. spot
Sr. senior
S.S., s.s. steamship
s.t. short ton
ster. sterling
St.Ex. stock exchange
stg. sterling
s.v. sub voce
T.A. telegraphic address
T.B. trial balance
tel. telephone
temp. temporary secretary
T.L., t.l. total loss
T.L.O. total loss only
TM multiple telegram
T.O. turn over
tr. transfer
TR telegram to be called for
TR, T/R trust receipt
TT, T.T. telegrahic transfer(cable)
TX Telex
UGT urgent
UR Uruguay Round
u.s.c. under separate cover
U/ws underwriters
v. volt
val. value

v.a.t. value-added tax
v.g. very good
VHF very high frequency
v.h.r. very highly recommended
w. watt
WA with bill
W.B. way bill
w.c. without charge
W.E.T. West European Time
wg. weight guaranteed
whse. warehouse
w.o.g. with other goods
W.P. weather permitting; without prejudice
w.p.a. with particular average
W.R. war risk
W/R, wr. warehouse receipt
W.W.D. weather working day
wt. weight
x.c. ex coupon
x.d. ex dividend
x.i. ex interest
x.n. ex new shares
y. year
yd. yard
yr. year
yrly. yearly

WEIGHTS AND MEASURES

U.S. UNIT	METRIC EQUIVALENT
mile	1.609 kilometers
yard	0.914 meters
foot	30.480 centimeters
inch	2.540 centimeters
square mile	2.590 square kilometers
acre	0.405 hectacres
square yard	0.836 square meters
square foot	0.093 square meters
square inch	6.451 square centimeters
cubic yard	0.765 cubic meters
cubic foot	0.028 cubic meters
cubic inch	16.387 cubic centimeters
short ton	0.907 metric tons
long ton	1.016 metric tons
short hundred weight	45.359 kilograms
long hundred weight	50.802 kilograms
pound	0.453 kilograms
ounce	28.349 grams
gallon	3.784 liters
quart	0.946 liters

U.S.UNIT	METRIC EQUIVALENT
pint	0.473 liters
fluid ounce	29.573 milliliters
bushel	35.238 liters
peck	8.809 liters
quart	1.101 liters
pint	0.550 liters

TEMPERATURE AND CLIMATE

Temperature Conversion Chart

DEGREES CELSIUS	DEGREES FAHRENHEIT
−10	14
−5	23
0	32
5	41
10	50
15	59
20	68
25	77
30	86
35	95
40	104

Average Temperature for Major Cities in Celsius (°C), Fahrenheit (°F), and Humidities (%)

	JAN (Winter)			APR (Spring)			JUL (Summer)			OCT (Autumn)		
	°F	°C	%	°F	°C	%	°F	°C	%	°F	°C	%
Seoul	33.4	0.8	66	52.1	11.2	59	79.5	26.4	81	58.1	14.5	65
Pusan	40.8	4.9	57	54.3	12.4	61	79.3	26.3	82	62.7	17.1	64
Taegu	36.1	2.3	67	54.1	12.3	61	82.4	28.0	78	59.3	15.2	69
Inch'eon	33.8	1.0	72	50.7	10.4	65	77.9	25.5	83	58.2	14.6	71
Mokp'o	39.7	4.3	73	52.8	11.6	69	80.9	27.2	80	62.6	17.0	68
Kangneung	37.9	3.3	55	52.8	11.6	60	79.1	26.2	81	58.6	14.8	60
Cheju	45.5	7.5	72	55.0	12.8	73	81.3	27.4	81	64.4	18.0	73

spring	봄	
	pon	
summer	여름	
	yeoreum	
autumn	가을	
	ka-eul	
winter	겨울	
	kyeo-ul	
hot	더운	
	teo-un	

hot and humid	덥고 무더운
	teopko mudeo-un
sunny	해가 난
	hae-ga nan
warm	따뜻한
	ttatteut'an
cool	선선한
	seonseonhan
windy	바람부는
	param-buneun
foggy	안개낀
	an-gae-kkin
snowing	눈이 오는
	nun-i o-neun
raining	비가 오는
	pi-ga o-neun
earthquake	지진
	chijin

COMMUNICATION CODES

Telephone

There are two ways to call. One is the operator-assisted call, and the other is direct dialing by using International Subscriber Dialing (ISD). When you make a call with operator-assistance, or collect call, dial 0077. Any other information regarding operator-assisted calls can be available through 0074. To dial direct to overseas, first dial the international code (001 or 002), and then the country code which is provided in this book, plus area code and individual phone number.

To dial direct to overseas, you have to have the international country code which is provided in this book.

International cables may be arranged by dialing 005.

In the city, public pay phones can be found in most building, at post offices, in hotels, and on the streets. The fee is 30 won for three minutes. Only three 10 won coins can be used to make a call. Plan carefully, because after the three minutes you will be automatically disconnected.

A long distance call can be made through public pay phones (gray color) at any post office, major hotel, airport, or railroad stations.

For international, local or long distance calls, telephone cards can be used. Telephone cards can be purchased at shops or banks at the price of 3,000 won, 5,000 won and 10,000 won.

telephone	전화
	cheonhwa
public phone	공중 전화
	kongjung jeonhwa
telephone directory	전화 번호부
	cheonhwa beonhobu
local call	시내 전화
	shinae jeonhwa

Korean for Business Traveler

long-distance call   장거리 전화
chang-geori jeonhwa
operator   교환수
kyohwansu

Area Codes within Korea

Seoul	02	Kumi	0546
Inch'eon	032	P'ohang	0562
Suweon	0331	Kyeongju	0561
Seongnam	0342	Taegu	053
Anyang	0343	Pusan	051
Kanghwa	0349	Ulsan	0522
Euijeongbu	0351	Masan	0551
Tongduch'eon	0361	Iri	0653
Ch'unch'eon	0354	Cheonju	0652
Weonju	0371	Kwangju	062
Ch'eolweon	03532	Mokp'o	0631
Kangneung	0391	Yeosu	0662
Taejeon	042	Seogwip'o	0642
Ch'eongju	0431	Cheju	0641
Ch'ungju	0441		

International Country Codes

Algeria	213	Luxembourg	352
Argentina	54	Malta	356
Australia	61	Mexico	52
Austria	43	Morocco	212
Belgium	32	Netherlands	31
Brazil	55	New Zealand	64
Canada	1	Norway	47
Chile	56	Philippines	63
Colombia	57	Poland	48
Denmark	45	Portugal	351
Finland	358	Russia	7
France	33	Saudi Arabia	966
Germany (East)	49	Singapore	65
Germany (West)	37	South Africa	27
Gibraltar	350	Spain	34
Greece	30	Sri Lanka	94
Hong Kong	852	Sweden	46
Hungary	36	Switzerland	41
Iceland	354	Taiwan	886
India	91	Thailand	255
Ireland	353	Tunisia	216
Israel	972	Turkey	90
Italy	39	United Kingdom	44
Japan	81	USA	1
Korea	82	Venezuela	58
Kuwait	965	Yugoslavia	38

POSTAL SERVICES

First, check with your hotel front desk to send your mail or telegrams. They may provide you information on postal services.

In Seoul, the Seoul Central Post Office and the International Post Office are located in Myeong-dong, a well known shopping and fashion district, between Namdaemun-ro and Ch'ungmu-ro. Local post offices are located in each district in the city. The central office is open 24 hours; the local offices are open Monday through Friday 9:00 A.M. to 6:00 P.M. and 9:00 A.M. to noon on Saturday. Stamps may be bought at a post office, souvenir shop, tobacco shop, or your hotel.

International Postal Rates (in won)

	Far East Asia	Southeast Asia	North America Europe Middle East	Africa Latin America
Airmail letters (up to 10 grams)	370	400	440	470
Aerogram	350	350	350	350
Postcard	300	300	300	300
Printed matter (up to 20 grams)	200	220	250	300
Registered mail	1,170	1,200	1,240	1,270

TIME ZONES

Use the following table to know the time difference between where you are and other major cities. Note, however, that during April through September, you will also have to take Daylight Savings Time into account. Since there are four time zones for the United States, eleven zones for the former Soviet Union and three for Australia, we've listed major cities for these countries. All of Korea is in the same zone.

-10 HOURS	-8 HOURS	-6 HOURS	-5 HOURS	GREENWICH MEAN TIME
Honolulu	Los Angeles San Francisco	Chicago Dallas Houston	Boston New York Washington, D.C.	Great Britain Iceland Ireland Portugal
+1 HOUR	+8 HOURS	+9 HOURS	+ADDITIONAL HOURS	
Austria Belgium Denmark France Germany	Hong Kong Kuala Lumpur Manila Shanghai	Beijing Japan Korea	Sydney (10) New Zealand (12)	

Hungary Italy Luxembourg Malta Monaco Netherlands Norway Poland Spain Sweden Switzerland Yugoslavia	Singapore				

MAJOR HOLIDAYS

January 1	New Year's Day	설날(양력설) *seol-nal (yangnyeok-seol)*
1st day of 1st lunar month	Folk Customs Day	민속의 날(음력설) *minsog-eui nal (eumnyeok-seol)*
March 1	Independence Movement Day	3·1절 *sam-il jjeol*
April 5	Arbor Day	식목일 *shingmogil*
8th day of 4th lunar month	Buddha's Birthday	석가탄일 *seokka t'an-il*
May 5	Children's Day	어린이날 *eorini-nal*
June 6	Memorial Day	현충일 *hyeonch'ung-il*
July 17	Constitution Day	제헌절 *cheheon-jeol*
August 15	Liberation Day	광복절 *kwangbok-cheol*
15th day of 8th lunar month	Ch'useok	추석 *ch'useok*
October 3	National Foundation Day	개천절 *kaech'eon-jeol*
December 25	Christmas	성탄절 *seongt'an-jeol*

CURRENCY INFORMATION

Korean Currency

The monetary unit in Korea is won (W). The bank notes are 100, 500, 1,000, 5,000, and 10,000 won bills; coins are 1, 5, 10, 50, 100, and 500 won.

The exchange rate is subject to change depending on the foreign exchange market, although the won is closely tied to the U.S. dollar. The current exchange rate is 803.00 won to the U.S. $1.00 as of September 1993.

Major Currencies of the World

Argentina	Argentinian Peso
Australia	Australian Dollar
Austria	Schilling
Belgium	Belgian Franc
Brazil	Cruzeiro
China (PRC)	Yuan
Colombia	Colombian Peso
Finland	Finnmark
France	Franc
Germany	Mark
Greece	Drachma
Hong Kong	Hong Kong Dollar
Iceland	Krone
India	Rupee
Indonesia	Rupiah
Ireland	Punt
Italy	Lira
Japan	Yen
Korea	Won
Malaysia	Ringgit
Mexico	Mexican Peso
Netherlands	Guilder
New Zealand	New Zealand Dollar
Norway	Norwegian Krone
Philippines	Peso
Portugal	Escudo
Russia	Rublic
Singapore	Singapore Dollar
Spain	Peseta
Sweden	Swedish Krone
Switzerland	Swiss Franc
Thailand	Baht
Turkey	Lira
United Kingdom	Pound Sterling
Venezuela	Bolivar
Yugoslavia	Dinar

Major Commercial Banks

Bank of Seoul
10-1, Namdaemun-ro 2-ga,
Chung-gu, Seoul
Tel:771-6000
Cable:SEOULTRUST
Telex:K23311
Fax:774-0428

Cho-Heung Bank
14, Namdaemun-ro 1-ga,
Chung-gu, Seoul
Tel:733-2000
Cable:CHOHEUNG BANK SEOUL
Telex:K23321
Fax:723-6475

Commercial Bank of Korea
111-1, Namdaemun-ro 2-ga,
Chung-gu, Seoul
Tel:775-0050

Cable:COMBANK SEOUL
Telex:K24611
Fax:754-9203

Hanil Bank
130, Nadaemun-ro 2-ga
Chung-gu, Seoul
Tel:771-2000
Cable:HANIL BANK SEOUL
Telex:K23823 HANIL BANK
Fax:753-9346

Korea First Bank
100, Kongp'yong-dong,
Chong ro-gu, Seoul
Tel:733-0070
Cable:FIRSTBANK SEOUL
Telex:K23685
Fax:733-0070

Shinhan Bank
120, T'aep'yeong-ro 2-ga,
Chung-gu, Seoul
Tel:756-0505
Cable:SHINHAN BANK
Telex:K25584
Fax:757-1024

Special Banks

Bank of Korea
110, Namdaemun-ro 3-ga,
Chung-gu, Seoul
Tel:759-4114
Cable:KOREA BANK SEOUL
Telex:KOREABK K24711
Fax:759-4890

Citizens National Bank
9-1, Namdaemun-ro 2-ga,
Chung-gu, Seoul
Tel:771-4000
Cable:CNBANK SEOUL
Telex:K23481
Fax:757-3679

Export-Import Bank of Korea
16-1, Yeoeuido-dong,
Yeongdeungp'o-gu, Seoul
Tel:784-1021
Cable:EXIMKOREA SEOUL

Telex:K26595
Fax:784-1030

Foreign Banks

Bank of America, NT & SA (U.S.)
192-18, Kwanhun-dong,
Chongro-gu, Seoul
Tel:733-2455

Bank of Montreal (Canada)
17-7, Namdaemun-ro 4-ga,
Chung-gu, Seoul
Tel:732-9206

Bank of Tokyo (Japan)
10-1, Eulji-ro 1-ga,
Chung-gu, Seoul
Tel:752-0111

Barclays Bank PLC (U.K.)
541, Namdaemun-ro 5-ga,
Chung-gu, Seoul
Tel:754-3681

Chase Manhattan Bank N.A. (U.S.)
50, Eulji-ro 1-ga,
Chung-gu, Seoul
Tel:758-5354

Chemical Bank (U.S.)
250, T'aep'yeong-ro 2-ga,
Chung-gu, Seoul
Tel:778-8941

Citibank N.A. (U.S.)
1, Chong-ro 1-ga,
Chongno-gu, Seoul
Tel:737-1114

Daiwa Bank (Japan)
5-1, Kongyong-dong,
Chongno-gu, Seoul
Tel:752-0831

General Information

MAJOR BUSINESS PERIODICALS

Newspapers

Korean Language

Chosun Ilbo
61, T'aep'yeong-ro 1-ga,
Chung-gu, Seoul
Tel:731-8341

Daily Sports
14, Chunghak-dong,
Chongro-gu, Seoul
Tel:732-4151

Dong-a Ilbo
139, Sejong-ro,
Chongno-gu, Seoul
Tel:361-0114

Han-Kyoreh Shinmun
116-25, Kongdeok-dong,
Map'o-gu, Seoul
Tel:710-0114

Hankook Ilbo
14, Chunghak-dong,
Chongro-gu, Seoul
Tel:732-8937

Joong-ang Daily News
7, Sunhwa-dong,
Chongro-gu, Seoul
Tel:751-5127

Korea Economic Daily
441, Chungnim-dong,
Chung-gu, Seoul
Tel:313-5511

Kyunghyang Daily News
22, Cheong-dong,
Chung-gu, Seoul
Tel:739-0035

Maeil Kyungje Shinmun
61, T'aep'yeong-ro 1-ga,
Chung-gu, Seoul
Tel:276-0201

Seoul Shinmun
61, T'aep'yeongro 1-ga,
Chung-gu, Seoul
Tel:735-7711

English Language

Korea Herald
1-12, Hoehyeon-dong 3-ga,
Chung-gu, Seoul
Tel 756-7711

Korea Times
14, Chunghak-dong,
Chongno-gu, Seoul
Tel 732-4161

Note: Most bookstores and hotels carry the *Asian Wall Street Journal*, the *Far Eastern Economic Review*, the *International Herald Tribune*, *Time*, *Newsweek*, and *U.S. News & World Report*. The *Pacific Stars and Stripes*, a U.S. military newspaper, is also available on U.S. Army posts.

RADIO AND TELEVISION STATIONS

Korea Broadcasting System (KBS)
18, Yeoeuio-dong,
Yeongdeungp'o-gu, Seoul
Tel:783-0513

Munhwa TV-Radio Broadcasting Corp. (MBC)
22, Cheong-dong,
Chung-gu, Seoul
Tel:780-0011

Seoul Broadcasting System (SBS)
10-2, Yeaeuido-dong,
Yeongdeungp'o-gu, Seoul
Tel:780-0006

Christian Broadcasting System (CBS)
136-46, Yeonji-dong,
Chongno-gu, Seoul
Tel:764-0413

ANNUAL TRADE FAIRS

This is a partial list of annual events. Changes may occur from year to year, as well as during the year. It is advisable to consult the Korea Exhibition Center (KOEX) of the Korea Trade Promotion Corporation (KOTRA) both in Korea and abroad for up-to-date information.

Seoul

March	International Electronics Packaging Production Exhibition and Conference
April	Korea International Food Technology Exhibition Korea International Packaging Exhibition Korea International Exhibition for Computers, Office Automation, Robots and Related Equipment Seoul Houseware and Home Automation Show
May	Korea International Safety and Security Exhibition Korea Exhibition of Photography Korea Electronics Parts and Equipment International Show International Exhibition for Environmental Pollution Control Korea International Textile Machinery Exhibition
June	Seoul International Arts and Craft Fair
August September	National Inventions Exhibition Korea World Travel Fair Seoul International Toy Fair Seoul International Stationery Fair Seoul International Gift Show Korea International Jewelry and Watch Fair
October	Korea Electronics Show Korean Business Fair

General Information

	Korea International Construction Exhibition
	International Exhibition for Sports and Leisure Goods
	Korea International Plastics, Machinery, Equipment and Material Exhibition
November	Korea International Welding Show
	Korea International Auto Parts and Accessories Exhibition
	Korea International Instrumentation Exhibition

For additional information contact the Korea Exhibition Center, Korea Trade Promotion Corporation.

Head Office
159-1, Samseong-dong,
Gangnam-gu, Seoul 135,
Korea
Tel:(02)551-0114
Cable:KOEXCEN
Telex:KOEXCEN K24594
Fax:(02)555-7414

New York Office
460 Park Ave., Suite 402
New York, N.Y. 10022, U.S.A.
Tel:(212)826-0900
Telex:62995 KOTRA NY
Cable:MOOGONG NEW YORK

Los Angeles Office
4801 Wilshire Blvd.
No. 230
Los Angeles, CA 90010, U.S.A.
Tel:(213)954-9500
Telex:674639LSA
Cable:MOOGONG LOSANGELES

Washington Office
1129 20th Street, N.W.,
Suite 410
Washington, D.C. 20036, U.S.A.
Tel:(202)857-7119
Telex:289608 KTCWUR
Cable:MOOGONG WASH D.C.

TRAVEL TIMES

Air Travel

Most international flights to Korea arrive at Kimp'o International Airport, which is 18 kilometers from the center of Seoul. The ride takes approximately 40 to 45 minutes.

Three airport express buses run between the airport and chamshil (Bus No. 600), the Express Bus Terminal (Bus No. 600-2), and the Sheraton Walker Hill Hotel (Bus No. 601). No. 600 departs the airport every 8 minutes from 5:20 A.M. to 10:00 P.M. No. 600-2, which runs the same route as No. 600 and operates every 20 minutes from 5:25 A.M. to 11:00 P.M. No. 601, via the city center, runs every 10 minutes. The one-way bus fare is 700 won.

The non-stop limousine bus service to the Korean City Air Terminal (KCAT), located south of the Han River and nearby the Trade Tower and Lotte World, is the most convenient for travelers. The bus runs every 10-15 minutes from 7:30 A.M. to 10 P.M. The one-way fare is 3,500 won. You can buy a ticket at the ticket counter on the first floor of each of the airport terminals, or you can pay the fare directly to the driver. Travel time is about one hour.

At Korea City Air Terminal (KCAT), there are check-in counters of Asiana Airlines, Northwest Airlines, Cathay Pacific Airlines, and Aeroflot Soviet Airlines. If you take one of these flights, you must check-in at least 1 hour and 40 minutes before departure of domestic flights and at least 2 hours and 30 minutes before departure of international flights. International airline passengers must be prepared to pay an airport tax of 8,000 won, and a domestic airport tax of 3,000 won is levied on all domestic flight passengers. Information: (02)551-0077/8, KCAT (159-6, Samseong-dong, Kangnam-gu, Seoul)

Taxis are plentiful, convenient, and reasonably priced to downtown Seoul.

Other information on transportation or sightseeing is available at the airport information desk. For flying by Korean Air (KAL) in Korea, contact the Head Office: 41-3, Seosomun-dong, Chung-gu, Seoul (02)7517-114. You may also call the following numbers for information and reservations:

Seoul	(02)756-2000
Pusan	(051)-463-2000
Cheju	(064)52-2000
For Asiana, call:	
Seoul	(02)774-4000
Pusan	(051)465-4000
Cheju	(064)43-4000

Approximate Flying Times to Korea

Bangkok - Tokyo - Seoul	8 hours, 10 minutes
Hong Kong - Seoul	3 hours, 30 minutes
Honolulu - Seoul	11 hours, 10 minutes
Kuala Lumpur - Seoul	7 hours, 5 minutes
London - Tokyo - Seoul	14 hours
Los Angeles - Anchorage - Seoul	14 hours, 10 minutes
Los Angeles - Seoul	13 hours, 20 minutes
Manila - Seoul	3 hours, 50 minutes
New York - Anchorage - Seoul	16 hours, 30 minutes
New York - Seoul	15 hours, 10 minutes
Singapore - Seoul	6 hours, 15 minutes
Taipei - Seoul	2 hours, 50 minutes
Tokyo - Seoul	2 hours, 20 minutes

Approximate Flying Times between Seoul and Major Cities in Korea

Cheju - Seoul	60 minutes
Chinju - Seoul	60 minutes
Kwangju - Seoul	50 minutes
Pusan - Seoul	50 minutes
Sokch'o - Seoul	40 minutes
Taegu - Seoul	50 minutes
Ulsan - Seoul	50 minutes
Yeosu - Seoul	40 minutes

Rail Travel

Traveling by train in Korea is very convenient and efficient. The railroad system operated by the Korean National Railroad has extensive connections from Seoul to other cities.

In Korea there are four types of trains:

Special Express	특급
	t'euk-keup
Express	급행
	keup-haeng
Ordinary Express	보통 급행
	pot'ong geup-haeng
Local Train	완행
	wan-haeng

The special express has two classes of seats, first and second. Express, Ordinary Express, and local trains have seats of second and third class. Seats on third class are unreserved.

First class seats	일등석
	il-tteung-seok
Second class seats	이등석
	i-deung-seok
Third class seats	삼등석
	sam-deung-seok

Information: Seoul (02)757-0086

Rail Travel Time between Seoul and Major Cities

Kangneung-Seoul	3 hours, 40 minutes
Kwangju-Seoul	4 hours, 30 minutes
Kyeongju-Seoul	4 hours, 20 minutes
Masan-Seoul	5 hours
Pusan-Seoul	5 hours, 30 minutes
Puyo-Seoul	3 hours, 30 minutes
Taegu-Seoul	4 hours
Taejon-Seoul	2 hours
Yosu-Seoul	7 hours

Subway

Seoul has an extensive subway system which provides a fast, efficient, and convenient way of getting around downtown and the suburbs. It connects with the outskirts of the city, Suweon, Anyang, and Inch'eon. The fares are 350 won for one zone, and 450 won for two zones.

Buses

Local buses are overcrowded throughout downtown Seoul. However, buses run very frequently and efficiently and are very convenient for traveling anywhere in the city. The fare is 290 won for a bus token.

City express buses called *chwaseok* (reserve-seat) buses are more comfortable. The fare is 600 won.

Express buses running on major highways are very convenient and efficient in traveling between major cities. Information: Seoul (02)757-2345

Taxis

Taxis are plentiful in Seoul and other cities. Taxis stop at designated taxi stands in front of department stores, hotels, railroad stations, and in certain areas downtown.

There are three types of taxis, the regular taxi (yellow or green), the call-taxi (usually beige), and the hotel taxi. The regular taxi has the meter showing the fare in digits. For the medium size taxi there is an initial charge of 1,000 won for the first 2 kilometers and 100 won for each additional 279 meters. If heavy traffic slows progress to less than 15 kilometers per hour 100 won is charged every 67 seconds in addition to the initial fare.

The call-taxi can be called by telephone anywhere downtown. Telephone: (02)414-0150/5. They charge 1,200 won for the first two kilometers and 100 won for each additional 400 meters. There is a 20 percent surcharge added from midnight to 4 A.M.

Hotel taxis are available at any major hotel.

Most of the taxi drivers speak English fairly well. Should you encounter a taxi driver who can't speak English, ask someone ahead of time to write down your destination in Korean.

Tipping is not traditionally practiced unless the driver does something special for you, such as waiting for a while or running errands at your request.

TRAVEL TIPS

On the Plane

1. Be aware that the engine noise is less noticeable in the front part of the plane. Try to sleep. Some frequent travelers bring along earplugs, eyeshades, and slippers.
2. Wear comfortable, loose-fitting clothing.
3. Walk up and down the aisles, when permitted, at least five minutes every hour to maintain body circulation.
4. Limit alcohol intake—altitude heightens the intoxicating effect.

Jet Lag

Disruption of the body's natural cycles can put a lingering damper on your vacation, so take the following precautions:
1. *Avoid loss of sleep* by taking a flight that will get you to your destination early in the evening, if at all possible. Get a good night's sleep at home the night before your departure.
2. *Rearrange your daily routine* and sleeping schedule to harmonize with a normal body clock at your destination.
3. *Avoid stress and last-minute rush.* You're going to need all your strength.

Shopping

Most downtown department stores are open from 10:00 A.M. to 7:30 P.M., weekdays, Saturdays, and holidays. Each department store is closed one day a week. Other smaller shops are open from 10:00 A.M., and remain open as late as 10:00 P.M. every day.

Besides department stores, there are various kinds of shopping places, such as arcades, specialized shopping districts, open air markets, and duty-free shops to attract tourists and shoppers.

Of the myriad arcades, Sogong Arcade, underground between the Seoul City Hall Plaza and Chosun Hotel and Myeong-dong, has a variety of stores carrying clothing, jewelry, records and tapes, antiques, and souvenirs. It is very convenient for those who stay at hotels in the center of downtown.

There are several shopping districts, such as It'aeweon, Insa-dong, and Myeong-dong. It'aeweon, which caters to foreign tourists, is occupied by many manufacturers' outlets carrying clothing, tennis shoes, and antiques. For shoppers who are interested in wooden chests, pottery, paintings, and antiques, Insa-dong (the so-called Mary's Alley) is an attractive place to go. There are many private art galleries and antique stores. This is a good place for browsing and window shopping for those who want to experience the world of Korean traditional arts. Myeong-dong is the major shopping district for high quality items and recent fashions. It is one of the busiest streets and the heart of fashion in Korea, especially for women. Many dress, silk, and boutique shops line the narrow and crowded streets with fabulous designs and colorful materials. With a flurry of fashion, Myeong-dong is a popular entertainment district.

There are a number of open air markets, such as Namdaemun Shijang (South Gate Market) and Tongdaemun Shijang (East Gate Market). There are many good buys to be found in leather goods, lacquerware, footwear, clothes, furniture, fabrics, ceramics, electrical appliances, and foods. Goods here are generally cheaper that those in other shopping districts.

Bargaining is customarily practiced at many stores, shops, and open air markets. But there is no discount at department stores, high quality boutiques, and arcades where a fixed price is posted on items.

Major credit cards, such as American Express, Visa, MasterCard, Diners Club, and Carte Blanche, are honored at department stores, shops, and stores, but check first before buying.

Clothing Sizes

Although sizing on items at stores in It'aeweon, or dress shops for foreign visitors is standard American or European, you should try on clothing before you buy it. You may find a good fit in most items, but waist or sleeves may sometimes be short or long. Sizes of suits and dresses for the domestic market are based on the metric system.

Drugstores

Pharmacies in Korea are quite different from drugstores in America. There are two kinds of pharmacies, Western and herb medicine. The Western pharmacy called *yang-yak-pang* or *yang-yak-kuk* (usually shortened to *yakbang* or *yak-kuk*) carry only Western medicines and toiletries. Western pharmacies can easily be found in all of the major cities. Herb medicine pharmacies called *han-yak-pang* or *han-yak-kuk* carry an amazing array of folk herb medicine and are rare downtown as well as in the countryside.

Rent-A-Car

There are car rental services for visitors who wish to drive around the country. The rental fee ranges from 26,000 won to 34,000 won for 12 hours; for 24 hours the charge would be 34,000 won and up to 46,800 won including insurance coverage.

Information and Reservations:

Arirang	Seoul	(02)790-1750
Daehan	Seoul	(02)585-0801
88	Seoul	(02)699-3885
Pusan	Pusan	(051)469-1100
Yongnam	Pusan	(051)469-5000
Cheju	Cheju	(064)42-3301
Halla	Cheju	(064)55-5000

A word of warning: Driving in downtown areas is not like driving in American cities. Streets are always crowded with cars, taxis, buses, and pedestrians. There is high risk involved with city driving. Don't consider driving unless you are prepared to take that risk.

Tipping

Traditionally, tipping has not been practiced in Korea. People in services such as taxi drivers, waiters, and waitresses don't expect tips. Most restaurants, hotels, and tourist facilities levy a 10 percent surcharge on their service. There are few exceptions, however. If someone runs errands especially for you (beyond their routine service) and no service charge is added to a check, 10 percent of the bill would be appropriate. At hotels or airports when one carries your baggage, a small tip would be appreciated.

Lost and Found Information Services

The central lost and found office in Seoul is the Citizen's Room, Metropolitan Police Bureau, 201-11, Naeja-dong, Chongro-gu, Seoul (02)778-4400, (02)755-9900.

Other lost and found services may be contacted at the following numbers:

Korea Broadcasting System (KBS)   (02)7803-311

General Information

Munhwa Broadcasting Corporation (MBC)	(02)724-6151
Seoul Railway Station	(02)755-7108
Kuro Railway Station	(02)633-0063
Shinseol-dong Subway Station	(02)744-2400

Emergencies

In case of emergency, dial 112 for the police and 119 for the fire department. In a hotel, the front desk or hotel manager can assist you calling a doctor or ambulance. On the street, ask a policeman or pedestrian for assistance, or go to a police box that can be found on every major thoroughfare. For foreigners, Asia Emergency Assistance provides a 24-hour emergency service. Tel. (02)790-7561.

MAJOR HOTELS

Hotels listed in this book have modern facilities comparable to those in America. Most hotels have Western-style rooms, but some hotels have both Western and traditional Korean rooms with *ondol* floors heated by a system of radiant pipes.

Hotels are classified into five classes according to quality, facilities, and service. They use the rose of Sharon, which is the Korean national flower, as a symbol of quality. Five flowers are the top rating and indicate super deluxe (SDX), four are deluxe (DLX), three are first class, two are second class, and one is third class. Facilities in SDX and DLX hotels include bars, cocktail lounges, coffee shops, restaurants, tennis courts, swimming pools, souvenir shops, game rooms, barber shops and beauty salons, laundries, and saunas.

Major international credit cards such as American Express, Diners Club, Visa, and MasterCard are accepted by most hotels.

Besides hotels there are traditional Korean-style inns called *yeogwan* (with the *ondol* floors). Accommodations and services are traditional, and provide a homelike atmosphere. You may easily find a comfortable *yeogwan* in cities and in the countryside. Although prices are relatively low compared to hotels, the *yeogwan* may appeal to those who wish to experience more of the country.

Seoul

Ambassador
186-54, Changch'ung-dong 2-ga,
Chung-gu
Tel: (02) 269-6111
Telex: K2369
Class: DLX

Capital
22-76, It'aeweon-dong,
Yongsan-gu
Tel: (02) 792-1122
Class: DLX

Hyatt Regency
747-7, Hannam-dong,
Yongsan-gu
Tel: (02) 797-1234
Telex: K24136
Class: SDX

King Sejong
61-3, Ch'ungmu-ro 2-ga,
Chung-gu
Tel: (02) 776-1811
Telex: K27265
Class: DLX

Koreana
61, T'aep'yeong-ro 1-ga,
Chung-gu

Tel: (02) 730-9911
Telex: K26241
Class: DLX

Lotte
1, Sogong-dong,
Chung-gu
Tel: (02) 771-1000
Telex: K28313
Class: SDX

Lotte World
40-1, Chamshil-dong,
Songp'a-gu
Tel: (02) 419-7000
Class: SDX

President
188-3, Eulchiro,
Chung-gu
Tel: (02) 753-3131
Telex: K27521
Class: SDX

Ramada Renaissance
676, Yeoksam-dong,
Kangnam-gu
Tel: (02) 555-0501
Class: SDX

Riverside
6-1, Chamweon-dong,
Seoch'o-gu
Tel: (02) 543-1001
Telex: K22063
Class: DLX

Seoul Hilton International
395, Namdaemun-ro 5-ga,
Chung-gu
Tel: (02) 753-7788
Telex: K26695
Class: SDX

Seoul Ramada Olympia
108-2, P'yeongch'ang-dong,
Cheongro-gu
Tel: (02) 353-5121
Telex: K23171
Class: DLX

Seoul Palace
63-1, Panp'o-dong,
Seoch'o-gu
Tel: (02) 532-5000
Telex: K2267
Class: DLX

Seoul Plaza
23, T'aep'yeong-ro 2-ga,
Chung-gu
Tel: (02) 771-2200
Telex: K26215
Class: SDX

Seoul Royal
6, Myeong-dong 1-ga,
Chung-gu
Tel: (02) 756-1112
Telex: K27239
Class: DLX

Sheraton Walker Hill
San 21, Kwangjang-dong,
Seongdong-gu
Tel: (02) 453-0121
Telex: K28517
Class: SDX

Shilla
202, Changch'ung-dong 2-ga,
Chung-gu
Tel: (02) 233-3131
Telex: K24160
Class: SDX

The Westin Chosun
87, Sogong-dong,
Chung-gu
Tel: (02) 771-0500
Telex: K24256
Class: SDX

Bukak Park
113-1, P'yeongch'ang-dong
Chongro-gu
Tel: (02) 352-7101
Class: 1st

Crown
34-69, It'aeweon-dong,
Yongsan-gu
Tel: (02) 797-4111

Telex: K25951
Class: 1st

Hamilton
119-25, It'aeweon-dong,
Yongsan-gu
Tel: (02) 794-0171
Telex: K24491
Class: 1st

Manhattan
13-3, Yeoeuido-dong,
Yeongdeungp'o-gu
Tel: (02) 780-8001
Telex: K24767
Class: 1st

Nam Seoul
602-4, Yeoksam-dong,
Kangnam-gu
Tel: (02) 552-7111
Telex: K25019
Class: DLX

New Kukje
29-2, T'aep'yeong-ro,
Chung-gu
Tel: (02) 732-0161
Telex: K24760
Class: 1st

New Seoul
29-1, T'aep'yeong-ro 1-ga,
Chung-gu
Tel: (02) 735-9071
Telex: K27220
Class: 1st

Pacific
31-1, Namsan-dong 2-ga,
Chung-gu
Tel: (02) 777-7811
Telex: K26249
Class: 1st

Poong Jun
73-1, Inhyeon-dong 2-ga,
Chung-gu
Tel: (02) 266-2151
Telex: K25687
Class: 1st

Sam Jung
604-11, Yeoksam-dong,
Kangnam-gu
Tel: (02) 557-1221
Telex: K26680
Class: 1st

Seokyo
354-5, Seogyo-dong,
Map'o-gu
Tel: (02) 333-7771
Telex: K26780
Class: 1st

Seoulin
149, Seorin-dong,
Chongro-gu
Tel: (02) 732-6000
Telex: K28510
Class: 1st

Tower
San 5-51, Chang ch'ung-dong 2-ga,
Chung-gu
Tel: (02) 236-2121
Telex: K28246
Class: DLX

Pusan

Commodore
743-80, Yeongju-dong,
Chung-gu
Tel: (051) 44-9101/7
Telex: K53717
Class: DLX

Crown
830-30, Peomil 1-dong,
Tong-gu
Tel: (051) 69-1241
Telex: K53422
Class: 1st

Hyatt Regency Pusan
1405-16, Chung-dong,
Haeundae-gu
Tel: (051) 743-1234
Class: SDX

Paradise Beach
1408-5, Chung-dong,
Haeundae-gu
Tel: (051) 742-2121
Class: SDX

Kuk Je
830-62, Peomil 2-dong,
Tong-gu
Tel: (051) 642-1330/4
Telex: K52096
Class: DLX

Sorabol
37-1, Taech'eong-dong 1-ga,
Chung-gu
Tel: (051) 463-3511/19
Telex: K53827
Class: DLX

The Westin Chosun Beach
737, U 1-dong,
Haeundae-gu
Tel: (051) 742-7411, (02) 771-0500
Telex: K53718
Class: SDX

Phoenix
8-1, Namp'o-dong 5-ga,
Chung-gu
Tel: (051) 245-8061/9
Telex: K53704
Class: 1st

Pusan
12, Tong-gwang-dong 2-ga,
Chung-gu
Tel: (051) 23-4301/9
Telex: K53657
Class: 1st

Royal
2-71, Kwangbok-dong,
Chung-gu
Tel: (051) 241-1051/5
Telex: K53824
Class: DLX

Taegu

Daegu Soosung
888-2, Tusan-dong,
Suseong-gu
Tel: (053) 763-7311
Telex: K54305
Class: 1st

Dong-in
5-2, Samdeok-dong 1-ga,
Chung-gu
Tel: (053) 46-5211/9
Telex: K54325
Class: 1st

Kumho
28, Haseo-dong,
Chung-gu
Tel: (053) 252-6001
Class: DLX

Prince
1824-2, Taemyeong 2-dong,
Nam-gu
Tel: (053) 628-1001
Class: DLX

Inch'eon

Olympos
13-2, Hang-dong 1-ga,
Chung-gu
Tel: (032) 762-5181
Telex: K24894
Class: 1st

Songdo Beach
812, Tongch'un-dong,
Nam-gu
Tel: (032) 865-1311/20
Class: DLX

Kangweon-do

Naksan Beach
3-2, Cheong-in-ri, Kanghyeon-myeon,
Yangyang-gun
Tel: (0396) 672-4000
Class: 1st

New Sorak
106-1, Seorak-dong,
Sokch'o

Tel: (0392) 34-7131/49
Class: 1st

Sorak Park
74-3, Seorak-dong,
Sokch'o
Tel: (0392) 34-7711
Class: DLX

Yongp'yeong
Dragon Valley
130, Yongsan-ri, Toam-myeon,
P'yeongch'ang-gun
Tel: (0374) 32-5757
Class: DLX

Ch'ungch'eongbuk-do

Ch'ungju Imperial
102-1, Hoam-dong,
Ch'ungju
Tel: (0441) 848-0470/9
Class: 1st

Songnisan
198, Sanae-ri, Naesongni-myeon,
Po-eun-gun
Tel: (0433) 42-5281/8
Class: 1st

Suanbo Sang Nok
292, Onch'eon-ri, Sangmo-myeon,
Chungweon-gun
Tel: (0441) 845-3500
Class: 1st

Ch'ungch'eongnam-do

Jeil
228-6, Onch'eon-dong,
Onyang
Tel: (0418) 44-6111/25
Class: 1st

Onyang
242-10, Onch'eon-dong,
Onyang
Tel: (0418) 545-2141
Class: 1st

Cheollabuk-do

Core
627-3, Seo-nosong-dong, Tokchin-gu,
Cheonju
Tel: (0652) 85-1100
Class: DLX

Naejangsan
71-14, Naejang-dong,
Cheonju
Tel: (0681) 535-4131/7
Class: 1st

Cheollanam-do

Chowon
1-9, Tae-eui-dong 2-ga,
Mokp'o
Tel: (0631) 43-0055
Class: 1st

Yeosu Beach
346, Ch'ungmu-dong,
Yeosu
Tel: (0662) 63-2011/5
Class: 1st

Kyeongsangbuk-do

Concorde
410, Shinp'yeong-dong,
Kyeongju
Tel: (0561) 745-7000
Class: SDX

Cignus
145-21, Yeongheung-dong,
P'ohang
Tel: (0562) 75-2000
Class: DLX

Hyundai
477-2, Shinp'yeong-dong,
Kyeongju
Tel: (0561) 748-2233
Class: SDX

Kolon
111-1, Ma-dong,
Kyeongju

Tel: (0561) 746-9001/11
Class: SDX

Kyeongju Hilton
370, Shinp'yeong-dong,
Kyeongju
Tel: (0561) 745-7788
Class: SDX

Kyeongju Chosun
410, Shinp'yeong-dong,
Kyeongju
Tel: (0561) 745-7701/9
Class: SDX

Kyeongsangnam-do

Diamond
283, Cheonha-dong, Tong-gu,
Ulsan
Tel: (0522) 32-7171
Class: DLX

Koreana
256-3, Seongnam-dong, Chung-gu,
Ulsan
Tel: (0522) 44-9911/20
Class: DLX

Cheju-do

Cheju KAL
1691-9, Ido 1-dong,
Cheju
Tel: (064) 43-6151
Class: DLX

Cheju Namseoul
291-30, Yeon-dong,
Cheju
Tel: (064) 42-4111/9
Class: DLX

Grand
263-15, Yeon-dong,
Cheju
Tel: (064) 47-5000
Class: SDX

Hyatt Regency
3039-1, Saektal-dong,
Seogwip'o
Tel: (064) 33-1234/40
Class: SDX

Lagonda
159-1, Yongdam 1-dong,
Cheju
Tel: (064) 58-2500
Class: DLX

Oriental
1197, Samdo 2-dong,
Cheju
Tel: (064) 52-8222
Class: DLX

Shilla
3039-3, Saektal-dong,
Seogwip'o
Tel: (064) 33-4466
Class: SDX

MAJOR RESTAURANTS

All of Seoul's major hotels have restaurants and coffee shops. Among them only a few provide authentic Korean cuisine. To enjoy Korean cuisine, try one or more of the downtown restaurants listed below.

Seoul

Korean restaurants

Korea House
P'il-dong
Tel: 267-8752

Hanilgwan
Myeong-dong
Tel: 776-3388

Pine Hill
Myeong-dong
Tel: 266-4486

Taewongak
Seongbuk-dong
Tel: 762-0161

Samch'eong-gak
Seongbuk-dong
Tel: 762-0151

Ever Spring Park
Yeong-dong
Tel: 543-8804

Nak San Garden
Tongsung-dong
Tel: 742-7470

Chinese restaurants

Arisan
Namsan
Tel: 793-7396

Dariwon
Namsan
Tel: 793-3615/6

China City
Shinsa-dong
Tel: 548-2222

Western restaurants

Banjul
Chongro
Tel: 733-1800

Chalet Swiss
It'aewon
Tel: 792-1723

La Cantina
Eulchiro
Tel: 777-2579

Ristorante Opera
Sejong
Tel: 723-7863

Japanese restaurants

Missouri
Sogong-dong
Tel: 778-1131

Seongjun
Sogong-dong
Tel: 755-1132

Namgang
Sogong-dong
Tel: 778-1141

Pusan

Korean restaurants

Bi Won
Pumin-dong
Tel: 244-1778

Byul Chung Ji
Kwangan-dong
Tel: 753-0660

Chun Hyang Won
Ch'oryang-dong
Tel: 27-0221

Dongrae Byul Jang
Onch'on-dong
Tel: 552-0157

Jung Ran Kak
Sujeon-dong
Tel: 42-1421
Kyo Mok Jang
Pumin-dong
Tel: 244-1297

Kyongju

Korean restaurants

Hwan Ho Jang
Sobu-dong
Tel: 2-3771

Kum Ho Kak
Hwango-dong
Tel: 2-7513

Song Rim Jang
Nodong-dong
Tel: 2-6101

Tong Myong Jang
Chinhyun-dong
Tel: 2-5492

Yo Sok Kung
Kyo-dong
Tel: 2-3347

Cheju-do

Korean restaurants

Beodunamu House
Yon-dong
Tel: 7-2361

Cheong Won Kak
Yon-dong
Tel: 7-2955

MAJOR DEPARTMENT STORES

Cosmos Department Store
83-5, Myeong-dong 2-ga,
Chung-gu, Seoul
Tel: (02) 776-0311

Galleria
148, Apkujeong-dong,
Kangnam-gu
Tel: (02) 515-3131/40
Closed on the 1st and 3rd Mondays

Grand Department Store
937, Taech'i-dong,
Kangnam-gu,
Tel: (02) 553-0101
Closed on the 1st and 3rd Mondays

Grand Prix Department Store
500, Taech'i-dong,
Kangnam-gu
Tel: (02) 553-3111
Closed on the 1st and 3rd Sundays

Hanshin Core
133 Block, Hagye-dong,
Noweon-gu
Tel: (02) 978-1919

Hyundai Department Store
224-11, Apkujeong-dong,
Kangman-gu
Tel: (02) 547-2233
Closed on Mondays

159-7, Samseong-dong,
Kangnam-gu

Tel: (02) 552-2233
Closed on Mondays

Lotte Shopping Center
1, Sogong-dong, Chung-gu
Tel: (02) 771-2500
Closed on Mondays

618, Yeongdeungp'o-dong,
Yeongdeungp'o-gu
Tel: (02) 632-2500
Closed on Monday

Lotte World
40-1, Chamshil-dong,
Songp'a-gu
Tel: (02) 411-2500
Closed on Mondays

Midop'a Department Store
123, Namdaemun-ro 2-ga,
Chung-gu
Tel: (02) 754-2222
Closed on the 2nd and 4th Wednesdays

892-71, Chegi-dong,
Tongdaemun-gu
Tel: (02) 960-2222
Closed on the 2nd and 4th Wednesdays

New Core Shopping Center
398-2, Panp'o 3-dong,
Seoch'o-gu
Tel: (02) 532-3311

Shinsegye Department Store
52-5, Ch'ungmu-ro 1-ga,
Chung-gu
Tel: (02) 754-1234
25-2 Kireum 3-dong,
Seongbuk-gu
Tel: (02) 984-1234

434-5, Yeongdeungp'o 4-ga,
Yeongdeungp'o-gu
Tel: (02) 676-1234
Closed on Mondays

Yeongdong Department Store
119, Nonhyeon-dong,
Kangnam-gu
Tel: (02) 544-3000
Closed on the 1st and 3rd Wednesdays

USEFUL ADDRESSES

Korea Trade Promotion Corporation

Head Office

159, Samseong-dong
Kangnam-gu, Seoul 135, Korea
Tel: (02) 550-1114
Fax: (02) 557-5784
Cable: KOEXCENTER
Telex: KOEXCEN K24594
FAX: (02)557-5784

Chicago
111 East Wacker Dr., Suite 519
Chicago, IL 60601
Tel: (312) 644-4323/4
Fax: (312) 644-4879
Telex: 253005 KOTRA CGO

Chicago (Exhibition Center)
1000 Tower Lane, Suite 110
Bensen Ville, IL 60106
Tel: (708) 350-0102
Fax: (708) 350-0747
Telex: 200-426 KAPEC CGO

Dallas
P.O. Box 58023
Dallas, TX 75258-0023
Tel: (214) 748-9341/2
Fax: (214) 748-4630
Telex: 732343 KOTRA DAL

Los Angeles
4801 Wilshire Blvd., No. 230
Los Angeles, CA 90010
Tel: (213) 954-9500
Fax: (213) 954-1707
Telex: 674639 LSA

Miami
One Biscayne Tower, Suite 1620
Miami, FL 33131
Tel: (305) 374-4648
Fax: (305) 375-9332
Telex: 515186 KTC UR MIA

New York
460 Park Ave., Suite 402
New York, NY 10022
Tel: (212) 826-0900
Fax: (212) 888-4930
Telex: 62995 KOTRA NY

Washington, D.C.
1129 20th St., N.W., Suite 410
Washington, D.C. 20036
Tel: (202)857-7919
Fax: (202) 857-7923
Telex: 289608 KTCW UR

Korea Foreign Trade Association (KFTA)

Head Office
Trade Tower, Korea World Trade Center
159-1, Samsung-dong, Kangnam-gu, Seoul
Tel: (02) 551-5114
Fax: (02) 551-5100, 5200
Telex: KOTRASO K24265

New York
Hahn Kook Center Bldg., Rm. 600
460 Park Ave.
New York, NY 10022
Tel: (212) 421-8804/6
Fax: (212) 223-3827
Telex: 425572 KTANY

Washington, D.C.
1800 K Street, N.W., Suite 700
Washington, D.C. 20006
Tel: (202) 828-4400/3
Fax: (202) 828-4404
Telex: 757427 KTAWSH

Korea Exhibition Center (KOEX)
Exhibition Center, Korea World Trade Center
159, Samsung-dong, Kanganm-gu, Seoul
Tel: (02) 551-0114
Fax: (02) 555-7414
Telex: K24594

Economic Associations

Federation of Korean Industries
28-1, Yeoeuido-dong,
Yeongdungp'o-gu, Seoul
Tel: 783-0821/6

Cable: KOB8USINESSMEN SEOUL
Telex: K25444
Fax: 784-1640

Korea Chamber of Commerce and Industry
45, Namdaemun-ro 4-ga,
Chung-gu, Seoul
Tel: 757-0757
Cable: KOREA CHAMBER SEOUL
Telex: K25728
Fax: 757-9475

Major Trading Companies

Daewoo Corp.
541, Namdaemun-ro 5-ga,
Chung-gu, Seoul
Tel: 779-0761
Cable: DAEWOO SEOUL
Telex: DAEWOO K23341/5

Hyosung Corp.
17-7, Namdaemun-ro 4-ga,
Chung-gu, Seoul
Tel: 780-0001
Cable: HYOSTAR SEOUL
Telex: HYOSTAR K23121/5

Hyundai Corp.
140-2, Kye-dong,
Chongno-gu, Seoul
Tel: 741-4141
Cable: HDSANSA SEOUL
Telex: HDCORP K23175

Kukje-ICC Corp.
191, Hangang-ro 5-ga,
Youngsan-gu, Seoul
Tel: 797-7111
Cable: KUKJECO SEOUL
Telex: KUKJE K27251

Lucky-Goldstar Int'l Corp.
537, Namdaemun-ro 5-ga,
Chung-gu, Seoul
Tel: 757-1234
Cable: FPIRCLOVER SEOUL
Telex: LGINTL K27266

Samsung Co., Ltd.
1250, T'aep'yeong-ro 2-ga,

Chung-gu, Seoul
Tel: 7518-114
Cable: STARS SEOUL
Telex: STARS K23657

Ssangyong Corp.
24-1, Cheo-dong 2-ga,
Chung-gu, Seoul
Tel: 270-8182
Cable: TWINDRA SEOUL
Telex: TWINDRA K24270

Sunkyong Ltd.
5-3, Namdaemun-ro 2-ga,
Chung-gu, Seoul
Tel: 771-88
Cable: SUNKYONG SEOUL
Telex: SNKYONG K24851

Tourist Information Services

Korean National Tourism Corporation
Head office (02) 757-6030
Kimp'o Airport (02) 662-2182
Cheju Airport (064) 7-0528
Kimhae Airport (051) 98-1100

Seoul

Seoul Tourist Information Center (02) 731-6337
Kimp'o International Airport Terminal (02) 662-9248
Seoul Railway Station (02) 779-3643
Seoul Express Bus Terminal (02) 598-4151
Chongno (02) 734-0023
Kwanghwamun (02) 734-0027
Myeong-dong (02) 779-3645
Namdaemun (02) 779-3644
Tongdaemun (02) 272-0348

Pusan

Railway Station (051) 463-4938
Pukwan Ferry Terminal (051) 463-3161

Kyeongju

Railway Station (0561) 2-3843
Pulguksa Temple (0561) 2-4747
Express Bus Terminal (0561) 2-9289

Korea Tourist Association Tel: (02) 734-2702/4
12 fl., Korea National Tourism Corp. Bldg.
10, Ta-dong,
Chung-gu, Seoul.

Korean Missions in the United States

Embassy
2450 Massachusetts Avenue, N.W.
Washington, D.C. 20008

Consulates General

Anchorage
101st, Benson Blvd. Suite 301,
Anchorage, AK 99508

Atlanta
229 Peachtree St.,
Suite 500, Cain Tower,
Atlanta, GA 30303

Chicago
500 North Michigan Avenue, Suite 600,
Chicago, IL 60611

Honolulu
2756 Pali Highway,
Honolulu, HI 96817

Houston
1990 Post Oak Suite 745
Houston, TX 77056

Los Angeles
5455 Willshire Blvd., Suite 1101
Los Angeles, CA 90036

New York
460, Park Ave., at 57th St., 5th Floor
New York, NY 10022

San Francisco
3500 Clay Street,
San Francisco, CA 94118

Seattle
Suite 1125, United Airlines Bldg.,
2033 6th Ave.,
Seattle, WA 98121

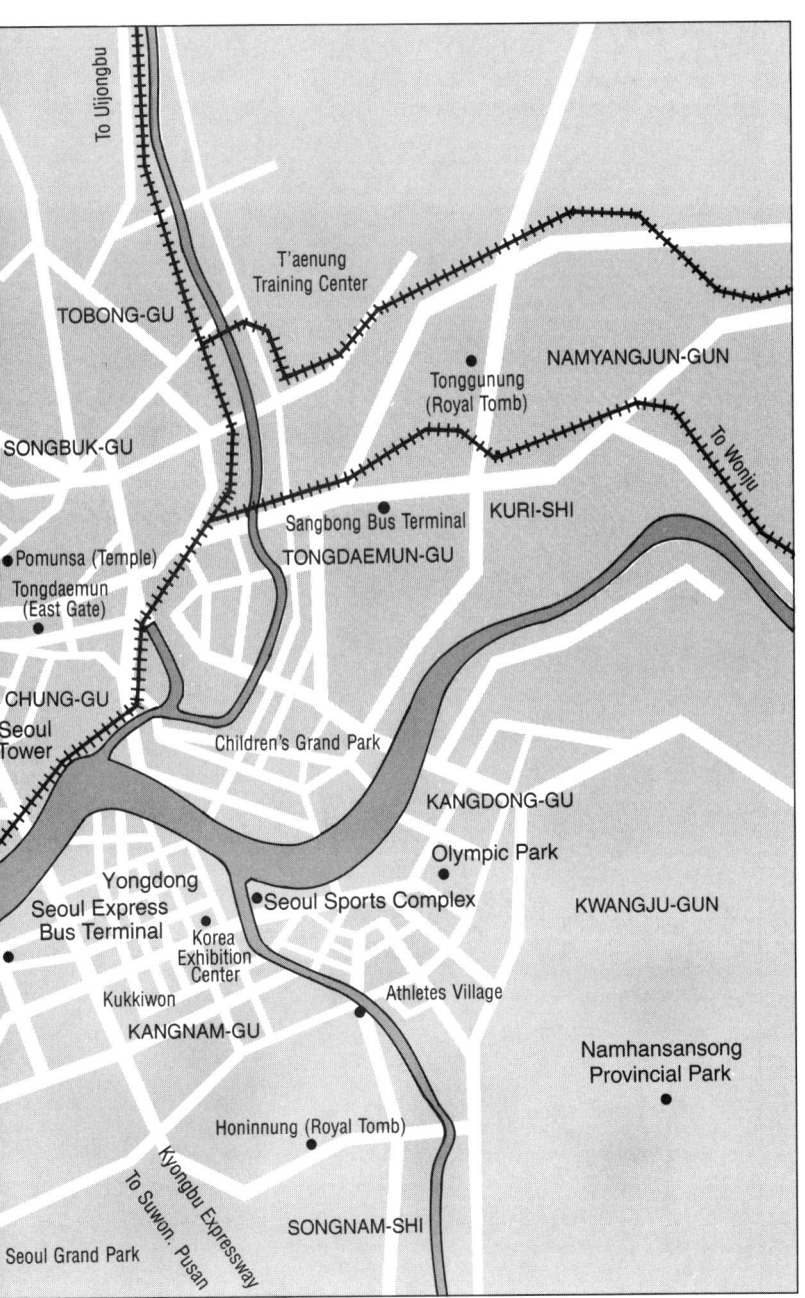

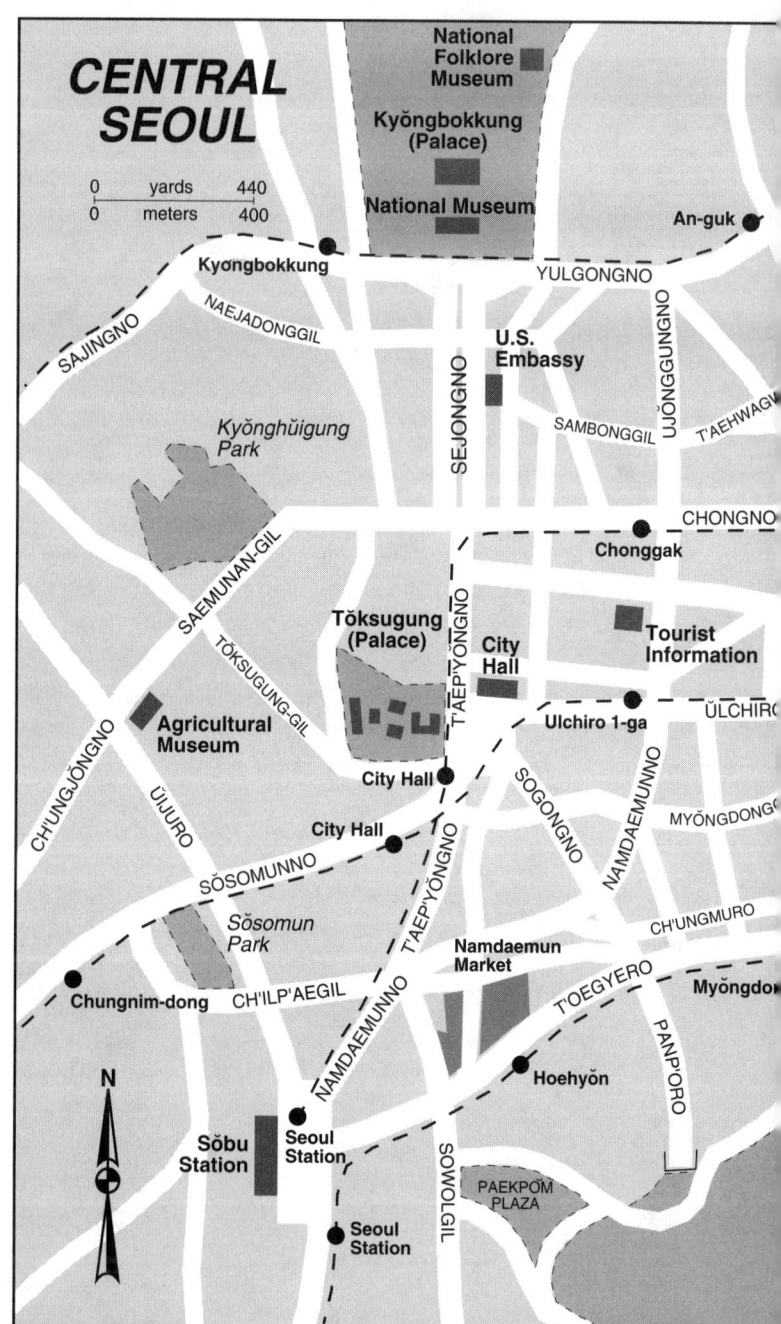

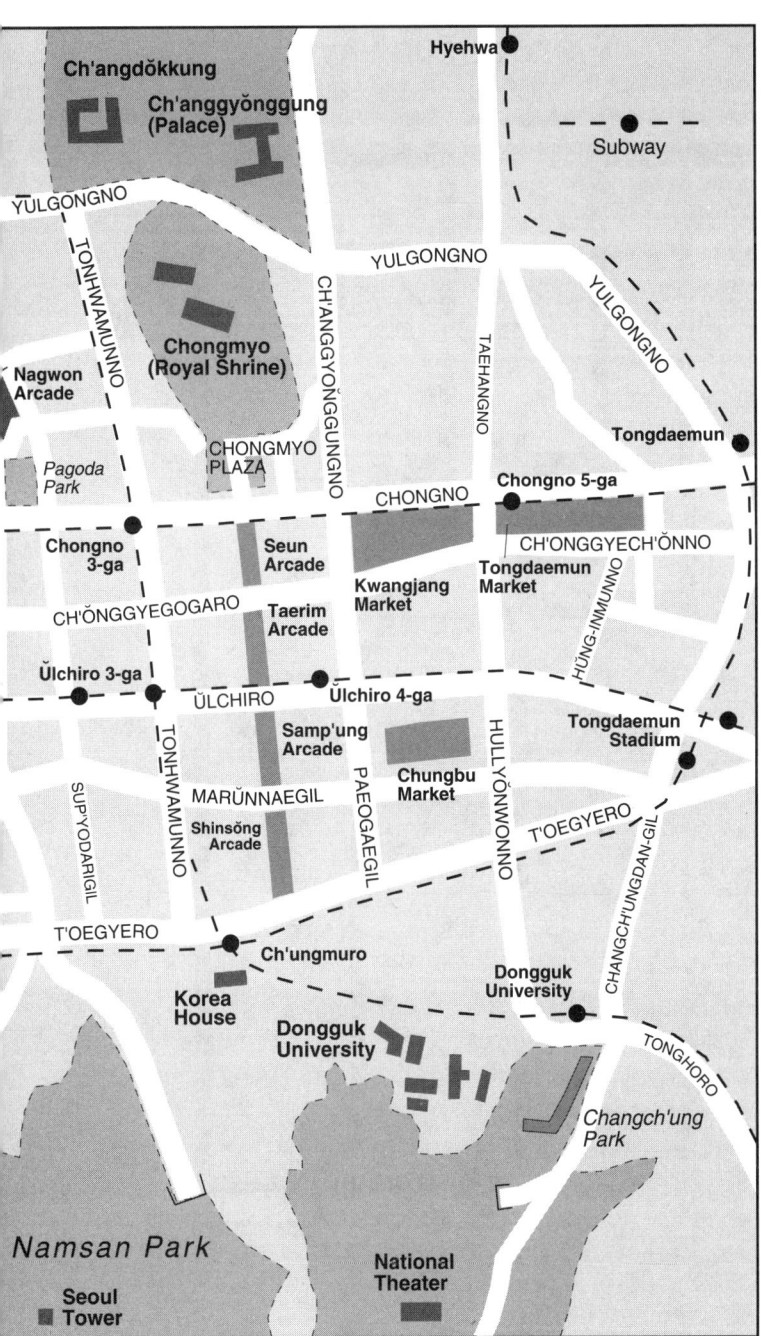

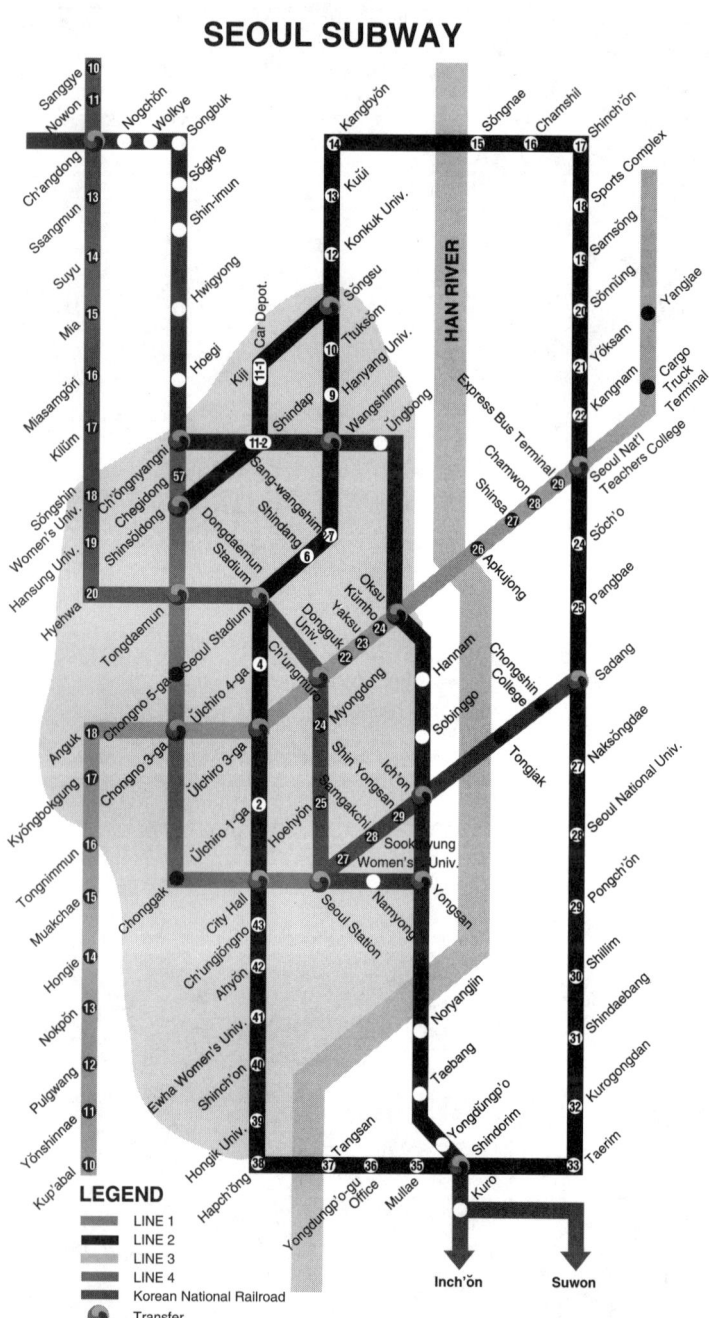

FOREIGN PHRASE BOOKS Series

Barron's new series gives travelers instant access to the most common idiomatic expressions used during a trip—the kind one needs to know instantly, like "Where can I find a taxi?" and "How much does this cost?"

Organized by situation (arrival, customs, hotel, health, etc.) and containing additional information about pronunciation, grammar, shopping plus special facts about the country, these convenient, pocket-size reference books will be the tourist's most helpful guides.

Special features include a bilingual dictionary section with over 2000 key words, maps of each country and major cities, and helpful phonetic spellings throughout.

Each book paperback, 256 pp., 3 3/4" x 6"

ARABIC AT A GLANCE, Wise (2979-8) $5.95, Can. $7.95
CHINESE AT A GLANCE, Seligman, Chen (2851-1) $6.95, Can. $9.95
FRENCH AT A GLANCE, 2nd, Stein & Wald (1394-8) $5.95, Can. $7.95
GERMAN AT A GLANCE, 2nd, Strutz (1395-6) $5.95, Can. $7.95
ITALIAN AT A GLANCE, 2nd, Costantino (1396-4) $5.95, Can. $7.95
JAPANESE AT A GLANCE, 2nd, Akiyama (1397-2) $6.95, Can. $8.95
KOREAN AT A GLANCE, Holt (3998-X) $8.95, Can. $10.95
RUSSIAN AT A GLANCE, Beyer (4299-9) $5.95, Can. $7.95
SPANISH AT A GLANCE, 2nd, Wald (1398-0) $5.95, Can. $7.95

Barron's Educational Series, Inc.
250 Wireless Blvd., Hauppauge, NY 11788
Call toll-free: 1-800-645-3476
In Canada: Georgetown Book Warehouse, 34 Armstrong Ave.
Georgetown, Ont. L7G 4R9, Call toll-free: 1-800-247-7160

Books may be purchased at your bookstore, or by mail from Barron's. Enclose check or money order for total amount plus sales tax where applicable and 10% for postage and handling (minimum charge $3.75, Canada $4.00). Prices subject to change without notice.
ISBN PREFIX: 0-8120

SPEAK A FOREIGN LANGUAGE LIKE A DIPLOMAT

FOREIGN SERVICE INSTITUTE MASTERING SERIES--*Level 1*

These kits are the same courses that the U.S. government uses to help foreign diplomats achieve foreign language fluency. **Each package features a textbook and 12 cassettes and is only $79.95, Can. $99.95**

Available in . . .
Mastering French ISBN: 7321-5
Mastering German ISBN: 7352-5
Mastering Greek ISBN: 7477-7
Mastering Hebrew ISBN: 7478-5
Mastering Italian ISBN: 7323-1
Mastering Japanese ISBN: 7633-8
Mastering Korean ISBN: 7480-7
Mastering Portuguese ISBN: 7479-3
Mastering Spanish ISBN: 7325-8

FOREIGN SERVICE INSTITUTE MASTERING SERIES--*Level 2*

This series begins where Level 1 leaves off. Level 2 is an intense, self-teaching program that takes serious students to a higher degree of fluency. Each package includes comprehensive tapes supplemented by a textbook. Hundreds of spoken drills, quizzes and written exercises for building and mastering grammar, vocabulary, pronunciation and conversational skills are offered. Each package: 12 Cassettes (Japanese 8) with book in boxed set, $79.95, Can. $99.95.

Available in . . .
French ISBN: 7918-3   **Japanese** ISBN: 7921-3
German ISBN: 7920-5   **Spanish** ISBN: 7919-1
Instruction textbooks for all Level 2 Titles may be purchased separately: **$15.95, Can. $19.95**

All prices are in U.S. and Canadian dollars, and subject to change without notice. At your bookstore or order direct adding 10% for postage (minimum charge $ .75 , Can. $4.00), N.Y. residents add sales tax.

Barron's Educational Series, Inc.
250 Wireless Blvd.
Hauppauge, NY 11788
Call toll-free: 1-800-645-3476
Canada: Georgetown Book Warehouse • 34 Armstrong Avenue
Georgetown, Ontario L7G 4R9 • Call toll-free: 1-800-247-7160